NATIONAL CHILD CARE SURVEY, 1990

A NATIONAL ASSOCIATION FOR THE EDUCATION OF YOUNG CHILDREN (NAEYC) STUDY

Conducted by The Urban Institute

Sandra L. Hofferth, April Brayfield, Sharon Deich, and Pamela Holcomb

Sponsored by:

Administration for Children, Youth and Families, Office of Human Development Services, U.S. Department of Health and Human Services

and

The National Association for the Education of Young Children

URBAN INSTITUTE REPORT 91–5

THE URBAN INSTITUTE PRESS
Washington, D.C.

599837

THE URBAN INSTITUTE PRESS
2100 M Street, N.W.
Washington, D.C. 20037

Editorial Advisory Board
William Gorham George E. Peterson
Craig G. Coelen Felicity Skidmore
Richard C. Michel Raymond J. Struyk
Demetra S. Nightingale B. Katherine Swartz

Copyright © 1991. The Urban Institute and the National Association for the Education of Young Children. All rights reserved. Except for short quotes, no part of this report may be reproduced or utilized in any form or by any means, electronic or mechanical, including photocopying, recording, or by information storage or retrieval system, without written permission from The Urban Institute Press.

National Child Care Survey, 1990 / Sandra L. Hofferth, April Brayfield, Sharon Deich, and Pamela Holcomb

1. Child care services--United States. 2. Child care services--United States--Statistics. 3. Child care services--Economic aspects--United States. I. Hofferth, Sandra L. II. Series: Urban Institute report; 91-5.

HQ778.7.U6N38 1991 90-27191
362.7'0973--dc20 CIP

(Urban Institute Reports; 91-5, ISSN 0897-7399)

ISBN 0-87766-505-2
ISBN 0-87766-504-4 (casebound)

Printed in the United States of America

Distributed by University Press of America

4720 Boston Way 3 Henrietta Street
Lanham, MD 20706 London WC2E 8LU
ENGLAND

BOARD OF TRUSTEES

David O. Maxwell
Chairman
Katharine Graham
Vice Chairman
William Gorham
President
Andrew F. Brimmer
James E. Burke
Marcia L. Carsey
Albert V. Casey
John M. Deutch
Richard B. Fisher
George J.W. Goodman
Fernando A. Guerra, M.D.
Ruth Simms Hamilton
Irvine O. Hockaday, Jr.
Michael Kaufman
Ann McLaughlin
Robert S. McNamara
Charles L. Mee, Jr.
Elliot L. Richardson
David A. Stockman
Mortimer B. Zuckerman

LIFE TRUSTEES

Warren E. Buffett
Joseph A. Califano, Jr.
William T. Coleman, Jr.
Anthony Downs
John H. Filer
Joel L. Fleishman
Eugene G. Fubini
Aileen C. Hernandez
Carla A. Hills
Vernon E. Jordan, Jr.
Edward H. Levi
Bayless A. Manning
Stanley Marcus
Arjay Miller
J. Irwin Miller
Franklin D. Murphy
Lois D. Rice
William D. Ruckelshaus
Herbert E. Scarf
Charles L. Schultze
William W. Scranton
Cyrus R. Vance
James Vorenberg

URBAN INSTITUTE REPORTS are designed to provide rapid dissemination of research and policy findings. Each report contains timely information and is rigorously reviewed to uphold the highest standards of policy research and analysis.

The Urban Institute is a nonprofit policy research and educational organization established in Washington, D.C., in 1968. Its staff investigates the social and economic problems confronting the nation and government policies and programs designed to alleviate such problems. The Institute disseminates significant findings of its research through the publications program of its Press. The Institute has two goals for work in each of its research areas: to help shape thinking about societal problems and efforts to solve them, and to improve government decisions and performance by providing better information and analytic tools.

Through work that ranges from broad conceptual studies to administrative and technical assistance, Institute researchers contribute to the stock of knowledge available to public officials and private individuals and groups concerned with formulating and implementing more efficient and effective government policy.

Conclusions or opinions expressed in Institute publications are those of the authors and do not necessarily reflect the views of other staff members, officers or trustees of the Institute, advisory groups, or any organizations that provide financial support to the Institute.

CHILD CARE PROJECT ADVISORY GROUP

Douglas Besharov, American Enterprise Institute
Virginia Cain, National Institute of Child Health and Human Development
Elizabeth Farquhar, U.S. Department of Education
Victoria Fu, Department of Family and Child Development, Virginia Polytechnic and State University
Ellen Galinsky, Families and Work Institute
Frederic Glantz, Abt Associates
Robert Granger, Manpower Demonstration Research Corp.
Jeanne Griffith, National Center for Education Statistics, Department of Education
Cheryl Hayes, National Commission on Children
Helena Hicks, Department of Health and Human Resources, State of Maryland
Beverly Jackson, National Black Child Development Institute
Sheila Kamerman, Columbia University School of Social Work
Ellen Kisker, Mathematica Policy Research
Joann Kuchak, Macro Systems
Joan Lombardi, Early Childhood Specialist
Mark Menchik, U.S. Office of Management and Budget
Frank Mott, Ohio State University, Center for Human Resource Research
Martin O'Connell, U.S. Bureau of the Census
Ann O'Keefe, U.S. Department of the Navy
Deborah Phillips, Department of Psychology, University of Virginia
Harriet Presser, Department of Sociology, University of Maryland
Philip K. Robins, Department of Economics, University of Miami
Nicholas Zill, Child Trends
Merrily Beyreuther, U.S. Department of Health and Human Services (DHHS)
Larry Guerrero, DHHS
Marlys Gustafson, DHHS
Patricia Hawkins, DHHS
Sharon McGroder, DHHS
William Prosser, DHHS
Ann Segal, DHHS
J.D. Andrews, National Association for the Education of Young Children (NAEYC)
Marilyn Smith, NAEYC
Barbara Willer, NAEYC

ABSTRACT

In October 1990 federal child care legislation was enacted to assist low- and moderate-income working families with their child care and other household expenses and to increase the supply and improve the quality of programs. Administrators of programs such as Head Start, the Social Services Block Grant, state grants for the Dependent Care Planning and Development Program, the Family Support Act of 1988, and the newly enacted Child Care and Development Block Grant now face the challenge of implementing these new programs and policies.

To implement these new programs and to promote high quality early childhood education, state and federal agencies needed a much greater understanding of child care trends and practices than was previously available. In the National Child Care Survey, 1990 (NCCS), a nationally representative sample of U.S. families with children under age 13 was interviewed by telephone with the aim of providing scientifically valid, reliable, and useful information on current use of child care and early childhood programs.

Statistics from this survey reveal that the primary source of child care for most families is parents, followed by relatives, center-based care, lessons (e.g., music, soccer practice), family day care, and nonrelatives in the child's home. Use of center-based programs has increased consistently over the past 25 years. Among families in which the mother works outside the home, center-based programs in 1990 cared for three out of ten preschool-age children, compared with one out of twenty in 1965. Half of all three- to four-year-olds are in such programs, regardless of whether or not the mother is employed.

PREFACE

The National Child Care Study is a public-private partnership, jointly sponsored by the National Association for the Education of Young Children (NAEYC) and the Head Start Bureau of the Administration for Children, Youth and Families (ACYF), Office of Human Development Services, Department of Health and Human Services.

The NAEYC is America's foremost professional association of early childhood professionals, representing nearly 75,000 individuals. NAEYC's primary goals are to improve professional practice in early childhood care and education and to build public understanding and support for high quality early childhood programs.

The ACYF is the agency within the federal government whose mission is to improve opportunities for the nation's children and families. A major focus of this effort is Head Start, a comprehensive community-based program serving more than half a million low-income children and their families annually.

This research partnership between NAEYC and ACYF reflects a recognition that child care has emerged as a focal point for work and family life in the United States and that issues related to the care of children span both private and public domains. The study was undertaken as a joint initiative in order to highlight our mutual commitment to children and their families as well as to assist the professionals who dedicate themselves to the betterment of children's lives.

Early in the conceptualization of the National Child Care Study, it became apparent that a study was needed which would characterize the entire child care marketplace, covering both parents and providers as well as all major forms of care. We were particularly concerned that the study cover informal arrangements between friends, neighbors and relatives as well as more formal segments of the child care market such as day care centers, preschools, Head Start centers, and family day care homes.

In order to more comprehensively address all aspects of child care demand and supply, ACYF entered into an interagency agreement with the Department of Education to coordinate the National Child Care Study with the National Profile of Child Care Settings study, which was initiated by the Education Department at about the same time. This partnership greatly extends the comprehensiveness, completeness and conceptual integration of the two studies, making possible a much clearer view of the national child care picture than would be possible from either study alone.

Another important partner to ACYF and NAEYC in the National Child Care Study is the Department's Office of the Assistant Secretary for Planning and Evaluation (ASPE) which funded a nationally representative substudy of low-income families. This enhanced sample allowed for a more complete and sophisticated analysis of the data from this important segment of the population.

The Department of Navy also joined the research as the sponsor of a substudy of military families. This substudy substantially enhances the research as a whole by providing a more complete picture of child care demand and supply along with a comparison of military and civilian child care to help identify the special needs of different types of families.

This collaborative approach to linking different sectors and facets of the national child care picture is particularly valuable because of the different needs of large subpopulations, the dramatic increase in numbers of working mothers over the past decade, and the restructuring of child care markets thought to be underway. We hope that results of this research will be useful to parents and providers, to program developers and administrators, to community child care organizations and civic groups, to employers, to legislators, and policymakers in federal, state, and local communities, and to all others who are attempting to respond to the changing needs and priorities of American families.

We are particularly grateful to our two research contractors who carried out with competence and dedication the many challenging demands of this research. The Urban Institute in Washington, D.C. was responsible for the research design, analysis, and reporting of data. Abt Associates carried out sampling and data collection from offices in Cambridge, Massachusetts, Amherst, Massachusetts and Chicago, Illinois. Their study teams also worked closely with colleagues at Mathematica Policy Research, Inc. who conducted the National Profile of Child Care Settings Study. We also thank our colleagues in federal agencies and private organizations for their many contributions to this study.

This report, the first of a series of analyses of child care and preschool enrollments in the United States in the 1990s, focuses on child care arrangements, cost of care, child care selection procedures, and parental perceptions of child care options and policies for children under age 13.

Subsequent reports and papers will address many of the same issues among low-income families and military families, and will provide the first nationally representative picture of family day care in the United States.

Barbara Willer
Co-Project Director
NAEYC

Patricia Divine-Hawkins
Co-Project Director
ACYF

CONTENTS

Abstract	v
Preface	vii
Executive Summary	1
1 Introduction	7
Background and Objectives of Study	7
Description of Data Collection	12
Description of Universe and Sample Selection	12
Procedures for Collection of Information	16
Overview of Report	19
2 Child Care Arrangements in the United States, 1990	21
National Estimates of Number of Mothers and Fathers with Children under Age 13	26
National Estimates of Primary Care Arrangements for All Children	27
Primary Child Care Arrangements for all Children under Age 13	27
National Estimates of Primary Care Arrangements for Youngest Child	42

Primary Care Arrangements for Youngest Child	42
Secondary Child Care Arrangements for Youngest Child	81
Other Arrangements for Youngest Child	97
Trends in Child Care Arrangements, 1965-90	97
Preschool-age Children with Employed Mother	97
School-age Children with Employed Mother	101
Hours in Primary Child Care Arrangement for Youngest Child	105
Preschool-age Children with Employed Mother	105
Preschool-age Children with Nonemployed Mother	107
Preschool-age Children with Single Father	112
School-age Children with Employed Mother	113
School-age Children with Nonemployed Mother	112
School-age Children with Single Father	113
Summary and Conclusions	114
Preschool-age Children	114
School-age Children	115
3 Parental Expenditures for Child Care	119
Proportion of Families Paying for Child Care Arrangements	120
Families Paying for the Primary Arrangement of the Youngest Child	120
Families Paying for Secondary Arrangement for Youngest Child	130

Hourly Expenditures for Youngest Child in Family	133
Expenditures for Primary Arrangements for Preschool-age Children	133
Expenditures for Primary Arrangements for School-age Children	145
Expenditures for Secondary Arrangements for Youngest Child	156
Weekly Expenditures for all Children in Family	160
Families with Youngest Child under Age Five	161
Families with Youngest Child Aged 5 to 12	168
Budget Shares: Percentage of Family Income Spent on Child Care	173
Families with Youngest Child under Age Five	174
Families with the Youngest Child Aged 5 to 12	179
Assistance in Paying for Child Care	183
Receipt of Direct Financial Assistance	183
Use of 1988 Child Care Income Tax Credit	184
Trends in Parental Expenditures Over Time	186
Employed Mothers with Preschool-age Child	188
Employed Mothers with School-age Children Only	193
Summary and Conclusions	196
4 Child Care Choice	**201**
Search for and Selection of Child Care Arrangements For Youngest Child	202

Other Types of Child Care
    Arrangements 202
Other Providers of Same Type of Care 207
Number of Other Providers Considered 211
Considered Both Alternative Arrangements
    and Alternative Providers of Same Type 213
Choice of Care Arrangements for Youngest
    Child 213
Locating Care 213
Decision Factors 215
Comparability with Previous Work 226
Length of Search for Current Arrangement 228
Satisfaction with Care Arrangements
    for Youngest Child 229
Preferences for Alternative Types of Care 232
Desire for Change 232
Preferred Alternatives 234
Reasons for Desiring a Change 241
Summary and Conclusions 245

5 Parental Perceptions of Care 249
Parental Perceptions of Care Used and Not
    Used 250
Expected Availability of Care--Nonusers 250
Distance to Care--Users and Nonusers 255
Price of Care 258
User Perceptions of Characteristics of Care 266
Group Size and Child/Staff Ratios 269
Provider Education and Training 271
Transportation 275
Parental Monitoring 279
Goal of the Program 279
Self-Care and Sibling Care 283
Use of Self-Care and Sibling Care 283

Age First Left Child to Care for Self	293
Factors Associated with Leaving Child in Self-Care	298
Age First Left Child in Care of Sibling	299
Summary and Conclusions	302

6 Previous Use of Child Care Arrangements — 305

Changes in Child Care Arrangements in Year Previous for Preschool Age Children	306
Episodes of Child Care Arrangements for Preschool-Age Children	313
Length of Current and Previous Arrangements	314
All Families	314
Types of Changes	325
Reason for Ending Previous Arrangements	328
First Use of Nonparental Care for Preschool-Age Children	328
Hours Spent In First Nonparental Care Arrangement	334
Summer Arrangements for School-Age Children	334
Summary and Conclusions	342

7 Employers and Child Care — 345

Child Care Failures and Time Lost From Work	345
Failures in Child Care Arrangements Causing Absenteeism from Work	346
Absenteeism from Work Caused by Child's Illness	354
Receipt of Employer Benefits by Parents	357
Leave Policies	370
Use of Leave Time	371
Summary and Conclusions	375

8 Opinions on Federal Child Care Policy: Families With Children Under Age 13 — 381
  Should Support be Targeted to Low-Income Families? — 383
  Does the Mother Have to be Employed? — 390
  Should School-Age Children be Included? — 399
  Should Employers Provide Child Care Benefits? — 403
  Summary And Conclusions — 407

9 Summary and Conclusions — 409
  Child Care Arrangements — 410
  Parental Expenditures — 413
  Choice and Satisfaction — 415
  Perceptions of Alternatives — 417
  Previous Child Care Arrangements — 419
  Employers and Child Care — 421
  Opinions on Child Care Policy — 423
  Conclusions — 425

Appendix A: Design Effects Tables for Survey Percentages — 429

Appendix B: Sample Bias From the Exclusion of Nontelephone Households — 437

Appendix C: Background on National Child Care Survey — 441

Appendix D: Care by Mother and Father — 449

References — 451

LIST OF TABLES AND FIGURES — 455

ACKNOWLEDGMENTS

Almost 5,000 parents and hundreds of providers in center-based and home-based programs provided information for this report. Without their patient and enthusiastic cooperation this study would not have been possible. We hope that the results prove useful for families making decisions regarding the care of their children and participation in the work force. We hope that researchers in the child care field will benefit for this up-to-date compendium. Finally, we hope that the results will be helpful to members of the policy community as they struggle to implement new child care and welfare legislation in the states.

We thank the members of our advisory board, who helped us develop this study as it is today by giving us valuable suggestions at critical junctures. Their names appear on an inside page of this volume.

Numerous individuals have made this project possible and have smoothed the way for us. These include Carol DeVita, the first Urban Institute Project Director on the study; Lee Bawden, Director of the Human Resource Policy Center at the Urban Institute; and Alexandra (Mike) Ferguson, Urban Institute Contract Administrator. We are grateful to Jennifer Pick, Beth Westerman, Douglas Wissoker, and KaLing Chan for their assistance during the design and early data analysis, and to Jennifer Berdahl and Mike Tilkin for computer analysis and preparation of the figures. Special thanks goes to Sonja Drumgoole, project secretary, who typed and retyped many hundreds of pages of manuscript and tables, and who kept calm in the midst of it all. We appreciate the Herculean efforts of Abt Associates staff, particularly Fred Glantz, Mike Battaglia, Diane Stoner, Bettina McGimsey, and Cathy Kaufman in bringing the project to fruition. We are indebted to the efforts of Molly B.C. Ruzicka for her editing. Finally, we wish to thank Pat Hawkins, Administration for Children, Youth and Families, and Barbara Willer, National Association for the Education of Young Children, for their foresightedness in starting such a project, their persistence in spite of problems, their courage in making hard decisions, and their continuing support throughout.

EXECUTIVE SUMMARY

Recent large-scale changes in maternal employment, accompanied by shifts in the child care practices of American families, have created the need for new national child care data. This need has become all the more pressing since the 1988 enactment of the Family Support Act and the October 1990 enactment of federal child care legislation to assist low- and moderate-income working families with their child care and other household expenses and to increase the supply and improve the quality of programs.

To implement and administer these programs and to promote high quality early childhood education for young children, a greater understanding of child care trends and practices was needed. In the National Child Care Survey, 1990 (NCCS), a nationally representative sample of U.S. families with children under age 13 was interviewed by telephone to learn about who cares for children, how much parents spend on child care, how parents choose arrangements and programs to care for their children, what they perceive their child care options to be, how frequently they change their arrangements, how American families balance work and family responsibilities, and parents' perceptions of public- and private-sector child care policies. This survey represents approximately 27 million households with children under age 13, or 3 out of 10 U.S. households.

Statistics from this survey reveal that the primary child care arrangement used by most families is parents (45 percent), followed by relatives (14 percent), center-based care (13 percent), lessons (e.g., music, soccer practice, 14 percent), family day care (7 percent), and paid care provided at home (3 percent). Use of center-based programs has increased consistently over the past 25 years. Among families in which the mother works outside the home, center-based programs in 1990 cared for three out of ten preschool-age children as a primary arrangement, compared with one out of twenty in 1965. Half of all three- to four-year-olds are enrolled in such programs, regardless of whether or not the mother is employed.

The study concludes that although many of the potential income-related differences in access to child care have been reduced through federal assistance, low-income families still bear a considerable burden in their attempts to raise children and support themselves. Public opinion strongly supports public policies to assist these families. Below are some of the findings of the survey.

CHILD CARE ARRANGEMENTS

Employed mothers and mothers of preschoolers are more likely to use nonparental care than are nonemployed mothers and mothers of school-age children. Even though most nonemployed mothers care for their children themselves, almost one out of three relies on center-based programs for 3- to 4-year-old children. Use of center-based programs for preschool-age children of employed mothers has increased over the past 25 years, from 6 percent in 1965 to 28 percent in 1990. At the same time, there has been a decline in use of in-home providers and relatives, while use of family day care has remained constant. Parental care as a primary arrangement has grown somewhat over the past 15 years. Many parents rely on activities such as lessons and sports, not only as educational and cultural supplements, but also as child care arrangements for children after school.

PARENTAL EXPENDITURES

In-home providers are the most expensive arrangement for employed mothers with a preschool-age child ($2.30 per hour). Relatives provide the least expensive care for employed mothers with a preschool child ($1.11 per hour), and center-based programs ($1.67 per hour) and family daycare providers ($1.35 per hour) fall in between. Employed mothers generally pay less per hour than nonemployed mothers, but their children spend more time in paid care than children of nonemployed mothers. Thus, employed mothers spend more on a weekly basis ($63 compared to $35 for nonemployed mothers with a preschool child).

Employed mothers with a preschool-age child spend $63 per week, about 11 percent of their weekly family income, on child care. Nonemployed mothers with a preschool-age child spend about 6 percent. Although less likely to pay for care, single mothers and poor families who pay for care spend a substantially greater share of their income on child care than two-parent or nonpoor families, regardless of employment status or the youngest child's age. For example, families with annual incomes under $15,000 pay 22-25 percent of their income on child care; in contrast, families with annual incomes of $50,000 or more pay only about 6 percent.

CHOICE AND SATISFACTION

Sixty-five percent of parents surveyed indicated that they learned about their primary care arrangement from friends, neighbors, or relatives; only 9 percent of parents found their current arrangement through a resource and referral service.

Quality was the characteristic cited most often by parents in selecting their current care arrangement for their youngest child. Families where the mother is employed cited quality more frequently than families where the mother is not employed. The aspect of quality most often cited was a provider-related characteristic such as a warm and loving manner, which was the most important factor for 70 percent of parents.

The reported level of satisfaction with child care arrangements is quite high, with 96 percent of those surveyed indicating they are either "very satisfied" or "satisfied" with their current care for their youngest child. Despite this, 26 percent indicated they would prefer an alternative type of care. This desire was highest among families where the mother is employed and the youngest child is not in school.

PERCEPTIONS OF ALTERNATIVES

The survey found that for the most part, parents are informed consumers when it comes to choosing child care arrangements. Parents' decisions in terms of location and cost also appear consistent from a rational decision-making perspective. Although many families use self-care and sibling care for their children, fewer than 2 percent report using these types of care as a primary arrangement. Regarding self-care, 3.5 million U.S. children under age 13 (7 percent) are in self-care on a regular basis, suggesting an increase in self-care or at least an increase in parents who report it since the early 1980s. However, self-care is likely to be of short duration, under two hours per day.

PREVIOUS USE OF CHILD CARE

Fewer than 3 out of 10 preschool or kindergarten children had no regular nonparental child care arrangement during the previous year. Younger children were more likely to start nonparental care than older children, who were more likely to be in the same nonparental care arrangement for the previous 12-month period. The most common reason for ending an arrangement was that it was no longer available or affordable.

The median length of all current child care arrangements is 12 months and that of all previous arrangements (used in the last 12 months) is 8 months. The median length of current arrangements increases with the age of the child until age 5, at which time it again declines, because many 5-year-olds have just begun kindergarten.

Sixty percent of respondents indicated that their youngest preschool child was regularly left in nonparental care prior to the start of school. Children of employed mothers and higher income parents started to use nonparental care at an earlier age.

EMPLOYERS AND CHILD CARE

Child care failures caused 15 percent of employed mothers to lose some time from work and 7 percent to miss at least one day of work during the last month. Low-income mothers appear to be especially affected. Many low-income jobs may not provide much flexibility in terms of work schedules, thus producing a higher incidence of absenteeism among low-income workers with child care problems. Failures of child care arrangements were more common among families relying on in-home care than among those using care outside the home.

Over half of the one-third of respondents who reported a sick child during the past month missed at least one day of work to stay home and care for their child. Child care failures due to the unavailability of the regular provider or a child's illness led one-quarter of women employed outside the home to miss at least a day of work in the past month.

According to NCCS data, 3 out of 10 families say that part-time work, unpaid leave, or flextime are available to them. One out of ten say that a workplace center is available to them, a figure twice as high as that reported by employers. Two-parent families (77 percent of the sample) have a higher probability of obtaining a child care benefit through either parent's employer. Many employer benefits are less available to low-income families than to high-income families.

Half of all mother took some leave after the birth of their youngest child, while only 3 out of 10 were paid during this absence. Most of those were paid through a combination of vacation and sick/disability pay; few mothers have paid parental leave available to them.

Chapter 1

INTRODUCTION

BACKGROUND AND OBJECTIVES OF STUDY

The need for new national child care data stems from recent large-scale changes in maternal employment, accompanied by shifts in the child care practices of American families. In the two decades from 1968 to 1988, the proportion of American children with mothers in the labor force rose from 39 percent to 60 percent, a 54 percent increase for the period (U.S. Bureau of Labor Statistics 1988). This trend is expected to continue. It is anticipated that by 1995 two-thirds of the nation's preschoolers and three-fourths of school-age children will have mothers who are employed (Hofferth and Phillips 1987).

The dramatic increase in working mothers has led to an increase in nonparental care for children while parents work, an increase visible for infants and toddlers as well as for preschoolers. At the same time, there has been a rapid increase in preschool enrollments of young children regardless of whether their mothers are employed. The proportion of three- to four-year olds enrolled in kindergarten or a preschool program doubled between 1970 and 1985, from

21 percent to 39 percent. And by age five, 87 percent of all children spend some time in school or a preschool program (U.S. Bureau of the Census 1988). For the school-age child, maternal employment has often meant self- or sibling care, although programs for the supervision of these children before and after school are beginning to appear.

Important policy debates at the federal level over the past several years led to the enactment in October 1990 of child care legislation to assist low- and moderate-income working families with their child care and other household expenses and to increase the supply and improve the quality of programs. In addition, Head Start has been expanding rapidly in accordance with the goal of serving all eligible, low-income children by 1994. At the federal and state levels, administrators of existing programs such as Head Start, the Social Services Block Grant, state grants for the Dependent Care Planning and Development Program, the Family Support Act of 1988, and the 1990 Child Care and Development Block Grant now face the important challenge of implementing these new programs and policies. The following illustrate some of the formidable tasks ahead:

- The increased labor force participation of mothers, expansion of Head Start, passage of the Family Support Act of 1988, and increasing evidence for the persistence of positive effects of preschool on disadvantaged children are intensifying the pressure on early childhood programs to meet the needs of employed mothers while providing developmentally appropriate experiences for children.

Introduction

- A crucial issue for Head Start is that of coordinating and linking programs designed to facilitate child development with those designed to facilitate maternal employment. The Head Start Program is typically a part-day, part-year, high-quality, comprehensive child development program for disadvantaged children. However, many Head Start parents are now employed, in training, or looking for work, and they need care for their children beyond the Head Start day. Accordingly, Head Start is seeking ways to establish "wraparound" programs in partnership with other federal, state, and local programs to better meet the needs of Head Start families and communities.

- As the Family Support Act of 1988 is implemented by the states, welfare parents with children age three or older (at the state's option, age one or older) will be required to work or engage in job training under the new JOBS program. To carry out this aspect of welfare reform, states will be required to provide child care for participants. The U.S. Department of Health and Human Services (DHHS) will provide assistance to states as they design their plans for meeting the child care needs of participants, including many Head Start families. Since states can reimburse parental expenditures up to the 75th percentile of local market rates, one of the more critical needs is for information on the price of care and on parental expenditures.

- The Social Services Block Grant, a federal program administered by the states, provides direct subsidies for the care of low-income children. An important issue for the states is how to conduct this program so that it best reflects the needs of families being served and complements other federal and state programs.

- The 1990 Child Care and Development Block Grant will provide $2.5 billion to the states over the next three years (1991-94) to help families pay for care and to expand the supply of care and education programs for preschool as well as school-age children.

- State grants for the Dependent Care Planning and Development Program, administered by the Administration for Children, Youth and Families (ACYF), provide funds for the planning, establishment, operation, or expansion of school-age child care programs as well as resource and referral services. As with other programs, the DHHS assists states in this function through information and technical support.

- In addition, families who prefer to have a parent care for the children at home are facing increased economic pressure to forego this option to meet other family needs. Child care policies and programs need to take account of this important group.

To implement and administer these programs and with the goal of promoting high quality early childhood education for young children, both the Department of Health and Human Services and the National Association for the Education of Young Children sought greater understanding of child care trends and practices than was previously available. There was a lack of sound information about the needs and resources of American families and about how they balance new demands of work and family life. In particular, little was known about the employment patterns of mothers or about the care of their children while they work. Information on child care arrangements for the children of employed mothers and information on preschool enrollments for all children came from separate and incompatible sources. While the data were available for children of nonemployed mothers, there were no previous national data on forms of care used by nonemployed mothers for infants and toddlers, for school-age children, or the variety of preschool programs in which three- to five-year-olds are enrolled. Likewise there were no national data on how parents choose the programs they are using, what alternatives are available to them, what their child care arrangements cost, and how they juggle employment and caring for their children. Accordingly, the purpose of the National Child Care Survey, 1990 (NCCS), described here, was to provide scientifically valid, reliable, and useful information on current use of child care and early childhood programs. This report provides a nationally representative picture of (1) who cares for children, (2) how much parents spend on child care, (3) how parents select their child care arrangements, (4) parents' perceptions about their child care options, (5) previous use of child care arrangements, (6) how American families balance their work and family responsibilities, and (7) parents' views on public- and private-sector child care policies.

The information this study collected from families with children under age 13, therefore, provides the first comprehensive picture of child care arrangements and early childhood program enrollments in the U.S.

DESCRIPTION OF DATA COLLECTION

Description of Universe and Sample Selection

DESIGN OF NATIONAL CHILD CARE SURVEY, 1990

The National Child Care Survey, 1990, has three components. The parent component consists of a national random-digit-dial computer-assisted telephone survey of households with one or more age-eligible children. The linked provider component consists of a follow-up computer-assisted telephone interview (CATI) with the child care provider of the youngest child in the household. The screened family day-care home component interviewed family day-care home providers that were identified during the random-digit-dialing screening for households with age-eligible children.

POTENTIAL RESPONDENT UNIVERSE

The potential respondent universe for the parent component comprised all households in the United States with one or more children aged 12 years and under. Approximately 27.6 million U.S. households met this criterion in 1990. The target population for the parent survey consisted of all

U.S. households with telephones. This population was stratified into three age groups according to the age of the youngest child: 0-2 years, 3-5 years, and 6-12 years.

The potential respondent universe of regulated and unregulated family day-care homes was covered by the family day-care home component of this study. The target population for this component was the same as for the parent component--all U.S. households with telephones.

Finally, the potential universe of out-of-home arrangements was covered in the linked provider component. The target population consisted of all out-of-home arrangements used by the youngest child in sample households. In 1988 there were an estimated 109,000 licensed family day-care homes in the United States, and an estimated 57,000 licensed and unlicensed day-care center/ Head Start and school-based programs. The total number of unlicensed family day-care homes has been estimated to be 10 times that of licensed homes.

Table 1.1 outlines the components of the National Child Care Survey, 1990, the approximate size of the potential respondent universes, the sample sizes, the response rate, and the number of interviews in each stratum.

SAMPLE SELECTION

A three-stage clustered sample design was used to draw the sampling frames. The first stage sampling frame consisted of all U.S. counties. A stratified first-stage sample of 100 counties/county groups was drawn with probability-proportional-to-size sampling. The measure of size was the number of children under five years of age, obtained from the most recent Census Bureau population estimates (1987). Both the National Child Care Survey, 1990, and

Table 1.1 SAMPLING FRAME AND RESPONSE RATES: NATIONAL CHILD CARE SURVEY, 1990

	Size of Universe (thousands)	Number of Calls	Screened Households	Eligible Households	Number of Interviews
Parent Component					
Age of Youngest Child:					
0–2	9,955	18,168	15,025	2,419	1,676
3–5	6,671	11,813	9,770	1,573	1,091
6–12	11,042	17,544	14,509	2,336	1,618
Other[a]	0	35	27	7	7
Total 0–12	27,668	47,560	39,331	6,333	4,392
R/E rate (%)[b]	—	—	82.7	16.1	69.4
Screened Provider Component					
Family day-care homes	1,000	47,560	36,443	222.6	162
R/E rate (%)[b]	—	—	76.6	0.61	72.8
Linked Provider Component					
Day-care center	57,000	578	325	190	142
R/E rate (%)[b]	—	—	56.2	58.5	74.7
Family day-care homes	1,000	778	343	147	108
R/E rate (%)[b]	—	—	44.1	42.8	73.5

Notes: Dash (—), inapplicable.

a. Seven cases were missing on age of youngest child.
b. R/E rate: Response/Eligibility rate.

the Profile of Child Care Settings Study of the U.S. Department of Education (Kisker et al. 1991) used the same first-stage sample of counties and county groups, so that the supply and demand studies were conducted in the same geographic areas around the country and at the same time.

At the second stage, the sampling frame consisted of all Mitofsky-Waksberg "primary units" (banks of 100 contiguous telephone numbers) in the 100 first-stage units (Waksberg 1978). A sample of 955 Mitofsky-Waksberg "primary units" was drawn at random from the 100 first-stage units.

At the third stage of sampling, the sampling frame was all household telephone numbers in these "primary units." A sample of telephone numbers was selected at random from each of these "primary units." The sample telephone numbers were dialed and an eligibility screening interview was attempted for residential numbers. The full interview was administered to households with one or more children under age 13.

Approximately 39,331 screening interviews were completed, and 4,392 interviews were conducted with 6,333 eligible households. This sample yielded 250 linked provider interviews. The identification of family day-care home providers during the household screening interview yielded 162 interviews with this type of provider.

ESTIMATION PROCEDURES AND DEGREE OF PRECISION

Each sample household was weighted by the reciprocal of its probability of selection. This basic sampling weight was adjusted for nonresponse within the Mitofsky-Waksberg "primary units" and for multiple telephone numbers among households with one or more children aged 12 years and under. The sample of responding households with one or more children aged 12 years and under was then poststratified to known population totals for various demographic and socioeconomic variables as a further adjustment for nonresponse, and also for noncoverage of nontelephone households. The resulting weights were used to project the sample to target populations and subgroups of interest. The present report is based on these weighted data, though the actual sample sizes on which analysis is based are provided throughout. In addition, approximate standard errors for percentages were calculated based upon appendix A, and only those statistically significant at $p < .05$ are reported herein.

Procedures for Collection of Information

OVERVIEW: PARENT SURVEY

Data were collected by means of telephone interviews with approximately 4,400 parents or guardians of children under age 13. Interviews were conducted by Abt Associates, under subcontract to The Urban Institute, from the firm's central telephone facility in Amherst, Massachusetts. Questionnaires were administered using computer-assisted telephone interviewing technology, whereby the questionnaire items appear on a computer screen and interviewers enter responses using the computer's keyboard. The majority of the questionnaire, including skip patterns, alternative question wordings, valid answer codes, and internal consistency checking, was programmed into the computer, so that interviewer and respondent errors were minimized. The weekly schedules of employment and child care, were, however, collected onto handwritten forms and entered into the computer by the interviewer after completion of the interview.

OVERVIEW: PROVIDER COMPONENTS

Parents were asked to provide the telephone numbers of their providers, and Abt Associates contacted and interviewed about 250 of these by telephone using CATI (linked provider component). Finally, in screening households to identify those with children under age 13 for the parent survey, providers who cared for other children in their own home were identified. Approximately 162 of these were interviewed, using the same instrument as that for the family day-care providers identified by parents (family day-care home component).

RESPONSE RATES

The National Child Care Survey, 1990, was conducted over a six-month period, beginning in late October 1989 and ending in May 1990. The provider component began in April 1990 and ended in June 1990.

Parent Survey. Although the survey was long (40 minutes on average) and some respondents terminated midway, we found that many parents were very interested in the survey, were eager to participate, and patiently answered the questions. There were two problems. First, the proportion of households containing a family with children under 13 (16 percent) was much lower than anticipated (30 percent). Second, although the screener response rate (83 percent) was close to that expected, the survey response rate (69 percent) was lower than originally predicted, making the overall response rate 57 percent. The lower eligibility rate suggests the possibility of hidden refusals by families with children who denied that they had children. The lower survey response rate reflects several factors, including the length of the interview and the well-documented increasing reluctance of the U.S. public to participate in telephone surveys (Groves and Lyberg 1988). Telephone surveys have many advantages over household surveys; however, the major disadvantage is the lower response rate.

Although undesirable, a response rate of the size obtained in this survey becomes a serious problem only if the nonresponses are biased in some way. To ensure that our results do not contain some unknown bias, we have made every effort to compare the results with data from household surveys collected in person, such as the U.S. Bureau of the Census' Survey of Income and Program Participation (SIPP) and the Current Population Survey (CPS). Based upon these comparisons, which are shown throughout the report, the results of the NCCS appear to be unbiased. Appendix B discusses the issue of sample bias resulting from the exclusion of nontelephone households.

Linked Provider Survey. We had great difficulty obtaining the names of providers from parents. A study conducted by the Centers for Disease Control found that only about 66 percent of parents were willing to name their provider (Louis Harris and Associates 1987). Once named, however, the completion rate was high, about 84 percent. We obtained telephone numbers from 44-56 percent of providers, and obtained interviews with 74 percent of those eligible.

We expected that some parents would be reluctant to name their provider for several reasons. First, parents are concerned about the safety of their children. To reassure reluctant parents, interviewers provided them with an "800" number to Abt Associates and offered to have the study director mail them a letter explaining the study's purpose. Some parents took advantage of this and telephoned the firm. Second parents may be worried about losing the provider if he or she were detected by either the local licensing authorities or the Internal Revenue Service. Assurance of confidentiality was very important. Interviewers asked only for telephone numbers, not the name or address of respondent or provider.

An additional problem was that many persons identified as providers at the first contact said they did not currently provide care or had never provided care. Many of these were probably refusals. Alternatively, given the length of time between when a phone number was obtained and second contact (as much as six months), it may be that the providers were, indeed, no longer providing care. Finally, providers, especially relatives, may disagree with parents as to whether they consider the care they provide as regular care.

Screened Provider Survey. The proportion of households containing a family day-care provider was less than 1 percent (.61 percent). Whether this statistic contains hidden refusals is not known. The response rate was 73 percent of those eligible. Again, the lengthy time between first contact with the household and follow-up may have reduced the eligibility rate.

OVERVIEW OF REPORT

This first chapter has reviewed the background and objectives of the National Child Care Survey, 1990, and described the data collection procedures. Chapter 2 provides an overview of the kinds of arrangements parents make for their children and the amount of time that children spend there. Chapter 3 reviews the extensive data on expenditures for child care arrangements and programs. Chapter 4 begins with an analysis of parental satisfaction, then moves to a discussion of parental choice of care. Chapter 5 provides a picture of what types of care parents see as available, how much they think they would cost, and what parents know about the arrangements they use for their children. Chapter 6 focuses on previous use of child care arrangements. Chapter 7 reviews what we know about the impact of child care problems on work and the availability of employer benefits to help employees balance the demands of work and family life. Chapter 8 examines parents' attitudes toward the government's role in child care. Chapter 9 summarizes the critical findings of the study.

Chapter

2

CHILD CARE ARRANGEMENTS IN THE UNITED STATES, 1990

This chapter describes the types of care and programs regularly used by families for an estimated 48 million children under age 13 during November 1989 to May 1990. The variety of family members and nonfamily individuals who care for children in families with an employed or a nonemployed mother is described, as well as the ways in which children are cared for in families headed by a father with no spouse or partner, or in which neither parent is present.

This report differs from previous child care reports in that it details care arrangements for children in families of both employed and nonemployed mothers. To make the data comparable to previous reports, all results are presented in conjunction with the employment status of the mother. In most cases, this is a crucial distinction, because the purpose of care and the characteristics associated with choice of arrangement have been found to differ based on maternal employment status. Inclusion of both types of families provides a comprehensive picture of the care arrangements and program enrollments of all children.

All children are cared for by a parent or guardian, usually their mother. If present, the mother typically assumes the primary responsibility of providing or arranging for the care of the child even if the father is also present and shares childrearing responsibilities. This report focuses on the regularly scheduled arrangements that mothers make for their children when they are not available and/or in order to provide an enriching experience for the child. Such arrangements may include care regularly provided by the father, relatives, friends, a family day care provider, or staff at a child care center or nursery school. It also includes children's regular participation in such activities as organized clubs, lessons, and/or sports. For the purposes of this report, all of the above situations are considered to be "child care arrangements," regardless of the reasons, because they may substitute for maternal care.

Respondents were asked to identify the "Programs children attend or people who care for each child on a regular basis, that is, at least once a week for the last two weeks." Occasional care was excluded. For the purpose of this report, fathers were considered a child care arrangement if identified by the mother as providing care for the child on a regularly scheduled basis when the mother is not present. Maternal care was coded as an arrangement only when no regular arrangements were reported so that all children have at least one child care arrangement. This is not meant to suggest that children in nonmaternal arrangements are not cared for by their mothers; in all but a few cases where the mother is not present these children experience alternative arrangements *in addition to* maternal care. Nor is this meant to suggest that fathers in two-parent families with mother care as the child care arrangement are not involved with their children. In such cases, fathers were simply not reported as having responsibility for providing care for the child on a regularly scheduled basis. As were mothers, single fathers were identified as the care arrangement if no other regular arrangement was reported.[1]

In this report, *primary arrangement* refers to the type of regular nonmaternal care used for the greatest amount of time according to the respondent. If there was no regular nonmaternal arrangement, maternal care was coded as the primary arrangement. *Secondary arrangement* refers to the care used for the next greatest amount of time as reported by the respondent. If there was a first but no second nonmaternal arrangement, then maternal care was coded as the second arrangement.

The number of hours children spent in each arrangement (excluding maternal care) during the previous week was collected separately in a weekly schedule of care. At this point a few discrepancies arose between respondents' designation of primary and secondary arrangements and the arrangement with the highest number of hours on the weekly schedule. One likely reason for this inconsistency is that the last week of care differed from other weeks; for example, if care was not used, or it was used fewer hours than usual, or another type of care was used. To maintain consistency with other studies, respondents' own designations of primary and secondary arrangements were used.

Throughout this report, children are described as being cared for *primarily* in a certain arrangement. This refers to the identified primary arrangement. As described above, for the purposes of this report, any nonmaternal regular arrangement is first considered to be the primary child care arrangement; maternal care is assumed to occur in addition to other arrangements.

Children who are cared for in child care centers, nursery schools, or (for school-age children) before- and after-school programs as a primary arrangement are typically referred to in this report as participating in "center-based programs," since this category includes a variety of different types of formal and informal programs for children generally in an institutional setting.

School is the primary activity and form of care for school-age children. Although previous reports have included school as child care for school-age children, we have excluded it from our tables, for the reason that not everyone reports school as an arrangement (even if the child is enrolled in school and the parent works during school hours). Although including school might be defensible if parental employment were the major concern, it is much less defensible when there is an interest in describing how children spend their time, regardless of parental employment. Therefore, we assumed all school-age children are enrolled in school and looked only at their nonschool arrangements. When school was listed as the primary arrangement for school-age children, secondary care was substituted in its place. Accordingly, the third form of care, if any, became the secondary arrangement. We believe that excluding school produces greater comparability across children than including it only for those respondents who mentioned it.

Figure 2.1 shows the proportion of children enrolled in school, by age. Almost no children under age four are enrolled in school, although a proportion are enrolled in a center-based program (from 10 percent of infants to 41 percent of three-year-olds). At age four, 51 percent are enrolled in a center-based program and 7 percent are in regular school. By age five, the enrollments are reversed: 70 percent are enrolled in school and 20 percent are in center-based programs. By age six, over 97 percent of children are enrolled in school. Although care arrangements for five-year-olds are similar in many ways to those of school-age children, five-year-olds are still likely to be in a part-day program (95 percent are enrolled in kindergarten, com-

Child Care Arrangements in the U.S., 1990 ■ 25

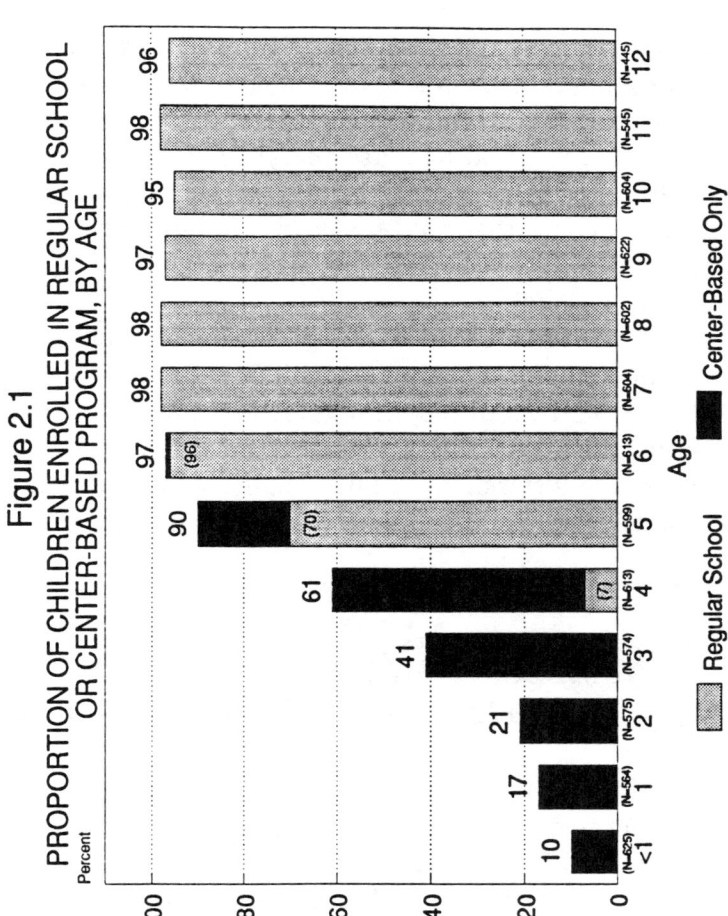

Figure 2.1
PROPORTION OF CHILDREN ENROLLED IN REGULAR SCHOOL OR CENTER-BASED PROGRAM, BY AGE

Source: National Child Care Survey 1990

pared with 32 percent of six-year-olds). In most cases, five-year-olds are included with school-age children; however, in cases where there are important differences, five-year-olds are separated from the older school-age children.

Data were initially obtained on child care arrangements for the four youngest children in the family. Fewer than 1 percent of all families had five or more children under age 13. To make the data comparable to data from previous child care studies, and because the youngest child was thought to have the strongest effect on choice of arrangements and activities of the family, the remainder of the survey obtained information primarily for the youngest child in the household.

Accordingly, this chapter first provides national estimates of the child care arrangements of all children under age 13. We then detail the arrangements of the youngest child, noting differences between the youngest child and all children, where differences occur. Finally, we also discuss the amount of time children spend in these arrangements.

NATIONAL ESTIMATES OF NUMBER OF MOTHERS AND FATHERS WITH CHILDREN UNDER AGE 13

In 1990 there were 27.6 million U.S. households with children under age 13. Fourteen million had a youngest child under age 5, and 13 million had a youngest child aged 5-12. Data were missing on age, family type, or care arrangements for a small proportion of households. Twenty-six million households contained a mother with a child under age 13. In 62 percent of these households the mother was employed the week previous, 54 percent of households had a youngest child under 5, and 72 percent of households had a youngest child aged 5-12 (table 2.1).[2]

In 1990 there were about half a million (449,000) single-father households. Of these, 133,000 had a youngest child under 5, and the remainder, 316,000, had a youngest child between 5 and 12 years of age.

Finally, there were about half a million households (462,000) with children under age 13 in which neither a mother nor father was present in the household. Of these, 176,000 had a youngest child under 5 and 286,000 had a youngest child between 5 and 12 years of age.

NATIONAL ESTIMATES OF PRIMARY CARE ARRANGEMENTS FOR ALL CHILDREN

In 1990 there were 47.7 million children in these 27.6 million households. Thirty-nine percent of these children (18.6 million) were under age 5, and 61 percent (29.1 million) were between 5 and 12 years of age.

Primary Child Care Arrangements for All Children under Age 13

Table 2.2 shows the primary child care arrangements for all children under age 13 by the employment status and presence of the mother. Note that the third and fourth columns describe children living with a mother, whereas children described in the two right-hand columns are living with their father or someone else.

Table 2.1　U.S. HOUSEHOLDS WITH CHILDREN UNDER AGE 13 (in thousands)

	Total	Children under 5	Children 5–12
Total households			
Number	27,668	14,463	13,203
Number of children[a]	47,718	18,579	29,139
Employed mothers			
Number	15,998	7,436	8,562
Percentage employed	62	54	72
Number of children[a]	26,675	9,319	17,356
Nonemployed mothers			
Number	9,711	6,321	3,390
Number of children[a]	19,487	8,881	10,606
Single fathers			
Number	449	133	316
Number of children[a]	795	151	644
No Parent			
Number	462	176	286
Number of children[a]	761	228	534
Missing Data	1,048	398	650

Source: National Child Care Survey, 1990

a. Fewer than 1 percent of households had five or more children. This study obtained information on the first five children, therefore effectively covering all U.S. children.

Table 2.2 PRIMARY CHILD CARE ARRANGEMENTS FOR ALL CHILDREN UNDER AGE 13

Child Care Arrangement #1, without School	Total (%)	Employed Mother (%)	Nonemployed Mother (%)	Father (%)	No Parent (%)
Center	13.1	16.6	8.6	14.4	5.3
Parent	44.9	34.9	60.9	21.5	8.1
Relative—child's home	7.0	8.5	4.8	10.6	8.0
Relative—other home	7.3	8.8	4.9	10.1	11.2
In-home provider	2.9	3.5	1.9	8.6	2.7
Family day care	6.9	10.8	1.6	8.3	5.0
Self-care	1.4	2.1	0.5	2.4	0.0
Lesson	13.8	12.8	15.6	7.7	9.9
Other	2.6	1.8	1.2	16.5	49.8
Total	100.0	100.0	100.0	100.0	100.0
Population estimate (in thousands)	47,718	26,675	19,487	795	761
Sample size	7,575	4,234	3,093	126	121

Source: National Child Care Survey, 1990

For 45 percent of children under age 13, the primary arrangement (excluding school) is care by a parent (table 2.2). For another quarter of these children, formal center-based care and activities such as lessons during their nonschool time constitute primary arrangements. For 14 percent of children, a relative is the primary arrangement and for 7 percent it is a family day-care provider. Only 3 percent are cared for by an in-home provider, and 1 percent are reported to care for themselves as a primary arrangement.

There are differences in primary arrangements by the employment status and presence of the mother, with a substantially larger proportion of children of nonemployed mothers primarily in the care of their parents (61 percent versus 35 percent). However, even so, almost 9 percent of children whose mothers are not employed outside the home are in a center as their primary arrangement (compared with 17 percent of the children of employed mothers). Children living with their father but not their mother are as likely to be cared for by another relative as by a parent. Children living with no parent are primarily cared for by someone else. A small proportion of such respondents listed "parent" as the primary caregiver; although these may include parents living elsewhere, in most cases these "parents" are guardians and not biological parents.

Because of the significant differences in care arrangements by age of the child, table 2.3 describes the primary child care arrangements for all children under 13 by the age of the child. The most striking finding in this table is the increased enrollment of preschoolers in center-based care with age. Only 7 percent of infants are enrolled in center-based programs, compared to one out of three preschoolers (ages 3-4). The number enrolled in center-based programs declines as children enter school. Age five clearly is a

Child Care Arrangements in the U.S., 1990

Table 2.3 PRIMARY CHILD CARE ARRANGEMENTS FOR ALL CHILDREN UNDER AGE 13, BY AGE

Child Care Arrangement #1, without School	Total Percentage (%)	<1 (%)	1–2 (%)	3–4 (%)	5 (%)	6–9 (%)	10–12 (%)
Center	13.1	7.3	14.6	33.0	21.4	9.1	2.6
Parent	44.9	59.4	48.8	37.1	43.2	45.7	41.6
Relative—child's home	7.0	7.4	6.8	4.2	5.9	7.2	9.2
Relative—other home	7.3	7.6	10.5	7.5	9.4	6.7	4.9
In-home provider	2.9	3.5	3.6	2.3	3.7	3.0	2.4
Family day care	6.9	10.1	11.8	10.1	7.6	4.9	2.6
Self-care	1.4	0.0	0.0	0.2	0.1	0.9	5.2
Lesson	13.8	1.2	1.2	3.2	7.4	20.2	28.4
Other	2.6	3.4	2.7	2.4	1.4	2.4	3.0
Total	100.0	100.0	100.0	100.0	100.0	100.0	100.0
Population estimate (in thousands)	47,718	3,927	7,175	7,477	3,755	15,358	10,025
Sample size	7,575	623	1,139	1,187	596	2,438	1,591

Source: National Child Care Survey, 1990

transition year, and is shown separately in the table. Five-year olds are enrolled in school (kindergarten), but usually for only a half day; depending on the employment status of their mother they may need additional child care. Thus, the extent of their care falls in between that of preschoolers and younger school-age children.

The age of the child and employment status of the mother are the most important factors determining the primary arrangement for the youngest child. The sections following describe the arrangements of children by both age and employment status of the mother.

PRESCHOOL-AGE CHILDREN WITH EMPLOYED MOTHER

Thirty percent of all preschool-age children with an employed mother are cared for primarily by a parent (table 2.4). Another 26 percent are in center-based care. Nineteen percent are in family day-care, and 18 percent are cared for by other relatives, either in the child's or the relative's home. Four percent are cared for by an in-home provider, and a small proportion are in other forms of care. It is remarkable that the proportion of preschool-age children cared for by a parent is not significantly different from the proportion cared for in center-based care as the primary arrangement.

Work Schedule. The employment schedule of the mother affects how children are cared for. Forty-four percent of children of part-time employed mothers are primarily cared for by a parent, whereas 22 percent of children of full-time employed mothers are cared for primarily by a parent (table 2.5). Center-based care is a more important arrangement for children of full-time employed mothers than for those of

Table 2.4 PRIMARY CHILD CARE ARRANGEMENTS FOR ALL CHILDREN UNDER AGE FIVE

Child Care Arrangement #1, without School	Total (%)	Employed Mother (%)	Nonemployed Mother (%)	Father (%)	No Parent (%)
Center	20.5	26.5	14.7	17.5	3.3
Parent	46.3	29.9	65.2	13.3	5.5
Relative—child's home	5.9	6.3	5.2	0.0	17.3
Relative—other home	8.7	11.3	5.5	26.5	12.3
In-home provider	3.0	3.7	2.2	13.2	0.0
Family day care	10.7	18.6	2.6	6.1	10.4
Self-care	0.1	0.1	0.0	0.0	0.0
Lesson	2.0	1.2	2.9	0.0	0.0
Other	2.8	2.3	1.7	4.7	0.0
Total	100.0	100.0	100.0	18.8	51.2
				100.0	100.0
Population estimate (in thousands)	18,579	9,319	8,881	151	228
Sample size	2,949	1,479	1,410	24	36

Source: National Child Care Survey, 1990

Table 2.5 PRIMARY CHILD CARE ARRANGEMENTS FOR ALL CHILDREN UNDER AGE FIVE, BY MOTHER'S EMPLOYMENT SCHEDULE

Child Care Arrangement #1, without School	Employed Total (%)	Full-time (%)	Employed Part-time (%)	Nonemployed (%)	Other (%)
Center	20.7	30.9	19.0	14.7	23.8
Parent	47.1	21.5	43.6	65.2	36.7
Relative—child's home	5.8	6.0	6.2	5.2	10.4
Relative—other home	8.5	11.9	10.8	5.5	9.1
In-home provider	3.0	3.4	3.5	2.2	8.2
Family day care	10.8	23.0	12.5	2.6	9.6
Self-care	0.1	0.2	0.0	0.0	0.0
Lesson	2.0	1.2	1.1	2.9	2.2
Other	2.0	2.0	3.3	1.7	0.0
Total	100.0	100.0	100.0	100.0	100.0
Population estimate (in thousands)	18,200	5,598	3,121	8,881	600
Sample size	2,889	889	495	1,410	95

Source: National Child Care Survey, 1990

part-time employed mothers. Thirty-one percent of preschool-age children are cared for primarily in center-based care if the mother is employed full-time, compared with 19 percent of children of mothers employed part-time. Twenty-three percent of children of full-time employed mothers are in family day-care, compared with 12 percent of children of part-time employed mothers.

Age of Child. Parent care declines and care by others increases as children of employed mothers grow older. One in three infants/toddlers is cared for primarily by a parent (table 2.6). As the child reaches preschool-age, one in four is cared for by a parent. Fourteen percent of infants, 21 percent of toddlers (2-3 years), and 37 percent of three- to four-year-old children with employed mothers are in center-based care. Twenty percent of infants and toddlers are cared for in family day-care; family day-care enrollment declines slightly among three- to four-year-olds as center-based care rises for that age group.

PRESCHOOL-AGE CHILDREN WITH NONEMPLOYED MOTHER

Sixty-five percent of the preschool-age children of nonemployed mothers are cared for primarily by a parent (table 2.4). This is not surprising. What is surprising is that still almost 15 percent of preschool children of nonemployed mothers are in center-based care as their primary arrangement during a typical week. About 11 percent are in relative care, and a small proportion is in other types of care such as in-home providers and lessons. In contrast to the children of employed mothers, only a small proportion of children of nonemployed mothers is enrolled in family day-care.

Table 2.6 PRIMARY CHILD CARE ARRANGEMENTS FOR ALL CHILDREN UNDER AGE 13, BY AGE, EMPLOYED MOTHER

Child Care Arrangement #1, without School	Total N Percentage	<1 (%)	1–2 (%)	3–4 (%)	5 (%)	6–9 (%)	10–12 (%)
Center	16.6	13.9	20.6	36.8	28.7	13.2	3.0
Parent	34.9	37.4	31.9	25.1	31.1	39.3	37.5
Relative—child's home	8.5	8.1	7.5	4.6	7.6	8.9	11.5
Relative—other home	8.8	11.2	12.9	9.9	11.3	8.1	5.4
In-home provider	3.5	5.1	4.1	2.9	3.6	3.5	3.2
Family day care	10.8	19.6	20.2	16.9	12.4	7.6	3.3
Self-care	2.1	0.0	0.0	0.3	0.3	1.3	6.8
Lesson	12.8	1.2	0.4	2.0	4.1	16.5	27.4
Other	1.8	3.3	2.7	1.5	1.1	1.5	1.9
Total	100.0	100.0	100.0	100.0	100.0	100.0	100.0
Population estimate (in thousands)	26,675	1,592	3,692	4,035	2,040	9,000	6,316
Sample size	4,234	253	586	641	324	1,429	1,003

Source: National Child Care Survey, 1990

Age of Child. The proportion of children of nonemployed mothers enrolled in center-based care is much lower than that for children of employed mothers, at all ages (table 2.7). However, this difference is smallest at ages 3-4, when most children are enrolled in a preschool program. Enrollment in family day-care also differs by maternal employment; however, in contrast to center-based care, only a small proportion of the children of nonemployed mothers is enrolled in family day-care, regardless of age.

SCHOOL-AGE CHILDREN WITH EMPLOYED MOTHER

Thirty-eight percent of all school-age children of employed mothers are cared for by parents as their primary arrangement (table 2.8). The next largest group, 19 percent, are in an activity such as lessons or sports; another 17 percent are in the care of a relative; 11 percent are in center-based care; and the remainder are in a variety of other forms of care.

Work Schedule. School-age children of full-time employed mothers are less likely to be cared for by a parent and more likely to be in other forms of care (table 2.9). For example, 14 percent of the children of full-time employed mothers are in center-based care, compared to 6 percent of the children of part-time employed mothers. Nineteen percent of the children of full-time employed mothers are in relative care, and 8 percent are in family day care, compared with 13 percent and 4 percent, respectively, of children of part-time employed mothers.

Age of Child. Age differences are also important for school-age children. The proportion of children in parental care declines and then increases again, as children age

Table 2.7 PRIMARY CHILD CARE ARRANGEMENTS FOR ALL CHILDREN UNDER AGE 13, BY AGE, NONEMPLOYED MOTHER

Child Care Arrangement #1, without School	Total N Percentage	<1 (%)	1-2 (%)	3-4 (%)	5 (%)	6-9 (%)	10-12 (%)
Center	8.6	2.9	8.5	29.4	12.3	2.0	1.8
Parent	60.9	76.5	68.7	53.7	60.2	58.8	52.9
Relative—child's home	4.8	6.8	6.0	3.2	3.6	4.6	4.6
Relative—other home	4.9	4.7	6.9	4.7	6.9	4.4	3.5
In-home provider	1.9	2.3	3.1	1.2	2.6	1.8	0.8
Family day care	1.6	3.4	2.6	1.9	1.6	0.8	0.4
Self-care	0.5	0.0	0.0	0.0	0.0	0.3	2.3
Lesson	15.6	1.2	2.2	4.7	12.2	26.7	32.5
Other	1.2	2.1	1.9	1.2	0.7	0.6	1.2
Total	100.0	100.0	100.0	100.0	100.0	100.0	100.0
Population estimate (in thousands)	17,487	2,272	3,363	3,246	1,592	5,764	3,250
Sample size	3,093	361	534	515	253	915	516

Source: National Child Care Survey, 1990

Table 2.8 PRIMARY CHILD CARE ARRANGEMENTS FOR ALL CHILDREN AGED 5-12

Child Care Arrangement #1, without School	Total (%)	Employed Mother (%)	Nonemployed Mother (%)	Father (%)	No Parent (%)
Center	8.4	11.3	3.5	13.7	6.2
Parent	43.9	37.7	57.2	23.4	9.2
Relative—child's home	7.7	9.7	4.4	13.1	4.0
Relative—other home	6.4	7.5	4.5	6.2	10.7
In-home provider	2.9	3.4	1.6	7.5	3.9
Family day care	4.5	6.6	0.8	8.8	2.7
Self-care	2.3	3.2	0.9	3.0	0.0
Lesson	21.4	19.0	26.3	8.4	14.1
Other	2.5	1.6	0.8	15.9	49.2
Total	100.0	100.0	100.0	100.0	100.0
Population estimate (in thousands)	29,139	17,356	10,606	644	534
Sample size	4,625	2,755	1,684	102	85

Source: National Child Care Survey, 1990

Table 2.9 PRIMARY CHILD CARE ARRANGEMENTS FOR ALL CHILDREN AGED 5–12, BY MOTHER'S EMPLOYMENT SCHEDULE

Child Care Arrangement #1, without School	Employed Total (%)	Full-time (%)	Employed Part-time (%)	Nonemployed (%)	Other (%)
Center	8.3	14.5	6.2	3.5	6.7
Parent	45.1	34.2	43.2	57.2	42.6
Relative—child's home	7.7	9.9	8.6	4.4	12.0
Relative—other home	6.4	9.3	4.4	4.5	5.6
In-home provider	2.7	3.5	3.3	1.6	3.2
Family day care	4.4	7.8	4.1	0.8	7.3
Self-care	2.3	3.5	2.7	0.9	2.5
Lesson	21.8	15.0	26.7	26.3	19.3
Other	1.3	2.1	0.9	0.8	0.8
Total	100.0	100.0	100.0	100.0	100.0
Population estimate (in thousands)	27,967	10,598	5,525	10,606	1,238
Sample size	4,439	1,682	877	1,684	197

Source: National Child Care Survey, 1990

(table 2.6). Although five-year-olds are enrolled in school, as stated earlier, they are in many ways like preschoolers in terms of their enrollment in center-based and family daycare--29 percent and 12 percent, respectively. Although there is some use of center-based before- and after-school care for 6- to 9-year-olds (13 percent), it is rarely used for older children (3 percent). At age 6, children begin to show sharp increases in enrollment in lessons--17 percent among 6- to 9-year-olds and 27 percent among 10- to 12-year-olds. The use of relative care, whether in-home or out-of-home, varies little by age of child. Finally, the proportion of children caring for themselves increases from almost none to almost 7 percent between ages 5 and 12.

SCHOOL-AGE CHILDREN WITH NONEMPLOYED MOTHER

Fifty-seven percent of school-age children of nonemployed mothers are cared for by parents as their primary care arrangement (table 2.8). The next most prevalent arrangement is lessons, accounting for 26 percent of children, followed by relative care, accounting for 9 percent of the arrangements of school-age children. Just under 4 percent of children of nonemployed mothers are in center-based care. The large proportion--26 percent--of school-age children of nonemployed mothers enrolled in lessons reduces the difference between children of employed and nonemployed mothers in the proportion primarily in parental care.

Age of Child. The proportion of children of nonemployed mothers in parental care as their primary arrangement declines consistently as the child ages (table 2.7). This is because the proportion of children enrolled in lessons increases dramatically as children age, from 12 percent of 5-year-olds to 32 percent of children between 10-12 years old. The proportion of children of nonemployed mothers in center-based care declines from 12 percent at age 5 to 2 percent at ages 10-12. There is little difference across ages in the other forms of care.

NATIONAL ESTIMATES OF PRIMARY CARE ARRANGEMENTS FOR YOUNGEST CHILD

Primary Care Arrangements for Youngest Child

In 42 percent of all families, parents are the primary care providers for their youngest child under 13 years of age (table 2.10) Relatives are next in prevalence, providing care in 18 percent of families. Centers are third in prevalence, accounting for 16 percent of primary care in families. Family day-care and lessons are next, each providing 9 percent of care. In-home providers are relatively rare, providing care for about 3 percent of youngest children.

Across families of all types, the proportion of youngest children in a center-based program as the primary arrangement rises to 37 percent at ages three to four, after which it falls to 28 percent at age five and to 12 percent from ages six to nine (table 2.11).

A comparison of table 2.2 and table 2.11 reveals that the distribution of children by age in primary arrangements is very similar for all children and for youngest children. Where age ranges are broader (e.g., under age five), the tables differ more because the distribution of the samples by age is not the same. Older children are underrepresented

Table 2.10 PRIMARY CHILD CARE ARRANGEMENT FOR YOUNGEST CHILD, BY FAMILY TYPE, ALL FAMILIES

Child Care Arrangement #1, without School	Total (%)	Employed Mother (%)	Nonemployed Mother (%)	Father (%)	No Parent (%)
Center	16.1	20.5	9.3	15.5	6.7
Parent	42.0	30.5	62.7	27.5	16.3
Mother	15.2	18.0	12.4	—	—
Father	29.3	17.0	48.5	—	—
Relative—child's home	8.8	9.7	6.5	17.6	15.5
Relative—other home	9.6	11.5	6.3	10.3	10.0
In-home provider	3.0	3.1	2.6	9.8	1.5
Family day care	8.7	12.8	2.0	4.9	10.8
Self-care	1.5	2.1	0.7	2.1	0.0
Lesson	8.6	8.4	8.5	4.4	20.6
Other	1.9	1.4	1.6	7.8	18.7
Total	100.0	100.0	100.0	100.0	100.0
Population estimate (in thousands)	26,618	15,997	9,711	449	462
Sample size	4,225	2,539	1,541	71	73

Source: National Child Care Survey, 1990

Table 2.11 PRIMARY CHILD CARE ARRANGEMENT FOR YOUNGEST CHILD, BY AGE

Child Care Arrangement #1, without School	Total (%)	<1 (%)	1–2 (%)	3–4 (%)	5 (%)	6–9 (%)	10–12 (%)
Center	16.1	7.0	15.4	37.2	27.6	11.5	3.0
Parent	42.0	57.8	46.7	32.4	33.5	40.9	36.9
Mother	18.3	24.3	19.9	13.5	12.4	18.8	17.9
Father	23.0	33.6	26.7	18.5	21.0	21.0	16.9
Relative—child's home	8.8	8.1	6.6	4.6	6.8	10.5	15.8
Relative—other home	9.6	8.3	11.6	8.9	12.4	9.6	6.8
In-home provider	3.0	3.6	3.2	2.2	1.8	4.0	1.7
Family day care	8.7	11.6	13.4	10.6	9.1	5.3	2.1
Self-care	1.5	0.1	0.4	0.2	0.0	0.9	8.2
Lesson	8.6	1.0	0.7	2.1	7.8	15.4	23.9
Other	1.9	2.4	2.1	1.7	1.1	1.9	1.5
Total	100.0	100.0	100.0	100.0	100.0	100.0	100.0
Population estimate (in thousands)	26,618	3,632	5,890	4,544	1,878	6,986	3,689
Sample size	4,225	576	935	721	298	1,109	586

Source: National Child Care Survey, 1990

in the sample of youngest children; therefore, differences are largest in the school-age analyses.

The age of the child and employment status of the mother are, as before, the most important factors determining the primary care arrangement for the youngest child. Therefore, the following discussion separates families by the age of the youngest child (under 5 years, 5-12 years) and by the employment status of the mother.

PRESCHOOL-AGE CHILDREN

In 45 percent of all families with the youngest child under age five, the parents (26 percent mother, 19 percent father) are the primary providers of care (table 2.12). Second is center-based care, which provides 20 percent of primary care. Relatives are third, providing 16 percent of primary care, with grandparents providing two-thirds to three-thirds of this care. Family day-care providers are fourth, providing 12 percent of primary care. The other forms of care as a primary arrangement are relatively rare.

PRESCHOOL-AGE CHILDREN WITH EMPLOYED MOTHER

As already indicated, the employment status of the mother makes a big difference in the type of primary care arrangement. For families with the youngest child under age five and an employed mother, center-based programs are used as often as parents in providing primary care for the youngest child while the mother works. In 28 percent of employed-mother families, parents (17 percent father, 11 percent mother) are primary providers during the working

Table 2.12 PRIMARY CHILD CARE ARRANGEMENT FOR YOUNGEST CHILD UNDER AGE FIVE

Child Care Arrangement #1, without School	Total (%)	Employed Mother (%)	Nonemployed Mother (%)	Father (%)	No Parent (%)
Center	20.3	28.3	11.4	18.6	4.3
Parent	44.9	27.7	67.2	16.9	2.0
Father	19.0	16.9	22.3	—	—
Mother	25.8	10.6	44.9	—	—
Relative—child's home	6.3	6.5	5.7	3.5	23.1
Relative—other home	9.9	12.7	6.3	17.6	11.5
In-home provider	3.0	2.8	3.0	15.0	0
Family day care	12.1	19.9	2.6	6.9	23.4
Self-care	0.2	0.1	0.4	0.0	0.0
Lesson	1.2	0.4	2.2	0.0	0.0
Other	2.0	1.6	1.1	21.4	35.8
Total	100.0	100.0	100.0	100.0	100.0
Population estimate (in thousands)	14,065	7,436	6,321	133	176
Sample size	2,233	1,180	1,003	21	28

Source: National Child Care Survey, 1990

day (table 2.12, figure 2.2). In another 28 percent of families, a center-based program is the primary care provider. After parents and centers, family day-care (20 percent) and relatives (19 percent) are next in importance. Grandparents provide about two-thirds to three-fourths of relative care. In-home providers are used relatively infrequently, with only about 3 percent of families relying on such nonrelative care. Thus, 47 percent of families depend on parents or a close relative for care for the youngest preschool child, and an almost equal percentage, 48 percent, depend on a preschool or family day-care program. Only 5 percent depend on in-home providers or other forms of care.

Work Schedule. Preschool-age children whose mothers are employed full-time are much less likely to be in the care of a parent than those whose mothers are employed part-time (15 percent versus 49 percent) (table 2.13, figure 2.2). Children of full-time employed mothers are also much more likely to be enrolled in a center-based program (35 percent versus 18 percent) or in a family day-care home (24 percent versus 13 percent) than children of mothers employed part-time.

Age of Child. There are strong differences in arrangements by age of the youngest child. Even when the mother is employed, 38 percent of parents of infants are their primary caregivers (table 2.14, figure 2.3). As the age of the youngest child increases, primary care by parents drops from 38 percent to 29 percent for toddlers (one to two years old) and to 21 percent for preschoolers (three to four years old). At the same time, care in a center-based program increases from 14 percent for infants, to 23 percent for toddlers, to 43 percent for preschoolers. Differences in the other categories of care by age of the youngest child are small.

48 ■ NATIONAL CHILD CARE SURVEY, 1990

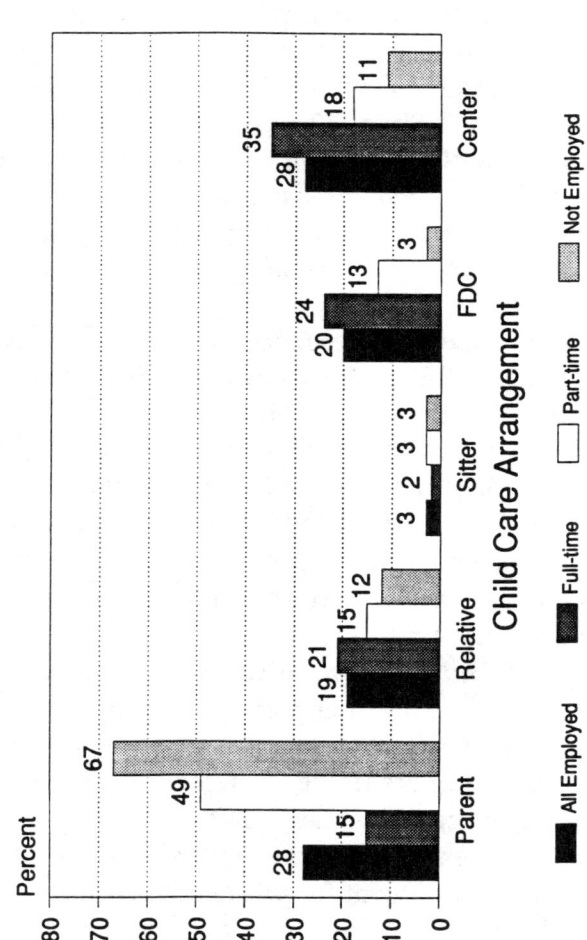

Figure 2.2
PRIMARY CARE, YOUNGEST PRESCHOOL CHILD
EMPLOYED AND NON-EMPLOYED MOTHERS

Source: National Child Care Survey 1990

Table 2.13 PRIMARY CHILD CARE ARRANGEMENT FOR YOUNGEST CHILD UNDER AGE FIVE, BY MOTHER'S EMPLOYMENT SCHEDULE

Child Care Arrangement #1, without School	Total (%)	Employed Full-time (%)	Employed Part-time (%)	Nonemployed (%)	Other (%)
Center	20.5	34.8	17.9	11.4	19.3
Parent	45.8	15.4	48.8	67.2	36.1
Father	19.4	10.9	29.1	22.3	13.0
Mother	26.4	4.5	19.6	44.9	23.1
Relative—child's home	6.1	7.1	4.1	5.7	12.5
Relative—other home	9.8	13.9	11.2	6.3	9.2
In-home provider	2.9	2.5	3.2	3.0	4.3
Family day care	12.0	24.0	13.0	2.6	16.1
Self-care	0.3	0.2	0.0	0.4	0.0
Lesson	1.3	0.5	0.2	2.2	1.2
Other	1.4	1.6	1.7	1.1	1.3
Total	100.0	100.0	100.0	100.0	100.0
Population estimate (in thousands)	13,756	4,537	2,389	6,321	500
Sample size	2,184	720	381	1,003	79

Source: National Child Care Survey, 1990

Table 2.14 PRIMARY CHILD CARE ARRANGEMENT FOR YOUNGEST CHILD, BY AGE, EMPLOYED MOTHER

Child Care Arrangement #1, without School	Total (%)	<1 (%)	1-2 (%)	3-4 (%)	5 (%)	6-9 (%)	10-12 (%)
Center	20.5	13.6	22.7	42.8	31.9	15.0	3.2
Parent	30.5	37.7	28.6	20.7	23.5	35.4	33.1
Father	18.0	22.5	18.4	12.1	13.5	20.2	18.6
Mother	12.5	15.2	10.2	8.6	10.0	15.1	14.1
Relative—child's home	9.7	9.0	6.7	4.9	1.5	11.1	17.4
Relative—other home	11.5	13.0	13.8	11.4	14.5	11.2	7.3
In-home provider	3.1	3.4	3.0	2.4	1.7	4.5	1.6
Family day care	12.8	20.4	22.6	16.5	13.9	6.8	3.1
Self-care	2.1	0.0	0.2	0.0	0.0	1.3	10.1
Lesson	8.4	0.5	0.3	0.6	6.5	13.6	22.4
Other	1.4	2.4	2.0	0.7	0.5	1.1	1.8
Total	100.0	100.0	100.0	100.0	100.0	100.0	100.0
Population estimate (in thousands)	15,997	1,529	3,152	2,754	1,148	4,835	2,579
Sample size	2,539	243	500	437	182	768	409

Source: National Child Care Survey, 1990

Figure 2.3
PRIMARY CARE FOR YOUNGEST CHILD <13
Employed Mothers

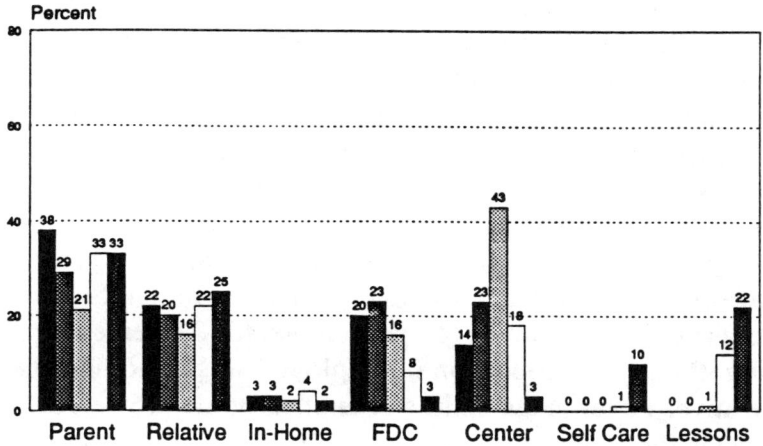

Non-Employed Mothers

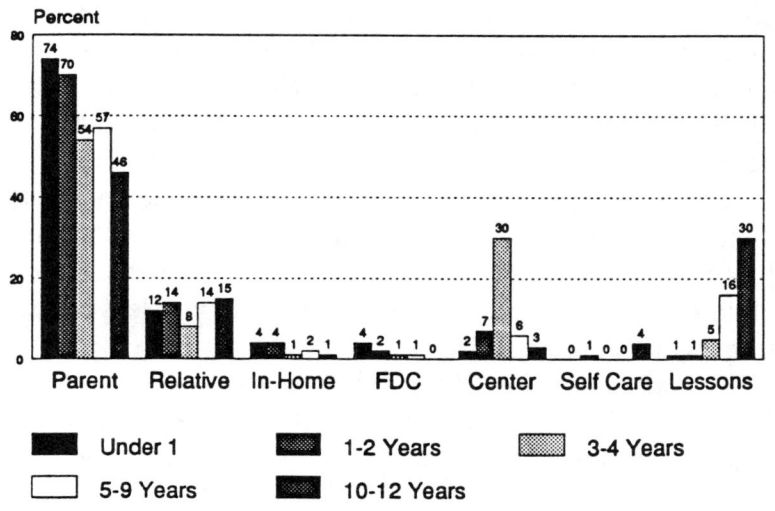

Source: National Child Care Survey, 1990

Demographic Characteristics. A number of characteristics of families with an employed mother are associated with greater or lesser enrollment of their youngest preschool-age child in centers. Non-Hispanic black families with an employed mother are almost twice as likely as white or Hispanic families to use a child care center, and are half as likely to use parent care (table 2.15). This may be explained by differences based on family structure. Black families are very likely to be headed by a single female. Mother-only families are, understandably, more likely than two-parent families to use a center (38 percent versus 26 percent) and less likely than two-parent families to use care by a parent (11 percent versus 31 percent). A slightly higher proportion of employed single mothers use relatives either in the child's or another home--26 percent--than is found among employed mothers in two-parent families (18 percent). Four out of five of these relatives are the child's grandparent.

Family size is one of the more important factors associated with care. Employed-mother families with three or more children under 13 years old are less likely to use center care or family day-care and are more likely to use parent care than families with one or two children under 13 years old.

There are significant differences in enrollments by the education of the mother, with employed mothers with a college or graduate degree more likely to enroll their youngest child in a center-based program than those with less education (figure 2.4a).

Income Level. Families with an employed mother and incomes of $50,000 or more per year (in some cases, those with incomes of $35,000 and over) differ in their child care arrangements from those with incomes under $50,000 per year (figure 2.4b). Families with higher incomes are more likely to have a child in a center or in family day-care, are less likely to use a parent or relative, and are more likely to use an in-home provider than families with lower incomes. This suggests that the higher the income, the more likely a family is to use market care. However, these differences are not statistically significant. In addition, the difference in enrollment in center-based care by poverty status is also not significant. Due to the extensive subsidization of programs for low-income children, families with incomes below the poverty line are as likely as wealthier families to enroll their children in center-based care.

The extent to which a mother can care for her youngest child when she works differs by occupations. Mothers in managerial and professional occupations are more likely to place their child in a center and less likely to use parent care than mothers in service occupations (not shown).

Residence. Compared with rural residents, employed mother families living in central cities and suburban areas are more likely to enroll their youngest preschool-age child in a center-based program. Employed mother families living in the South have the highest proportion of youngest children in center-based care--36 percent. The comparable proportions are 28 percent in the West, 25 percent in the Northeast and only 17 percent in the Midwest. Families in the South use less parental care as a primary arrangement than those in other regions. Families in the Midwest use more parental care and family day-care. Families in the Northeast use more care by relatives. Western families appear to be about average on their use of all types of care (table 2.15).

Table 2.15 PRIMARY CHILD CARE ARRANGEMENT FOR YOUNGEST CHILD UNDER AGE FIVE, BY FAMILY AND AREA CHARACTERISTICS, EMPLOYED MOTHER

	Parent (%)	Relative (%)	In-home Provider (%)	FDC[a] (%)	Center (%)	Other (%)	Total %	Population Estimate (thousands)	Sample Size
White	31	17	3	22	26	1	100	5,436	863
Black	14	27	0.1	11	45	3	100	989	157
Hispanic	25	30	4	15	23	3	100	664	105
<high school	31	33	0.5	12	22	2	100	456	72
High school	27	24	2	19	25	3	100	2,847	452
Some college	32	16	1	25	25	1	100	1,787	284
College	28	14	4	20	32	2	100	1,419	225
Graduate school	19	11	8	18	44	0	100	707	112
Mother only	11	26	3	19	38	3	100	1,208	192
Mother and father	31	18	3	20	26	2	100	6,007	954
<$15,000	31	24	0	16	25	4	100	1,074	170
$15,000–$24,999	30	23	2	16	27	2	100	1,226	195
$25,000–$34,999	29	24	1	20	23	3	100	1,222	194
$35,000–$49,999	31	15	4	20	29	1	100	1,713	272
$50,000+	21	14	5	26	34	0	100	1,712	272

Child Care Arrangements in the U.S., 1990

Central city	28	19	3	17	32	1	100	2,994	475
Suburban	24	20	2	23	28	3	100	2,413	383
Rural	33	19	4	21	22	1	100	1,808	287
West	31	16	2	20	28	3	100	1,331	211
South	21	20	3	18	36	2	100	2,754	437
Midwest	34	16	2	30	17	1	100	1,715	272
Northeast	30	25	5	13	25	2	100	1,415	225
1 child	21	21	2	22	32	2	100	3,181	505
2 children	28	19	3	21	27	2	100	2,829	449
3 or more children	44	16	5	14	18	3	100	1,205	191
Age:									
<1 year	38	22	4	20	14	2	100	1,495	237
1–2 years	29	21	3	23	22	2	100	3,061	486
3–4 years	21	16	2	16	43	2	100	2,659	422
Above poverty	28	18	3	20	29	2	100	6,022	956
Below poverty	29	26	0	16	22	7	100	664	105

Source: National Child Care Survey, 1990

a. FDC, family day care.

56 ■ NATIONAL CHILD CARE SURVEY, 1990

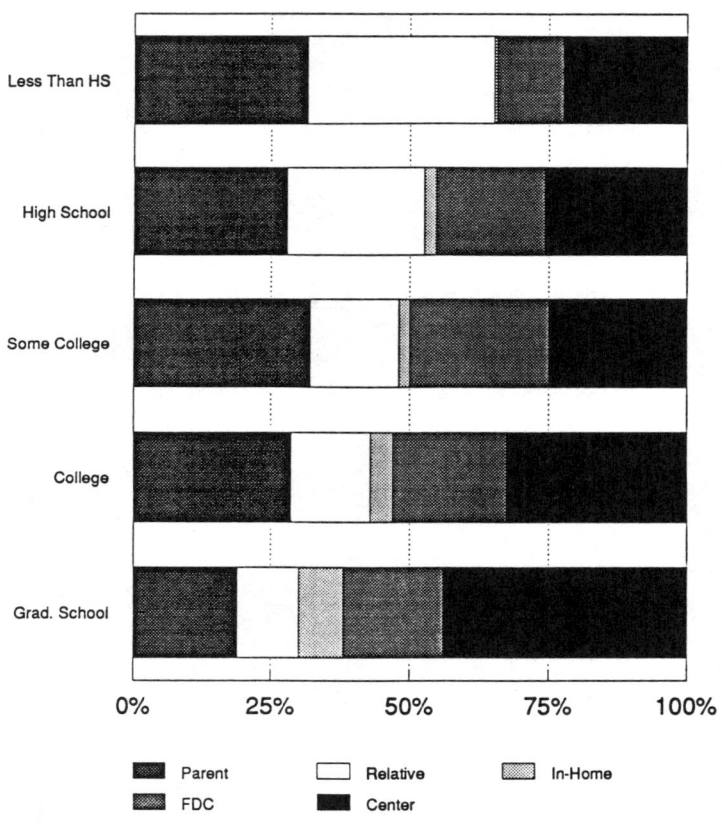

Figure 2.4a
PRIMARY CARE FOR YOUNGEST PRESCHOOL CHILD
BY EDUCATION, EMPLOYED MOTHERS

Source: National Child Care Survey 1990

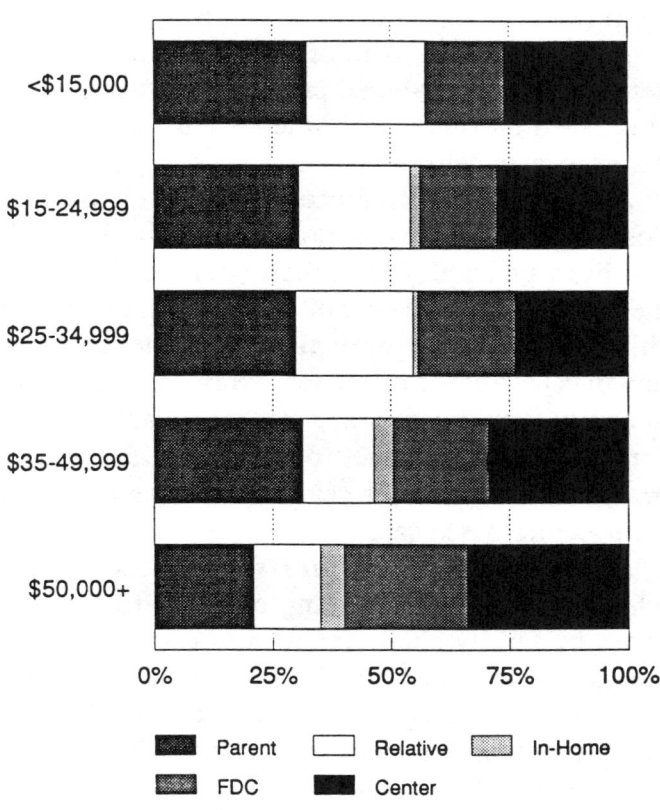

Figure 2.4b
PRIMARY CARE FOR YOUNGEST PRESCHOOL CHILD
BY INCOME, EMPLOYED MOTHERS

Source: National Child Care Survey 1990

PRESCHOOL-AGE CHILDREN WITH NONEMPLOYED MOTHER

In families with a youngest child under age five and the mother is not employed outside the home, 67 percent of parents (22 percent father, 45 percent mother) care for their preschool-age children themselves as a primary arrangement (table 2.12, figure 2.2). Thirty-three percent are in some nonparental form of care, primarily relatives (12 percent) and center-based programs (11 percent). For nonemployed mothers, in-home care by a nonrelative is a minor form of care.

Age of Child. Differences by age of child among families with nonemployed mothers are similar to those for families with employed mothers (table 2.16, figure 2.3). As the age of the youngest child increases, the proportion of children in primary parental care declines and the proportion in center-based care rises. Only 2 percent of infants of nonemployed mothers are in center-based care, as are 7 percent of toddlers (one- to two-year-olds). However, 30 percent of three- to four-year-olds of nonemployed mothers are in center-based care.

Demographic Characteristics. Among families in which the mother is not employed, there are also differences by family characteristics in primary care arrangements chosen. For example, families in which the mother has at least a college degree are the most likely to enroll their preschool-age child in a center-based program (table 2.17, figure 2.5a). There are no significant differences by race or marital status in the use of a center as the primary form of care for their youngest preschooler among mothers not employed outside the home. Fourteen percent of nonemployed single mothers use a center-based program, compared with 11 percent of two-parent families with a

Table 2.16 PRIMARY CHILD CARE ARRANGEMENT FOR YOUNGEST CHILD, BY AGE, WITH NONEMPLOYED MOTHER

Child Care Arrangement #1, without School	Total (%)	<1 (%)	1–2 (%)	3–4 (%)	5 (%)	6–9 (%)	10–12 (%)
Center	9.3	2.2	7.2	29.6	19.3	1.6	2.9
Parent	62.7	74.1	70.0	54.0	52.7	58.8	46.5
Father	20.3	26.1	22.5	17.1	11.5	17.7	17.8
Mother	42.4	48.0	47.5	36.9	41.1	41.0	28.7
Relative—child's home	6.5	7.7	6.1	2.6	4.8	7.5	11.0
Relative—other home	6.3	4.8	8.1	5.3	9.7	5.9	4.1
In-home provider	2.6	3.7	3.6	1.2	0.9	2.7	1.0
Family day care	2.0	4.2	2.2	1.2	0.6	1.3	0.0
Self-care	0.7	0.2	0.6	0.5	0.0	0.3	3.7
Lesson	8.5	1.5	1.1	4.9	10.4	18.7	30.1
Other	1.6	1.6	1.1	0.9	1.6	3.1	0.8
Total	100.0	100.0	100.0	100.0	100.0	100.0	100.0
Population estimate (in thousands)	9,711	2,055	2,634	1,632	680	1,799	911
Sample size	1,541	326	418	259	108	285	145

Source: National Child Care Survey, 1990

Table 2.17 PRIMARY CHILD CARE ARRANGEMENT FOR YOUNGEST CHILD UNDER AGE FIVE, BY FAMILY AND AREA CHARACTERISTICS WITH NONEMPLOYED MOTHER

	Parent (%)	Relative (%)	In-home Provider (%)	FDC[a] (%)	Center (%)	Other (%)	Total %	Population Estimate (thousands)	Sample Size
White	68	11	4	3	12	2	100	4,538	720
Black	60	21	1	2	8	8	100	763	121
Hispanic	69	11	0	2	14	4	100	797	127
< high school	64	21	2	0.5	9	4	100	1,038	165
High school	74	11	2	3	8	2	100	2,555	406
Some college	65	11	4	3	12	5	100	1,384	220
College	56	8	5	5	21	5	100	931	148
Graduate school	61	8	9	3	14	5	100	259	41
Mother only	44	28	2	6	14	6	100	1,086	172
Mother and father	72	9	3	2	11	3	100	5,082	807
<$15,000	62	15	2	4	12	5	100	1,576	250
$15,000–$24,999	80	8	2	0.5	6	4	100	1,016	161
$25,000–$34,999	71	12	3	2	9	3	100	915	145
$35,000–$49,999	74	12	2	4	7	1	100	1,068	170
$50,000+	50	10	7	3	25	5	100	886	141

Central city	61	14	3	2	14	6	100	2,675	425
Suburban	70	11	4	3	9	3	100	2,054	326
Rural	73	12	2	4	9	0	100	1,440	229
West	66	14	2	3	10	5	100	1,655	263
South	66	10	3	4	12	5	100	1,739	276
Midwest	72	12	2	2	10	2	100	1,541	245
Northeast	63	13	6	2	12	4	100	1,233	196
1 child	66	15	3	3	10	3	100	2,047	325
2 children	65	11	3	3	14	4	100	2,373	377
3 or more children	71	11	3	2	8	5	100	1,748	377
Age:									
<1 year	74	13	4	4	2	3	100	1,996	317
1–2 years	70	14	4	2	7	3	100	2,588	411
3–4 years	53	8	1	1	30	7	100	1,585	252
Above poverty level	70	10	3	2	12	3	100	4,215	669
Below poverty level	57	20	0.7	5	12	5	100	1,154	183

Source: National Child Care Survey, 1990

a. FDC, family day care.

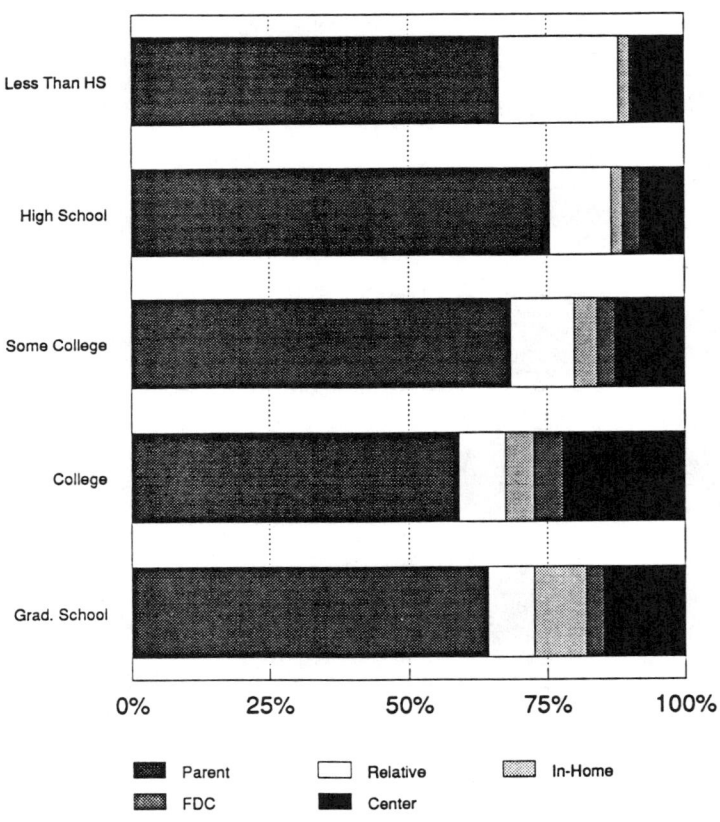

Figure 2.5a
PRIMARY CARE FOR YOUNGEST PRESCHOOL CHILD
BY EDUCATION, NON-EMPLOYED MOTHERS

Source: National Child Care Survey 1990

nonemployed mother. In contrast, there are large differences in parent care as the primary arrangement by marital status. Only 44 percent of nonemployed single mothers rely on no regular arrangements besides parent care compared with 72 percent of two-parent families with a nonemployed mother. A high proportion of single mothers uses relatives either in the child's or another home--28 percent of nonemployed single mothers, compared to 9 percent of nonemployed mothers in two-parent families. Four out of five of these relatives are the child's grandparent.

Income Level. Families with high income levels are more likely than families with low or middle-level incomes to use a center-based program for their youngest child (figure 2.5b). However, families at the lowest income level are slightly more likely than families with middle-level incomes to use a center-based program, again a likely result of the availability of subsidies for low-income children.

Residence. Compared with rural residents, residents of central cities are more likely to enroll their youngest preschool-age child in a center-based program. There are few regional differences in enrollment in centers among families with a nonemployed mother. The only major difference is the greater use of in-home providers by families living in the Northeast.

PRESCHOOL-AGE CHILDREN WITH SINGLE FATHER

Single fathers of preschoolers are as likely to care for their child themselves as a primary arrangement as are married fathers. A father is primary caregiver for 17 percent of preschoolers (table 2.12). Care by a relative (primarily a

64 ■ NATIONAL CHILD CARE SURVEY, 1990

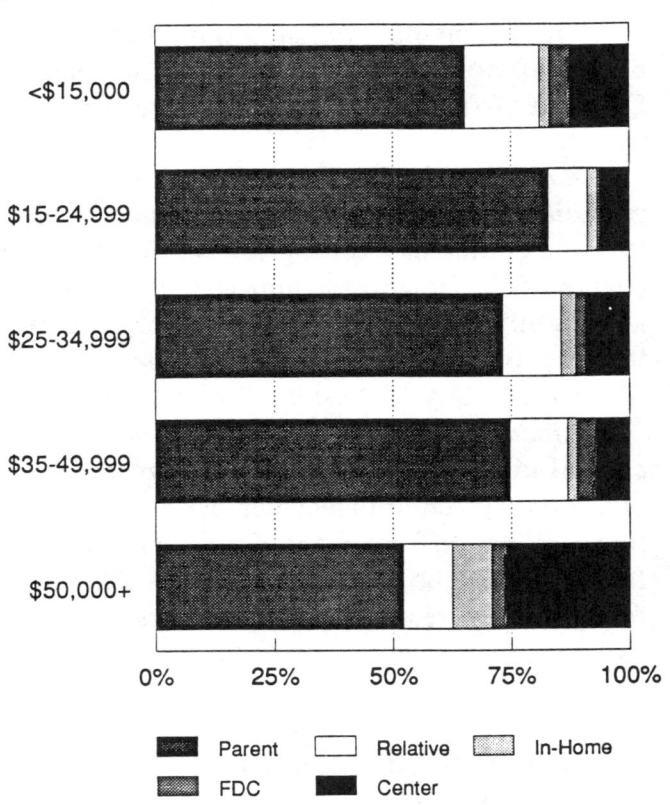

Figure 2.5b
PRIMARY CARE FOR YOUNGEST PRESCHOOL CHILD
BY INCOME, NON-EMPLOYED MOTHERS

Source: National Child Care Survey 1990

grandparent, not shown) constitutes a large category, accounting for 21 percent of youngest preschoolers. Center care is next in importance, providing care for 19 percent of youngest preschoolers. In-home providers constitute 15 percent of care for the youngest child in these families. The large "other" category reflects a number of unknown arrangements used for children of single fathers.

SCHOOL-AGE CHILDREN

Among families with no preschool-age children, nonparental care is even more common than among families with preschool-age children. This is because a substantial proportion of school-age children spend time in lessons, which in many cases serve as child care. In families with the youngest child of school age, 39 percent of children are cared for primarily by parents before or after school, 21 percent are cared for by relatives, 17 percent take lessons, 11 percent are cared for in centers, 5 percent are cared for in family day-care, and 3 percent care for themselves (table 2.18).

SCHOOL-AGE CHILDREN WITH EMPLOYED MOTHER

Among families with an employed mother, 33 percent of school-age children are in the primary care of a parent before or after school, 23 percent are in the care of a relative, 15 percent take lessons, 14 percent are cared for in a center-based program before or after school, 7 percent are cared for in a family day-care home, 3 percent are cared for

Table 2.18 PRIMARY CHILD CARE ARRANGEMENT FOR YOUNGEST CHILD, AGED 5–12

Child Care Arrangement #1, without School	Total (%)	Employed Mother (%)	Nonemployed Mother (%)	Father (%)	No Parent (%)
Center	11.4	13.7	5.5	14.1	8.2
Parent	38.6	33.1	54.3	31.9	25.1
Father	17.6	18.8	16.5	—	—
Mother	19.8	14.1	37.7	—	—
Relative—child's home	11.5	12.5	7.9	23.5	10.8
Relative—other home	9.2	10.5	6.2	7.3	9.1
In-home provider	3.0	3.3	1.9	7.6	2.4
Family day care	4.9	6.6	0.8	4.0	3.0
Self-care	2.9	3.8	1.1	3.0	0.0
Lesson	16.8	15.3	20.1	6.3	33.2
Other	1.7	1.2	2.2	2.2	8.1
Total	100.0	100.0	100.0	100.0	100.0
Population estimate (in thousands)	12,553	8,562	3,390	316	286
Sample size	1,993	1,359	538	50	45

Source: National Child Care Survey, 1990

by an in-home provider, and 4 percent are in self-care (table 2.18, figure 2.6).

Age of Child. As with families of preschool-age children, there are large differences in child care usage between families with older and younger school-age children. Among families with an employed mother, about one out of three uses primary parental care for their school-age children, regardless of the child's age (table 2.14, figure 2.3). However, thirty-two percent of families whose youngest child is 5 years old use a center-based before-/after-school program, compared with 15 percent of families with a 6- to 9-year-old and only 3 percent of families with a 10- to 12-year-old. The other main difference is in the use of self-care. Although no 5-year-olds and only 1 percent of youngest children 6-9 are in self-care, 10 percent of youngest children aged 10-12 are in self-care. Four times as many 5-year-olds and twice as many 6- to 9-year-old as 10- to 12-year-old youngest children are cared for by a family day-care provider (14 percent and 7 percent versus 3 percent, respectively). Finally, over one-third more 10- to 12-year-olds as 6- to 9-year-olds and twice as many 6- to 9-year-olds as 5-year-olds take lessons (22 percent compared with 14 percent and 7 percent, respectively). Many parents use lessons as a way to care for school-age children after school, as well as to expand their academic, physical, social, and cultural skills.

Work Schedule. Compared to those with a mother employed part-time, school-age children with a mother employed full-time are less likely to be cared for primarily by a parent (30 percent, full-time, versus 39 percent, part-time), are more likely to be in the care of a relative (26 percent versus 18 percent), are twice as likely to be enrolled in a center-based before-/after-school program (17 percent versus 8 percent), and are half as likely to be taking lessons

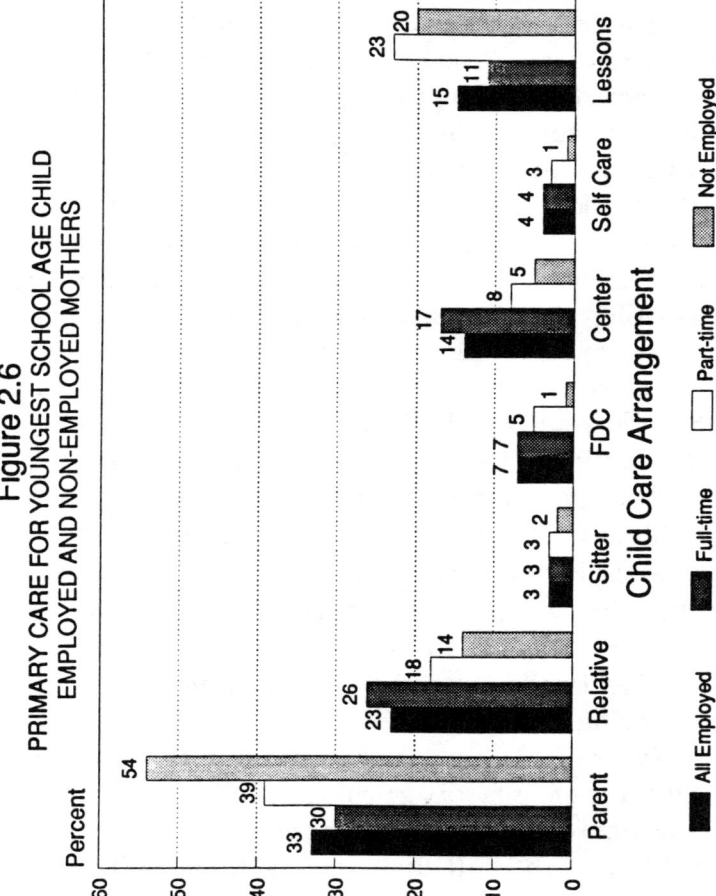

Figure 2.6
PRIMARY CARE FOR YOUNGEST SCHOOL AGE CHILD
EMPLOYED AND NON-EMPLOYED MOTHERS

Source: National Child Care Survey 1990

after school (11 percent versus 23 percent) (table 2.19, figure 2.6).

Demographic Characteristics. The biggest difference in use of parental care is between families with and without a father present. Two-parent families are three times more likely than single mothers to rely on parent care (39 percent versus 13 percent) (table 2.20). This may explain the apparent difference in use of parent care use between non-Hispanic blacks and others, since black families are more likely to be headed by a single mother.

There are sharp differences in enrollments in before-/after-school programs by the education of the mother, but not by income or race. Families in which the mother has less than a high school education are less likely to enroll their children in a before-/after-school program in a center than are mothers with a high school education (4 percent versus 13 percent) and are substantially less likely to enroll their children in a before-/after-school program in a center than mothers with graduate school training (4 percent versus 19 percent) (figure 2.7a).

Highly educated mothers are also considerably more likely than other mothers to enroll their school-age children in lessons (21-22 percent of youngest children of mothers with a college degree compared with 11-14 percent of youngest children of mothers with less than a college degree).

Income. Families with incomes in the $25,000-$50,000 range are more likely than other families to use primarily parent care for their school-age children (figure 2.7b). In contrast to enrollments in before-/after-school programs, which do not differ significantly by income, use of lessons is tied to income. Only 8 percent of children in families with incomes under $15,000 take lessons, compared with 20 percent of children in families with incomes of $50,000

Table 2.19 PRIMARY CHILD CARE ARRANGEMENT FOR YOUNGEST CHILD, AGED 5–12, BY MOTHER'S EMPLOYMENT SCHEDULE

Child Care Arrangement #1, without School	Total (%)	Employed Full-time (%)	Employed Part-time (%)	Nonemployed (%)	Other (%)
Center	11.4	17.2	8.0	5.5	5.6
Parent	39.1	29.6	39.3	54.3	41.0
Father	18.2	18.4	21.2	16.5	12.6
Mother	20.8	11.1	18.0	37.7	28.4
Relative—child's home	11.2	14.1	10.0	7.9	7.6
Relative—other home	9.2	11.4	8.0	6.2	12.1
In-home provider	2.9	3.3	3.4	1.9	2.5
Family day care	5.0	7.5	4.9	0.8	5.1
Self-care	3.0	4.5	2.6	1.1	1.1
Lesson	16.6	11.1	23.1	20.1	22.1
Other	1.5	1.3	0.7	2.2	3.0
Total	100.0	100.0	100.0	100.0	100.0
Population estimate (in thousands)	11,957	5,559	2,491	3,390	517
Sample size	1,898	882	395	538	82

Source: National Child Care Survey, 1990

Child Care Arrangements in the U.S., 1990 ■ 71

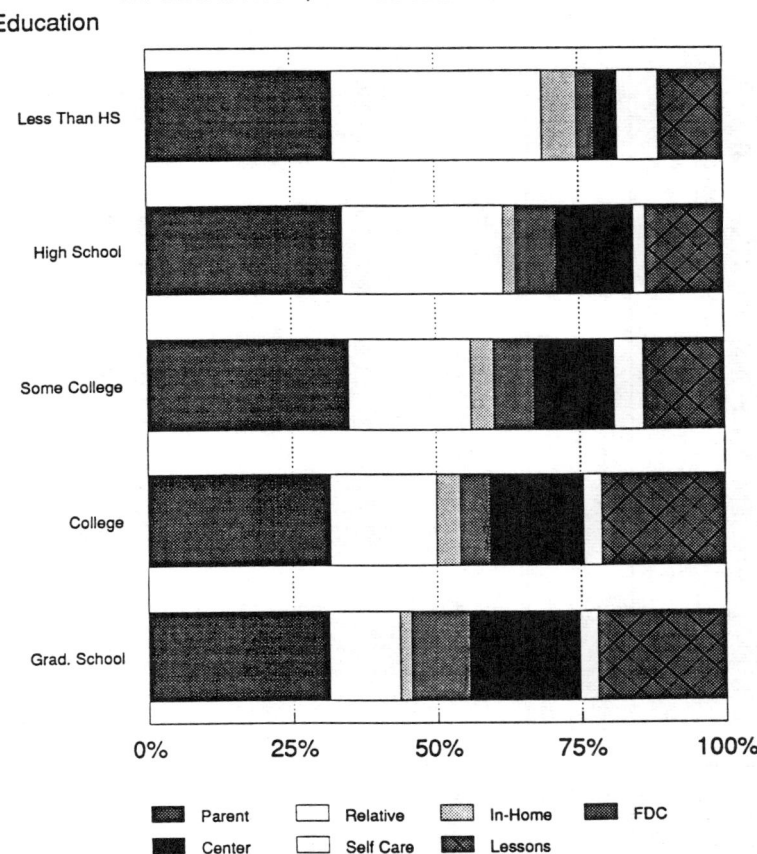

Figure 2.7a
PRIMARY CARE FOR YOUNGEST SCHOOL AGE CHILD
BY EDUCATION, EMPLOYED MOTHERS

Source: National Child Care Survey 1990

Table 2.20 PRIMARY CHILD CARE ARRANGEMENT FOR YOUNGEST CHILD AGED 5–12, BY FAMILY AND AREA CHARACTERISTICS, WITH EMPLOYED MOTHER

	Parent (%)	Relative (%)	In-home Provider (%)	FDC[a] (%)	Center (%)	Self-care (%)	Lessons (%)	Other (%)	Total %	Population Estimate (thousands)	Sample Size
White	35	19	2	7	14	4	18	1	100	6,424	1,020
Black	26	42	3	6	14	3	6	0	100	1,135	180
Hispanic	30	31	13	8	8	2	9	0	100	639	101
< high school	32	36	6	3	4	7	11	1	100	588	93
High school	33	27	2	7	13	2	13	3	100	3,336	530
Some college	35	21	4	7	14	5	14	0	100	2,236	355
College	31	18	4	5	16	3	21	2	100	1,316	209
Graduate school	31	12	2	10	19	3	22	1	100	869	138
Mother only	13	35	6	13	17	4	10	2	100	1,869	297
Mother and father	39	20	2	5	13	3	17	1	100	6,476	1,028
<$15,000	28	33	6	10	9	4	8	2	100	1,278	203
$15,000–$24,999	30	35	2	6	15	5	6	1	100	1,274	202
$25,000–$34,999	39	20	2	6	14	2	16	1	100	1,286	204
$35,000–$49,999	38	19	2	5	13	3	18	2	100	1,653	262
$50,000+	31	17	4	6	16	4	20	2	100	1,329	370

Child Care Arrangements in the U.S., 1990

Central city	30	25	5	8	16	2	12	2	100	2,858	454
Suburban	34	18	3	6	15	4	19	1	100	3,099	492
Rural	35	28	1	6	10	4	15	1	100	2,389	379
West	34	16	2	8	20	3	14	3	100	1,627	258
South	32	26	4	6	14	3	15	0	100	3,134	497
Midwest	34	21	3	7	11	4	18	2	100	1,901	302
Northeast	33	28	3	6	10	5	15	0	100	1,683	267
1 child	30	25	3	6	13	5	15	3	100	4,925	782
2 children	36	20	3	6	15	1	18	1	100	2,780	441
3 or more children	40	22	8	9	11	2	8	0	100	640	102
Age:											
5–9 years	33	22	4	8	18	1	12	2	100	5,855	929
10–12	33	26	2	3	3	10	23	0	100	2,490	395
Above poverty level	33	22	3	7	15	3	16	1	100	6,844	1,086
Below poverty level	27	41	8	9	8	6	2	0	100	678	108

Source: National Child Care Survey, 1990

a. FDC, family day care.

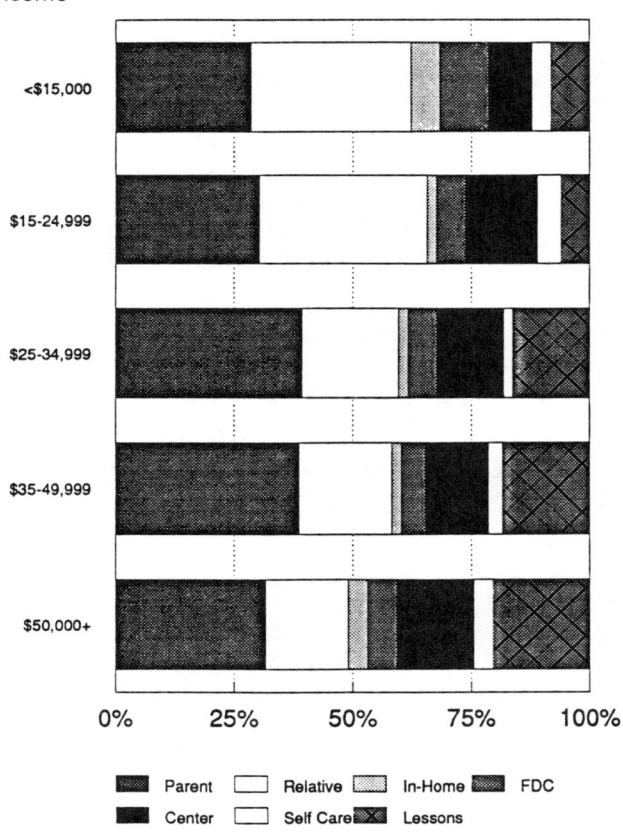

Figure 2.7b
PRIMARY CARE FOR YOUNGEST SCHOOL AGE CHILD
BY INCOME, EMPLOYED MOTHERS

Source: National Child Care Survey 1990

or higher. The lack of a statistically significant impact of income on center-based enrollment and its significant impact of impact on lessons shows how subsidization can equalize access to these programs for children in low income families.

Residence. Regional differences in use of school-age programs in centers are apparent. The West has the highest proportion of youngest school-age children enrolled (20 percent), and the Northeast has the lowest (10 percent) (table 2.20).

SCHOOL-AGE CHILDREN WITH NONEMPLOYED MOTHER

Among families with a nonemployed mother, 54 percent of youngest school-age children are in the care of a parent before or after school, 20 percent take lessons, and 14 percent are in the care of relatives (table 2.18, figure 2.6) as their primary arrangement. Only a small proportion (6 percent) of school-age children are cared for in before-/after-school programs in centers if their mothers are not employed. Finally, 3 percent are in the care of an in-home provider or family day-care provider, and 1 percent are in self-care.

Age of Child. A larger proportion of nonemployed mothers of 6- to 9-year-olds care for their children primarily themselves than do nonemployed mothers of 10- to 12-year-olds (59 percent compared with 47 percent) (table 2.16). This is because of the increased use of lessons for older children. Thirty percent of youngest children 10-12 years of age take lessons, compared with 19 percent of youngest children 6-9 and 10 percent of 5-year-old youngest children. Clearly, lessons become a more important part of the school-age child's experience as he or she approaches adolescence. Four percent of 10- to 12-year-old youngest children are in self-care, compared with almost none of 5- to 9-year-old youngest children. Clearly, age 5 is the final year for center-based care for school-age children of nonemployed mothers (19 percent). Only 2 to 3 percent of school children ages 6 and older are in center-based programs.

Demographic Characteristics. There are few differences in use of exclusive parental care for school-age children by demographic characteristics of nonemployed mother families. Hispanic families appear to be more likely than families of other ethnic groups to use only parental care, and less-educated mothers are more likely than more-educated mothers to use parental care only (table 2.21, figure 2.8a). Families with three or more children under 13 years old are more likely than smaller families to use only parental care. Hispanic and low-income families are less likely to use before-/after-school programs in centers (figure 2.8b). Large families and families with a mother with a low level of education and low levels of income are least likely to send children to lessons. The group with the highest use of lessons consists of families with a mother who had some graduate school education--41 percent. The groups with the lowest use of lessons are non-Hispanic black (9 percent) and mother-only families (6 percent).

SCHOOL-AGE CHILDREN WITH SINGLE FATHER

The majority of school-age children with a single father are in the primary care of a parent or relative in the child's home (55 percent) (table 2.18). An additional 7 percent are cared for by a relative in the relative's home. Fourteen

Figure 2.8a
PRIMARY CARE FOR YOUNGEST SCHOOL AGE CHILD
BY EDUCATION, NON-EMPLOYED MOTHERS

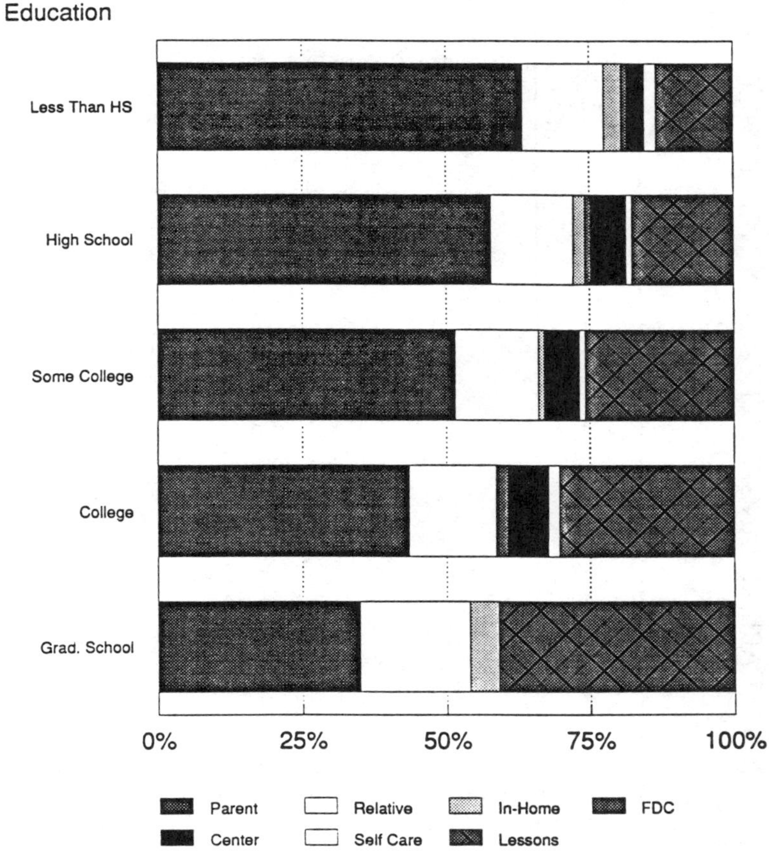

Source: National Child Care Survey 1990

Table 2.21 PRIMARY CHILD CARE ARRANGEMENT FOR YOUNGEST CHILD AGED 5–12 BY FAMILY AND AREA CHARACTERISTICS, WITH NONEMPLOYED MOTHER

	Parent (%)	Relative (%)	In-home Provider (%)	FDC[a] (%)	Center (%)	Self-care (%)	Lessons (%)	Other (%)	Total %	Population Estimate (thousands)	Sample Size
White	51	14	2	1	6	1	24	4	100	2,429	386
Black	52	22	4	0	8	1	9	4	100	458	73
Hispanic	67	12	0	1	1	3	16	0	100	357	57
< high school	62	14	3	1	3	2	13	2	100	561	89
High school	56	14	2	1	6	1	17	3	100	1,396	222
Some college	50	14	1	0	6	1	25	3	100	821	130
College	43	15	0	2	7	2	30	1	100	390	62
Graduate school	35	19	5	0	0	0	41	0	100	113	18
Mother only	43	27	5	2	9	2	7	5	100	674	107
Mother and father	56	11	1	1	4	1	24	2	100	2,607	414
<$15,000	53	23	4	2	6	0	10	2	100	743	118
$15,000–$24,999	60	5	0	1	7	1	20	5	100	482	77
$25,000–$34,999	56	13	0	1	3	1	25	1	100	539	86
$35,000–$49,999	49	13	1	0	4	2	30	1	100	606	96
$50,000+	51	11	2	1	6	2	27	0	100	512	81

Child Care Arrangements in the U.S., 1990

Central city	53	19	2	1	6	2	17	0	100	1,230	195
Suburban	52	9	2	1	6	1	26	3	100	1,101	175
Rural	56	14	3	1	4	1	19	2	100	950	151
West	56	9	1	1	5	2	23	3	100	617	98
South	57	14	3	1	4	1	18	2	100	1,147	182
Midwest	47	20	1	2	8	1	21	0	100	969	154
Northeast	56	10	2	0	5	2	24	1	100	547	87
1 child	53	15	2	1	5	1	22	1	100	1,657	263
2 children	50	14	2	1	7	2	22	2	100	1,180	187
3 or more children	64	11	1	1	4	0	14	5	100	443	70
Age:											
5–9 years	56	14	2	1	6	0	17	4	100	2,386	379
10–12 years	46	15	1	0	3	4	31	0	100	894	142
Above poverty level	54	11	1	1	6	1	24	2	100	2,199	349
Below poverty level	52	27	5	0	4	0	10	2	100	582	92

Source: National Child Care Survey, 1990

a. FDC, family day care.

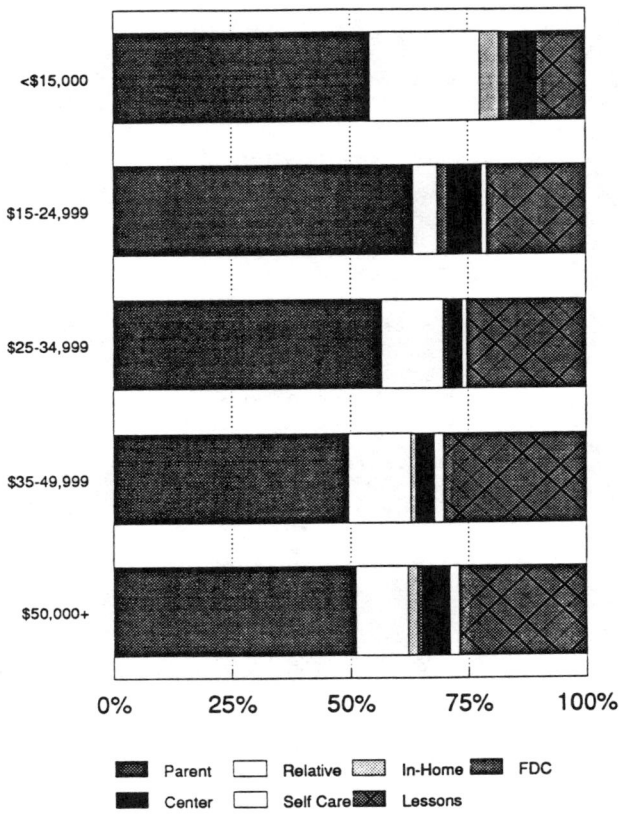

Figure 2.8b
PRIMARY CARE FOR YOUNGEST SCHOOL AGE CHILD
BY INCOME, NON-EMPLOYED MOTHERS

Source: National Child Care Survey 1990

percent are cared for in a before-/after-school program, and 8 percent are cared for by an in-home provider in the child's home.

Secondary Child Care Arrangements for Youngest Child

Across all families, 28 percent have only one arrangement for their children (table 2.22). The existence of a second arrangement varies depending on the type of primary arrangement. Almost half of those who said that a parent cared for the children have only one arrangement, whereas under 10 percent of those whose first arrangement is family day-care have only one arrangement.

Among those families with a second arrangement (100 percent minus 28 percent, or 72 percent), parents are listed as the second arrangement in two of three cases (table 2.23). Relatives are also important sources of care; 13 percent of families use relative care for their youngest child as a second arrangement. Lessons are third in importance, at 10 percent. Only 4 percent of children are in a center-based program as a second arrangement. However, this varies greatly by age of youngest. Ten percent of three- to four-year-old children are in center-based second arrangements, compared with 2 percent of infants.

PRESCHOOL-AGE CHILDREN WITH EMPLOYED MOTHER

Among families with a preschool-age child and an employed mother, 82 percent (100 percent minus 18 percent with only one arrangement) have a second arrangement

Table 2.22 PROPORTION OF ALL HOUSEHOLDS WITH ONLY ONE ARRANGEMENT, BY TYPE OF ARRANGEMENT

Primary Arrangement	Total (%)	Mother Employed (%)	Nonemployed Mother (%)	Father (%)	No Parent (%)
Center	12.8	12.6	14.7	0.0	0.0
Parent	47.5	41.8	51.2	60.0	87.3
Relative—child's home	15.6	13.3	15.1	14.0	70.1
Relative—other home	12.2	12.4	11.6	0.0	26.2
In-home provider	11.9	5.6	26.6	0.0	0.0
Family day care	9.1	7.7	18.2	0.0	35.4
Self-care	26.4	18.6	69.3	0.0	0.0
Lesson	8.2	10.3	3.2	59.0	11.9
Other	71.8	57.4	77.2	71.1	100.0
All	28.1	21.3	38.1	27.1	52.6
Population estimate (in thousands)	7,503	3,400	3,703	122	243
Sample size	1,191	540	588	19	39

Source: National Child Care Survey, 1990

Table 2.23 SECONDARY CHILD CARE ARRANGEMENT FOR YOUNGEST CHILD, BY AGE, ALL FAMILIES

Child Care Arrangement #2, without School	Total (%)	<1 (%)	1–2 (%)	3–4 (%)	5 (%)	6–9 (%)	10–12 (%)
Center	4.0	2.2	3.1	9.7	7.7	1.7	1.6
Parent	65.0	78.4	73.9	61.6	65.7	57.5	54.3
Relative—child's home	7.0	4.7	7.0	6.9	3.7	7.6	9.6
Relative—other home	6.0	5.8	7.2	6.0	7.3	5.7	3.6
In-home provider	2.3	3.8	2.3	3.5	1.7	1.7	0.5
Family day care	2.7	2.4	3.1	2.4	4.5	3.3	0.9
Self-care	1.5	0.0	0.0	0.3	0.0	0.8	9.2
Lesson	9.9	0.2	1.6	8.2	9.4	20.2	18.1
Other	1.7	2.5	1.8	1.3	0.0	1.6	2.1
Total	100.0	100.0	100.0	100.0	100.0	100.0	100.0
Population estimate (in thousands)	19,150	2,473	4,524	3,619	1,280	4,643	2,611
Sample size	2,953	389	708	558	197	701	400

Source: National Child Care Survey, 1990

(table 2.24). Two out of three (67 percent) of these second arrangements are parents (table 2.25, figure 2.9). Fifteen percent of preschool-age youngest children are cared for by relatives as a secondary arrangement, whereas 6 percent are in centers.

Primary Arrangement. The percentage of those with parental care as a second arrangement ranges from 52 percent of those using a parent, to 64 percent of those using a center; 70 percent to 80 percent of those using a relative, family day-care provider, or in-home provider; and 100 percent of those with lessons (not shown) as the primary arrangement (figure 2.10). A relative serves as the second most frequent arrangement for families with a youngest child in a center, in parent or relative care, or cared for by a family day-care provider as the primary arrangement. Surprisingly, a center-based program is a common second arrangement for those cared for first by a parent or an in-home provider. These are probably part-day programs. In-home providers and family day-care providers are much less likely to be secondary forms of care than primary forms.

Work Schedule. There are no significant differences in type of second arrangements by the employment schedule of the mother (not shown).

Age of Child. Enrollment in secondary arrangements by age is similar to that in primary arrangements.

PRESCHOOL-AGE CHILDREN WITH NONEMPLOYED MOTHER

Sixty-eight percent of families with a preschool-age child and a nonemployed mother have a second arrangement (table 2.24). Of these, 77 percent of second arrangements

Table 2.24 PROPORTION OF HOUSEHOLDS WITH ONLY ONE ARRANGEMENT, BY TYPE OF ARRANGEMENT, YOUNGEST UNDER AGE FIVE

Primary Arrangement	All (%)	Mother Employed (%)	Nonemployed Mother (%)	Father (%)	No Parent (%)
Center	10.4	11.3	8.0	0.0	0.0
Parent	37.1	30.8	40.2	0.0	0.0
Relative—child's home	17.1	17.6	11.4	0.0	63.1
Relative—other home	10.9	11.9	9.7	0.0	0.0
In-home provider	10.5	3.6	19.4	0.0	0.0
Family day care	10.9	8.9	21.3	0.0	0.0
Self-care	100.0	100.0	100.0	0.0	42.6
Lesson	24.2	46.8	18.9	0.0	0.0
Other	71.3	59.9	67.9	64.2	100.0
All	24.6	17.5	32.0	13.7	60.3
Population estimate (in thousands)	3,458	1,304	2,022	18	106
Sample size	549	207	321	3	17

Source: National Child Care Survey, 1990

Table 2.25 SECONDARY CHILD CARE ARRANGEMENT FOR YOUNGEST CHILD UNDER AGE FIVE

Child Care Arrangement #2, without School	Total (%)	Employed Mother (%)	Nonemployed Mother (%)	Father (%)	No Parent (%)
Center	5.1	6.4	3.2	12.5	0.0
Parent	70.8	66.8	77.1	53.5	56.9
Relative—child's home	6.4	6.6	5.9	14.4	15.6
Relative—other home	6.5	7.6	4.8	13.1	0.0
In-home provider	3.1	3.4	2.6	5.0	0.0
Family day care	2.7	3.5	1.5	1.5	0.0
Self-care	0.1	0.2	0.0	0.0	0.0
Lesson	3.5	3.1	4.3	0.0	0.0
Other	1.8	2.4	0.6	0.0	27.5
Total	100.0	100.0	100.0	100.0	100.0
Population estimate (in thousands)	10,616	6,132	4,299	115	70
Sample size	1,685	973	682	18	11

Source: National Child Care Survey, 1990

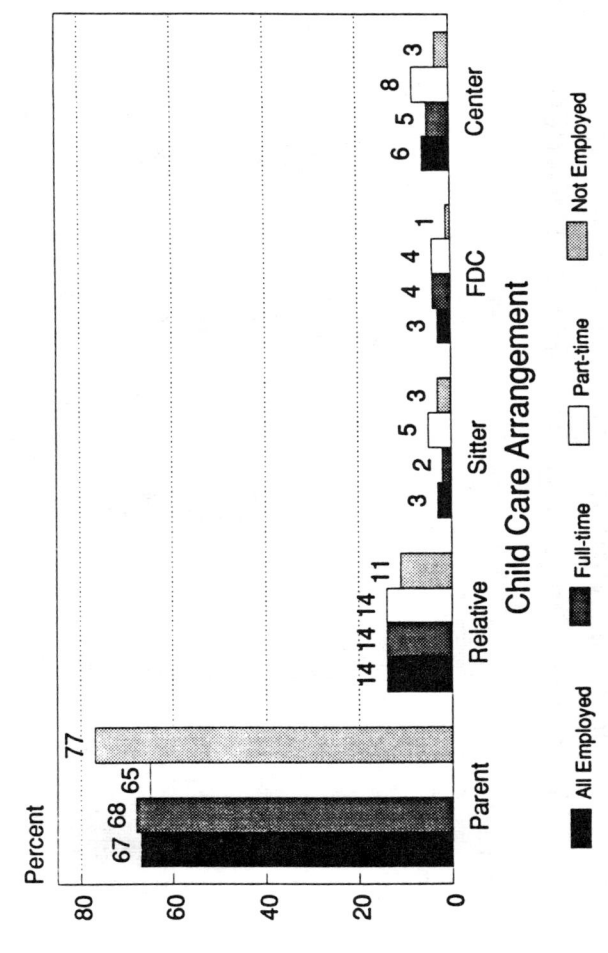

Figure 2.9
SECONDARY CARE, YOUNGEST PRESCHOOL CHILD
EMPLOYED AND NON-EMPLOYED MOTHERS

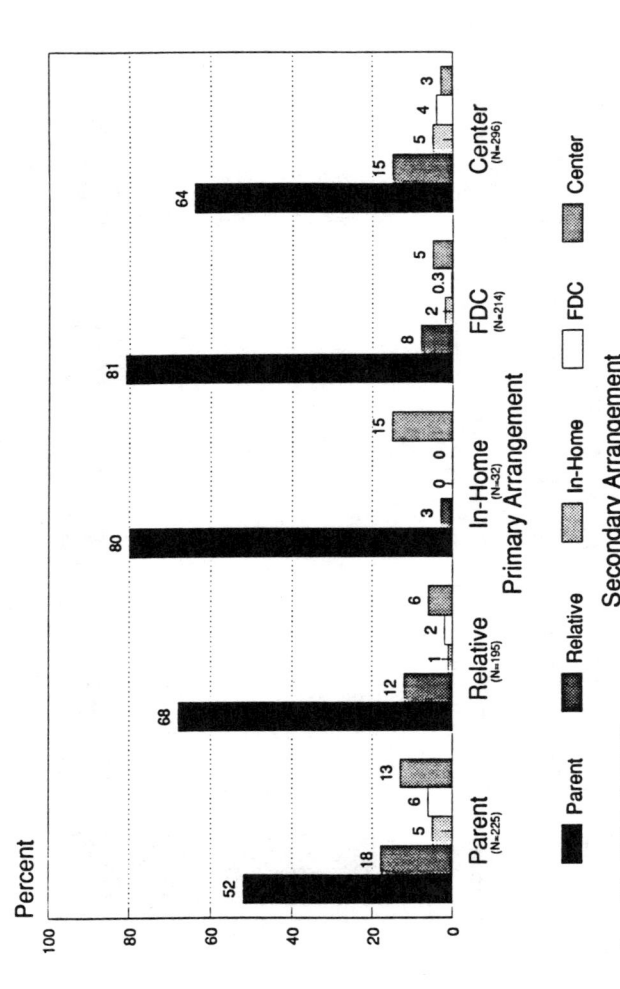

are parents (table 2.25). As for children of employed mothers, after parents (67 percent) relatives are the next most common secondary care arrangement (14 percent). In-home providers also serve as a common second arrangement for nonemployed mothers (3 percent), as do lessons (4 percent), and centers (3 percent).

Primary Arrangement. The proportion of families in which parents serve as the second arrangement ranges from 58 percent for those whose primary arrangement is a center to 85 percent for those whose primary arrangement is a parent (figure 2.11). A substantial proportion of nonemployed mothers cite a center as a second arrangement if the first arrangement is an in-home provider (12 percent). A high proportion of secondary care is provided by a relative, even if the first arrangement is a relative. Finally, lessons provide a substantial proportion of secondary care (20 percent) when the primary arrangement is care in a center or preschool (not shown).

SCHOOL-AGE CHILDREN WITH EMPLOYED MOTHER

Seventy-six percent of school-age children with an employed mother have a second arrangement (100 percent minus 24 percent with only one arrangement) (table 2.26). Fifty-five percent of these children are cared for by a parent (table 2.27, figure 2.12). Lessons (19 percent) are clearly the next most common second arrangement for school-age children, followed by relative care (14 percent). Self-care is also mentioned as a second arrangement by almost 4 percent.

Primary Arrangement. The proportion of children whose parents are the second arrangement varies from 36

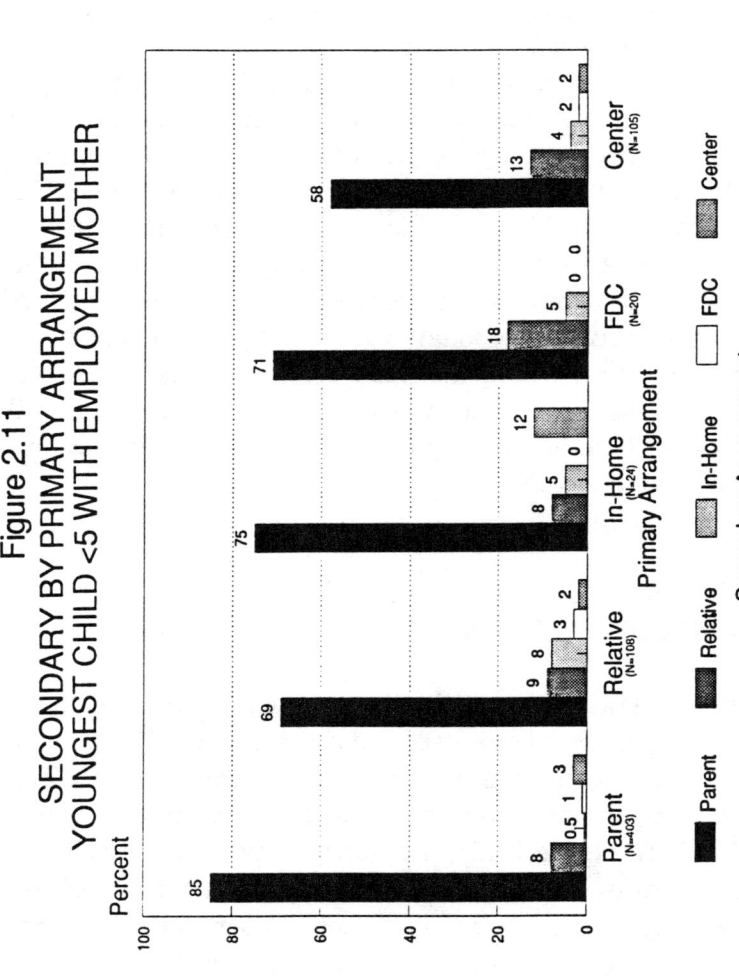

Figure 2.11
SECONDARY BY PRIMARY ARRANGEMENT
YOUNGEST CHILD <5 WITH EMPLOYED MOTHER

Table 2.26 PROPORTION OF HOUSEHOLDS WITH ONLY ONE ARRANGEMENT, BY TYPE OF ARRANGEMENT, YOUNGEST CHILD AGED 5–12

	All (%)	Employed Mother (%)	Nonemployed Mother (%)	Father (%)	No Parent (%)
Center	17.8	14.8	40.6	0.0	0.0
Parent	61.1	49.6	76.5	73.4	91.5
Relative—child's home	14.6	11.4	20.0	14.8	79.2
Relative—other home	13.9	13.0	15.2	0.0	46.6
In-home provider	13.5	7.1	47.6	0.0	0.0
Family day care	4.1	4.4	0.0	0.0	0.0
Self-care	19.5	16.7	47.5	0.0	0.0
Lesson	6.9	9.4	0.0	59.0	11.9
Other	72.5	54.6	86.5	100.0	100.0
All	32.2	24.5	49.6	32.8	47.9
Population estimate (in thousands)	4,044	2,096	1,682	104	137
Sample size	642	333	267	16	22

Source: National Child Care Survey, 1990

Table 2.27 SECONDARY CHILD CARE ARRANGEMENT FOR YOUNGEST CHILD AGED 5–12

Child Care Arrangement #2, without School	Total (%)	Employed Mother (%)	Nonemployed Mother (%)	Father (%)	No Parent (%)
Center	2.6	2.8	2.4	0.0	0.0
Parent	57.7	54.6	68.5	56.6	74.0
Relative—child's home	7.6	8.2	5.6	11.5	0.0
Relative—other home	5.3	5.4	4.7	2.9	12.6
In-home provider	1.3	1.5	0.2	3.6	1.4
Family day care	2.7	3.4	0.4	0.0	4.8
Self-care	3.3	3.5	2.4	6.1	0.0
Lesson	17.9	19.2	14.0	16.4	7.2
Other	1.5	1.4	1.9	2.9	0.0
Total	100.0	100.0	100.0	100.0	100.0
Population estimate (in thousands)	8,535	6,465	1,708	213	149
Sample size	1,355	1,026	271	34	24

Source: National Child Care Survey, 1990

Child Care Arrangements in the U.S., 1990 93

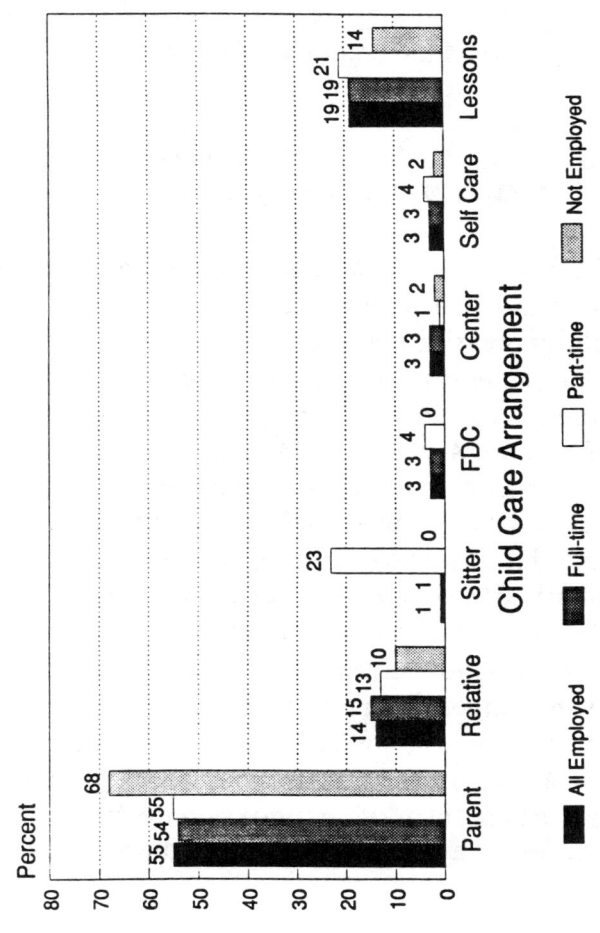

Figure 2.12
SECONDARY CARE, YOUNGEST SCHOOL AGE CHILD
EMPLOYED AND NON-EMPLOYED MOTHERS

Source: National Child Care Survey 1990

percent for those whose primary caregiver is a parent to 74 percent of those whose primary care is a lesson (figure 2.13). Relative care as a secondary arrangement is common among those whose first arrangement is a center, relative, or self-care. Self-care is relatively common among those whose first arrangement is lessons (7 percent) or care by a relative in the child's home (8 percent).

SCHOOL-AGE CHILDREN WITH NONEMPLOYED MOTHER

Of school-age children with a nonemployed mother, 50 percent have a second arrangement (table 2.26). Sixty-eight percent of that secondary care is parent care (table 2.27). Lessons are next (14 percent), with relative care third in importance (10 percent).

Primary Arrangement. The proportion of children whose parents are secondary caregivers ranges from 44 percent for those who are cared for primarily by a relative in the child's home to 90 percent of those using lessons as a primary after-school arrangement (figure 2.14). Lessons are also clearly the most important secondary source of care for school-age children of nonemployed mothers. Use of lessons ranges from 54 percent of children cared for primarily by an in-home provider to none of those whose primary arrangement is a family day-care provider. Lessons are a major form of secondary care for those cared for primarily by a relative, a parent, or those in self-care.

Child Care Arrangements in the U.S., 1990

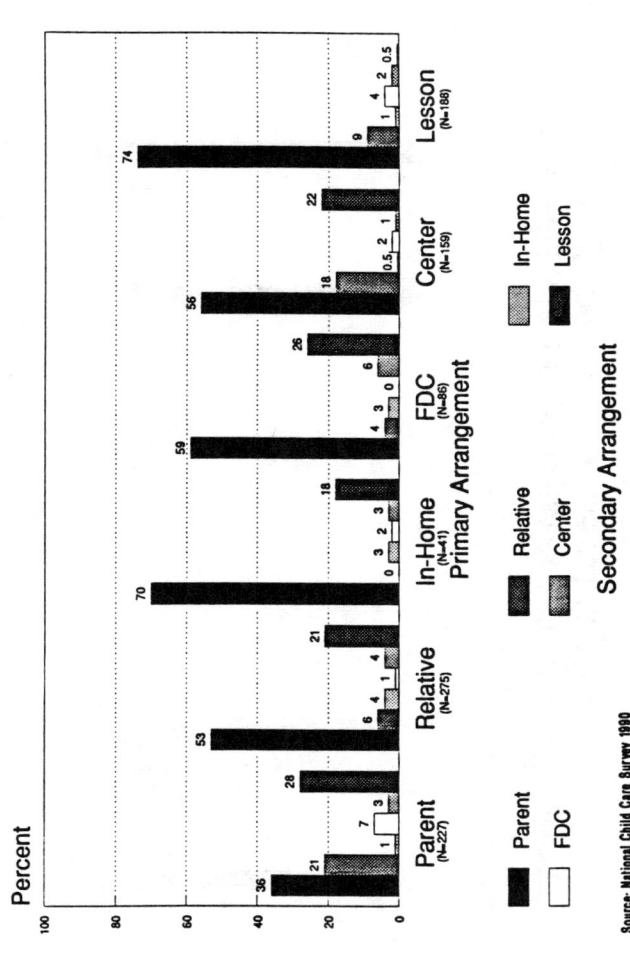

Figure 2.13
SECONDARY BY PRIMARY ARRANGEMENT
YOUNGEST CHILD 5-12 WITH EMPLOYED MOTHER

Source: National Child Care Survey 1990

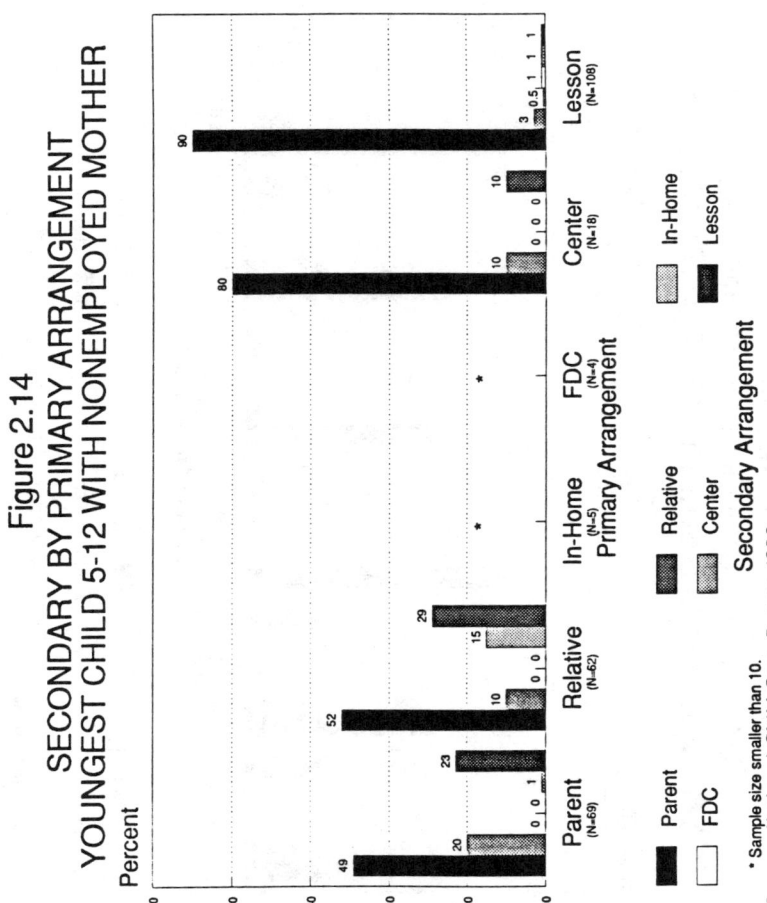

Figure 2.14
SECONDARY BY PRIMARY ARRANGEMENT
YOUNGEST CHILD 5-12 WITH NONEMPLOYED MOTHER

* Sample size smaller than 10.
Source: National Child Care Survey 1990

Other Arrangements for Youngest Child

Sixty-three percent of the sample have one or two arrangements. In this study we, in effect, increased the number of arrangements that parents have by one, since their final arrangement is always "parent cares for child." Therefore, the third and fourth arrangements are worth examining. Table 2.28 shows that the proportion whose arrangement is parental care rises dramatically with the arrangement number. Seventy-six percent of third arrangements and 90 percent of fourth arrangements consist of parental care. Since only one-quarter of the 36 percent of families who have three or more providers list a nonparental arrangement as third, we have summarized 91 percent of families' nonparental arrangements by looking at the first two arrangements.

TRENDS IN CHILD CARE ARRANGEMENTS, 1965-90

Preschool-age Children with Employed Mother

For the last 25 years, the U.S. Bureau of the Census has been collecting data on the child care arrangements of preschool-age children of employed mothers. The National Child Care Survey extends this series to 1990. The primary arrangements for the youngest child for families with an employed mother from Census Bureau estimates for 1965, 1977, 1982, and 1985, and the 1990 National Child Care Survey, are shown in table 2.29 and figure 2.15.

Table 2.28 NUMBER OF ARRANGEMENTS FOR YOUNGEST CHILD, ALL HOUSEHOLDS

Number of Arrangements	%	Cumulative Percentage	% Whose Nth Arrangement Is Parent	Population Estimate (in thousands)	Sample Size
1	28.1	28.1	42.0	7,503	1,191
2	35.4	63.5	65.0	9,429	1,497
3	25.3	88.8	76.3	6,743	1,070
4+	11.2	100.0	90.1	2,978	473
All	100.0			26,653	4,231

Source: National Child Care Survey, 1990

Table 2.29 PRIMARY CHILD CARE ARRANGEMENT FOR YOUNGEST PRESCHOOL CHILD, EMPLOYED MOTHER, 1965–90

	1965 (%)	1977 (%)	1982 (%)	1985 (%)	1990 (%)
Parent	29	25	25	23	28
Father	—	14	15	15	17
Mother	—	11	10	8	11
Relative	33	31	30	25	19
Grandparent	—	—	23	16	12
In-home provider	15	7	6	5	3
Family day care	16	23	23	22	20
Center	6	13	15	25	28
Other	1	1	1	—	2
Total	100	100	100	100	100
Population estimate (in thousands)	2,561	3,987	5,086	6,666	7,436

Source: Low and Spindler, 1968; U.S. Bureau of the Census, 1982, 1983, 1987; National Child Care Survey, 1990

Note: Dash (—), data not available. Census Bureau data from 1986–87 could not be included in the table, since the most recent publication only reports figures for all children in the family, not for the youngest child under age five. This is not a serious problem, since the estimates from that report do not differ much from the estimates from the 1985 report.

100 ■ NATIONAL CHILD CARE SURVEY, 1990

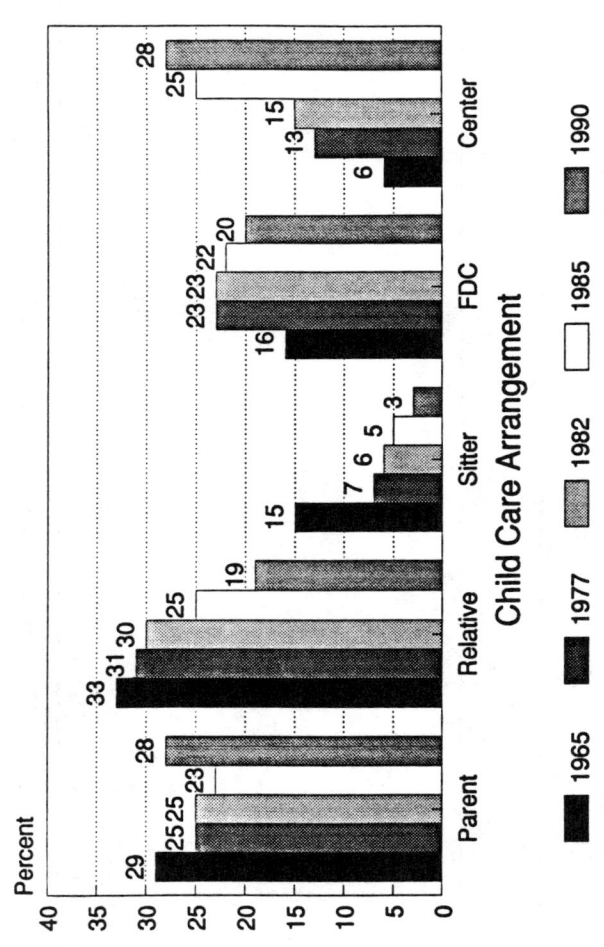

Figure 2.15
PRIMARY CARE, YOUNGEST PRESCHOOL CHILD,
EMPLOYED MOTHERS, 1965-1990

Source: National Child Care Survey 1990

Trends that had emerged over the course of previous surveys continued between 1985 and 1990. During these five years, there was a continued decline in care by a relative other than parents (from 25 percent to 19 percent), a decline in care by an in-home provider (from 5 percent to 3 percent), a decline in care in family day-care homes (from 22 percent to 20 percent), and an increase in enrollment in center-based programs (from 25 percent to 28 percent). The only surprising finding is an apparent increase in care by parents, from 23 percent to 28 percent. This increase balances the large decline in care by a relative over the same period. Therefore, the proportion of children cared for either by a parent or by a relative stayed about the same as in 1985.

Probably the most interesting finding is that the proportion of children cared for in a center-based program now surpasses all other forms of care except care by a parent, which it now equals. The second conclusion is that care by a relative continues its consistent downward trend and care by a center its consistent upward trend manifested over the past 25 years. Care by parents and family day-care have not moved in a consistent manner over the period.

Since this is the first time questions on child care arrangements have been asked all for children, we have no comparable time series of data on the child care arrangements of nonemployed mothers.

School-age Children with Employed Mother

Prior to 1984-85 the Census Bureau did not survey the child care arrangements for school-age children of employed mothers (U.S. Bureau of the Census 1982, 1983).

Therefore, a lengthy time series is not available for school-age children. For 1984-85 the Census Bureau did report on child care arrangements of school-age children 5-14 years old (U.S. Bureau of the Census 1987). However, school was included as an arrangement while the mother was working. Since all school-age children are in school, but respondents did not always cite school as child care, the reports of primary arrangements were inconsistent across families. The Census Bureau also reported secondary arrangements for school-age children for those who reported school as the primary arrangement, and it is this comparison we make. Therefore, the figures from the 1984-85 data are not exactly comparable to those from the NCCS, which uses the second arrangement for school-age children who mentioned school as first; otherwise the first arrangement is used as reported.

The NCCS data and the data from the 1984-85 Survey of Income and Program Participation (SIPP) differ substantially (table 2.30, figure 2.16). The NCCS found more school-age children in the care of parents and centers, but fewer in family day-care and self-care than the earlier survey. The proportion in in-home provider care is about the same as in the earlier year. Certainly the increase in use of before-/after-school care in centers is consistent with the reported increase in such programs, and, thus, may reflect a real increase. Detailed examination of trends awaits a reanalysis of SIPP data, based upon the deletion of school as a care arrangement for school-age children.

Table 2.30 PRIMARY NONSCHOOL CHILD CARE ARRANGEMENT FOR YOUNGEST SCHOOL-AGE CHILD, EMPLOYED MOTHER, 1985–90

	All Children 1984–85 (%)	Youngest Child	
		Including Lessons, 1990 (%)	Excluding Lessons, 1990 (%)
Parent	22	33	39
Relative	34	23	27
In-home provider	4	3	4
Family day care	13	7	8
Center	7	14	16
Self-care	20	4	4
Lessons	—	15	—
Other	—	1	2
Total	100	100	100
Population estimate (in thousands)	5,037	8,562	7,255

Source: U.S. Bureau of the Census, 1987; National Child Care Survey, 1990

Note: Dash (—), data not available.

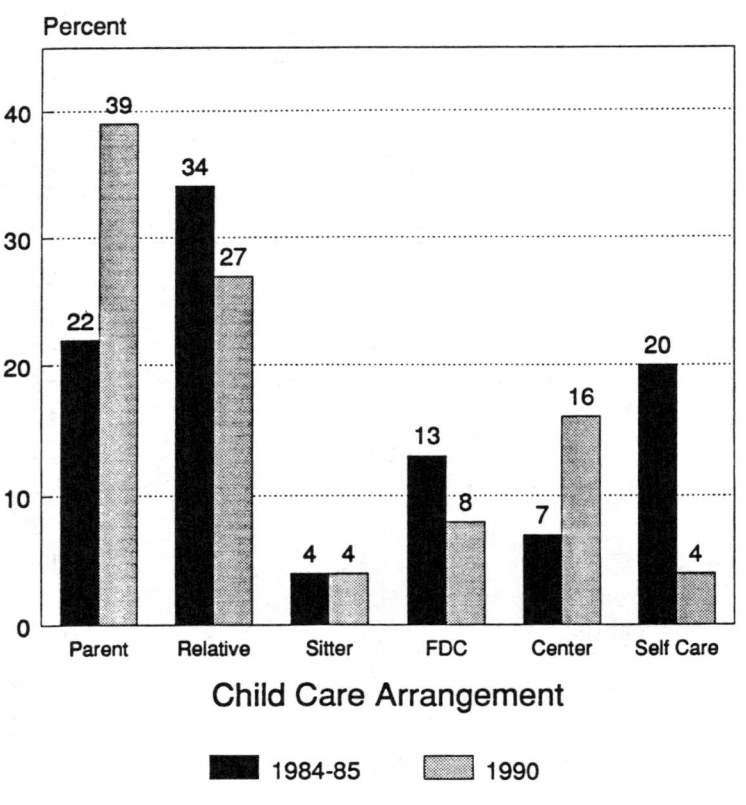

Figure 2.16
PRIMARY CARE FOR YOUNGEST SCHOOL AGE CHILD, EMPLOYED MOTHERS, 1985-1990

Source: National Child Care Survey 1990

HOURS IN PRIMARY CHILD CARE ARRANGEMENT FOR YOUNGEST CHILD

Preschool-age Children with Employed Mother

The youngest preschool-age child (0-4) of an employed mother spent a mean amount of 35 hours in primary care during the week previous, including all types of care except care by the mother, regardless of whether the parents paid for that care (table 2.31, lower panel). The number of hours varies sharply depending on the type of child care. Preschool-age children in a center-based program or a family day-care home are there for an average of 37 hours per week, compared with children in the care of a relative, an in-home provider, or a parent (spouse or partner), who are in care for about 30 hours a week (table 2.31, lower panel).

Age of Child. The younger the child, the more hours on average the child spends in the primary arrangement. Among preschool-age children of employed mothers, children under age three spend an average of 36 hours per week in care, compared with 33 hours for children ages three to four (table 2.31). There is no difference in hours of care between infants and toddlers. There are some differences by type of care. Infants and toddlers in center-based care programs are in care for almost 42 hours per week, the highest of any group of children. In contrast, infants and toddlers in the care of a parent or relative are in care about 30 hours per week. The hours spent by infants in a family day-care home are almost as great as those spent in a center. The hours an infant spends with an in-home provider are only slightly smaller. However, the time toddlers spend in the care of an in-home provider is lower than that

Table 2.31 HOURS PER WEEK, PRIMARY CHILD CARE ARRANGEMENT FOR YOUNGEST CHILD, EMPLOYED MOTHER

	Center		Relative		In-Home Provider		FDC[a]		Parents		Other		All	
	Mean	N	Mean	N	Mean	N	Mean	N	Mean	N	Mean	N	Mean	N
Age of Child (years)														
Under 1	41.92	30	30.45	40	*	7	40.91	44	32.49	49	*	2	35.89	172
1–2	41.56	96	34.22	92	28.56	14	37.11	99	29.51	84	*	3	35.53	387
3–4	34.19	168	29.62	61	23.32	8	35.51	66	31.63	49	*	1	32.96	353
5	30.70	50	18.26	32	*	3	23.13	24	17.55	19	*	9	22.70	137
6–9	13.87	95	14.14	145	10.09	31	13.28	50	13.11	120	3.89	92	11.77	533
10–12	*	7	8.47	83	*	5	*	6	16.94	63	5.21	119	9.08	283
Age of Child (years)														
0–4	37.37	294	31.99	193	29.37	29	37.41	208	30.88	181	*	6	34.60	912
5–12	19.21	152	12.84	260	11.14	39	15.71	80	14.72	201	4.68	219	12.54	952
All	31.18	446	20.99	453	18.88	69	31.41	288	22.38	383	5.19	226	23.33	1864

Source: National Child Care Survey, 1990

Note: Asterisk (*) denotes fewer than 10 cases.

a. FDC, family day care.

of infants in such care. Surprisingly, preschoolers (aged 3-4) spend much less time in each of the primary forms of care. This may be because this age group is in a secondary form of care as well; for example, preschoolers may be enrolled in a nursery school program and in the care of an in-home provider the rest of the day. Children 3-4 years old spend an average of 33 hours a week in care, ranging from 34 hours in a center to 23 hours in the care of an in-home provider.

Demographic Characteristics. The hours children are in care also vary with the characteristics of the family (table 2.32). Children in one-parent families spend more time in child care than children in two-parent families (40 hours versus 33 hours per week). Black children spend more time in care than white or Hispanic children, probably because they are more likely to be in one-parent families.

Income. There is little difference by income or poverty status in hours spent in the primary arrangement among preschool-age children with an employed mother.

Residence. Children in the South spend more time in care (40 hours per week) compared with children in other regions (who average 31-32 hours per week). Children in urban areas spend slightly more time in care than those in rural areas.

Preschool-age Children with Nonemployed Mother

Preschool-age children whose mothers are not employed outside the home still average about 20 hours per week in the primary arrangement (table 2.33). This amount varies from 29 hours per week with a parent to 14-18 hours per week with an in-home provider, center, or family day-care home.

Table 2.32 WEEKLY CHILD CARE HOURS, BY AGE OF YOUNGEST AND MOTHER'S EMPLOYMENT STATUS

	0–4 Years Old (hours/week)						5–12 Years Old (hours/week)					
	Employed		Not Employed		Total		Employed		Not Employed		Total	
	Mean	N	Mean	N	Mean	N	Mean	N	Mean	N	Mean	N
White	33.31	687	19.86	308	29.15	996	11.75	744	5.42	177	10.53	921
Black	40.17	132	24.51	48	36.00	180	16.99	116	12.04	19	16.30	135
Hispanic	36.21	74	18.58	49	27.17	123	13.95	75	8.50	17	12.95	92
Other	37.44	16	20.86	4	34.41	20	11.18	16	1.00	1	10.83	16
Less than high school	40.62	52	21.18	60	30.24	112	9.28	61	9.21	21	9.26	82
High school	34.72	362	24.16	147	31.67	509	13.59	381	5.81	87	12.15	467
Some college	33.29	217	19.84	104	28.94	320	13.77	250	5.78	60	12.23	310
College	34.73	183	15.56	77	29.05	260	10.77	162	4.57	32	9.74	194
Graduate school	33.74	95	9.54	21	29.37	116	10.40	96	10.31	14	10.39	110
Mother only	40.12	150	26.20	74	35.51	225	14.84	210	10.94	34	14.29	244
Mother and father	33.53	759	18.93	334	29.07	1,093	11.91	741	5.33	179	10.63	920

Child Care Arrangements in the U.S., 1990

<$15,000	36.78	132	25.24	109	31.55	242	14.80	140	11.68	38	14.13	178
$15,000–$24,999	36.38	144	21.19	67	31.57	210	14.61	144	4.59	29	12.94	173
$25,000–$34,999	31.36	163	18.78	53	28.29	216	12.17	155	4.60	35	10.77	190
$35,000–$49,999	32.39	214	17.97	66	29.00	280	11.30	185	3.71	45	9.81	230
$50,000+	36.84	227	12.20	79	30.49	306	11.41	268	5.81	46	10.60	314
Central city	36.26	372	18.39	199	30.03	570	12.27	329	5.75	80	11.00	409
Suburban	34.03	308	19.92	124	29.99	432	12.33	349	6.00	76	11.19	426
Rural	32.75	230	25.06	86	30.65	316	13.19	272	7.22	57	12.16	329
West	31.00	159	18.14	112	25.68	271	14.13	191	6.62	40	12.84	231
South	39.58	351	24.99	103	36.28	454	11.84	333	6.36	65	10.95	398
Midwest	31.78	215	23.14	96	29.10	311	12.20	215	6.20	72	10.69	288
Northeast	31.59	185	14.88	98	25.82	283	12.16	211	5.65	37	11.58	248
1 child	37.11	416	21.49	142	33.13	558	11.77	561	6.42	109	10.90	669
2 children	33.56	356	19.25	163	29.07	518	13.33	319	6.04	82	11.83	401
3 or more children	29.81	138	20.13	104	25.66	241	15.26	71	6.02	23	13.03	94
Above poverty level	34.44	770	18.71	293	30.10	1,063	12.43	786	4.74	153	11.18	939
Below poverty level	35.69	80	22.06	74	29.12	155	13.94	74	13.50	31	13.81	105

Source: National Child Care Survey, 1990

Table 2.33 HOURS PER WEEK, PRIMARY CHILD CARE ARRANGEMENT FOR YOUNGEST CHILD, NONEMPLOYED MOTHER

	Center		Relative		Sitter		FDC[a]		Parents		Other		All	
	Mean	N	Mean	N	Mean	N	Mean	N	Mean	N	Mean	N	Mean	N
Age of Child (years)														
Under 1	*	7	16.24	29	*	8	*	9	21.53	59	*	2	18.51	113
1–2	16.71	28	13.98	40	*	8	*	8	29.00	74	*	6	21.73	164
3–4	14.02	68	16.50	16	*	3	*	3	40.82	33	2.33	12	19.67	136
5	10.89	10	5.56	10	*	1	*	1	*	7	3.44	12	8.68	41
6–9	*	1	12.55	19	*	3	*	3	7.20	23	2.86	51	6.00	101
10–12	*	3	6.37	15	*	1	*	0	4.37	10	4.60	43	5.34	73
Age of Child (years)														
0–4	15.13	103	15.22	85	14.15	19	17.97	20	28.70	166	4.08	19	20.17	413
5–12	10.78	15	8.84	44	*	5	*	4	8.53	40	3.63	106	6.29	215
All	14.58	118	13.04	130	12.65	24	16.34	23	24.75	207	3.70	126	15.42	627

Source: National Child Care Survey, 1990

Note: Asterisk (*) denotes fewer than 10 cases.

a. FDC, family day care.

Age of Child. Hours of care vary only slightly according to the age of the youngest preschool-age child, with toddlers (one to two years of age) in care the most hours per week (22), and infants in care the fewest hours (18) (table 2.33). Preschoolers (three to four years of age) spend 20 hours per week in care. After parent care, infants spend the most time in the care of relatives, at 16 hours per week. Few infants of nonemployed mothers are enrolled in center-based care.

Demographic Characteristics. Children with a nonemployed single mother spend more time in care (26 hours per week) than than those in two-parent families with a nonemployed mother (19 hours) (table 2.32). Preschool-age children of less well-educated nonemployed mothers spend more hours in care than children of better-educated mothers.

Income. Children who are poor or in low-income families spend more hours in care than those in nonpoor, higher-income families. The differences between families with incomes under $15,000 and those whose incomes equal or exceed $50,000 are the largest. The low-income children are probably enrolled in subsidized programs.

Residence. Preschool-age children in the South and Midwest spend more hours in primary care than those in other regions. Likewise, preschool-age children in rural areas spend more hours in care than their counterparts in urban areas.

Preschool-age Children with Single Father

Preschool-age children with a single father spend an average of almost 39 hours per week in care (not shown), about the same as that of children with a single employed mother (table 2.32). Sample sizes are too small for analyses by age or type of care.

Other Characteristics. There are too few households headed by a single father to evaluate differences in care by other characteristics.

School-age Children with Employed Mother

School-age children of employed mothers spend an average of almost 13 hours per week in a primary arrangement (table 2.31). This amount ranges from 19 hours per week if enrolled in a center or preschool to 11 hours per week if in the care of an in-home provider.

Age of Child. The hours spent in care vary by age of the school-age child. Younger school-age children spend many more hours in care (14 hours per week on average) than older school-age children (9 hours per week on average). Average hours for the 5- to 9-year-olds range from almost 20 hours per week in a center-based program to 10 hours per week with an in-home provider. Average hours for 10- to 12-year-olds range from almost 17 hours per week with an in-home provider or parent to 7 hours per week in a day-care home.

Demographic Characteristics. Black children and children in one-parent families spend more hours in care than other children (table 2.32).

Income Levels. Low-income children spend more hours in care than children in other families. Differences by poverty status are small.

Residence. School-age children in the West spend more hours in care than children in all other regions. There are few differences by urban residence.

School-age Children with Nonemployed Mother

School-age children whose mothers are not employed outside the home spend 6 hours per week in a primary arrangement on average, ranging from 11 hours in a center to 4 hours in other arrangements (table 2.33). Differences by age are small among these children.

Income Levels. Children in families below the poverty level and whose family incomes are below $15,000 annually spend more time in care than children above the poverty level or whose family incomes are above $15,000 (table 2.25).

Residence. Although there are no meaningful regional differences in hours, children living in rural areas spend slightly more time in care than children living elsewhere.

School-age Children with Single Father

Few school-age children are cared for by their single father. However, among children who are, primary care hours are high--21 hours per week on average (not shown). Since most of these fathers are employed, the most appropriate comparison is with school-age children of employed mothers. The hours these children spend in care is much higher than for the children of employed mothers (15 hours per week on average). This suggests much less reluctance on the part of single fathers to use alternative forms of child care--or, perhaps, their better economic position enables them to rely on nonparental care to a greater extent.

SUMMARY AND CONCLUSIONS

Preschool-age Children

The most important findings regarding the primary care arrangements of preschool-age children in 1990 are, first, that parents use regular nonparental arrangements for children, regardless of the employment status of the mother. Of course, there are large differences in use of nonparental care according to the employment status of the mother, with 85 percent of families with a full-time employed mother and 50 percent of families with a part-time employed mother using some type of nonparental arrangement. Even so, 33 percent of families with a mother who is not employed outside the home use some regular arrangement or program for their youngest preschool-age child.

Second, among families with an employed mother, care in a center-based program is common; no other arrangement serves so high a proportion of preschool-age children.

Third, for preschool-age children, we noted the continued increase in center-based care, the decline in care by a nonrelative in the child's home, and the dramatic decline in care by another relative. Use of family day-care is holding steady or declining slightly. However, parent care appears to have increased somewhat over the past 15 years. This reflects an increase in time spent caring for their children by both fathers and mothers.

Finally, we examined the amount of time children spend in different types of arrangements by age and family characteristics. Many analysts assume that children in nonparental care are uniformly in care for 40 hours a week. This is clearly not the case. Preschool children average 35 hours in their primary arrangement if their mother is employed and 20 hours if she is not. There are some surprising results. For example, infants who are in center-based care actually spend more hours a week in care than older children. This is probably because parents who leave an infant in center care are different from other mothers: they may be low-income or single parents and, thus, need to work more hours, or they may be career oriented and want to work more hours.

School-age Children

There are two major findings concerning primary arrangements for school-age children. First, the coverage of school-age children in centers, particularly children from five to nine years of age, appears to have risen since 1984-85, perhaps reflecting an increase in the availability of school-age, center-based before- and after-school programs.

Second is the large proportion of school-age children enrolled in lessons. When the survey was pretested, we discovered that a number of parents relied heavily on lessons, not only as educational and cultural supplements but also as child care arrangements for their children after school. As a result, questions were asked specifically about the use of lessons.

Of substantial policy importance is the relationship between income and enrollment in center-based programs. Although there were some differences in enrollments in preschool and before- and after-school programs in centers based on income, these differences were relatively small. Children (of employed or nonemployed mothers) whose family incomes were in the lowest income quartile were, even if not as likely as high-income children to be enrolled, much more likely to be enrolled than children in families in the next income quartile. This suggests that although subsidization has not completely eliminated differences of income (other confounding factors, such as maternal education, are also linked to use of center care), still, it has reduced a large part of the differential between the highest- and lowest-income families. Consistent with the National Child Care Staffing Study (Whitebook et al. 1989), the children of middle-income nonemployed mothers are the least likely to be enrolled in center-based programs.

This is not the case, however, with lessons. For example, among school-age children of employed mothers, 21 percent of children whose family incomes are $50,000 or more take lessons. In contrast, only 5 percent of children whose incomes are under $15,000 take lessons. Among children of nonemployed mothers, the difference is just as great. Twenty-nine percent of children of mothers whose family income is $50,000 or above take lessons, compared with 12 percent of children in households with incomes under 15,000 annually. These differences reflect the educational levels of mothers as well; therefore, the relationship between education and income needs to be examined in a multivariate framework. What is not known is the effect on children of taking lessons. Lessons provide a structured after-school activity, as well as cultural education, socialization, and the opportunity to practice physical and intellectual skills. This may be an important aspect of the lives of school-age children, one in which, apparently, there are sharp differences by socioeconomic levels.

Notes, chapter 2

1. For more detailed definitions of these arrangements, see appendices C and D to this report.

2. Data cited from this chapter's tables are typically rounded off to the nearest whole number.

Chapter

3

PARENTAL EXPENDITURES FOR CHILD CARE

Parents are constrained by both time and money in deciding how to care for their children. This chapter characterizes who pays and how much they pay for child care, including all possible forms of child care (i.e., parental, relative, and nonrelative care). Fundamentally, the amount that parents spend on child care is limited by their ability to pay. Thus, information about hourly expenditures for the youngest child and weekly expenditures for all children in the family is supplemented here with data on the share of family income spent on child care. The chapter also presents details on the proportion of working families that receive direct financial assistance with their child care expenses and the degree to which parents claimed the Child and Dependent Care Federal Income Tax Credit for the 1988 tax year. The chapter concludes by examining trends in parental expenditures over time.

PROPORTION OF FAMILIES PAYING FOR CHILD CARE ARRANGEMENTS

Although most parents are the primary caregivers for their children, and thus pay nothing for child care, some families spend a substantial amount of money on child care services. Besides monetary payments, families may pay for child care through a nonmonetary arrangement such as providing room and board or exchanging child care services. Most notably, not all families with an employed mother pay for child care. Likewise, not all mothers staying home fulltime choose parental care as the primary arrangement for their children. Consequently, many nonemployed mothers also pay for child care services.

Families Paying for the Primary Arrangement of the Youngest Child

PRESCHOOL-AGE CHILDREN

Maternal Employment Status. The proportion of families who pay for the primary care arrangement (regardless of the type of arrangement) of their youngest child under age five varies by the employment status of the mother (figure 3.1). Fifty-six percent of employed mothers pay for child care (not shown). Full-time employed mothers (i.e., those employed 35 hours or more per week), are more likely than part-time employed mothers to pay for child care. Sixty-eight percent of full-time employed mothers make monetary payments to the primary care provider for their youngest preschool-age child, whereas 33 percent of part-

Parental Expenditures for Child Care ■ 121

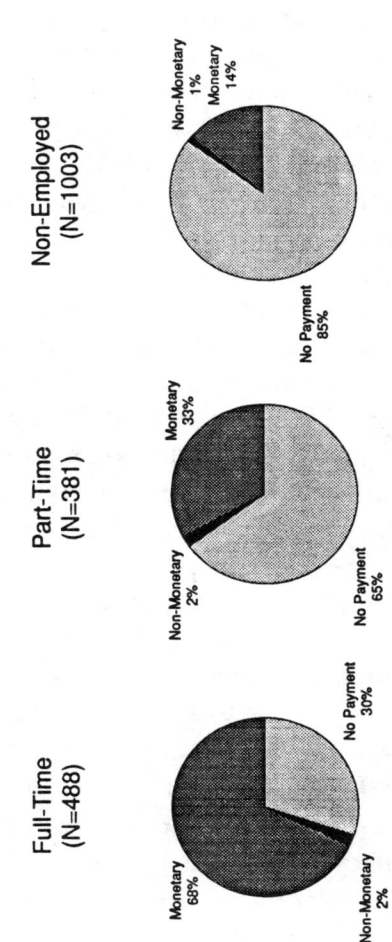

Figure 3.1
Distribution of Payment for Primary Arrangement
By Maternal Employment Status,
Youngest Child Under Five

Full-Time (N=488)
Monetary 68%
Non-Monetary 2%
No Payment 30%

Part-Time (N=381)
Monetary 33%
Non-Monetary 2%
No Payment 65%

Non-Employed (N=1003)
Monetary 14%
Non-Monetary 1%
No Payment 85%

Source: National Child Care Survey 1990

time employed mothers pay for these services. In turn, part-time employed mothers are more likely than nonemployed mothers to pay for child care. Only 14 percent of nonemployed mothers pay for the primary arrangement of their youngest preschool-age child, 1 percent have nonmonetary arrangements, and over 84 percent pay nothing at all. The low proportion of nonemployed mothers paying for child care is partially explained by the high proportion of nonemployed mothers relying on parental care as the primary arrangement for their youngest preschool-age child (see chapter 2).

Type of Primary Arrangement. Needless to say, a parent almost never pays his or her spouse for providing child care for a preschool-age child (figure 3.2). However, the majority of families using centers, in-home providers, or family day-care providers as a primary arrangement pay for these services, regardless of maternal employment. On the other hand, families are less likely to pay relatives, especially if the mother is not employed. For employed mothers with a preschool-age child, 94 percent of those using family day-care home providers, 93 percent of those using in-home providers, and 90 percent of those using centers as a primary arrangement pay for child care. The proportion of nonemployed mothers paying in-home providers and family day-care providers is similar to that of employed mothers. However, a smaller proportion of nonemployed mothers pay for center-based care compared with employed mothers, perhaps reflecting public subsidies to low-income families. Although almost 36 percent of employed mothers relying on relatives as a primary arrangement make monetary payments, only 12 percent of nonemployed mothers using relatives as a primary arrangement pay for care.

Figure 3.2

Percentage Paying for Primary Arrangement
By Type of Arrangement and Maternal Employment Status,
Youngest Child Under Five

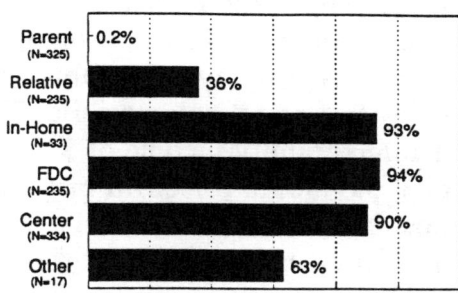

Employed Mothers

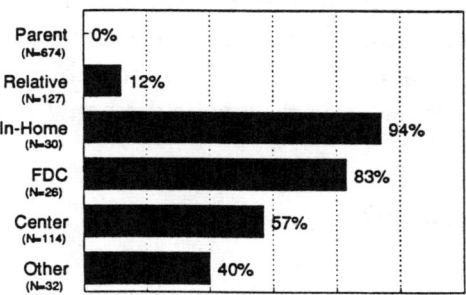

Non-Employed Mothers

Source: National Child Care Survey 1990

Time Spent in Primary Arrangement. The proportion of full-time versus part-time employed mothers paying for any type of child care is partly a function of the number of hours spent in care (figure 3.3). Among preschool-age children who spend under 20 hours per week in a nonmaternal primary care arrangement, only 33 percent of their families pay for this care. In contrast, the proportion is nearly double (65 percent) for preschool-age children spending 20 or more hours per week in a nonmaternal primary arrangement.

Family Income. High-income families are much more likely to pay for child care than low-income families, regardless of maternal employment status. Among employed mothers with a preschool-age child, 70 percent of those with an annual family income of $50,000 or more make monetary payments for child care, whereas 42 percent of those with an annual family income under $15,000 pay for child care services (not shown). Among those with a mother who is not employed, 38 percent of high-income families ($50,000 or more) and only 8 percent of low-income families (under $15,000) pay for child care (not shown). Thus, high-income mothers who are not employed are just as likely to pay for child care as low-income mothers who work outside the home.

SCHOOL-AGE CHILDREN

Maternal Employment Status. Employed mothers with their youngest children aged 5 to 12 are less likely to pay for their primary nonschool arrangement than those with a preschool-age child (36 percent versus 56 percent, not shown). Moreover, among families with no preschool-age children, the proportion of full-time employed mothers

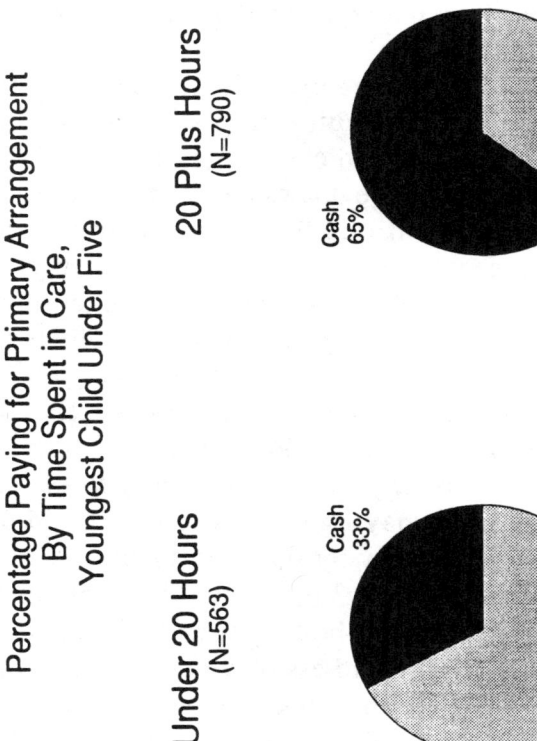

Figure 3.3
Percentage Paying for Primary Arrangement By Time Spent in Care, Youngest Child Under Five

Source: National Child Care Survey 1990

paying (37 percent) is not significantly different from that of part-time employed mothers (33 percent) (figure 3.4). Nonemployed mothers with a youngest child aged 5 to 12 are more likely to pay for the primary nonschool arrangement than those with a preschool-age child. Twenty percent of nonemployed mothers with no preschool-age children pay for the primary arrangement, under 1 percent make nonmonetary payments, and the majority (79 percent) pay nothing.

Type of Primary Arrangement. Like families with a preschool-age child, those with youngest school-age children most often pay for child care when centers, in-home providers, or family day-care homes are used as the primary nonschool arrangement (figure 3.5). However, both employed and nonemployed mothers with a youngest child aged 5 to 12 are less likely to pay relatives than those with a preschool-age child. Among nonemployed mothers who rely on in-home providers, those with no preschool-age children are less likely to pay for care (39 percent) than those with a preschool-age child (94 percent).

Time Spent in a Primary Nonschool Arrangement. The proportion of families paying for any type of child care does not significantly vary by the time spent in care for school-age children (figure 3.6). Since most school-age children spend less than 20 hours per week in a primary nonschool arrangement regardless of maternal employment status (see chapter 2), the amount of time spent in care does not affect whether or not a family pays for care.

Family Income. Among employed mothers, the difference in the proportion paying for child care between high-income ($50,000 or more) and low-income families (under $15,000) is not as large for those whose youngest child is of school age compared to families with a preschool-age child. For employed mothers with school-age children

Parental Expenditures for Child Care ■ 127

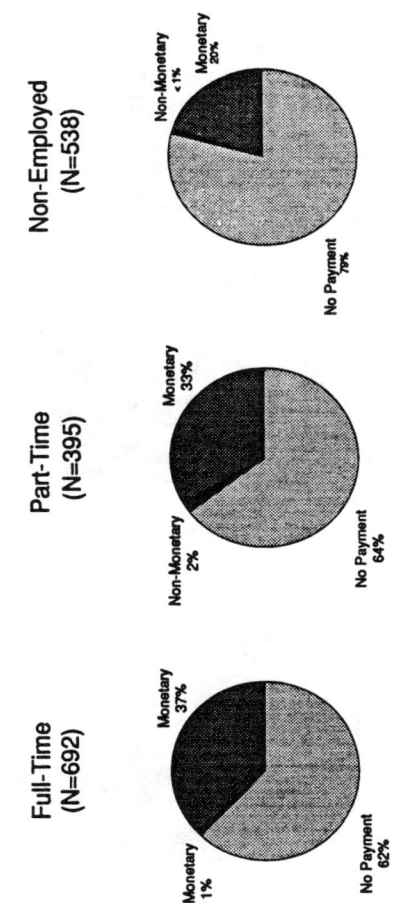

Figure 3.4
Distribution of Payment for Primary Arrangement
By Maternal Employment Status,
Youngest Child Age 5-12

Source: National Child Care Survey 1990

Figure 3.5

Percentage Paying for Primary Arrangement
By Type of Arrangement and Maternal Employment Status,
Youngest Child Age 5-12

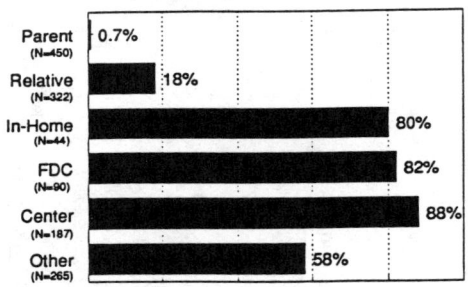

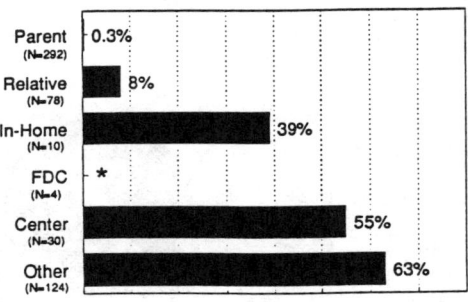

* Fewer than 10 cases.
Source: National Child Care Survey 1990

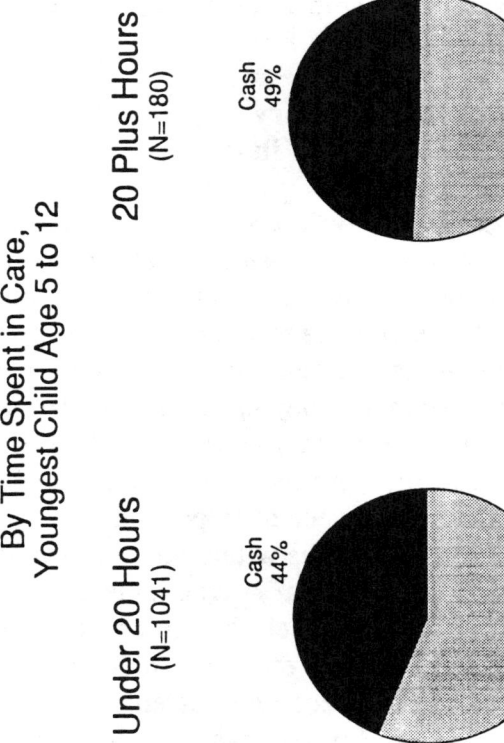

Figure 3.6
Percentage Paying for Primary Arrangement
By Time Spent in Care,
Youngest Child Age 5 to 12

Under 20 Hours (N=1041)
- Cash 44%
- Non-cash 56%

20 Plus Hours (N=180)
- Cash 49%
- Non-cash 51%

Source: National Child Care Survey 1990

only, 43 percent of high-income families and 33 percent of low-income families pay for child care. Among nonemployed mothers, the difference in the proportion paying for child care between high-income and low-income families is about the same for school-age children as for preschool-age children. Thirty-three percent of high-income families with a nonemployed mother pay for child care, while 10 percent of low-income families with a nonemployed mother pay for child care.

Families Paying for Secondary Arrangement for Youngest Child

Parents typically rely on themselves as the secondary providers of child care (see chapter 2). Thus, the vast majority of the families using secondary arrangements for their youngest preschool-age child pay nothing for this care, regardless of maternal employment status (figure 3.7). The proportion of mothers paying for a secondary arrangement ranges from 9 percent for nonemployed mothers to 19 percent for part-time employed mothers, with full-time employed mothers in between at 15 percent.

The proportion of families with a youngest child aged 5 to 12 who pay for a secondary arrangement is similar to that for families with a preschool-age child (figure 3.8). Both full-time and part-time employed mothers are slightly more likely to pay for a secondary arrangement than nonemployed mothers. Approximately 20-21 percent of employed mothers pay for a secondary arrangement for their youngest child aged 5 to 12, whereas 11 percent of nonemployed mothers pay.

Parental Expenditures for Child Care ■ 131

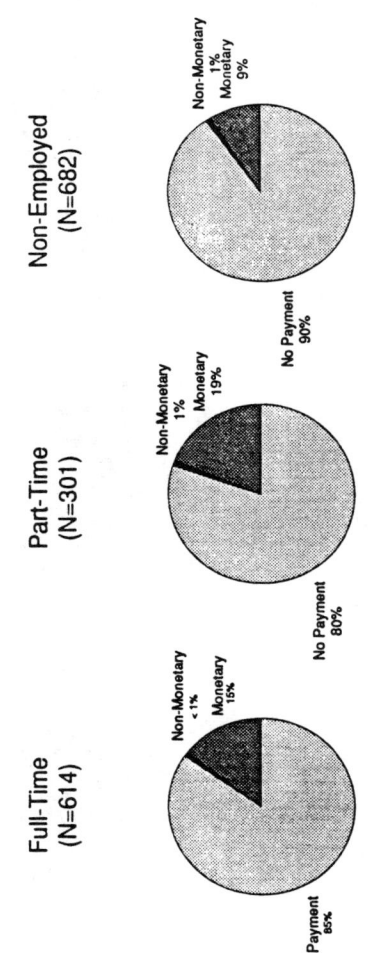

Figure 3.7
Distribution of Payment for Secondary Arrangement
By Maternal Employment Status,
Youngest Child Under 5

Source: National Child Care Survey 1990

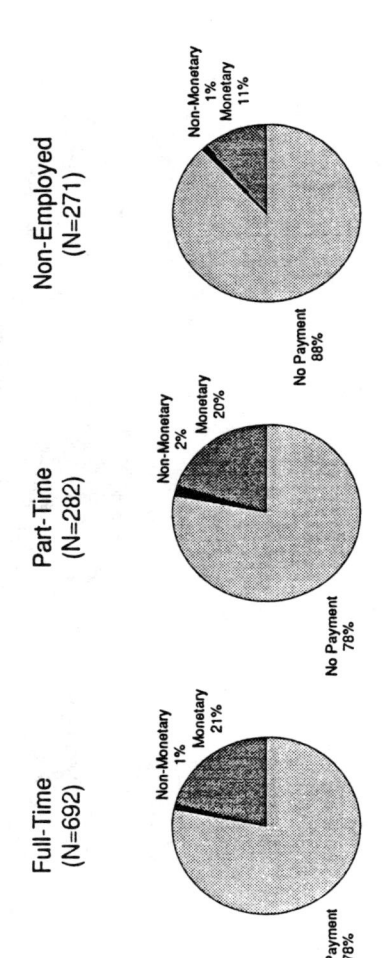

Figure 3.8
Distribution of Payment for Secondary Arrangement
By Maternal Employment Status,
Youngest Child Age 5-12

Source: National Child Care Survey 1990

HOURLY EXPENDITURES FOR YOUNGEST CHILD IN FAMILY

Parents were asked "How much does your household usually pay for each arrangement for the youngest child?" Parents could respond in terms of hourly, daily, weekly, monthly, or annual payments. If more than one child under 13 years old lived in the household, parents were also asked how many other children in the family were included in this payment. First, to control for the differing amounts of time children spend in paid care, we converted parental expenditures to hourly payments according to the number of hours and days the youngest child spent in the corresponding arrangement. Next, if the payment included other children in the family, the hourly expenditure was divided by the number of children included in the payment. Estimates of hourly expenditures include only those families who pay for child care.

Expenditures for Primary Arrangements for Preschool-age Children

FAMILIES WITH EMPLOYED MOTHER

Average Hourly Expenditure. Of those paying for care, families with an employed mother spend $1.56 per hour on average for the primary arrangement of the youngest child under 5 years old (figure 3.9). Nearly 64 percent of employed mothers pay less than $1.50 per hour, whereas only 2 percent pay $5 or more per hour (table 3.1).[1] However, part-time employed mothers pay more per hour

Figure 3.9

Mean Hourly Expenditure for Youngest Child Under 5 By Maternal Employment Status, Those Paying for Care Only

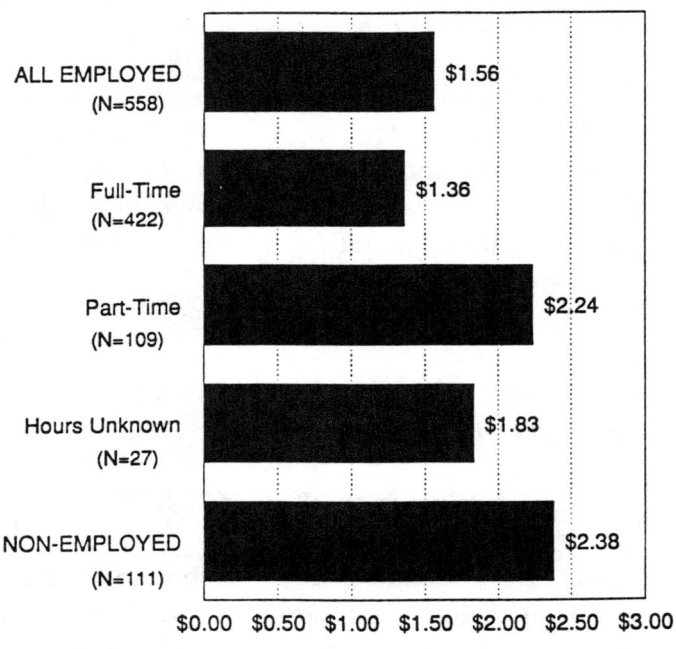

Source: National Child Care Survey 1990

Table 3.1 PERCENTILE DISTRIBUTION OF MEAN HOURLY EXPENDITURE FOR PRIMARY CARE ARRANGEMENT FOR YOUNGEST CHILD UNDER AGE FIVE, EMPLOYED MOTHERS PAYING FOR CARE ONLY

	Number	Under $1	$1 to <$1.50	$1.50 to <$2	$2 to <$2.50	$2.50 to <$3	$3 to <$4	$4 to <$5	$5 and Over	Mean Dollars	Mean Hours
All Employed:	558	30.6	33.1	16.2	8.8	3.4	4.2	1.4	2.4	1.56	37.47
Full-time	442	34.2	34.0	17.0	7.8	2.4	3.0	1.0	0.8	1.36	41.68
Part-time	109	19.1	28.7	14.3	12.1	6.1	9.4	3.6	6.6	2.24	23.31
Hours unknown	27	21.4	36.5	12.3	10.9	7.7	1.0	0.0	10.1	1.83	28.46
Primary Arrangement:											
Center	262	24.8	29.8	21.0	11.9	4.5	3.8	1.7	2.5	1.67	38.30
Relative	76	59.1	22.1	11.2	2.6	2.5	0.4	0.0	2.1	1.11	37.27
In-home provider	26	22.3	27.2	20.7	2.3	2.9	5.0	5.2	14.3	2.30	30.96
Family day care	189	29.1	43.0	11.4	7.5	2.3	5.5	1.2	0.0	1.35	37.75
Other	5	*	*	*	*	*	*	*	*	*	*
Age of Youngest:											
Under 1 year	87	28.7	37.7	13.8	9.0	3.1	6.4	0.4	0.9	1.45	40.51
1 to 2 years	227	33.7	31.0	16.2	6.7	3.7	3.5	1.7	3.5	1.61	38.86
3 to 4 years	244	28.4	33.3	17.0	10.6	3.1	3.9	1.6	2.0	1.54	35.08

(*continued*)

Table 3.1 (Continued)

	Number	Under $1	$1 to <$1.50	$1.50 to <$2	$2 to <$2.50	$2.50 to <$3	$3 to <$4	$4 to <$5	$5 and Over	Mean Dollars	Mean Hours
Race/Ethnicity:											
White	425	25.7	34.1	18.1	9.5	3.7	5.2	1.5	2.1	1.60	36.24
Black	78	59.1	27.7	5.3	2.4	1.3	0.0	0.8	3.4	1.32	43.40
Hispanic	45	27.8	34.1	13.6	12.8	3.0	2.4	2.3	4.0	1.53	37.78
Other	9	*	*	*	*	*	*	*	*	*	*
Family Structure:											
Single mother	98	46.5	31.1	14.3	4.6	0.5	1.1	1.0	0.8	1.14	41.68
Two parents	460	27.3	33.5	16.6	9.6	4.0	4.8	1.5	2.7	1.64	36.57
Family Size:											
1 child	274	20.8	36.8	18.1	12.4	3.6	3.9	1.9	2.4	1.64	39.87
2 children	225	39.5	29.1	15.3	4.2	3.2	4.6	1.3	2.8	1.54	35.78
3 or more children	59	42.3	30.4	10.6	9.5	2.6	3.3	0.0	1.3	1.23	32.76
Mother's Education:											
Less than high school	26	53.9	33.4	9.8	1.9	0.0	1.0	0.0	0.0	0.95	43.16
High school	203	34.9	39.3	14.7	6.0	1.6	1.0	1.5	1.0	1.33	38.70
Some college	129	31.4	35.9	13.4	10.1	3.1	1.8	1.4	3.0	1.53	37.77
College	123	26.1	25.2	22.6	6.2	5.6	7.7	1.1	5.5	1.88	35.36
Graduate school	75	17.8	24.8	17.1	19.7	4.9	12.7	2.6	1.1	1.87	35.03

Family Income:									
<$15,000	68	59.5	25.6	7.8	6.6	0.0	0.0	0.5	0.0	0.95	38.62
$15,000–$24,999	75	42.4	42.2	9.5	3.4	0.0	1.1	0.0	1.4	1.26	40.66
$25,000–$34,999	90	34.9	34.1	12.9	5.7	7.6	2.1	0.7	2.0	1.43	34.85
$35,000–$49,999	134	22.5	33.8	22.5	7.5	0.7	5.0	2.4	5.5	1.88	35.37
$50,000+	168	20.2	31.9	18.0	14.6	5.9	5.4	2.1	1.9	1.69	39.26
Missing	23	13.1	25.4	25.7	9.4	4.5	20.4	1.4	0.0	1.88	32.88
Poverty Status:									
Below	35	73.81	14.66	5.54	1.94	0.0	0.0	1.1	3.0	1.29	36.71
Above	481	27.91	34.29	16.98	9.17	3.68	3.85	1.5	2.6	1.58	37.59
Missing	43	26.23	34.05	15.79	9.98	2.39	10.88	0.8	0.0	1.48	36.74
Urbanicity:									
Central city	230	23.8	32.9	18.1	8.8	5.8	5.4	1.6	3.5	1.70	38.70
Suburban	200	29.8	30.3	19.4	11.6	1.2	4.6	2.2	0.8	1.53	37.59
Rural	129	44.0	37.6	7.8	4.3	2.2	1.2	0.0	2.9	1.33	35.07
Region:									
West	101	23.9	30.0	24.1	9.4	4.0	4.4	2.0	2.2	1.60	35.78
South	227	40.8	34.4	11.5	7.6	1.1	1.1	1.1	2.4	1.42	41.45
Midwest	128	23.9	47.9	16.1	5.9	2.6	2.4	0.5	0.7	1.34	36.45
Northeast	102	23.1	14.2	18.9	14.4	8.7	12.9	2.9	4.9	2.09	31.55

Source: National Child Care Survey, 1990

Note: Asterisk (*) denotes fewer than 10 cases.

($2.24), but for fewer hours on average, than full-time employed mothers ($1.36). This difference in hourly expenditures implies that either full-time employed mothers seek arrangements that offer a lower price per hour, or part-time employed mothers pay a penalty for purchasing fewer hours of care. Preschool-age children of all employed mothers spend an average of 37 hours per week in a paid primary arrangement. However, preschool-age children of full-time employed mothers spend an average of 42 hours per week, whereas children of part-time employed mothers spend an average of only 23 hours per week in a paid primary arrangement.

Type of Primary Arrangement. In-home care by a non-relative is the most expensive type of care, at a mean expenditure of $2.30 per hour for an average of 31 hours per week (figure 3.10). Over 14 percent of employed mothers using an in-home provider as the paid primary arrangement for preschool-age children spend $5 or more per hour (table 3.1). Twenty-two percent of these families spend less than $1 per hour. Child care provided by a relative is the least expensive type of primary arrangement for employed mothers with a preschool-age child. Employed mothers pay $1.11 per hour for an average of 37 hours per week for relative care. Nearly 60 percent of employed mothers using relative care as the primary arrangement spend less than $1 per hour. Only 2 percent of these families spend $3 or more per hour. Employed mothers pay $1.35 per hour for family day-care homes as the primary arrangement, with preschool-age children spending an average of 38 hours per week in this arrangement. Twenty-nine percent of these families pay under $1 per hour, and none spend $5 or more per hour. Employed mothers relying on centers as the primary arrangement for their preschool-age children pay $1.67 per hour for an average of

Figure 3.10

Mean Hourly Expenditure for Youngest Child Under 5
By Type of Primary Arrangement,
Employed Mothers Paying for Care Only

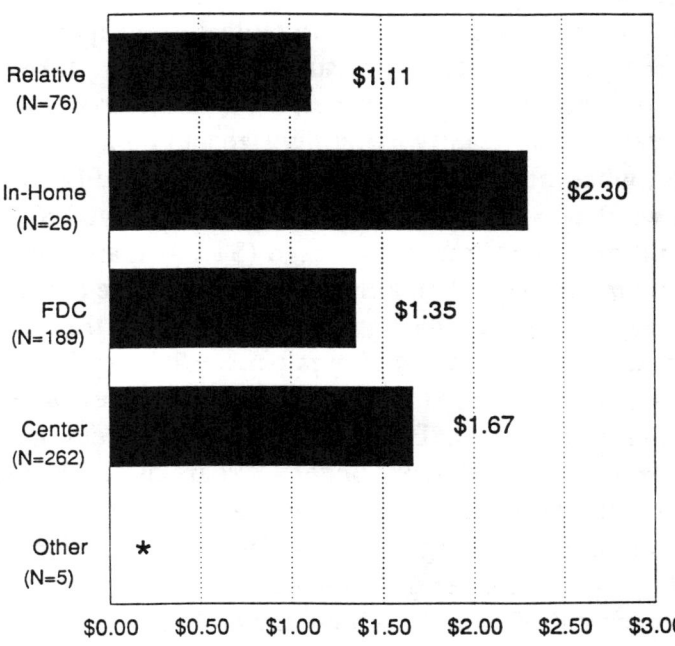

* Fewer than 10 cases.
Source: National Child Care Survey 1990

38 hours per week. Twenty-five percent of these families spend less than $1 per hour, and fewer than 3 percent pay $5 or more per hour for center-based care.

Age of Youngest Child. Employed mothers appear to spend less per hour for infant care ($1.45) than for toddler ($1.61) or preschooler ($1.54) care (table 3.1). However, once the type of arrangement and other family characteristics are considered, these differences are not statistically significant (not shown.)[2]

Family Demographic Characteristics. The initial differences in hourly expenditures based on race/ethnicity and mother's education, detailed in table 3.1, disappear when other family characteristics such as income are taken into account (not shown). However, the mean hourly expenditure varies significantly by family size and family structure, even when other factors are held constant. Figure 3.11 shows that two-parent families with employed mothers spend more per hour on average ($1.64) than employed single mothers ($1.14), although preschool-age children of employed single mothers spend slightly more time in paid primary arrangements (42 hours per week on average) than those in two-parent families (37 hours per week on average) (table 3.1). Employed mothers pay less per hour as the number of children under 13 years old in the family increases, especially when the number of children expands from two to three (figure 3.11). Employed mothers with only one child spend $1.64 per hour for the primary arrangement of their preschool-age child for an average of 40 hours per week; those with two children pay $1.54 per hour for an average of 36 hours per week; and those with three or more children pay $1.23 per hour for an average of 33 hours per week.

Family Income. Employed mothers generally spend more per hour on the care of their youngest preschool-age

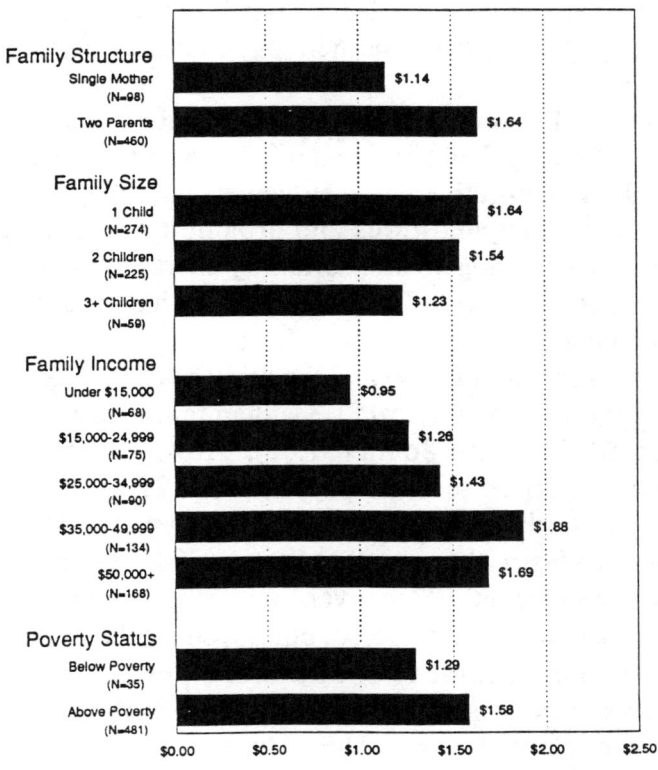

Figure 3.11

Average Hourly Expenditure for Youngest Child Under 5, Employed Mothers Paying for Care Only

Source: National Child Care Survey 1990

child as their family income increases, with a leveling off to a slight drop in cost per hour for the highest levels of income (figure 3.11). Likewise, employed mothers living above the poverty line spend more per hour on primary child care arrangements ($1.58) than employed mothers living below the poverty line ($1.29) for a similar average amount of time (i.e., 38 and 37 hours per week, respectively) (figure 3.11). Twenty-eight percent of nonpoor employed mothers pay under $1 per hour, whereas 74 percent of poor employed mothers pay under $1 per hour (table 3.1).

Residence. Rural employed mothers spend less per hour on average ($1.33) than suburban ($1.53) or urban ($1.71) employed mothers (table 3.1). However, the relationship between hourly expenditures and urbanicity disappears once the type of arrangement and family characteristics are considered (not shown). Table 3.1 shows that employed mothers living in the northeastern United States generally spend more per hour ($2.09) and the midwestern employed mothers spend less per hour ($1.34) than those residing in the West ($1.60) or the South ($1.42). However, the percentage of employed mothers paying under $1 per hour is highest for southern families (41 percent) compared to those in the West (24 percent), Midwest (24 percent), or Northeast (23 percent). Moreover, once other factors such as family income are considered, employed mothers living in the Northeast tend to spend more per hour than employed mothers living in other regions of the United States (results not shown). The average amount of time spent in a paid primary arrangement also varies by region among employed mothers with a preschool-age child (table 3.1). Children in the Northeast spend fewer hours per week in paid primary care (32 hours) than those living in the West (36 hours), Midwest (36 hours), or South (41 hours).

FAMILIES WITH NONEMPLOYED MOTHER

Average Hourly Expenditure. Of those who pay for care, families with a nonemployed mother spend $2.38 per hour on average for the primary arrangement of their youngest child under 5 years old (figure 3.9). Nearly 11 percent of these families spend $5 or more per hour in contrast to 2 percent of the families with an employed mother. Although nonemployed mothers spend more per hour than employed mothers, their preschool-age children spend less time in paid primary care on average (13 hours per week) than those of employed mothers (37 hours per week).

Type of Primary Arrangement. On average, center-based care is the least expensive arrangement for nonemployed mothers, at a mean hourly cost of $1.89 for an average of 12 hours per week (figure 3.12). The mean hourly payment for in-home care by a nonrelative is $2.08 for an average of 13 hours per week among nonemployed mothers. For family day-care, the average cost is $2.20 per hour for an average of 14 hours per week. Other arrangements such as lessons and sports are the most expensive form of care for nonemployed mothers, at $5.14 per hour for an average of 5 hours per week.

Age of Youngest Child. Nonemployed mothers, unlike employed mothers, appear to spend more per hour for infant care ($2.93) than for toddler ($1.93) or preschooler care ($2.46). However, differences in hourly expenditures based on the age of the youngest preschool-age child are not statistically significant among either employed or nonemployed mothers, once other family characteristics are taken into account (results not shown).

Other Characteristics. Race/ethnicity, mother's education, family structure, family size, family income, or

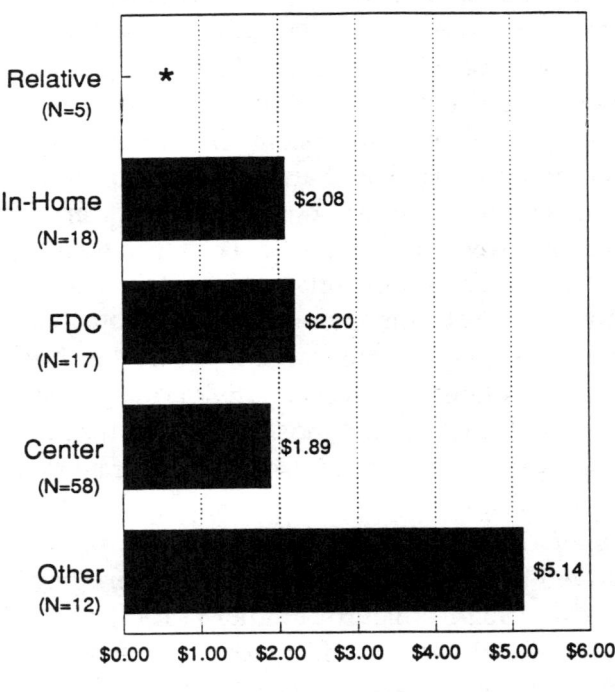

Figure 3.12

Mean Hourly Expenditure for Youngest Under Five
By Type of Primary Arrangement,
Non-Employed Mothers Paying For Care Only

* Fewer than 10 cases.
Source: National Child Care Survey 1990

residence do not independently affect hourly expenditures net of other factors such as type of primary arrangement (not shown).

SINGLE-FATHER FAMILIES

Single fathers pay slightly less per hour than employed single mothers. Of those who pay for care, single fathers spend $.96 per hour on average for the primary arrangement of the youngest child under five years old (not shown). Sixty-five percent of these fathers pay under $1 per hour, whereas 9 percent pay $3 or more per hour. The average amount of time spent in a paid primary arrangement by preschool-age children with a single father is 41 hours per week. The number of single fathers with a youngest child under five years old is too small to permit further cross-classifications by type of primary arrangement, age of youngest child, family demographic characteristics, family income, or residence.

Expenditures for Primary Arrangements for School-age Children

FAMILIES WITH EMPLOYED MOTHER

Average Hourly Expenditure. Of those who pay for care, employed mothers spend $2.78 per hour for about 13 hours of care per week on average for the primary care arrangement (excluding school) of a youngest child aged 5 to 12 (figure 3.13). Forty-two percent pay less than $1.50 per hour, whereas 14 percent pay $5 or more per hour (table

Figure 3.13

Mean Hourly Expenditure for Youngest Child Age 5 to 12
By Maternal Employment Status,
Those Paying for Care Only

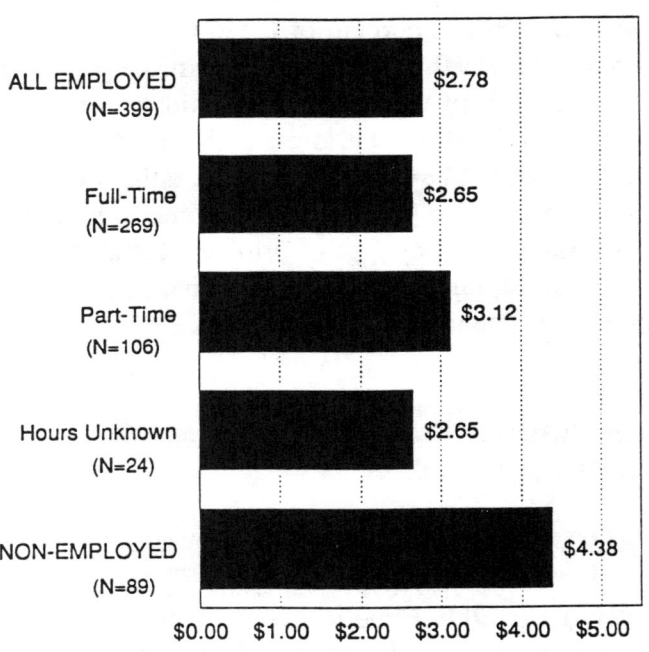

Source: National Child Care Survey 1990

3.2). Like employed mothers with a preschool-age child, part-time employed mothers with only school-age children pay more per hour ($3.12), but for half as many hours of care, than full-time employed mothers (figure 3.13). School-age children of full-time employed mothers spend an average of 16 hours per week in a paid primary arrangement, whereas those of part-time employed mothers spend an average of 8 hours per week in a paid primary arrangement. There is no significant difference in hourly payments between full-time and part-time employed mothers after the type of primary arrangement is taken into account (not shown).

Type of Primary Arrangement. As for preschool-age children, in-home care by a nonrelative is the most expensive arrangement for school-age children with an employed mother, at a mean rate of $3.49 per hour for an average of 14 hours per week (figure 3.14). Almost 23 percent of employed mothers relying on in-home providers as the main nonschool arrangement spend $5 or more per hour, and 21 percent spend under $1 per hour (table 3.2). Relatives ($2.31) and family day-care providers ($2.32) are the least expensive types of nonschool arrangements, with children in both of these arrangements averaging 17 hours of paid care per week. Fifty percent of employed mothers relying on relative care spend less than $1.50 per hour, whereas 9 percent spend $5 or more per hour. Thirty-two percent of employed mothers relying on family day-care providers spend less than $1.50 per hour, and fewer than 7 percent pay $5 or more per hour. Employed mothers using center-based care pay $2.52 per hour for an average of 19 hours per week. Thirty-five percent of these mothers spend less than $1.50 per hour, and 6 percent spend $5 or more per hour.

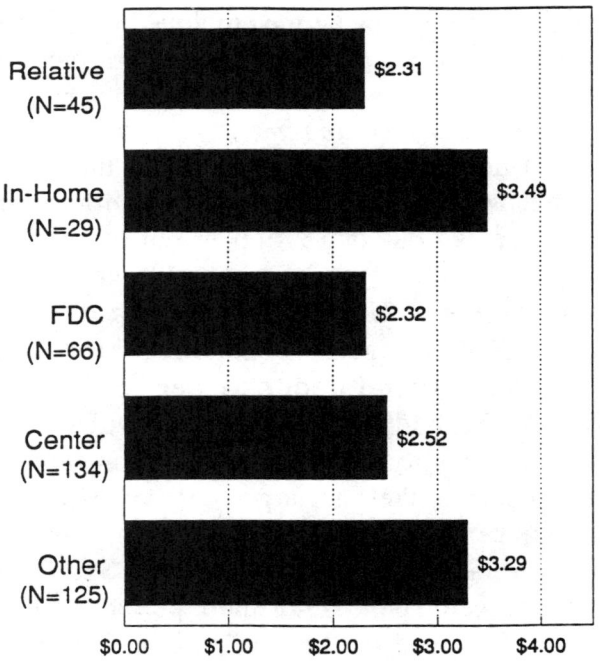

Figure 3.14

Mean Hourly Expenditure for Youngest Child Age 5 to 12
By Type of Primary Arrangement,
Employed Mothers Paying For Care Only

Source: National Child Care Survey 1990

Table 3.2 PERCENTILE DISTRIBUTION OF MEAN HOURLY EXPENDITURE FOR PRIMARY CARE ARRANGEMENT FOR YOUNGEST CHILD AGED 5 TO 12, EMPLOYED MOTHERS PAYING FOR CARE ONLY

	Number	Under $1	$1 to <$1.50	$1.50 to <$2	$2 to <$2.50	$2.50 to <$3	$3 to <$4	$4 to <$5	$5 and Over	Mean Dollars	Mean Hours
All Employed:	399	21.8	19.9	9.4	11.8	7.1	11.0	4.8	14.1	2.78	13.44
Full-time	269	18.1	22.1	7.4	12.8	8.5	13.5	5.0	12.7	2.65	16.10
Part-time	106	31.2	13.8	11.5	10.9	2.8	7.3	4.7	17.7	3.12	7.74
Hours unknown	24	21.4	3.0	22.9	4.9	10.8	0.0	2.2	14.8	2.65	8.84
Primary Arrangement:											
Center	134	12.3	23.2	12.3	13.2	11.0	16.5	5.3	6.2	2.52	19.47
Relative	45	17.8	32.0	4.0	18.3	9.0	5.7	3.7	9.4	2.31	16.82
In-home provider	29	21.3	9.5	8.7	16.5	2.2	12.1	6.9	22.9	3.49	14.19
Family day care	66	7.1	25.0	17.2	19.0	4.4	16.6	4.0	6.8	2.32	16.55
Other	125	41.2	12.0	4.4	3.1	4.9	3.9	4.4	26.1	3.29	3.97
Age of Youngest:											
5 to 9 years	322	18.2	21.6	10.7	11.7	7.1	13.0	4.8	12.9	2.75	15.18
10 to 12 years	77	36.7	13.0	4.1	12.3	7.3	2.8	4.4	19.5	2.86	6.15

(continued)

Table 3.2 (Continued)

	Number	Under $1	$1 to <$1.50	$1.50 to <$2	$2 to <$2.50	$2.50 to <$3	$3 to <$4	$4 to <$5	$5 and Over	Mean Dollars	Mean Hours
Race/Ethnicity:											
White	329	20.6	20.6	8.3	12.1	8.1	10.8	5.1	14.3	2.75	12.53
Black	37	28.9	14.0	11.2	14.9	0.0	21.4	0.0	9.6	2.78	19.33
Hispanic	25	28.0	23.4	21.4	4.7	0.0	0.0	8.1	14.3	2.74	17.78
Other	8	*	*	*	*	*	*	*	*	*	*
Family Structure:											
Single mother	107	17.5	26.7	9.8	16.3	8.9	7.8	4.6	8.4	2.33	17.03
Two parents	291	23.4	17.5	9.3	10.1	6.5	12.2	4.8	16.3	2.94	12.11
Family Size:											
1 child	221	18.5	19.8	7.1	13.1	8.0	12.4	5.5	15.6	3.05	11.30
2 children	146	28.0	17.7	11.2	9.0	7.4	10.0	4.6	12.0	2.39	15.71
3 or more children	32	16.0	31.2	17.4	15.6	0.0	6.2	0.0	13.7	2.59	17.79
Mother's Education:											
Less than high school	10	23.69	37.82	6.25	13.5	7.5	11.2	0.0	0.0	1.53	16.00
High school	147	25.03	21.84	7.73	13.3	4.7	9.0	3.8	14.6	2.61	15.42
Some college	106	18.53	22.95	6.93	13.5	7.6	13.2	7.1	10.1	2.69	13.67
College	77	26.45	13.17	10.63	10.5	3.7	11.9	5.4	18.4	3.13	10.49
Graduate school	57	11.54	16.29	17.73	6.5	16.1	11.2	3.1	17.5	3.13	11.66

Family Income:									
<$15,000	52	26.4	27.3	10.0	17.6	3.6	9.4	0.0	5.8	1.90	16.24
$15,000–$24,999	46	20.5	35.4	6.7	17.1	4.9	5.3	2.7	7.4	2.05	21.01
$25,000–$34,999	58	17.4	18.9	17.2	9.5	9.9	5.5	5.2	16.4	2.89	12.11
$35,000–$49,999	84	23.1	23.9	4.5	12.5	6.9	7.8	7.2	14.1	2.62	11.26
$50,000+	133	18.7	12.7	11.8	9.3	9.2	14.2	6.1	18.0	3.42	12.50
Missing	26	36.0	4.6	0.0	6.7	2.0	30.6	2.2	17.9	2.78	9.24
Poverty Status:									
Below	17	12.8	28.1	23.8	31.1	0.0	4.3	0.0	0.0	1.55	16.33
Above	345	20.4	21.1	9.6	11.6	7.7	10.0	5.3	14.4	2.83	13.65
Missing	37	39.3	5.2	1.6	4.8	5.4	24.1	1.6	18.0	2.80	10.11
Urbanicity:									
Central city	149	16.4	19.0	8.0	11.4	12.5	13.0	3.9	15.8	3.16	13.07
Suburban	151	24.5	17.6	11.1	10.2	5.6	13.0	5.0	13.2	2.64	14.05
Rural	100	25.7	24.9	9.0	14.8	1.5	5.1	5.7	13.2	2.41	13.05
Region:									
West	95	23.7	20.6	9.6	8.4	8.9	11.5	4.8	12.4	2.55	15.51
South	144	23.5	19.9	9.5	16.4	3.2	13.1	5.7	8.8	2.63	13.84
Midwest	89	20.7	26.8	9.0	7.5	6.3	7.2	4.3	18.2	2.83	12.46
Northeast	70	17.0	10.4	9.6	12.4	14.1	10.9	3.2	22.4	3.31	11.01

Source: National Child Care Survey, 1990

Note: Asterisk (*) denotes fewer than 10 cases.

Age of Youngest Child. The mean hourly payment for younger school-age children (5 to 9 years old) does not differ significantly from that for older school-age children (10 to 12 years old), although children ages 5 to 9 generally spend more time in paid arrangements than older children (table 3.2).

Family Demographic Characteristics. The mean hourly expenditure on (nonschool) care arrangements of school-age children varies by family structure and family size, but not by race/ethnicity or mother's education. Although white school-age children spend less time per week in paid care on average (13 hours) than black (19 hours) or Hispanic (18 hours) children, the mean hourly expenditure is approximately the same across families of different races/ethnicities (table 3.2). Figure 3.15 shows that two-parent families with an employed mother spend more per hour ($2.94 on average) for the care of their youngest school-age child than employed single mothers ($2.33). However, school-age children of employed single mothers spend more time on average in paid nonschool arrangements (17 hours per week) than those of mothers with partners (12 hours per week). Unlike those with preschool-age children, employed mothers with two children under 13 years old pay less on average ($2.39) for the care of their school-age child than those with only one child ($3.05) or those with three or more children under 13 years old ($2.59).

Family Income. Like those with a preschool-age child, employed mothers with a youngest child aged 5 to 12 pay more per hour as their family income increases (figure 3.15). Eighteen percent of high-income families (i.e., those earning $50,000 or more) spend $5 or more per hour, whereas 6 percent of low-income families (i.e., those earning under $15,000) spend $5 or more per hour (table 3.2).

Figure 3.15

Average Hourly Expenditure for Youngest Child Age 5 to 12,
Employed Mothers Paying for Care Only

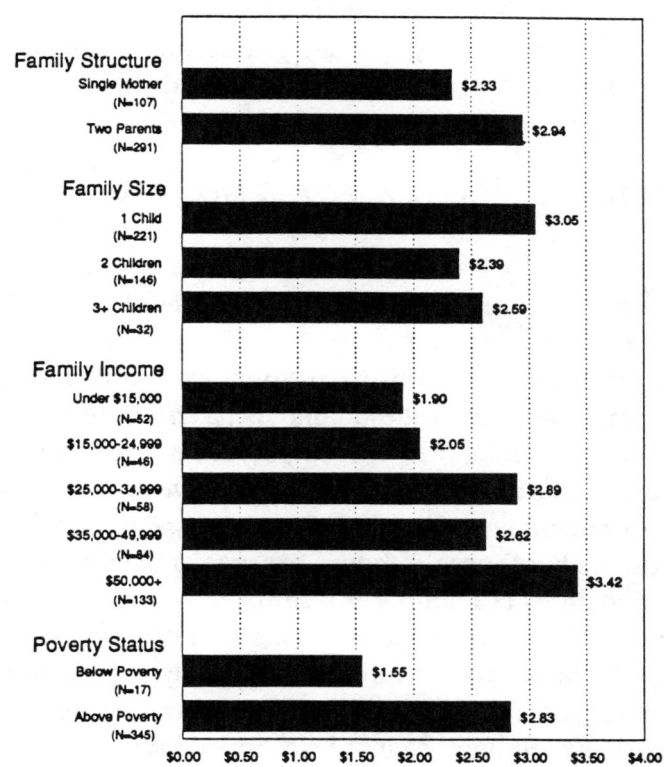

Source: National Child Care Survey 1990

Likewise, employed mothers living above the poverty line spend more per hour ($2.83) on nonschool care arrangements than those living below the poverty line ($1.55) (figure 3.15). Over 20 percent of nonpoor employed mothers pay $4 or more per hour, while none in poverty pay $4 or more per hour (table 3.2).

Residence. The mean hourly expenditure for employed mothers with no preschool-age children does not vary significantly by residence, either in terms of urbanicity or region, when other family characteristics such as income and family size are taken into account (not shown).

FAMILIES WITH NONEMPLOYED MOTHER

Average Hourly Expenditure. Of those who pay for care, nonemployed mothers without a preschool-age child spend $4.38 per hour on average for the primary (nonschool) arrangement of their youngest child (figure 3.13). Over 20 percent of these families pay $5 or more per hour (not shown) in contrast to 14 percent of the families with an employed mother (table 3.2). However, school-age children of nonemployed mothers generally spend less time in paid (nonschool) care (4 hours per week) than those of employed mothers (13 hours per week).

Type of Primary Arrangement. Since an overwhelming majority of school-age children of nonemployed mothers use alternative arrangements like lessons and sports, the mean hourly expenditure cannot be estimated separately for centers, in-home providers, family day-care providers, or relatives owing to small sample sizes (see chapter 2).

Age of Youngest Child. As for employed mothers, the mean hourly expenditure for younger school-age children (ages 5 to 9) does not differ significantly from the mean hourly expenditure for older school-age children (ages 10 to 12) among nonemployed mothers (not shown).

Family Characteristics. The estimates of the mean hourly expenditure classified by race/ethnicity or family income are tenuous because the number of nonwhite or low-income, nonemployed mothers is very small. Moreover, family structure, family size, and mother's education do not independently influence hourly expenditures, net of all other family characteristics or residence (not shown).

Residence. Nonemployed mothers with their youngest child aged 5 to 12 and living in central cities spend substantially more per hour ($8.96) on nonschool arrangements than those living in suburban ($2.39) or rural ($2.39) areas. Thirty-seven percent of central city dwellers pay $5 or more per hour, while 12 percent of suburban families and 19 percent of rural families pay $5 or more per hour. The mean hourly expenditure does not significantly vary by regional residence among nonemployed mothers without a preschool-age child when urbanicity and family characteristics are taken into account (not shown).

SINGLE-FATHER FAMILIES

Single fathers with their youngest child aged 5 to 12 spend approximately the same amount for their primary care arrangement as employed single mothers (excluding school), paying $2.32 per hour for an average of 25 hours per week (not shown). Seventeen percent of these fathers pay $5 or more per hour, whereas 46 percent pay less than $1.50 per hour. The small number of single fathers in this sample prohibits further cross-classifications.

Expenditures for Secondary Arrangements for Youngest Child

PRESCHOOL-AGE CHILDREN

Maternal Employment Status. Table 3.3 shows that employed mothers pay less per hour ($2.11) for secondary arrangements than nonemployed mothers ($3.75). Yet, preschool-age children of employed mothers spend more time in paid secondary arrangements on average (13 hours per week) than those of nonemployed mothers (8 hours per week). In fact, few nonemployed mothers pay for a secondary arrangement for a preschool-age child. Four percent of employed mothers pay $5 or more, whereas 19 percent of nonemployed mothers pay $5 or more for secondary arrangements. The mean hourly expenditure for full-time employed mothers does not differ significantly from that of part-time employed mothers, although preschool-age children of full-time employed mothers spend more time in a paid secondary arrangement than those of part-time employed mothers--17 hours versus 9 hours per week.

Type of Secondary Arrangement. Centers are more expensive than relatives, in-home providers, or family daycare providers as a secondary arrangement for preschool-age children (table 3.3). Employed mothers pay a mean amount of $2.08 per hour for an average of 17 hours of center care. Care provided by a relative is the least expensive secondary arrangement for a preschool-age child with an employed mother, at $1.34 per hour for an average of 13 hours of relative care.

SCHOOL-AGE CHILDREN

Maternal Employment Status. Employed mothers pay less per hour on average ($4.03) than nonemployed mothers ($7.57) for secondary arrangements for their youngest child aged 5 to 12 (table 3.3). School-age children of employed mothers generally spend more time in a paid secondary arrangement (5 hours per week) than those of nonemployed mothers (2 hours per week). Like those with a preschool-age child, nonemployed mothers with only school-age children rarely pay for a secondary arrangement. Twenty-two percent of employed mothers pay $5 or more for secondary arrangements, whereas 25 percent of nonemployed mothers pay $5 or more for secondary arrangements. Full-time employed mothers ($4.17) pay slightly more per hour on average than part-time employed mothers ($3.63), whereas their children spend about the same amount of time in a paid secondary arrangement (5 hours versus 4 hours, respectively).

Type of Secondary Arrangement. For school-age children in paid secondary arrangements, 66 percent with employed mothers are *not* cared for by relatives, centers, in-home providers, or family day-care providers. These children rely on more expensive alternative services like lessons and sports activities (table 3.3). Thus, the average hourly expenditure for secondary arrangements for school-age children is higher than that for preschool-age children.

Table 3.3 PERCENTILE DISTRIBUTION OF MEAN HOURLY EXPENDITURE FOR SECONDARY CARE ARRANGEMENT FOR YOUNGEST CHILD, BY AGE OF CHILD AND MATERNAL EMPLOYMENT STATUS, MOTHER PAYING FOR CARE ONLY

	Number	Under $1	$1 to <$1.50	$1.50 to <$2	$2 to <$2.50	$2.50 to <$3	$3 to <$4	$4 to <$5	$5 Over	Mean Dollars	Mean Hours
					Youngest Child under Age Five						
All Employed:	123	23.8	13.8	16.1	13.9	10.0	10.4	7.4	4.4	2.11	13.06
Full-time	66	29.2	18.7	17.4	10.7	1.8	10.9	5.4	6.0	2.03	16.65
Part-time	48	20.8	6.6	13.0	17.7	23.3	6.1	11.6	1.0	2.11	9.17
Type of Arrangement:											
Center	48	13.5	13.6	23.6	18.0	14.0	10.5	5.8	1.0	2.08	16.81
Relative	17	54.2	5.8	7.8	22.5	0.0	0.0	9.8	0.0	1.34	12.68
In-home provider	21	18.5	28.0	14.2	11.3	15.8	0.0	9.9	2.3	1.78	8.60
Family day care	17	29.7	20.9	13.8	10.6	13.7	7.8	3.4	0.0	1.63	20.30
Other	20	22.9	0.0	9.4	2.2	0.0	32.8	10.2	22.5	3.64	2.85
Nonemployed	46	13.90	20.12	4.90	5.27	13.84	11.90	10.9	19.2	3.75	7.58

Parental Expenditures for Child Care

Youngest Child Aged 5–12

	N										
All Employed:	177	24.6	7.0	9.7	12.1	6.5	9.2	9.1	21.8	4.03	4.71
Full-time	122	23.6	5.4	12.5	10.4	8.4	11.6	7.8	20.3	4.17	5.03
Part-time	48	27.8	9.5	4.0	16.3	2.7	2.1	13.7	24.0	3.63	4.12
Type of Arrangement:											
Center	19	15.9	13.2	21.8	9.6	0.0	19.9	8.2	11.4	3.06	7.57
Relative	13	5.1	3.8	18.4	25.8	13.2	0.0	15.2	18.3	3.05	6.19
In-home provider	7									*	*
Family day care	22	6.0	16.7	19.6	32.4	0.0	7.7	12.4	5.1	2.25	9.45
Other	116	32.3	4.1	3.9	7.8	6.7	9.4	8.4	27.4	4.72	2.92
Nonemployed	24	15.7	9.5	13.4	11.9	3.9	14.6	5.8	25.1	7.57	2.20

Source: National Child Care Survey, 1990

Note: Asterisk (*) denotes fewer than 10 cases.

WEEKLY EXPENDITURES FOR ALL CHILDREN IN FAMILY

Although focusing on hourly payments for the youngest child in the family allows one to control for children spending differing amounts of time in paid care, a look at total weekly expenditures for all children in the family and for all child care arrangements gives a better picture of the total financial responsibilities parents face in purchasing child care.

In the survey, if parents had more than one child under 13 years old, they were also asked, "How much does your household pay for all of the arrangements and activities used by all the children under age 13 in the household?" Parents could respond in terms of hourly, daily, weekly, monthly, or annual payments. For those few parents who listed their expenditures by the hour or day, their total weekly expenditure was estimated according to the age of their youngest child and the average number of hours and days per week spent by all youngest children in the sample under age 5, as well as between ages 5 and 12, in a paid primary arrangement. For one-child families, the total weekly expenditure is the sum of weekly payments across all arrangements. Estimates of weekly expenditures are made only for those families who pay for any child care services.

Families with Youngest Child under Age Five

FAMILIES WITH EMPLOYED MOTHER

Average Weekly Expenditure. Employed mothers with their youngest child under five years old make average weekly payments of $63 for the care of all children in the family (figure 3.16). Full-time employed mothers have higher average weekly expenditures than part-time employed mothers--$68 compared to $51.

Type of Primary Arrangement of Youngest Child. The mean total weekly expenditure for all children in the family varies by the type of primary arrangement of the youngest preschool-age child (figure 3.17). Employed mothers who rely on parents or relatives for the primary care of their youngest child spend less per week for the care of all their children than those who rely on other types of primary arrangements for their youngest preschool-age child. Employed mothers using in-home providers as the primary arrangement for their youngest preschool-age child have the highest weekly child care expenditures, at $94 on average.

Race/Ethnicity. Mean weekly expenditures differ slightly by the race/ethnicity of the family (table 3.4). Overall, employed black mothers spend less per week ($54) on the care of all their children when the youngest child is under five years old than Hispanic mothers ($56), white mothers ($65), or mothers of other races/ethnicities ($64). Black mothers with a preschool-age child spend less per week than white mothers, even when other factors like family structure and income are taken into account (not shown).

Family Demographic Characteristics. The initial difference in mean weekly expenditures between single mothers ($55) and two-parent families ($65) is not statistically

Figure 3.16

Mean Weekly Expenditure for All Children in the Family
By Maternal Employment Status,
Mothers With Youngest Child Under 5 Paying for Care Only

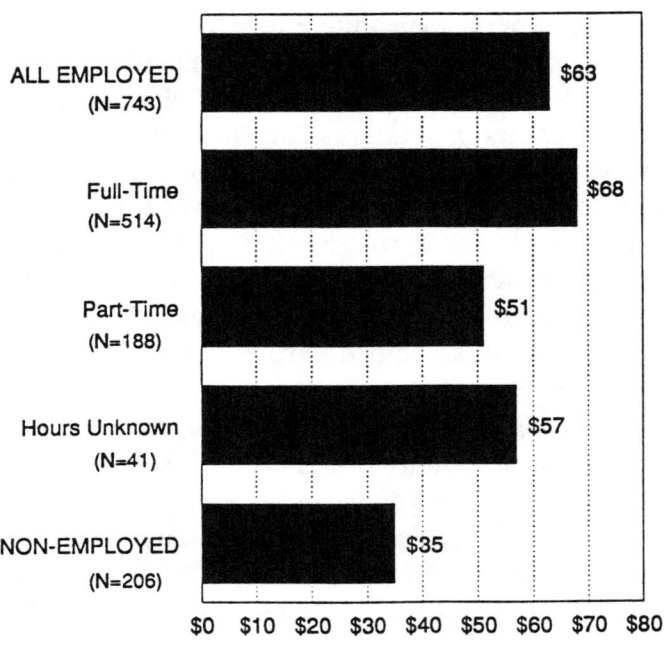

Source: National Child Care Survey 1990

Figure 3.17

Mean Weekly Expenditure for All Children in the Family
By Primary Arrangement of Youngest Child,
Employed Mothers With Youngest Child Under 5
Paying For Care Only

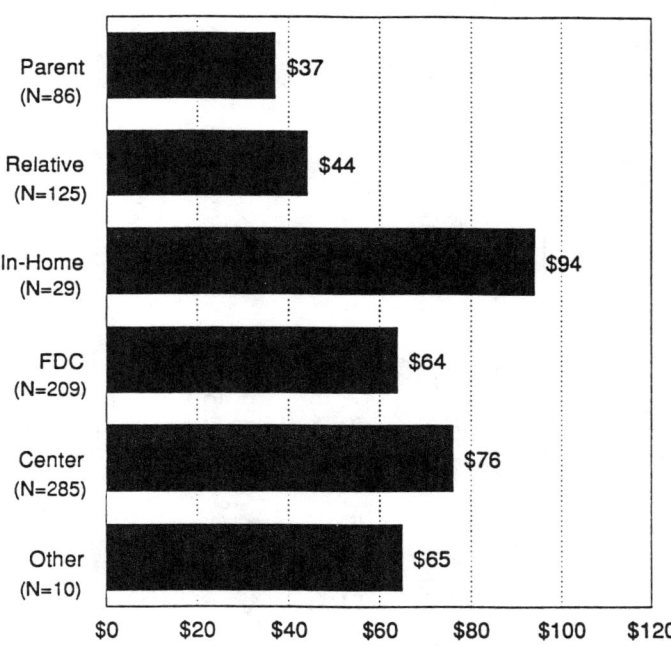

Source: National Child Care Survey 1990

Table 3.4 MEAN WEEKLY CHILD CARE EXPENDITURE FOR ALL CHILDREN AND PERCENTAGE OF TOTAL WEEKLY INCOME FOR YOUNGEST CHILD UNDER AGE FIVE, BY RACE, POVERTY, AND FAMILY INCOME, EMPLOYED MOTHERS PAYING FOR CARE ONLY

	White (N)	Black (N)	Hispanic (N)	Other (N)	Total (N)
Total cost ($)	65.43 (575)	54.19 (92)	55.69 (61)	64.02 (15)	63.21 (743)
Percentage of income	9.68	13.51	11.06	17.25	10.43
Below Poverty:					
Total ($)	42.29 (25)	28.41 (21)	*	*	37.27 (53)
Percentage of Income	23.56	17.39	*	*	23.21
Above Poverty:					
Total ($)	66.74 (504)	61.99 (63)	55.80 (55)	73.13 (12)	65.45 (633)
Percentage of Income	8.47	9.54	8.99	11.38	8.68
Under $15,000:					
Total ($)	39.70 (48)	35.42 (30)	37.62 (11)	*	37.92 (92)
Percentage of Income	25.11	23.73	22.33	*	24.79

$15,000–$24,999:					
Total ($)	51.35 (75)	47.59 (11)	47.23 (13)	*	50.70 (99)
Percentage of Income	13.47	12.04	11.86	*	13.22
$25,000–$34,999:					
Total ($)	49.22 (97)	57.73 (17)	47.13 (15)	*	50.71 (132)
Percentage of Income	8.52	9.94	8.23	*	8.78
$35,000–$49,999:					
Total ($)	64.90 (153)	57.26 (64)	*	*	64.53 (177)
Percentage of Income	7.91	6.98	*	*	10.22
$50,000 or More:					
Total ($)	85.74 (177)	85.37 (17)	78.97 (14)	*	85.11 (212)
Percentage of Income	6.26	6.10	5.99	*	6.20

Source: National Child Care Survey, 1990

Note: Asterisk (*) denotes fewer than 10 cases in category.

significant, after other factors such as family size and income are held constant (not shown). Employed mothers with two children under age 13 spend more per week than either those with three children or only one child, regardless of race/ethnicity. Average weekly expenditures are also greater for employed mothers with higher levels of education than for those with lower levels of education (figure 3.18). For example, employed mothers with a bachelor's degree and no additional schooling spend $70 per week, whereas employed mothers without a high school diploma spend approximately $44 per week. The relationship between mother's education and weekly expenditures persists even when the effect of family income is taken into account (not shown).

Family Income. Among those with a preschool-age child, employed mothers with higher family incomes spend substantially more per week for the care of all their children than employed mothers with lower family incomes, especially compared to those living in poverty (figure 3.18). Regardless of race/ethnicity, mothers with a family income of $50,000 or more typically spend more than twice as much as mothers with a family income under $15,000 (table 3.4).

Residence. Employed mothers living in central cities pay more per week for total child care expenses on average ($75) than those living in suburban ($60) or rural ($47) areas (figure 3.18). Although weekly expenditures vary by urbanicity, regional differences disappear when other family characteristics such as income are considered (not shown).

Parental Expenditures for Child Care

Figure 3.18

Mean Weekly Expenditure For All Children in the Family, Employed Mothers with Youngest Child Under 5 Paying for Care Only

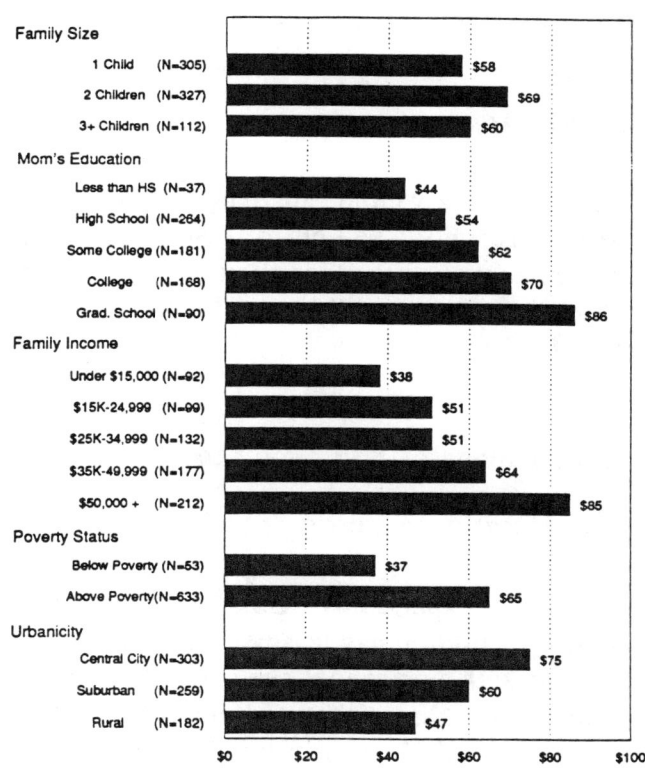

Source: National Child Care Survey 1990

FAMILIES WITH NONEMPLOYED MOTHER

Nonemployed mothers with a preschool-age child spend half of what employed mothers spend on total child care--an average of $35 weekly--because of their heavier reliance on parental care (figure 3.16). Among nonemployed mothers, weekly child care expenditures do not vary significantly by the characteristics of the youngest child or by family structure or residence (not shown).

SINGLE-FATHER FAMILIES

The mean total of weekly child care expenditures for single fathers with a preschool-age child is $48 (not shown). Single fathers pay slightly less than employed single mothers ($55) but substantially more than nonemployed single mothers ($29) (not shown).

Families with Youngest Child Aged 5 to 12

FAMILIES WITH EMPLOYED MOTHER

Average Weekly Expenditure. Employed mothers with no preschool-age children pay less per week for child care ($30) than those with a preschool-age child ($63, table 3.4) because they are purchasing fewer hours of care (figure 3.19). Likewise, full-time employed mothers with no preschool-age children also have higher average weekly expenditures ($33) than their part-time employed counterparts ($22).

Type of Primary Arrangement of Youngest Child. Mean total weekly expenditures are greater for employed mothers

Parental Expenditures for Child Care ■ 169

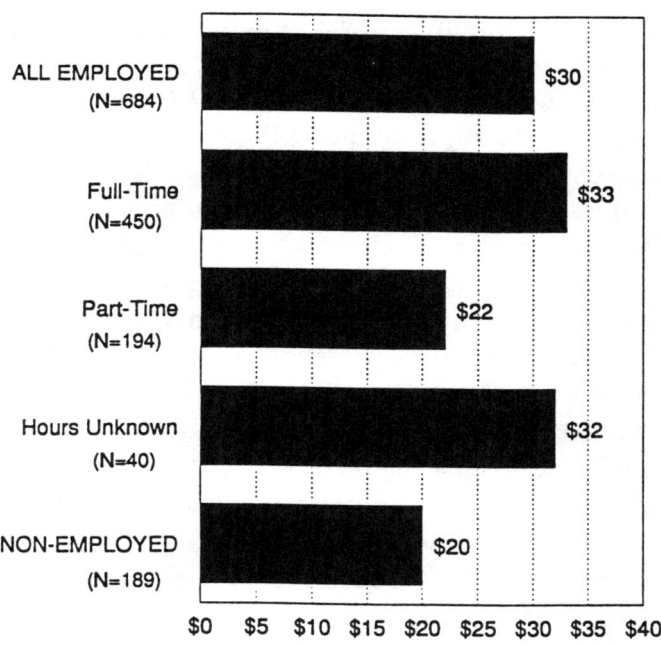

Figure 3.19

Mean Weekly Expenditure for All Children in the Family
By Maternal Employment Status,
Mothers With Youngest Child 5 to 12 Paying for Care Only

Source: National Child Care Survey 1990

using centers, in-home providers, and family day-care homes as the primary before- and after-school arrangement for their youngest child than for those relying on parents or relatives (figure 3.20). Using lessons or sports as the youngest child's primary before-/after-school arrangement appears to lower the weekly cost of child care.

Race/Ethnicity. There is little variation by race/ethnicity in mean weekly expenditures among employed mothers with a youngest child ages 5 to 12. Employed Hispanic mothers pay $28; employed white mothers pay $30; employed black mothers pay $33; and employed mothers of other races/ethnicities pay $34 per week on average (not shown).

Family Demographic Characteristics. Single employed mothers spend approximately the same amount on child care each week as employed mothers living with a partner (not shown). However, employed mothers with only one child have smaller total weekly expenditures than those with two or three children under 13 years old (figure 3.21). Moreover, employed mothers without a preschool-age child, like those with a preschool-age child, tend to spend more on a weekly basis as their educational level increases. Employed mothers who have some educational experience beyond a bachelor's degree spend $43 a week on average, whereas those who have not completed high school spend $17 per week on average (figure 3.21).

Family Income. Weekly expenditures on child care do not vary significantly by family income or poverty status among employed mothers without a preschool-age child (figure 3.21).

Residence. Employed mothers with a youngest child aged 5 to 12 living in central cities ($35) and suburban areas ($31) generally have higher average weekly child care expenses than those living in rural areas ($21) (not shown).

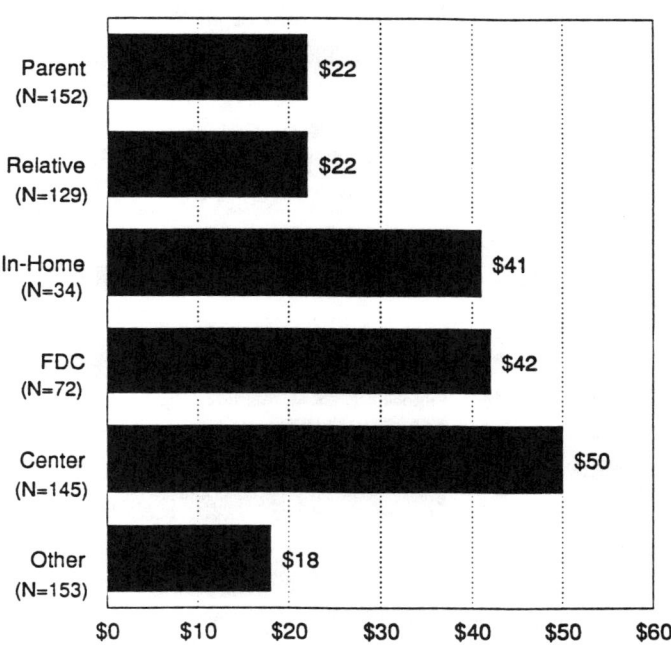

Figure 3.20

Mean Weekly Expenditure for All Children in the Family By Primary Arrangement of Youngest Child, Employed Mothers With Youngest Child Age 5 to 12 Paying For Care Only

Source: National Child Care Survey 1990

Figure 3.21

Mean Weekly Expenditure For All Children in the Family, Employed Mothers with Youngest Child Age 5 to 12 Paying for Care Only

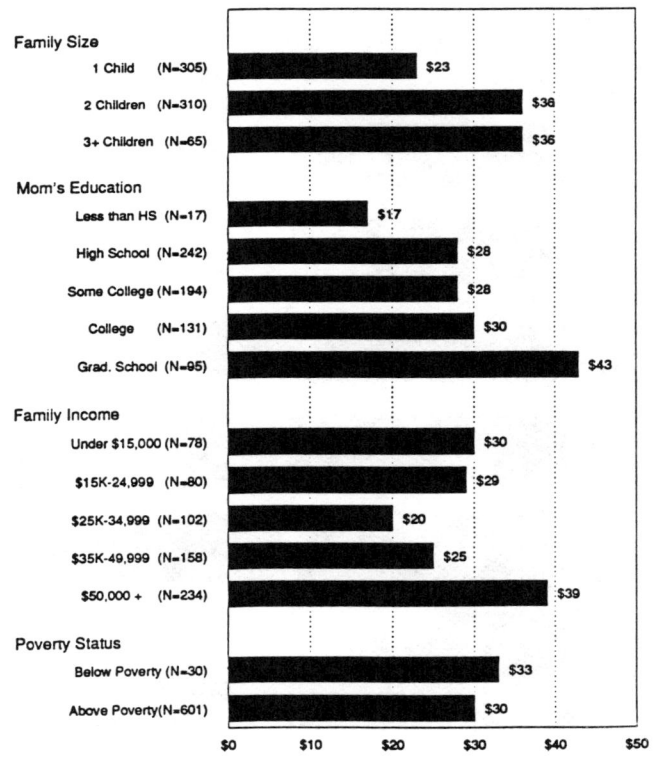

Source: National Child Care Survey 1990

Even when the effects of family income and other factors are considered, rural employed mothers pay less per week (not shown). Weekly expenditures do not vary significantly by regional residence (not shown).

FAMILIES WITH NONEMPLOYED MOTHER

Like employed mothers, nonemployed mothers with no preschool-age children spend less per week on total child care (average of $20, figure 3.19) than those with at least one preschool-age child ($35, figure 3.16). The small number of nonwhite, nonemployed mothers with a youngest child aged 5 to 12, especially those with low income or education, prohibits additional cross-classifications.

SINGLE-FATHER FAMILIES

Unlike single fathers with a preschool-age child, single fathers with their youngest child aged 5 to 12 pay slightly more per week for child care ($39) than either employed single mothers ($34) or nonemployed single mothers ($25) (not shown).

BUDGET SHARES: PERCENTAGE OF FAMILY INCOME SPENT ON CHILD CARE

Although the absolute amount of money spent on child care is important, one needs to examine the proportion of the family budget spent on child care to understand the relative cost of care for American families. Parents' ability to pay is limited by the total amount of their financial resources. Moreover, the larger the share of family income spent on child care, the less money there is for other goods and services. Thus, for each family in the sample, we have calculated the percentage of their weekly family income that constitutes total weekly child care expenses for all children.

Families with Youngest Child under Age Five

FAMILIES WITH EMPLOYED MOTHER

Average Budget Share. Employed mothers with a youngest child under five years old spend 10 percent of their family income on the care of all their children, with no difference between full-time and part-time employed mothers (figure 3.22). This overall average share is not significantly different from the average share estimated for 1985 (Hofferth 1988). The U.S. Bureau of the Census (1990) reported that 7 percent to 8 percent of monthly family income was spent on child care in 1986-87 by employed mothers with the youngest child under five years old. However, the Census Bureau calculated the average child care budget share not on a family-by-family basis, but as the ratio of the sum of weekly expenditures across all families over the sum of weekly income across all families. Therefore, the Census Bureau's estimate of the average proportion of family income spent on child care is not comparable to our family-based measure.

Race/Ethnicity. Employed nonwhite mothers generally spend a larger percentage of their family income on child care than employed white mothers (table 3.4). Race/ethnic

Parental Expenditures for Child Care 175

Figure 3.22

Mean Percentage of Family Income Spent on Child Care
By Maternal Employment Status,
Mothers With Youngest Child Under 5 Paying for Care Only

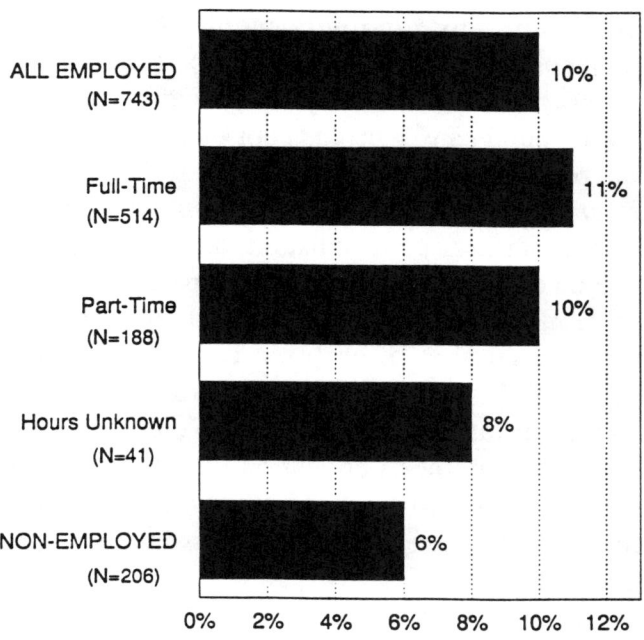

Source: National Child Care Survey 1990

differences in budget shares disappear once family income and other factors are taken into account (not shown).

Family Income. Although low-income employed mothers are less likely to pay for child care and pay a smaller amount per week for it than high-income employed mothers, those with a family income under $15,000 who pay for care spend a substantially larger share of their financial resources on child care than employed mothers with higher family incomes, regardless of race/ethnicity (figure 3.23). Nonpoor white mothers with a preschool-age child spend 8 percent of their family income on child care, whereas poor white mothers spend 24 percent of their family income on child care (table 3.4). Likewise, nonpoor black mothers spend nearly 10 percent of their family income on child care, whereas poor black mothers spend 17 percent of their budget on child care.

Other Family Characteristics. Employed mothers with a husband/partner spend substantially less of their family income on child care (9 percent) compared with employed single mothers (21 percent). Mean budget shares do not vary by the number of children in the family when the youngest child is under age five (figure 3.24). Finally, the percentage of family income spent on child care decreases as the level of mother's education increases (figure 3.24). This relationship disappears after the effect of family income on child care budget shares is taken into account (not shown).

Residence. There is little variation in the percentage of family income spent on child care by residence (region and urbanicity) among employed mothers with a preschool-age child (not shown). This finding suggests that residential differences in family income explain some of the regional and urban variations in weekly expenditures found earlier.

Parental Expenditures for Child Care

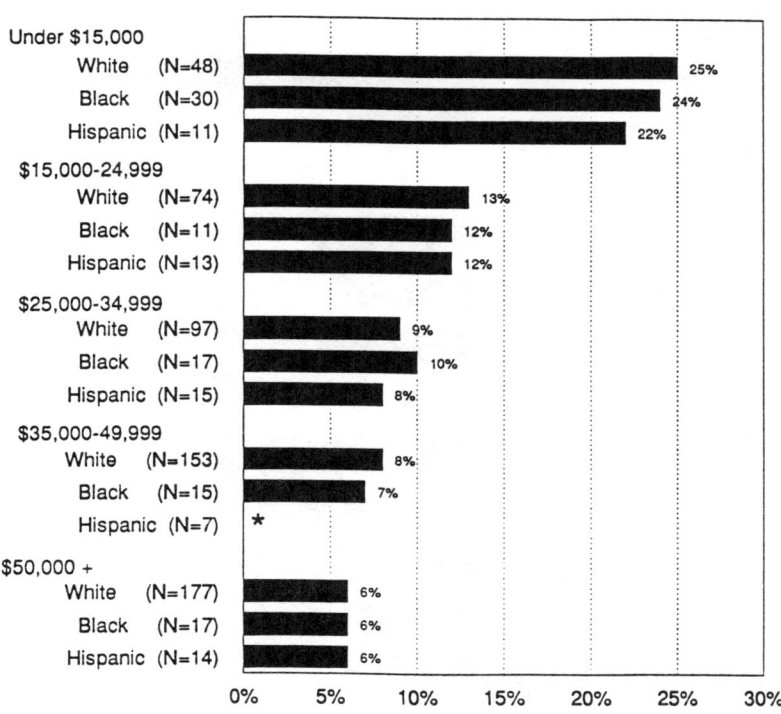

Figure 3.23

Mean Percentage of Family Income Spent on Child Care
By Race/Ethnicity and Family Income,
Employed Mothers with Youngest Child Under 5
Paying for Care Only

* Fewer than 10 cases.
Source: National Child Care Survey 1990

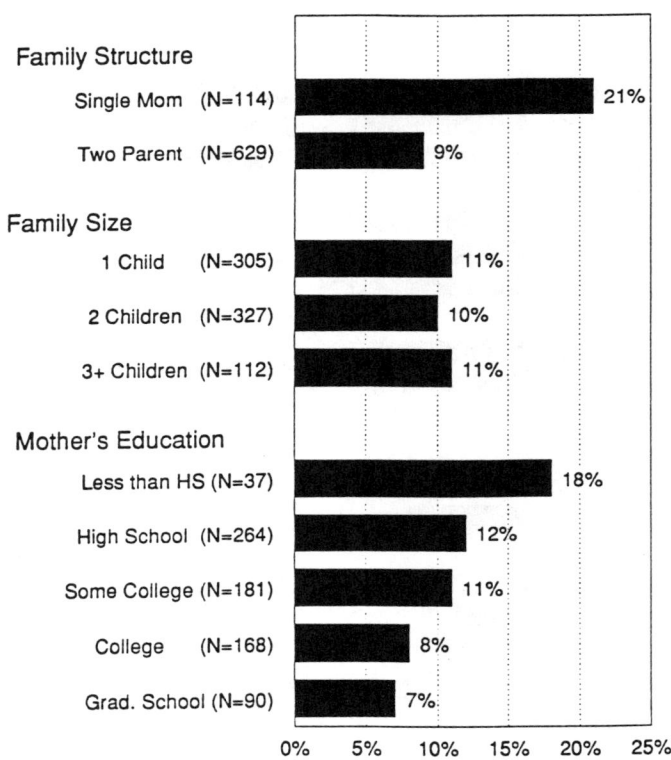

Figure 3.24

Mean Percentage of Family Income Spent on Child Care, Employed Mothers with Youngest Child Under 5 Paying for Care Only

Source: National Child Care Survey 1990

FAMILIES WITH NONEMPLOYED MOTHER

Nonemployed mothers with a youngest child under age five spend about 6 percent of their income on child care, which is four percentage points lower than that of employed mothers (figure 3.22).

SINGLE-FATHER FAMILIES

Single fathers with a preschool-age child spend approximately the same percentage of income on child care (18 percent) as single mothers who are employed (21 percent) or nonemployed (19 percent) (not shown).

Families with the Youngest Child Aged 5 to 12

FAMILIES WITH EMPLOYED MOTHER

Average Budget Share. Employed mothers with a youngest child aged 5 to 12 spend proportionately less of their family budget on child care than those with a preschool-age child (figure 3.25). Employed mothers with a school-age child as the youngest in the family spend just over 6 percent of their family income on child care, whereas those with a preschool-age child spend 10 percent of their family income. The former figure is lower than the 9 percent mean child care budget share reported for 1985 (Hofferth 1988).

Race/Ethnicity. Employed white mothers whose youngest child is of school age appear to spend a smaller percentage of their family income on child care than their nonwhite counterparts. However, these differences disap-

180 ■ NATIONAL CHILD CARE SURVEY, 1990

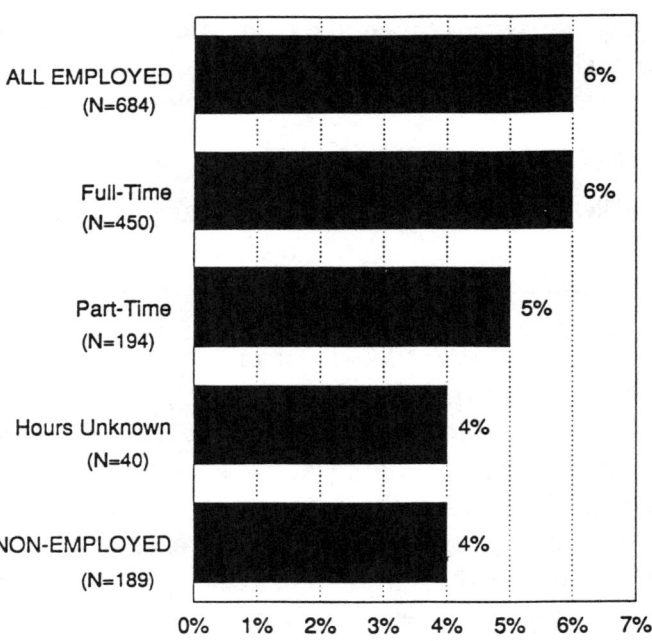

Figure 3.25

Mean Percentage of Family Income Spent on Child Care
By Maternal Employment Status,
Mothers With Youngest Child 5 to 12
Paying for Care Only

Source: National Child Care Survey 1990

pear after the effect of family income is taken into account (not shown).

Family Income. Like those with a preschool-age child, employed mothers whose youngest child is of school age spend a greater share of their budget on child care as their family income declines (figure 3.26). For example, nonpoor employed mothers spend only 4 percent of their family income on child care, whereas poor employed mothers spend almost 23 percent of their budget on child care.

Other Family Characteristics. Employed mothers with a husband/partner spend a smaller share of their total family income on child care (4 percent) than employed single mothers (12 percent) (figure 3.26). Moreover, single mothers spend a greater share of their financial resources on child care even when the effect of family income is held constant (not shown). Mean budget shares vary slightly by the number of children under 13 years old, with employed mothers spending a greater share when they have more children (figure 3.26). Unlike employed mothers with a preschool-age child, child care budget shares do not differ according to the mother's level of education for those with their youngest child 5 to 12 years old (figure 3.26).

Residence. The percentage of family income spent on child care does not vary significantly by residence among employed mothers without a preschool-age child (not shown).

FAMILIES WITH NONEMPLOYED MOTHER

The gap between employed and nonemployed mothers in terms of the percentage of family income spent on child care is smaller among those with a youngest child aged 5 to 12 than among those with a preschool-age child.

Figure 3.26

Mean Percentage of Family Income Spent on Child Care, Employed Mothers with Youngest Child Age 5 to 12 Paying for Care Only

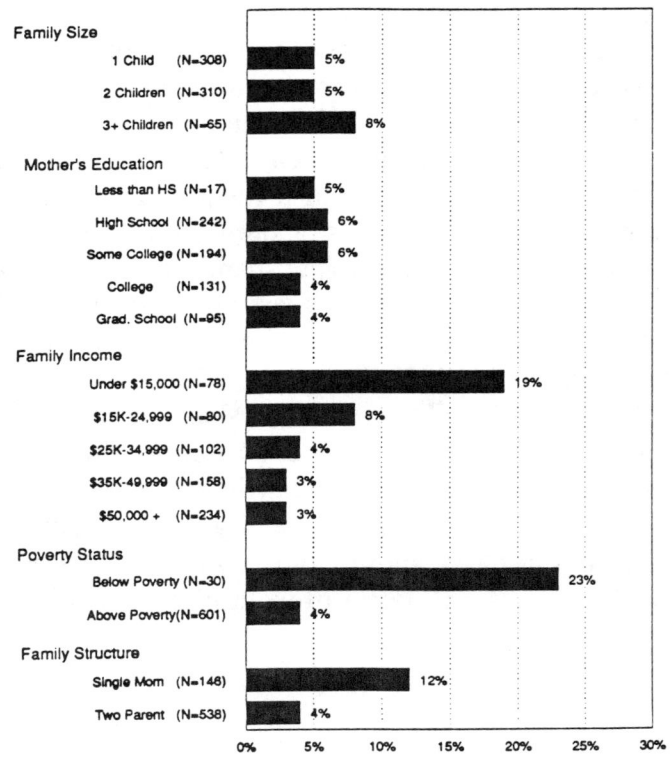

Source: National Child Care Survey 1990

Nonemployed mothers whose youngest child is of school age spend almost 4 percent of their family income on child care, whereas employed mothers spend almost 6 percent (figure 3.25).

SINGLE-FATHER FAMILIES

Unlike single fathers with a preschool-age child, single fathers with a youngest child between 5 and 12 years old spend a smaller share of their income on child care (7 percent) than single mothers who are employed (12 percent) or nonemployed (14 percent) (not shown).

ASSISTANCE IN PAYING FOR CHILD CARE

Receipt of Direct Financial Assistance

Nearly 5 percent of the families who pay for child care reported that they receive help from an agency or another person outside their household to pay for the care of their youngest child (not shown). Forty-six percent of these families reported that they receive direct financial assistance specifically for the primary arrangement of their youngest child, of which 57 percent of these families rely on center-based care. Of those families receiving assistance for their youngest child's primary arrangement, 66 percent reported that they receive governmental subsidies; 21 percent receive financial aid from friends or relatives; 3 percent receive assistance from employers; and 10 percent receive help from other sources.

Direct financial assistance does not vary by maternal employment status or according to whether or not the family is headed by a single father. Single fathers are just as likely as employed or nonemployed mothers to receive financial aid. However, single mothers are more likely to receive financial help than single fathers because of differences in income. Forty-seven percent of families with annual incomes under $15,000 receive direct financial assistance for child care (figure 3.27).

Use of 1988 Child Care Income Tax Credit

Parents were also asked whether or not they claimed the federal Child and Dependent Care Credit for the 1988 tax year. Twenty-two percent of all families in the sample reported that they used the child care tax credit in 1988, whereas 5 percent did not know or could not remember whether or not they used the tax credit (not shown). Nearly 31 percent of all families with an employed mother (and 39 percent of those paying for care) claimed the 1988 child care income tax credit, with another 6 percent reporting that they did not know if they used the tax credit in 1988 (not shown).

The percentage of families with an employed mother reporting that they used the tax credit for 1988 is lower than the preliminary Internal Revenue Service figures for 1987 (see Robins 1990). This discrepancy is partly because of differences in the sampling base. The IRS reports that 43 percent of working mothers with children under age 18 claimed the Child and Dependent Care Credit in 1987. However, the National Child Care Survey sampled only those families with the youngest child under 13 years old. Moreover, the published figures from IRS also note a slight

Figure 3.27

Percentage Receiving Direct Financial Assistance
For the Care of the Youngest Child
By Family Income

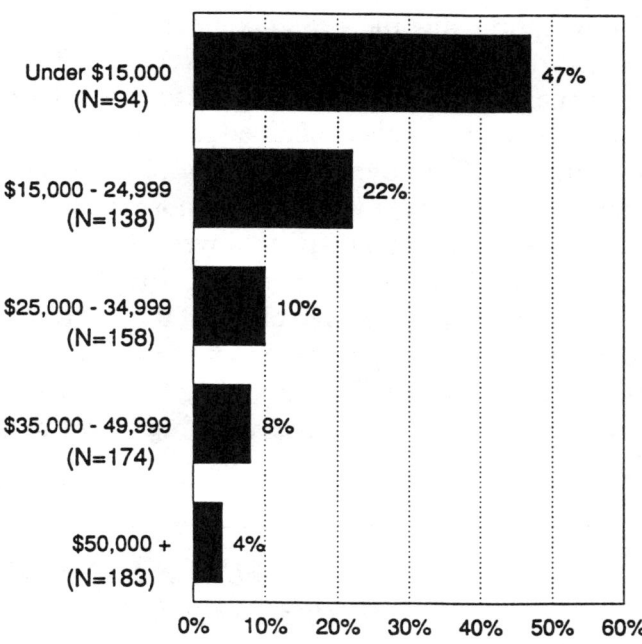

Source: National Child Care Survey 1990

decline in the percentage claiming the tax credit from 1986 (47.3 percent) to 1987 (43.1 percent). Tax reform and changes in restrictions of its use may have reduced the proportion claiming the tax credit. Therefore, the 1988 estimate from the NCCS may be a continuation of a more general trend.

Among families with an employed mother, a higher percentage of those with preschool-age children (35 percent) reported that they claimed the 1988 tax credit than families whose youngest child is school-aged (27 percent) (figure 3.28). Families with two children under age 13 were more likely to report using the 1988 tax credit (37 percent) than families with only one child (27 percent) or those with three or more children (25 percent). However, two-parent families and single mothers claimed the 1988 tax credit to a similar degree. Employed mothers with graduate school education (48 percent) were much more likely to report using the 1988 tax credit than employed mothers who have not finished high school (16 percent). Employed mothers were also more likely to have claimed the 1988 child care tax credit as their family income increases, with 33 percent of nonpoor working families claiming the tax credit compared with 17 percent of poor working families (figure 3.28).

TRENDS IN PARENTAL EXPENDITURES OVER TIME

Analyzing trends in child care expenditures according to the type of child care arrangement provides information on how the child care market operates over time. However,

Figure 3.28

Percentage of Employed Mothers
Using 1988 Child Care Income Tax Credit

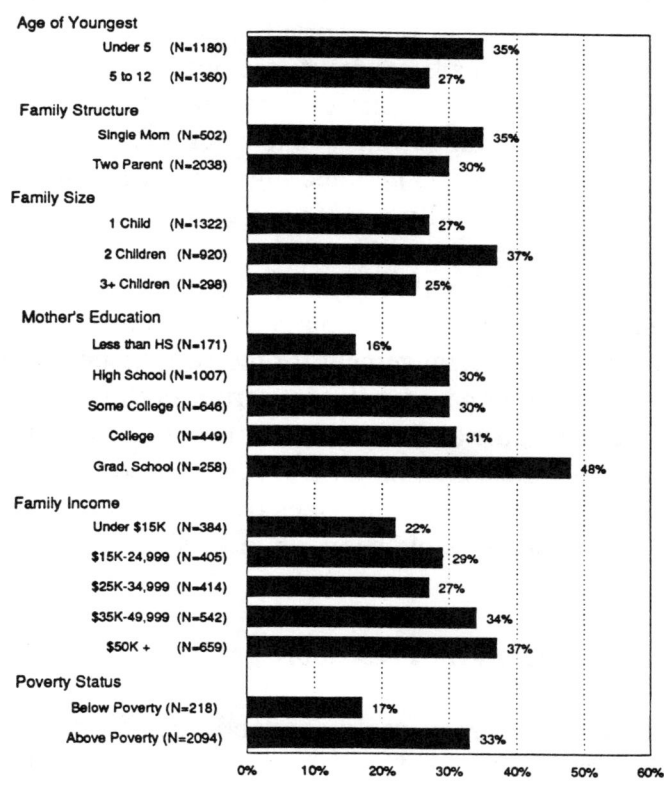

Source: National Child Care Survey 1990

previous data on the amount that parents pay for child care is not always suited to this task. For example, the U.S. Bureau of the Census' Survey of Income and Program Participation (SIPP) asked only about total child care expenses for all children and not specifically about the care for one particular child in the family. Therefore, use of SIPP data limits generalizations about expenditures per arrangement to families with only one child and one arrangement. Since these families are a small subset of all families in the United States, their child care payments are not representative of the expenditures of all American families. Large families spend less per hour for the youngest child's care than small families (figure 3.11). Selecting one-child families, therefore, may artificially inflate per child estimates of parental expenditures on care.

For the purposes of this report, data from the 1990 National Child Care Survey on hourly and weekly expenditures for the primary arrangement for the youngest child in the family were compared with data from both the 1985 National Longitudinal Survey of Youth and the 1975 National Child Care Consumer Survey. The older data were adjusted for changes in prices over time, to reflect what the same dollars would be worth in 1990.

Employed Mothers with Preschool-age Child

Between 1975 and 1985, weekly expenditures for center-based care for the youngest preschool-age child decreased slightly for employed mothers, whereas expenditures for family day-care increased by about 14 percent, expenditures on relative care increased by about 20 percent, and expenditures on in-home providers increased by 170 percent (figure 3.29). Between 1985 and 1990, weekly

Parental Expenditures for Child Care ■ 189

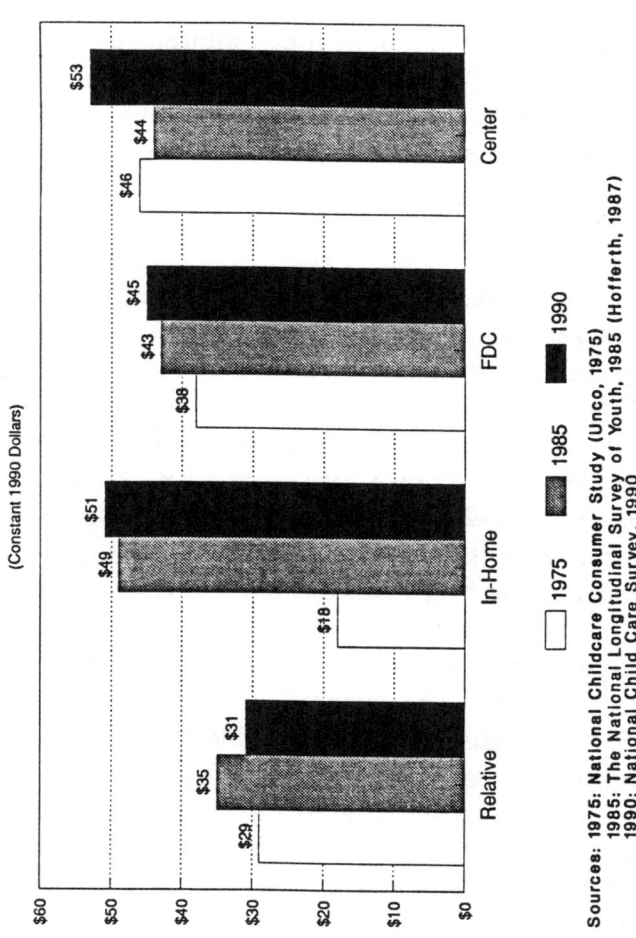

Figure 3.29
Mean Weekly Payment for Youngest Child Under 5,
Employed Mothers Paying for Child Care
1975-1990
(Constant 1990 Dollars)

Sources: 1975: National Childcare Consumer Study (Unco, 1975)
1985: The National Longitudinal Survey of Youth, 1985 (Hofferth, 1987)
1990: National Child Care Survey, 1990

expenditures on care in the child's home by a nonrelative or relative did not increase in real terms. However, child care expenses rose by 4 percent for employed mothers relying on family day-care providers and by 21 percent for those using center-based care.

Since the amount of time children spend in care varies systematically by arrangement, weekly expenditures on child care can be misleading. Figure 3.30 presents mean hourly payments for the youngest child under five years old among employed mothers paying for child care. The trend in hourly expenditures is somewhat different than the trend in weekly payments. There was an increase in per-hour expenditures for all types of child care arrangements between 1975 and 1985. Moreover, this increase was greatest for relatives and in-home providers (58 percent and 52 percent, respectively). There was a 5 percent per hour increase in hourly expenditures for family day-care and a 14 percent increase for center care. However, between 1985 and 1990, in-home provider care was the only type of arrangement that notably increased in per hour expenditures, rising by 24 percent. In contrast, hourly expenditures on center-based care rose only seven cents per hour, expenditures on relative care declined, and expenditures on family day-care remained stable.

What caused the apparent increase in weekly expenditures between 1985 and 1990? Figure 3.31 shows that between 1985 and 1990 the average number of paid hours per week that children spent in a day-care center increased from 35 to 38, an increase of 8 percent; this partly explains the rise in weekly expenditures over this period. The decline in the hourly cost of relative care is consistent with the increase in paid hours and the stability of weekly expenditures for this category. Although expenditures on family day-care rose slightly, they were not as high as

Parental Expenditures for Child Care

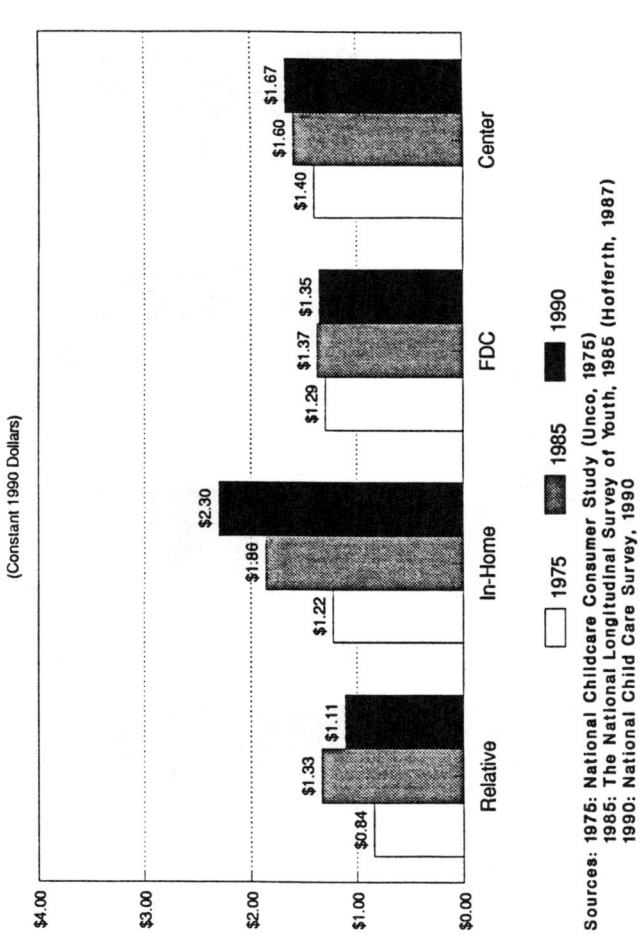

Figure 3.30
Mean Hourly Payment for Youngest Child Under 5,
Employed Mothers Paying for Child Care
1975-1990
(Constant 1990 Dollars)

Sources: 1975: National Childcare Consumer Study (Unco, 1975)
1985: The National Longitudinal Survey of Youth, 1985 (Hofferth, 1987)
1990: National Child Care Survey, 1990

192 ■ NATIONAL CHILD CARE SURVEY, 1990

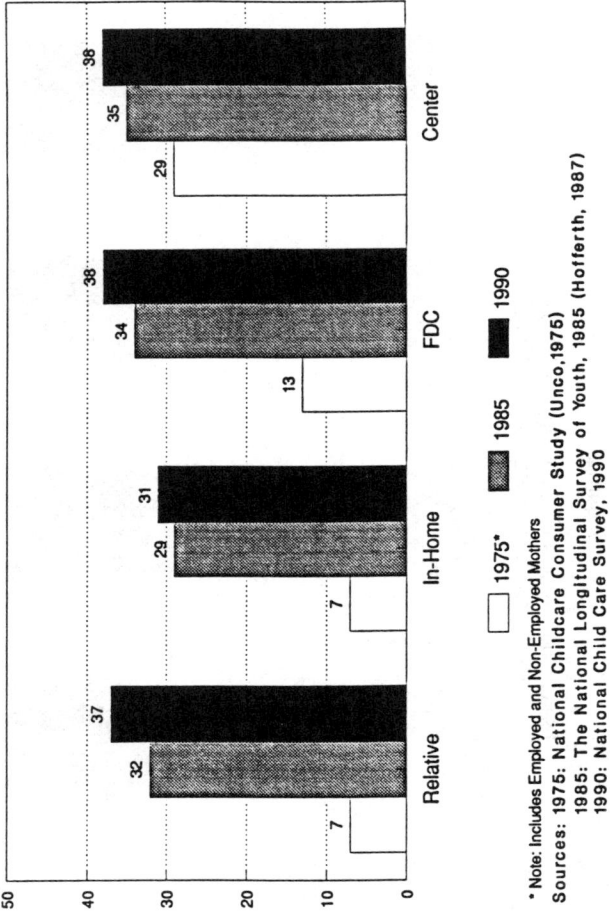

Figure 3.31
Mean Hours in Care for Youngest Child Under 5,
Employed Mothers Paying for Child Care
1975-1990

* Note: Includes Employed and Non-Employed Mothers
Sources: 1975: National Childcare Consumer Study (Unco,1976)
1985: The National Longitudinal Survey of Youth, 1985 (Hofferth, 1987)
1990: National Child Care Survey, 1990

expected based on the lack of change in hourly expenditures and the increase in hours in paid care. Although these trends do not fully account for changes in weekly expenditures, they indicate that parents' use of child care has changed. Not only are children spending more time in center-based care, but they are also spending more time in other types of paid nonparental care.

Employed Mothers with School-age Children Only

Weekly payments for school-age children declined slightly in real terms between 1975 and 1985 for those using relative care (figure 3.32). However, weekly expenditures remained constant for family day-care, and they declined substantially for center-based care. Between 1985 and 1990 there were apparent declines in weekly expenditures for care by a relative or a family day-care provider. Weekly expenditures on center-based care stayed constant in real terms. Weekly payments to in-home providers rose significantly between 1975 and 1990, to become the highest priced care on a weekly basis.

The story is somewhat different if hourly expenditures are examined (figure 3.33). Between 1975 and 1985, expenditures per hour increased dramatically for all forms of care for school-age children. Between 1985 and 1990, expenditures again rose for relatives and for family day-care providers. Hourly expenditures for center-based care did not rise between 1985 and 1990, suggesting that the increased supply of center-based care for school-age children between 1975 and 1985 was sufficient to meet the demand between 1985 and 1990.

Apparently, between 1985 and 1990 the average number of hours spent by school-age children in a child care center

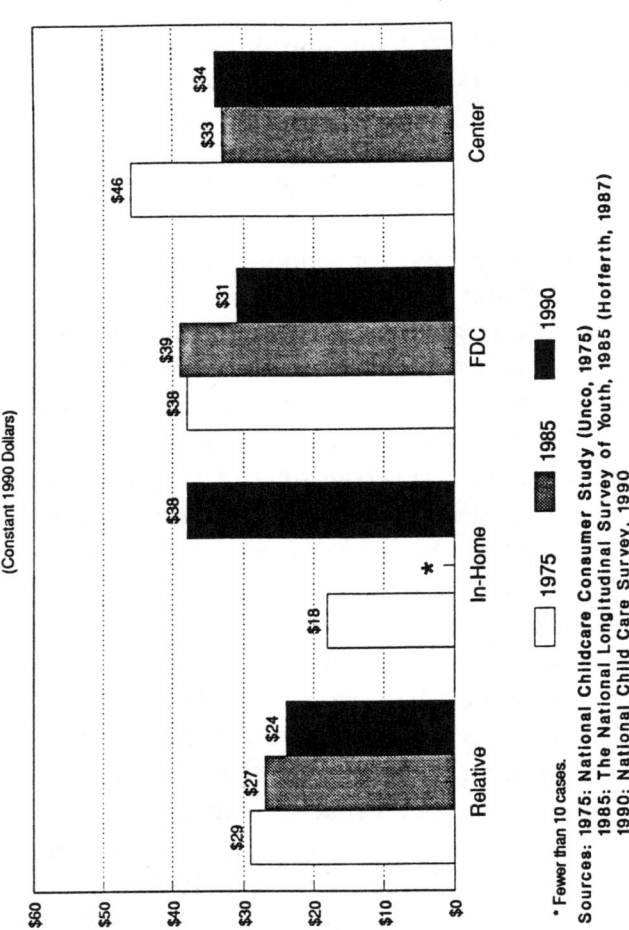

Figure 3.32
Mean Weekly Payment for Youngest Child 5 to 12,
Employed Mothers Paying for Child Care
1975-1990
(Constant 1990 Dollars)

* Fewer than 10 cases.
Sources: 1975: National Childcare Consumer Study (Unco, 1975)
1985: The National Longitudinal Survey of Youth, 1985 (Hofferth, 1987)
1990: National Child Care Survey, 1990

Parental Expenditures for Child Care ■ 195

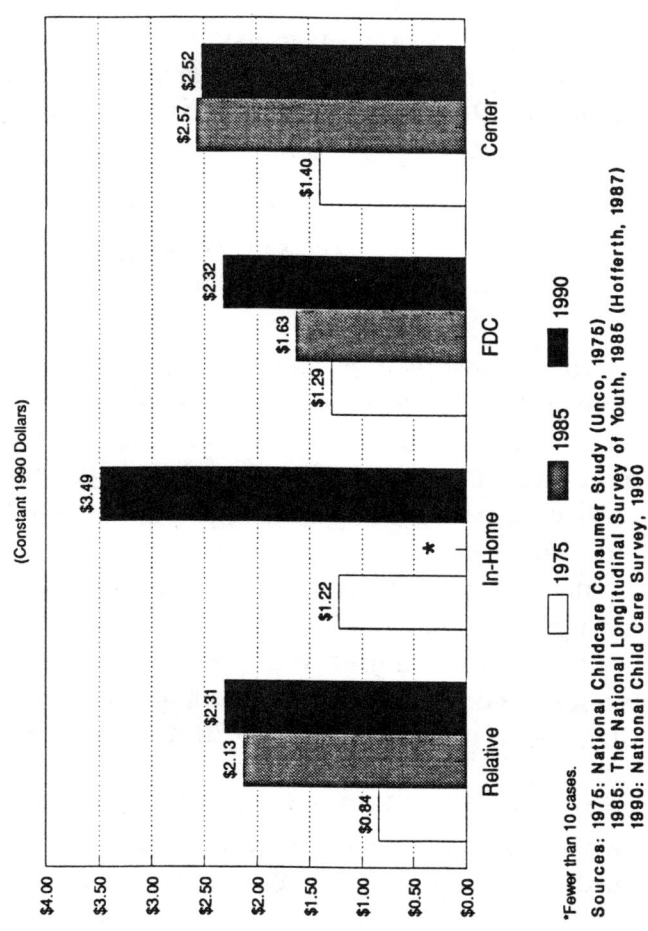

Figure 3.33
Mean Hourly Payment for Youngest Child 5 to 12,
Employed Mothers Paying for Child Care
1975-1990
(Constant 1990 Dollars)

*Fewer than 10 cases.
Sources: 1975: National Childcare Consumer Study (Unco, 1976)
1985: The National Longitudinal Survey of Youth, 1985 (Hofferth, 1987)
1990: National Child Care Survey, 1990

declined (figure 3.34). Unfortunately, the distribution of children by age is not the same in the 1985 National Longitudinal Survey of Youth (Hofferth 1988) as in the 1990 National Child Care Survey; therefore, we cannot presume that the mean hours are comparable. Certainly, however, this decrease in hours is consistent with the increase in hourly expenditures for center-based care that occurred between 1985 and 1990 and the stability of weekly expenditures.

SUMMARY AND CONCLUSIONS

Although most parents care for their children themselves, many parents spend a substantial amount of money on child care services. This study finds that employed mothers are more likely than nonemployed mothers to pay for child care services, especially if the youngest child is under five years old. Moreover, there is a strong relationship between the amount of time a preschool-age child spends in a primary arrangement and whether or not the family pays for care. Preschool-age children who spend 20 hours or more per week in a nonparental primary arrangement are more likely than those in care for under 20 hours to pay for these services.

Among those families that pay for child care, employed mothers generally pay less per hour than nonemployed mothers for the primary arrangement of their youngest child, regardless of the child's age. However, children of employed mothers typically spend more time in paid care than children of mothers who are not employed. Therefore, employed mothers pay more on a weekly basis. In-home providers, at an average cost of $2.30 per hour for

Parental Expenditures for Child Care ■ 197

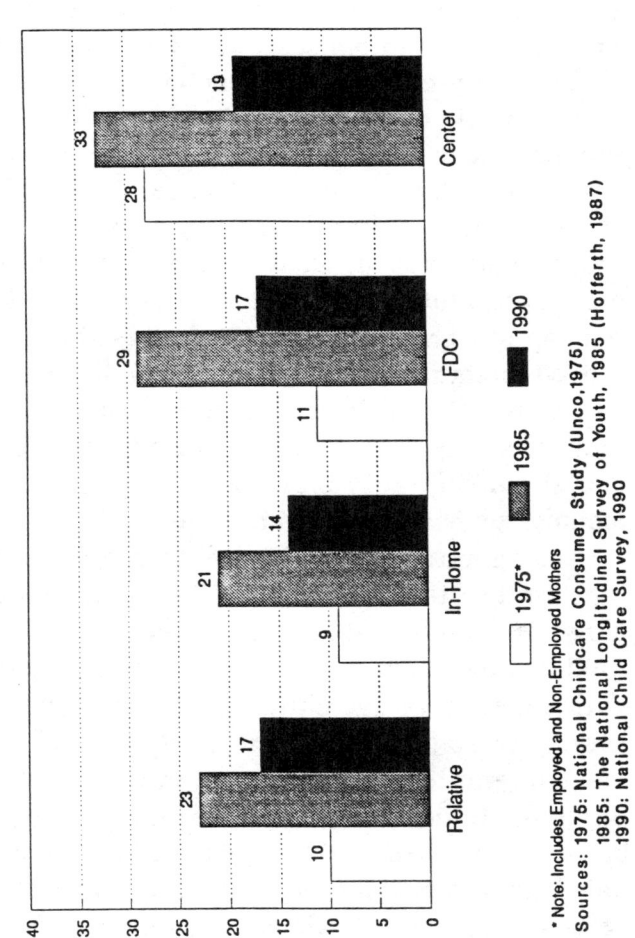

preschool-age children and $3.49 per hour for school-age children, are the most expensive arrangement used by employed mothers. Parents pay $1.67 per hour for center-based care and $1.35 per hour for family day care for preschool children. As expected, relatives provide the least expensive form of paid care for employed mothers with a preschool-age child, at $1.11 per hour on average.

When all children in the family are considered, employed mothers pay more per week than mothers who are not employed, regardless of the age of the youngest child. For example, among those with a preschool child, employed mothers spend an average of $63 per week and nonemployed mothers spend an average of $35 per week. Among those whose youngest child is of school age, employed mothers spend $30 and nonemployed mothers $20 per week. Regardless of maternal employment status, families whose annual incomes are above the poverty level spend considerably more per week than those whose incomes are below the poverty level.

Among those that pay for child care, families pay about 7 percent of their weekly family income on child care. However, families differ according to the proportion of total income spent on child care services. Among those with a preschool-age child, employed mothers spend an average of 10 percent of their family income on child care and nonemployed mothers spend a corresponding 6 percent. In contrast, the difference in budget shares between employed mothers and nonemployed mothers with only school-age children is minuscule, at 5 percent and 4 percent, respectively. Generally, single mothers and poor families spend a substantially larger share of their budget on child care, regardless of the youngest child's age or maternal employment status. For example, poor employed mothers with a preschool-age child spend 23 percent of their family income on care child. Yet, their high-income counterparts spend only 6 percent of their budget on child care expenses. Single fathers with a preschool-age child spend approximately the same share of income on child care as single mothers. However, single fathers with the youngest child aged 5 to 12 spend a smaller share of their budget than employed single mothers, but a larger share than single mothers who are not employed.

Only 5 percent of those who do pay for child care receive any direct financial assistance with these expenses. However, 31 percent of families with an employed mother reported using the federal Child and Dependent Care Credit in 1988. Notably, families with incomes above the poverty level are more likely to have claimed the tax credit than those with incomes below poverty.

Hourly expenditures on family day-care and center-based care for preschool-age children remained constant between 1985 and 1990, after having increased only sightly over the previous decade. In contrast, expenditures on care in a child's home by a nonrelative rose tremendously both in the last five years and in the previous decade. Expenditures on all types of care for school-age children had their greatest increase between 1975 and 1985 and continued to rise through 1990 for all but center-based care, which stabilized between 1985 and 1990. Parents pay considerably more per hour for school-age children than for preschool-age children, but they actually pay less per week because they purchase fewer hours of care.

Several questions about parental expenditures require further research. For instance, is there some rule of thumb that families use to decide jointly on the number of hours of care and their weekly expenditures? Also, if prices rise, do families simply substitute nonpaid forms of care for market care so as to maintain expenditures no higher than a certain level, or do they adjust their labor market behavior accordingly?

Notes, chapter 3

1. Percentages cited from this chapter's tables are typically rounded off to the nearest whole number.

2. In this chapter ordinary least squares regression equations were used to estimate the effects of the characteristics of the youngest child, of the mother, and of the family on parental child care expenditures. This procedure allows us to evaluate the net effect of one variable while simultaneously controlling for the effects of other factors.

Chapter

4

CHILD CARE CHOICE

The previous chapters have described the types of child care arrangements that families use and how much they spend. From a policy perspective it is important to know if these arrangements reflect preferences or the underlying constraints of availability and affordability. Accordingly, this chapter explores two issues: how parents search for and select a care arrangement for their youngest child and how satisfied parents are with their current arrangements. This chapter is divided into four sections. The first section describes the overall child care search and selection process; the second section focuses more specifically on factors involved in choosing a particular arrangement; the third section reviews parents' satisfaction with their current care arrangements; and the fourth section explores parents' preferences for an alternative type of care and their reasons for desiring a change.

SEARCH FOR AND SELECTION OF CHILD CARE ARRANGEMENTS FOR YOUNGEST CHILD

To date, little research has been conducted on the process of searching for and selecting child care arrangements. To better understand this process, the National Child Care Survey, 1990 (NCCS) asked parents a series of questions about (1) the various types of arrangements they considered, (2) the number of providers of the *same* type who were considered, (3) the number of other types of providers who were considered, (4) parents' perceptions of their current arrangements, and (5) the amount of time that elapsed between locating the provider and starting the child in care.

These questions were asked of all families in the survey--including those using formal arrangements such as centers, family day-care providers, relatives, and self- and sibling care, as well as those who indicated having no regular care arrangement for their youngest child. School-age children for whom school was reported to be the primary arrangement were excluded; therefore, the school-age sample is small.

Other Types of Child Care Arrangements

Overall, 37 percent of families sought alternative child care arrangements (table 4.1).

Maternal Employment Status. The proportion of parents who considered other types of child care arrangements varies with the employment status of the mother. Families where the mother is employed were far more likely to consider a variety of care types. Forty-three percent of these families versus 26 percent of families where the mother is not employed considered alternative modes of care (table 4.1).

Type of Current Care. The current type of care used by parents influences whether *other* types are considered. Among families with employed mothers using formal types of arrangements--in-home providers, centers, or family daycare providers--almost 50 percent indicated considering other types of care. In comparison, about 30 percent of employed mother families using care by relatives, partners, self/sibling, or caring for children themselves considered alternate types (figure 4.1).

Families in which the mother is not employed are generally less likely to consider other types of providers, regardless of the type they currently use. For example, about 50 percent of families with employed mothers considered other types of arrangements compared with only 20 percent to 30 percent of those with nonemployed mothers (table 4.1).

Family Income. Overall, the proportion of families considering alternative types of care did not vary with income. However, for families with incomes of $25,000 or more per year and an employed mother, alternative types of care were considered more frequently than in comparable families where the mother is not employed (figure 4.2). For families with incomes below $25,000, the differences by employment status were not large enough to be statistically significant.

Race. The proportion of families who seriously considered other types of providers did not vary by race.

Table 4.1 TYPES OF CARE SERIOUSLY CONSIDERED, BY MATERNAL EMPLOYMENT STATUS

Seriously Consider Alternative Types?	In-Home Provider (%)	Other Relative (%)	Partner (%)	Family Day Care (%)	Center (%)	Self/ Sibling (%)	Respondent (%)	All (%)
All								
Yes	49	29	23	49	47	32	27	37
No	51	71	77	51	53	68	73	63
Total	100	100	100	100	100	100	100	100
Sample size	322	654	223	324	414	111	376	2,423
Mom Employed Last Week								
Yes	52	30	28	52	54	34	27	43
No	48	70	72	48	46	66	73	57
Total	100	100	100	100	100	100	100	100
Sample size	265	606	117	278	331	89	59	1,535
Mom Not Employed Last Week								
Yes	37	23	17	30	17	24	27	26
No	63	77	83	70	81	76	73	74
Total	100	100	100	100	100	100	100	100
Sample size	57	312	106	46	83	22	50	512

Source: National Child Care Survey, 1990

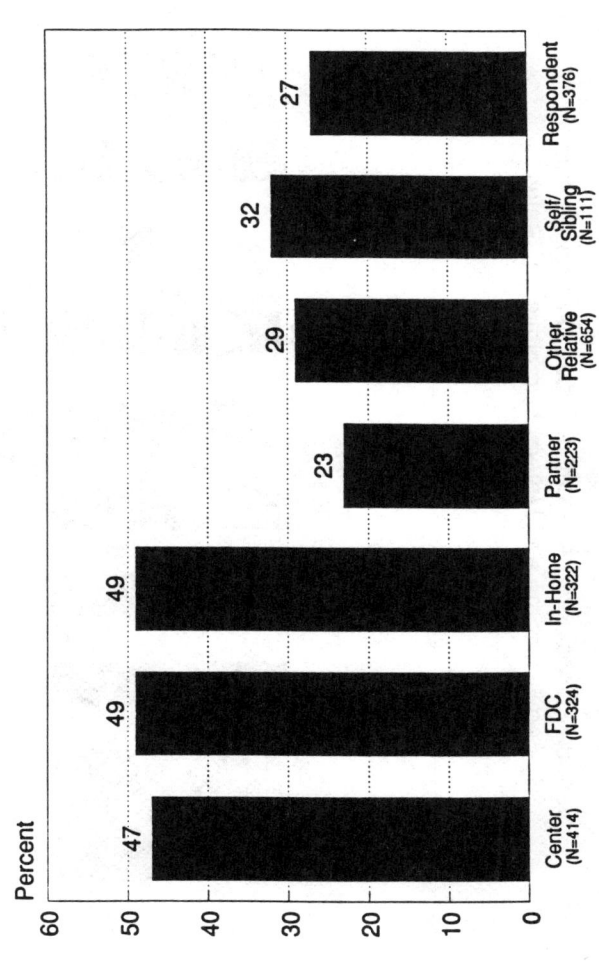

Figure 4.1
Seriously Considered Alternative Types of Arrangements By Current Type of Care, Employed Mothers

Source: National Child Care Survey 1990

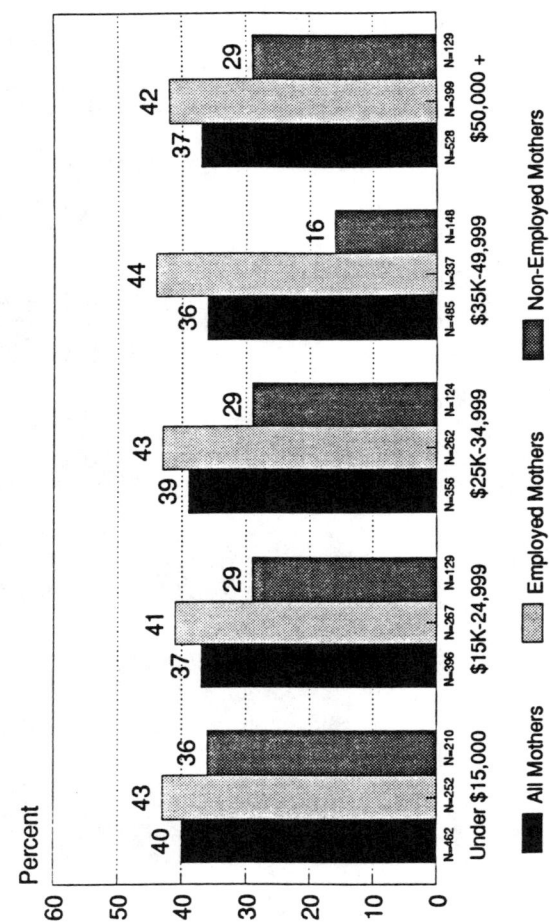

Figure 4.2
Seriously Considered Alternative Types of Arrangements
By Family Income and Maternal Employment Status

Source: National Child Care Survey 1990

Age of Youngest Child. Parents whose youngest child is between 10 and 12 years of age considered alternative types of providers less often than parents of younger children. Twenty-four percent of families with the youngest child 10-12 years of age considered alternative types of providers, as compared to a range of 34-44 percent for families with younger children (figure 4.3).

In addition, in families where the youngest child is under 10 years of age, alternative types of providers were considered more often if the mother is employed than if not employed (figure 4.3).

Types of Care Considered. Parents who evaluated other types of arrangements were asked what these were. Center-based care was the type most often considered (49 percent, figure 4.4), followed by a family day-care or in-home provider (26 percent), parental care (11 percent), care by another relative (10 percent), and "other" (3 percent). These findings did not vary with the employment status of the mother, age of the child, or type of care currently used.

Other Providers of Same Type of Care

Families using centers, in-home providers, or family day-care providers were asked if they had seriously considered other providers of the same type to care for their youngest child. Sixty percent of families interviewed only the provider they chose while 40 percent investigated other providers (figure 4.5).

Maternal Employment Status. Whether or not alternatives were considered varied with the employment status of the mother. In families where the mother was employed, 42 percent considered such alternatives; in families where

208 ■ NATIONAL CHILD CARE SURVEY, 1990

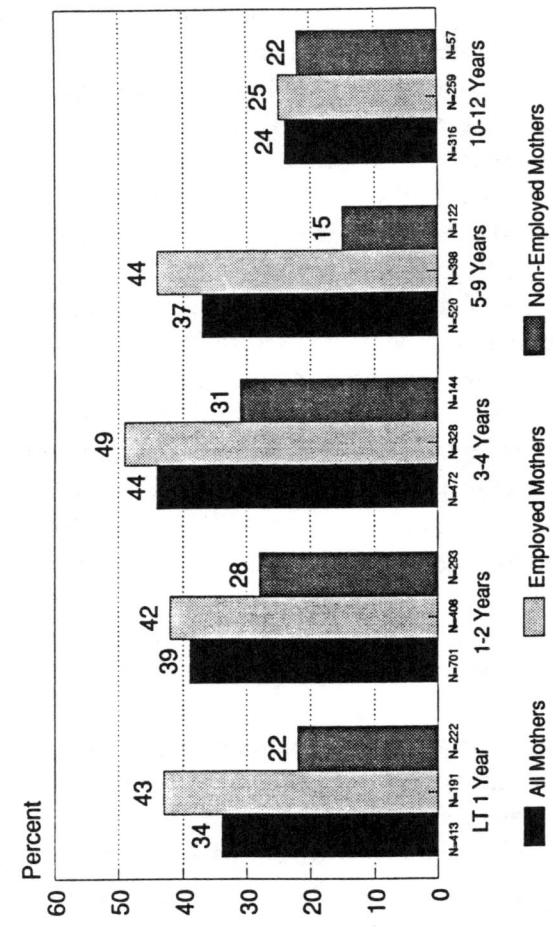

Figure 4.3
Seriously Considered Alternative Types of Arrangements
By Age of Youngest and Maternal Employment Status

Source: National Child Care Survey 1990

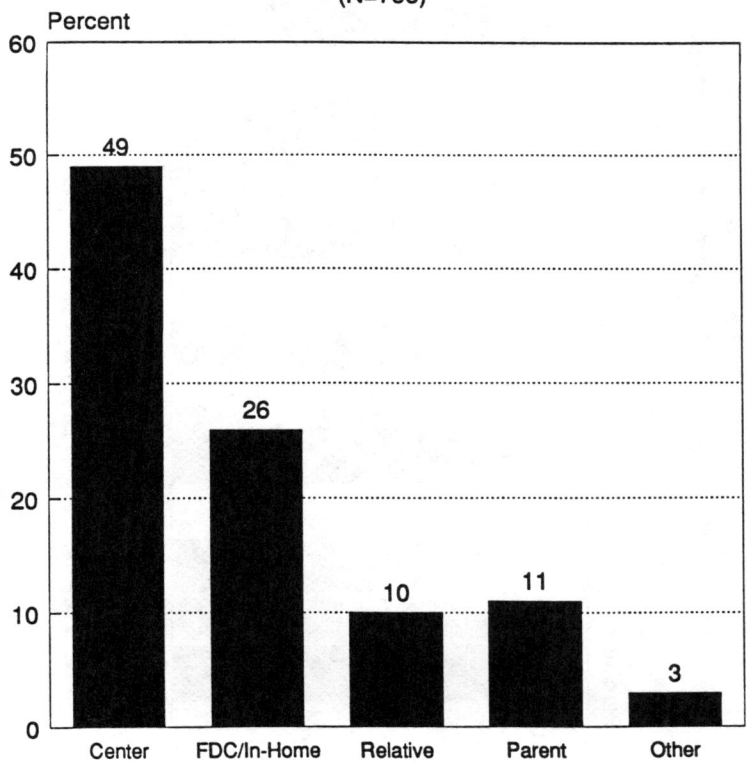

Figure 4.4

Alternative Types of Providers Considered (N=793)

Source: National Child Care Survey 1990

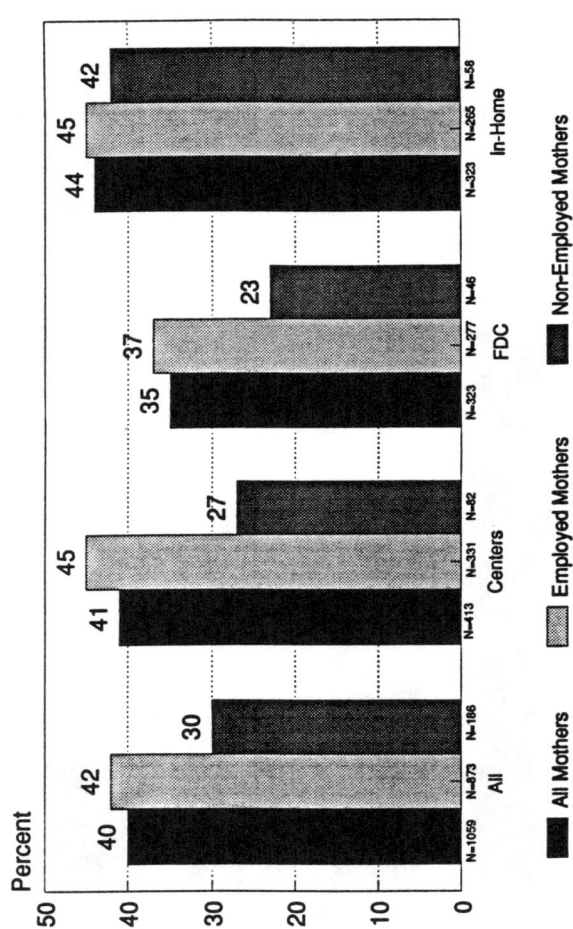

Figure 4.5
Seriously Considered Other Providers
By Current Type of Care and Employment Status of the Mother

the mother was not employed, only 30 percent seriously considered alternative providers (figure 4.5).

Type of Current Care. Whether parents considered multiple providers of the same type varied by the type of care currently used. As figure 4.5 shows, 44 percent of families using in-home providers seriously considered other providers of the same type; 41 percent of families using centers considered other centers; and 35 percent of those using family providers considered alternative providers. Although these differences appear large, they are not statistically significant.

Differences by the employment status of the mother were not statistically significant except in the case of centers, where 45 percent of families with an employed mother but only 27 percent of families with a nonemployed mother considered other providers of the same type (figure 4.5).

Age of Youngest Child. There were no significant differences in the proportion of families who considered multiple providers of the same type by the age of the youngest child.

Number of Other Providers Considered

For parents who considered other providers of the same type, information was collected on how many other providers were considered. Approximately 70 percent of these parents indicated seriously considering between one and three other providers (figure 4.6). Only 12 percent of the respondents indicated seriously considering six or more providers. Sample sizes were too small for further subgroup analysis.

**Figure 4.6
Number of Other Providers Considered
(N=436)**

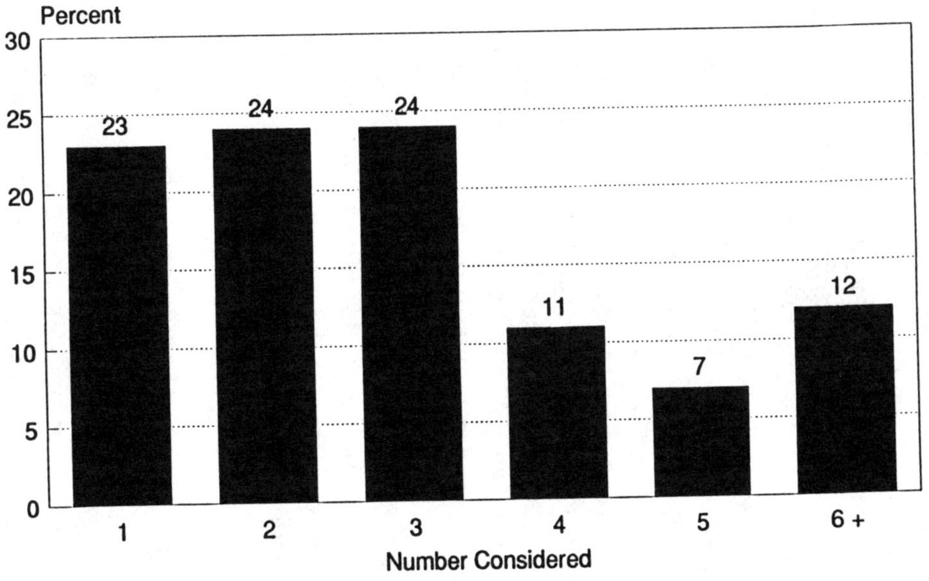

Number Considered	Percent
1	23
2	24
3	24
4	11
5	7
6+	12

Source: National Child Care Survey 1990

Considered Both Alternative Arrangements and Alternative Providers of Same Type

Approximately 26 percent of families using centers, in-home providers, or family day-care providers considered both other types of arrangements *and* other providers of the same type (not shown). The sample size for this group was insufficient for further subgroup analysis.

CHOICE OF CARE ARRANGEMENTS FOR YOUNGEST CHILD

Locating Care

Families using center-based care, in-home providers or family day-care providers were asked how they first learned about the care arrangement they are currently using. The majority (66 percent) responded that they learned of their provider from friends, neighbors, or relatives (figure 4.7). The next most common response was from newspapers, advertisements, or bulletin boards (13 percent). Only 9 percent of respondents indicated that they found their current provider through a resource and referral service. The low percentage that located a provider through such a service may reflect lack of availability of the service rather than the usefulness of such services when available. These findings are similar regardless of the employment status of the mother, age of the child, or family income.

Type of Care. Although the majority of all families using centers, in-home providers or family day-care providers indicated locating care through friends, neighbors, or

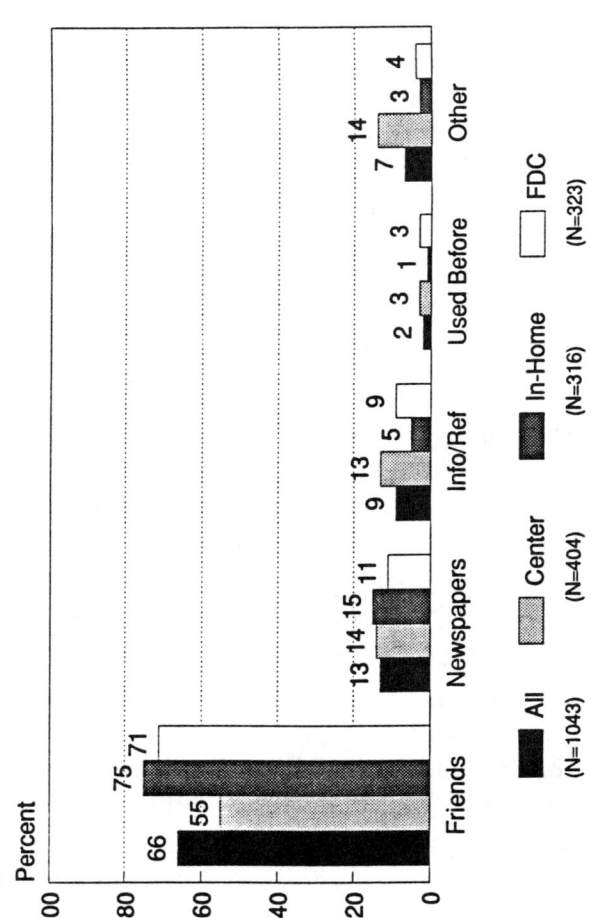

Figure 4.7
How First Learned of Current Child Care Arrangement For Youngest Child

relatives, the proportion was higher for those using in-home providers or family providers (75 percent) compared to those using centers (55 percent) (figure 4.7). The sample sizes for the other categories were too small to test for significant differences.

Decision Factors

The 40 percent of families who indicated considering alternative types of care or alternative providers of the same type were asked two questions regarding what factors were most important in choosing their current arrangement: "Why did you choose the [current arrangement] for your youngest child?" and "What was the most important thing you considered?" Interviewers were instructed to code responses into one of the following categories: cost, convenient hours, convenient location, quality, availability, prefers care by relative, and other. All parents were also asked to specify the second most important reason for choosing the arrangement.

MOST IMPORTANT REASON

Thirty-seven percent of all parents indicated some aspect of quality of care as being most important in their choice of arrangements (figure 4.8, table 4.2). Another 30 percent of parents indicated that they prefer care by a relative. (The extent to which this reflects a desire for quality, convenience, or some other factor is unclear.) After quality and relatives, parents cited convenient location (10 percent) and reasonable cost (9 percent) as the most important factors.

216 ■ NATIONAL CHILD CARE SURVEY, 1990

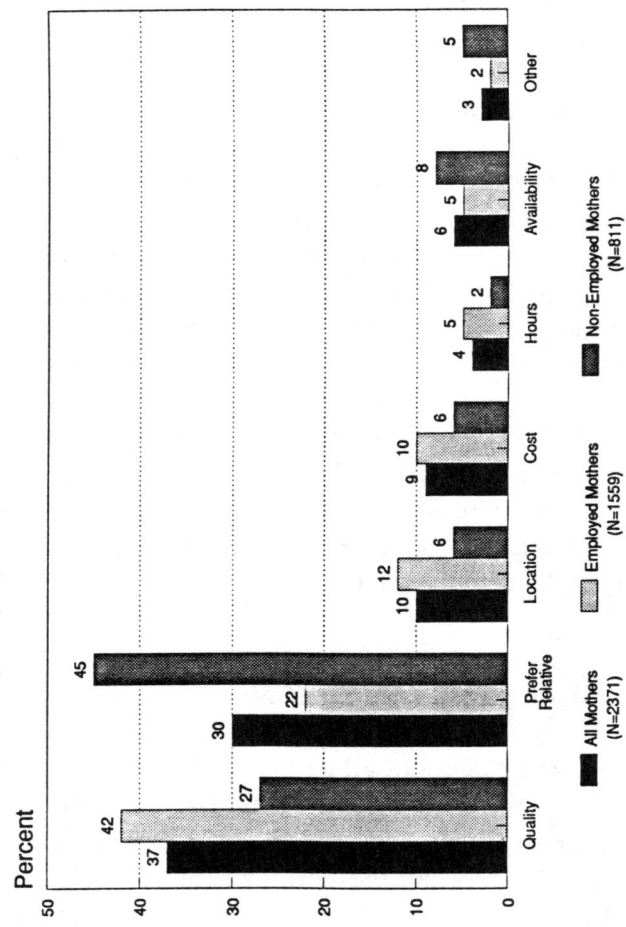

Figure 4.8
Most Important Factor in Choice of Current Arrangement
By Employment Status of Mother

Source: National Child Care Survey 1990

Table 4.2 MOST IMPORTANT REASON FOR CHOICE OF CURRENT CARE ARRANGEMENT, BY TYPE OF CARE

Most Important Reason for Choice of Arrangement	In-home Provider (%)	Other Relative (%)	Partner (%)	Family Day Care (%)	Center (%)	Self/Sibling (%)	Respondent (%)	All (%)
Cost	6	10	15	8	6	13	11	9
Hours	4	4	4	—	6	10	1	4
Location	17	8	4	13	17	12	0	10
Quality	59	20	19	61	59	13	20	37
Availability	7	6	5	6	6	7	6	6
Prefers relative	5	50	51	7	—	32	55	30
Total	100	100	100	100	100	100	100	100
Sample size	318	647	219	324	401	101	362	2,371

Source: National Child Care Survey, 1990

Maternal Employment Status. Regardless of maternal employment status, quality was the most important characteristic of care in choosing an arrangement. However, families where the mother is employed cited quality more frequently than families with a nonemployed mother (42 percent versus 27 percent) (figure 4.8). In families where the the mother is not employed, the most important factor in choosing a care arrangement is preference for a relative (45 percent versus 22 percent).

Type of Care. The reason for selecting the current arrangement varies with the type of arrangement used. As shown in table 4.2, approximately 60 percent of those families using in-home providers, family day-care, or center-based care indicated that quality is the most important factor in the decision. For those using care by a relative or caring for the children themselves, only 20 percent indicated quality as the most important reason for choosing the arrangement. This did not vary with the employment status of the mother.

Age of Youngest Child. Parents with a youngest child between the ages of 10 and 12 years indicated quality as a reason for choice of care arrangement far less often than did parents of younger children (20 percent versus 39 percent, respectively) (not shown).

Family Income. The most important factor in choosing the child care arrangement varied with the income of the family. For families with incomes below $15,000 per year, a lower percentage indicated quality (26 percent) than did families with incomes above $50,000 per year (47 percent) (figure 4.9). Families with incomes in the middle ranges indicated quality more often than families with lower incomes; however, only the differences between the highest and lowest income groups were significant.

Child Care Choice

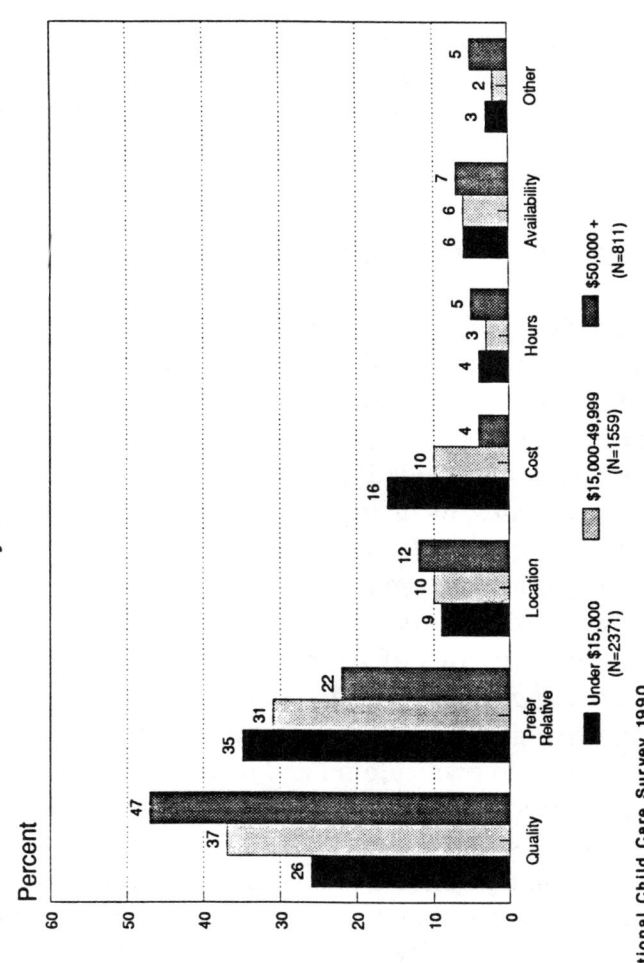

Figure 4.9
Most Important Factor in Choice of Current Arrangement By Income

Source: National Child Care Survey 1990

In addition, families with incomes below $15,000 indicated cost as the most important reason for choosing an arrangement far more often than families in the highest income group--16 percent versus 4 percent, respectively (figure 4.9). The middle income group also indicated cost less often than the lowest income families, but these differences were not statistically significant.

Race. There were no significant differences by race in the main reason for choosing a child care arrangement.

ASPECTS OF QUALITY

Since quality can mean different things to different people, parents who indicated that quality (as defined by a precoded list of possible responses) was the major factor were asked what aspect of quality was most important. Parental responses were coded into four categories: *child-related characteristics,* including child/staff ratios, group sizes, and age ranges; *provider-related characteristics,* including a warm and loving teaching/parenting style, reliability, training and credentials, experience or provider is a parent, recommendations of friends and/or relatives; *program-related characteristics,* including preparation for school, cognitive and social development, religious instruction, instruction in own culture; and *facility-related characteristics,* including toys, equipment, homelike setting, and health and safety issues.

Figure 4.10 shows that over 70 percent of all parents cited provider-related characteristic as the most important dimension of quality. Of these, a warm and loving manner was most frequently mentioned (35 percent) (figure 4.11). After provider-related characteristics, child-related characteristics of care and facilities were most important

Child Care Choice ■ 221

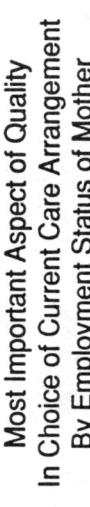

Figure 4.10

Most Important Aspect of Quality
In Choice of Current Care Arrangement
By Employment Status of Mother

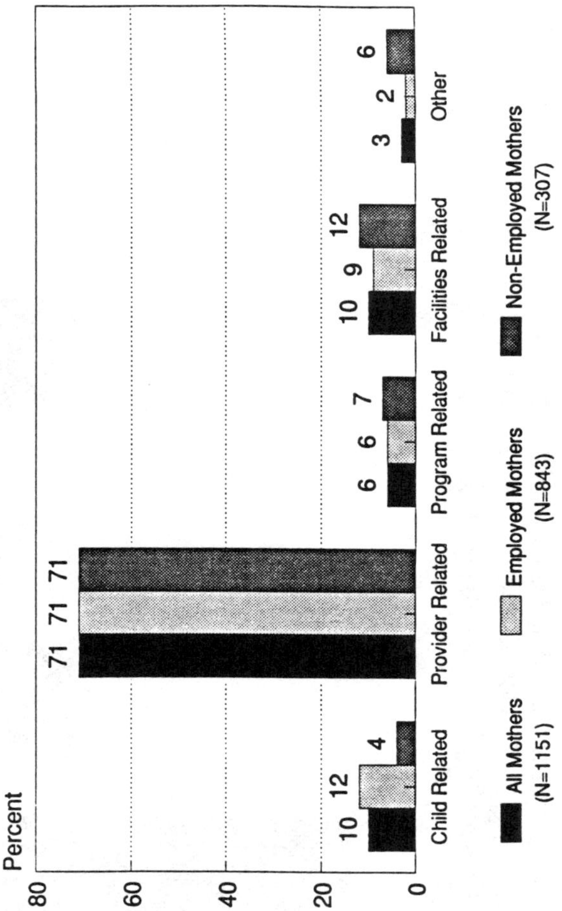

Source: National Child Care Survey 1990

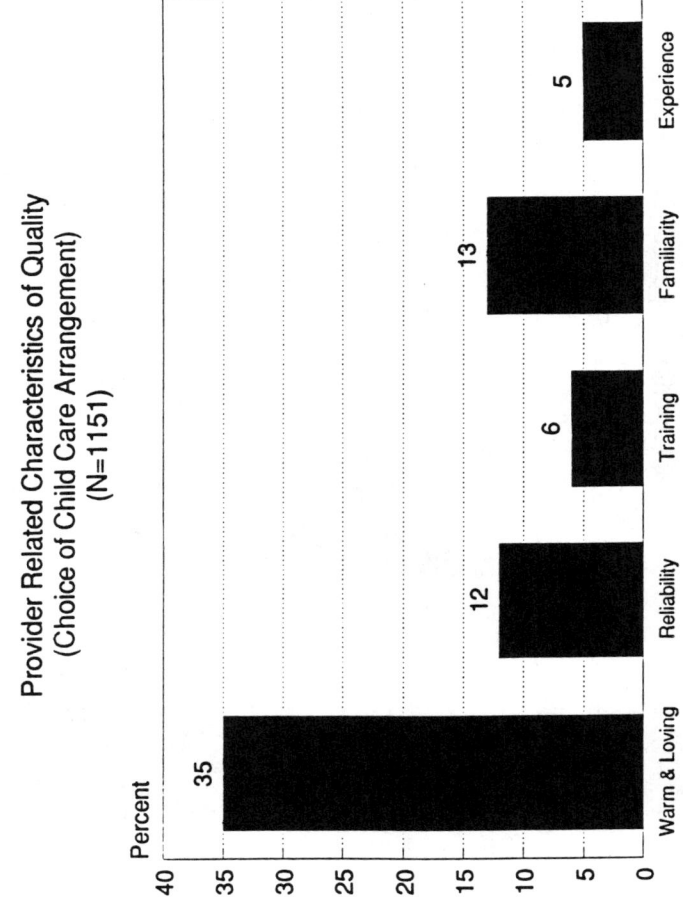

Figure 4.11
Provider Related Characteristics of Quality
(Choice of Child Care Arrangement)
(N=1151)

Source: National Child Care Survey 1990

Child Care Choice 223

(10 percent each) (figure 4.10). Employed mothers were more likely to cite child-related factors, particularly child/staff ratio, and less likely to cite facilities than nonemployed mothers.

Just over half of those indicating quality as the reason for choosing care indicated a *second aspect of quality*. Again, provider-related characteristics were most important to parents (57 percent) (figure 4.12). In fact, 60 percent of parents who indicated provider-related characteristics as the first response and who named a second aspect also listed these as the second response. As was the case for the first response, a warm and loving manner was the most frequent response (not shown). After provider-related characteristics, facilities were next in importance. Employed mothers were more likely to cite child-related characteristics and less likely to cite provider-related characteristics than nonemployed mothers.

SECOND MOST IMPORTANT REASON

Parents were also asked to indicate their *second most important reason* for choosing their current care arrangement. Half of the parents indicated that there was no other reason. For the other 50 percent, quality was again the most important factor (29 percent) (figure 4.13). Although quality was still the modal choice for the second reason, other reasons become more important. After quality, parents indicated that location was the next most important reason (19 percent) (figure 4.13). This differs from the response to the question asking for the *most* important reason which indicates that preference for a relative was second in importance after quality.

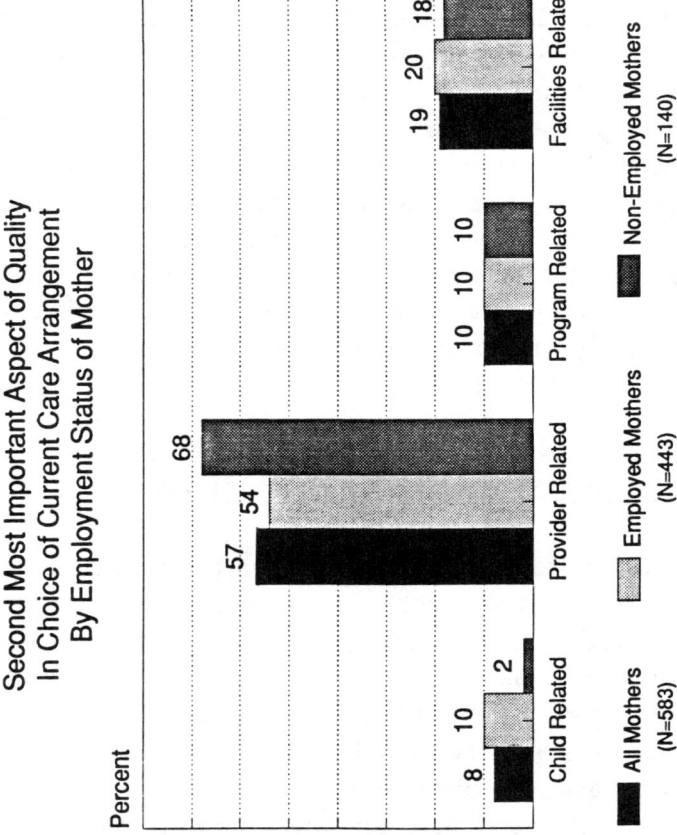

Figure 4.12
Second Most Important Aspect of Quality
In Choice of Current Care Arrangement
By Employment Status of Mother

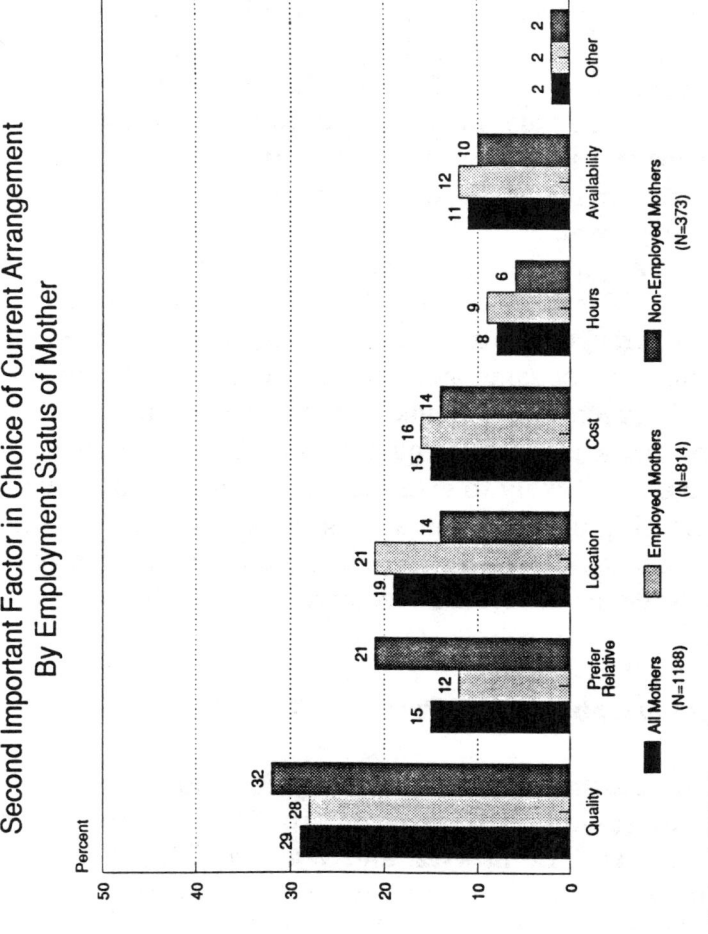

Figure 4.13
Second Important Factor in Choice of Current Arrangement By Employment Status of Mother

Source: National Child Care Survey 1990

Maternal Employment Status. The proportion of families indicating quality as the second most important factor did not vary greatly with the employment status of the mother, unlike the findings for the primary reason. However, families where the mother is not employed still said they prefer a relative more often than those where the mother is employed--21 percent compared to only 12 percent (figure 4.13). In addition, families with an employed mother mentioned location almost twice as often as the secondary reason, compared to those citing location as the primary reason, for choosing a particular care arrangement.

Age of Youngest Child, Type of Care, Family Income, Race. The second most important reason for choosing a care arrangement did not vary with the age of the youngest child, type of care, family income, or race of the family.

First Reason. Parents who indicated more than one reason and who indicated quality as the most important reason were most likely to give location as the second reason for selecting their current arrangement. Those who did not indicate quality as the most important reason were likely to indicate quality for the second reason (see figure 4.14).

Comparability with Previous Work

The reasons cited in this study for choosing child care arrangements differ from findings in other studies (Johansen, Leibowitz, and Waite 1990; UNCO 1975). However, the various survey questions were different. The 1986 wave of the National Longitudinal Study of the Class of 1972 asked respondents, "What things influenced you most in choosing child care arrangements for your child?" Respondents were asked to check all the items that applied

Child Care Choice ■ 227

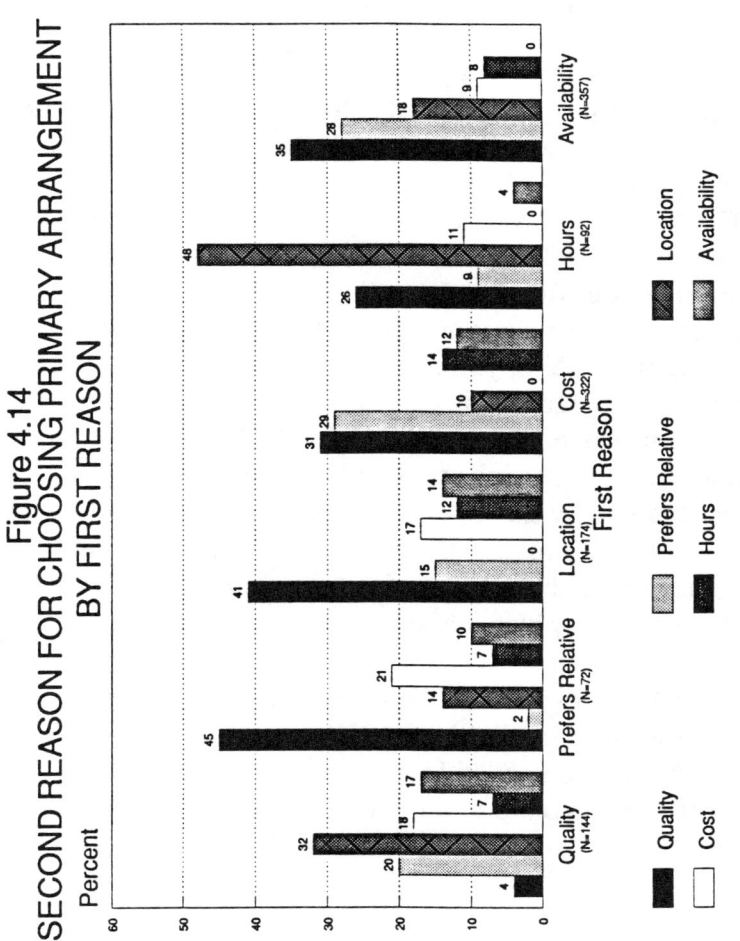

Figure 4.14
SECOND REASON FOR CHOOSING PRIMARY ARRANGEMENT BY FIRST REASON

Source: National Child Care Survey 1990

from a predesignated list that included: cost, hours day-care is available, distance from home, type of program offered, type of educational materials used, training of staff, distance from workplace, child knows caregiver, and recreational equipment. Although "quality" was not cited in the list, some of its components (but only a limited set) were included (type of program, type of educational materials, and staff training). Based on this list, respondents indicated that their choices were driven primarily by convenience and cost (Johansen et al. 1990).

The National Child Care Survey, 1990 (NCCS), replicating the 1975 UNCO approach, asked parents the following open-ended questions: "Why did you choose the [current arrangement] for your youngest child?" and "What was the most important thing you considered?" Interviewers coded two answers into predesignated categories, of which "quality" was one.[1] In addition, the NCCS question occurs after a series of questions concerning alternate providers. It is possible that by the time parents have to choose between several selected providers, factors such as cost and convenience have already been taken into account. On the other hand, parents may also initially screen out poor-quality care as well.

These findings indicate the importance of the wording of survey questions in eliciting the factors influencing choice. More research is needed in general to identify the importance of various factors in the child care decision-making process.

Length of Search for Current Arrangement

Finally, NCCS respondents were asked, "How long was it between the time you started trying to arrange child care and the time you had a commitment for this arrangement?" The median time to commitment for all families was approximately five weeks (figure 4.15).

Maternal Employment Status. For families where the mother is employed, the median time to commitment was seven weeks compared to four weeks for families where the mother is not employed (not shown).

Type of Care. There was no variation in median time to commitment by type of care.

Age of Youngest Child. The median time to commitment varied with the age of the child, ranging from four weeks for children 1-2 years old to almost nine weeks for those between 9 and 12 years (figure 4.15).

Family Income. The median time to commitment did not vary significantly with the income of the family.

Race. The median time to commitment did not vary by race.

SATISFACTION WITH CARE ARRANGEMENTS FOR YOUNGEST CHILD

The next two sections of this chapter explore parental satisfaction with current care and preferences for alternative care arrangements. Understanding these issues will allow researchers and policymakers to design and implement child care policies and programs that are responsive to the needs of families. Although this information is crucial, measurement of parental preferences for child care arrangements is quite difficult. The literature provides two approaches (Sonenstein 1991). The first assumes that the market for child care operates like any other economic

230 ■ NATIONAL CHILD CARE SURVEY, 1990

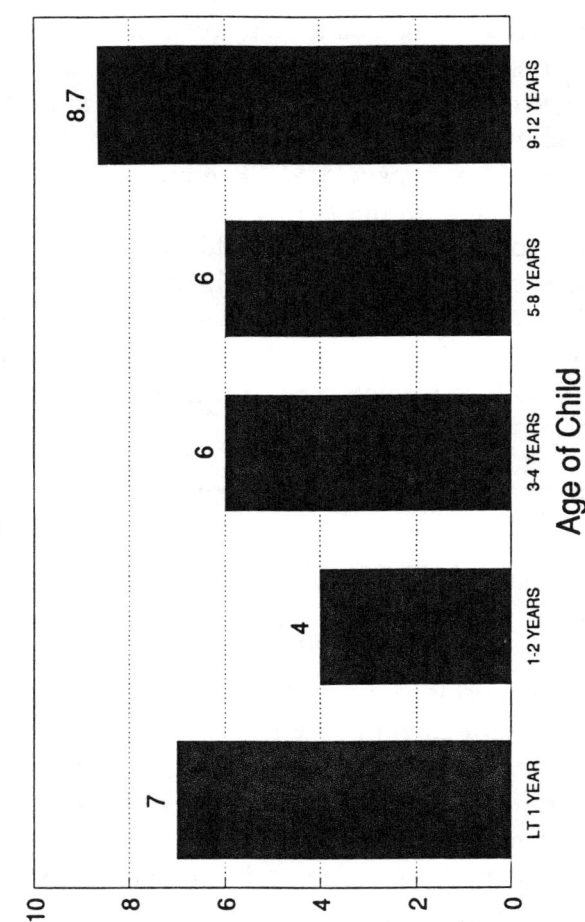

Figure 4.15
Weeks to Commitment by Age
(Youngest Child)

Source: National Child Care Survey 1990

market in which consumers choose an arrangement that maximizes their preferences subject to a budgetary constraint. In this case, if the market is operating efficiently, the arrangement chosen can be assumed to reflect parental preferences.

The second method assumes that the child care market is not operating efficiently and that the supply of care is somehow constrained. Under this scenario, parental preferences must be measured by asking parents hypothetical questions regarding the type of child care arrangement they would choose in the absence of constraints. Although this second approach provides a way to gauge preferences in the absence of an efficient market, there is no assurance that parents' behavior would match their stated preferences should the opportunity become available.

The NCCS utilized both approaches in gathering data on parental preferences for child care arrangements. This section of the chapter discusses parents' overall satisfaction. This method is not without problems (mentioned later here), but it does provide information comparable to previous work and allows for comparisons over time. The section following this one describes use of the second approach.

NCCS parents who used any regular care arrangement for their youngest child or had preschool-age children who they cared for themselves were asked questions about how satisfied they were with their care arrangements. Parents were asked "How satisfied are you with your [current arrangement]?" The following responses were read by the interviewer: "very satisfied," "satisfied," "not completely satisfied," or "dissatisfied." Overall, the reported level of satisfaction with child care arrangements appears to be quite high, with 96 percent of those surveyed in the NCCS responding that they were either "very satisfied" or "satisfied" with the primary care arrangement for their youngest child (table 4.3). These findings did not vary with the employment status of the mother, the type of care used, family income, age of the child, or race.

These findings are consistent with earlier studies on child care. The 1975 National Childcare Consumer Study (UNCO 1975), for example, using the identical question, found that 94 percent of all parents were "very satisfied" or "satisfied" with their current care arrangements (table 4.3) Results from such a general satisfaction question are open to criticism stemming from the concern that parents do not want to admit that their child care arrangement is unsatisfactory. On the other hand, the results support the theoretical approach mentioned earlier (Sonenstein 1989) that argues that arrangements in use reflect preferences, since parents will terminate unsatisfactory arrangements.

PREFERENCES FOR ALTERNATIVE TYPES OF CARE

Desire for Change

Although 96 percent of parents indicated that they are "very satisfied" or "satisfied" with their current care arrangement, 26 percent answered yes when asked, "Assuming you could have any type or combination of care arrangements . . . would you prefer some other type or combination of types instead of what you have now?" (table 4.3). As is the case with the satisfaction questions, the NCCS results are almost identical to those of the Childcare Consumer Study (UNCO

Table 4.3 COMPARISON OF SATISFACTION/PREFERENCE DATA, 1975 AND 1990

	National Childcare Consumer Study, 1975 (%)	National Child Care Survey, 1990 (%)
How satisfied are you with current arrangement?		
Very satisfied	74	79
Satisfied	20	17
Not completely satisfied	5	3
Dissatisfied	1	1
Assuming you could have any type of care, would you prefer an alternate type?		
Yes	24	26
No	76	74
What type would you prefer?		
Center	56	49
Parent	3	13
Relative	19	12
In-home provider	16	1
Family day care	3	20
Self/Sibling	1	0
Lessons	NA[a]	3
School	2	3
Total	100	100

Source: National Child Care Survey, 1990

a. NA, "lessons" was not included as a category in the 1975 study.

1975), which found that 24 percent of families indicated a preference for an alternative type of care arrangement (Hofferth and Phillips 1987).

Maternal Employment Status. The desire for alternative care arrangements was far higher among families with an employed mother (30 percent) than among families where the mother was not employed (19 percent) (figure 4.16).

Type of Care. Preferences for an alternative type of care varies with the current type of care. Families using centers were *least* likely to want to change modes (26 percent), whereas those families using in-home providers or self-/sibling care were *most* likely to desire a change in modes (37-38 percent) (figure 4.17). There were no other significant differences by types of care.

Age of Youngest Child. In general, age of the youngest child was not a significant factor in the desire to change arrangements; however, there were differences in the desire to change arrangements by age when employment status is also considered (figure 4.16). Among families where the youngest child is under the age of one and the mother is employed, 35 percent would prefer alternative care; when the mother is not employed, only 16 percent would prefer to change arrangements.

Race/Ethnicity. There were no significant differences in preference for an alternative type of care by race.

Family Income. Family income was not related to the desire to change arrangements.

Preferred Alternatives

For those families desiring a change, the mode of care they are most likely to prefer is a center or preschool (49 percent) (figure 4.18). After centers, parents prefer family

Child Care Choice ■ 235

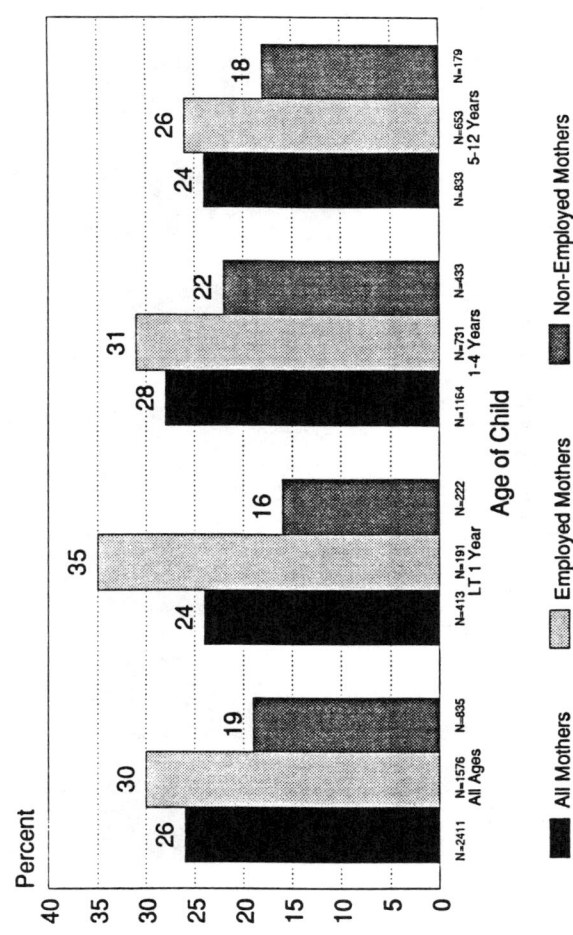

Figure 4.16
Families Preferring Alternative Type or Combination of Care By Age of Youngest Child and Employment Status of Mother

Source: National Child Care Survey 1990

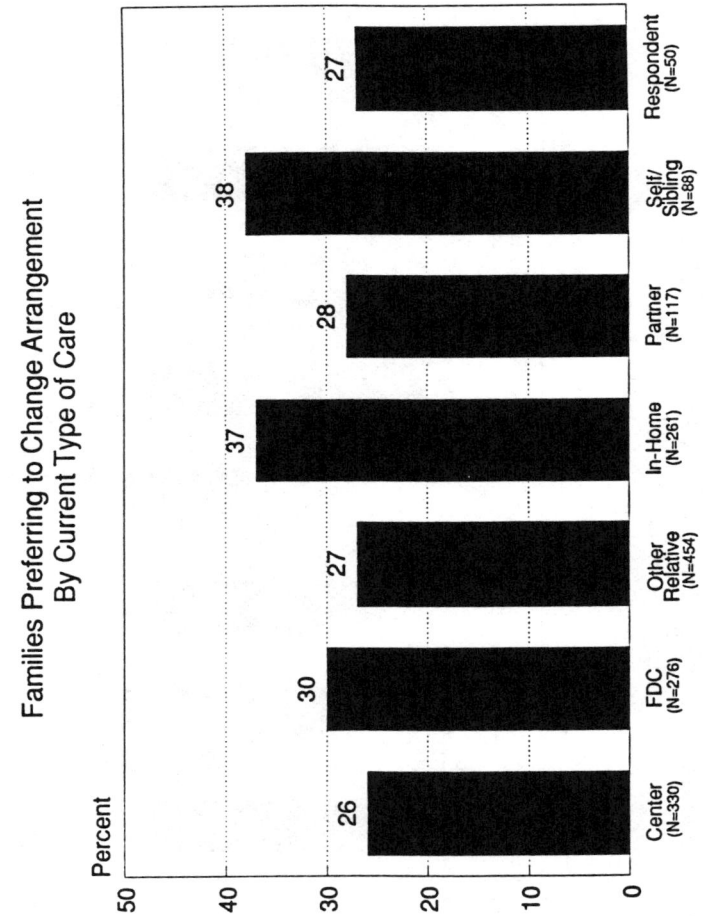

Figure 4.17
Families Preferring to Change Arrangement
By Current Type of Care

Source: National Child Care Survey 1990

Child Care Choice ■ 237

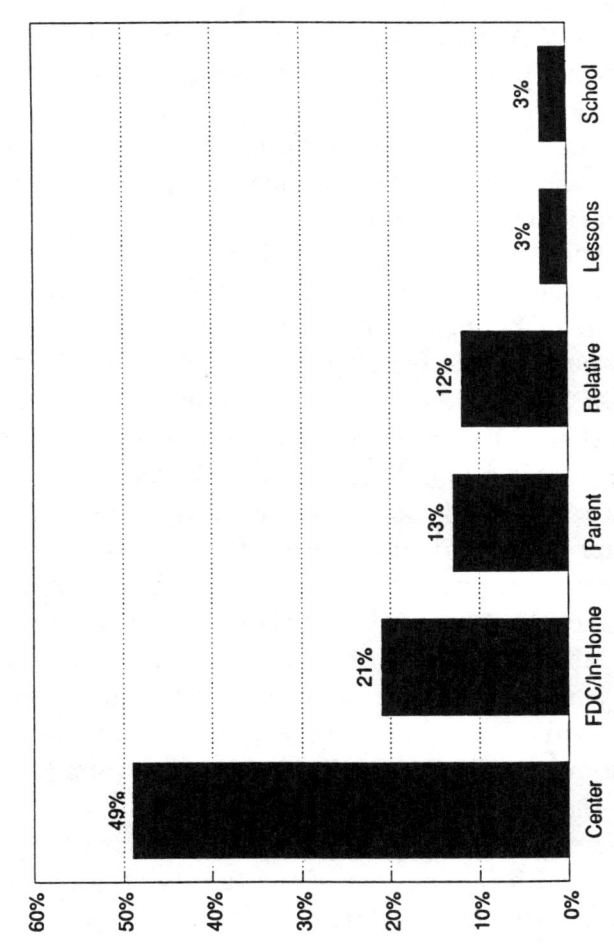

Figure 4.18
Preferred Alternative Type of Care
(N=600)

Source: National Child Care Survey 1990

day-care homes (21 percent). Here too, the findings are consistent with the 1975 UNCO study indicating that among families wanting to change modes of care, the most desired type of care was center-based care (table 4.3). As table 4.3 indicates, the only significant change between 1975 and 1990 has been a shift away from preference for an in-home provider to preference for a family day-care provider.

Maternal Employment Status. The alternative type of care that a family prefers does not vary with the employment status of the mother.

Type of Care. The alternative type of care that a family prefers does not vary with the type of care being used.

Age of Youngest Child. The age of the youngest child may be related to the alternative type of care desired. Four out of 10 families in which the youngest child is less than one year old reported wanting to change to center-based care (figure 4.19). In families where the youngest child is between one and four, almost 6 out of 10 reported wanting center care. This probably reflects a true difference in preferences of parents regarding care for children of different ages; however, it could also reflect a difference in the availability of center care for children. In families where the youngest child is under one year old, the next most frequently desired alternative mode of care was care by an in-home provider or family day-care provider (33 percent) (not shown).

Family Income. The preferred alternative type of care varies with the income of the family (figure 4.20). For families with incomes below $25,000 per year, 66 percent indicated preferring care in a center. This compares to 43 percent of families with incomes between $25,000 and $49,999 and 29 percent for families with incomes of $50,000 and over (figure 4.20).

Child Care Choice ■ 239

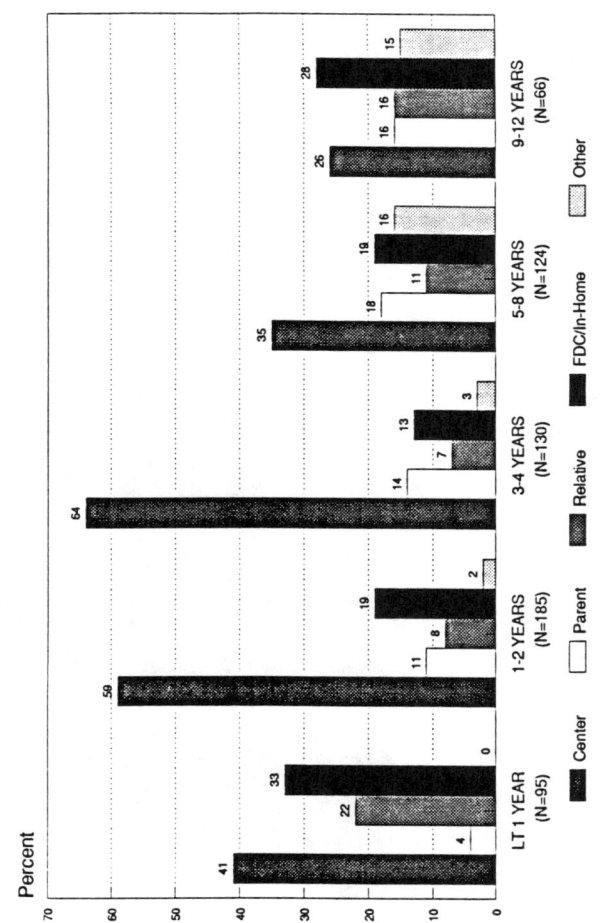

Figure 4.19
Preferred Alternative Type of Care
by Age of Youngest Child

Source: National Child Care Survey 1990

240 ■ NATIONAL CHILD CARE SURVEY, 1990

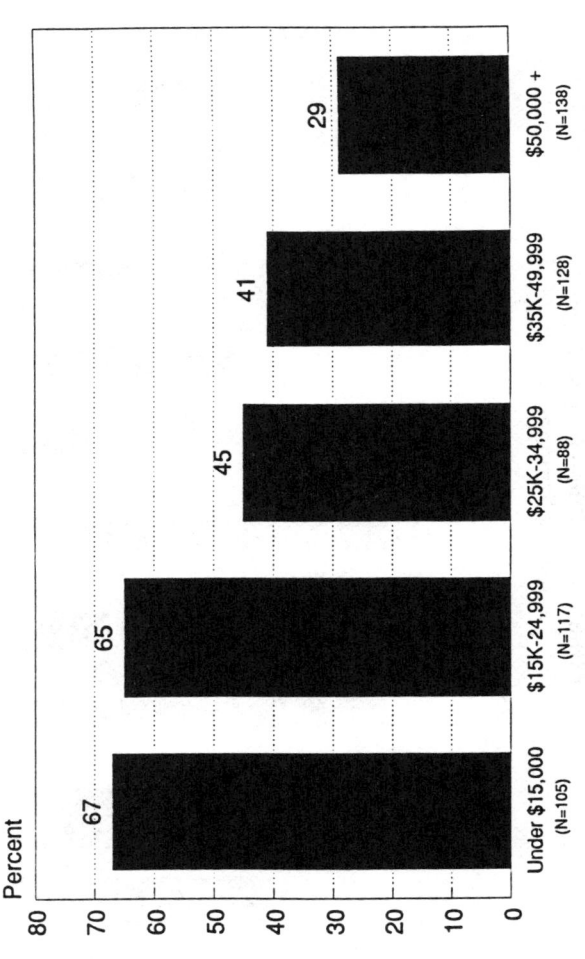

Race. There is no significant difference in type of care preferred by race.

Reasons for Desiring a Change

When asked why they would prefer an alternative mode of care, the majority of parents cited reasons of quality (60 percent) (figure 4.21, table 4.4) The aspects of quality most often cited were program related (figure 4.22). Within this category, cognitive and/or social and emotional development were mentioned most often by 21 percent of parents. Another 17 percent of parents indicated preparation for school as the reason for desiring an alternative care arrangement (not shown).

Maternal Employment Status. The reason for desiring an alternative type of care does not vary with the employment status of the mother. Quality is clearly first for both groups. However, the aspects of quality that are important to employed mothers differ from those important to nonemployed mothers. As figure 4.22 shows, the most important category of quality for employed mothers is program-related characteristics--43 percent compared to 28 percent for nonemployed mother. For nonemployed mothers the most important category of quality aspects is provider-related characteristics--35 percent--compared to 24 percent for employed mothers. Differences by employment status of the mother also can be seen in the child-related category, where 27 percent of nonemployed mothers but only 17 percent of employed mothers indicated these reasons were most important in the desire to change arrangements.

Age of Youngest Child. Although the majority of NCCS respondents cited quality as the reason they would prefer an

Table 4.4 MOST IMPORTANT REASON FOR PREFERRING DIFFERENT ARRANGEMENT, BY AGE OF YOUNGEST CHILD

First Reason for Preferring Alternative Arrangement	<1 yr. (%)	1–2 yrs. (%)	3–4 yrs. (%)	5–8 yrs. (%)	9–12 yrs. (%)	All (%)
Cost	4	4	4	2	9	4
Hours	6	5	4	10	0	5
Location	16	11	6	14	11	11
Quality	42	66	73	55	55	60
Availability	11	3	2	6	11	6
Prefers Relative	18	8	9	9	8	10
Other	4	3	2	3	5	3
Total	100	100	100	100	100	100
Sample size	93	173	124	110	60	560

Source: National Child Care Survey, 1990

Child Care Choice

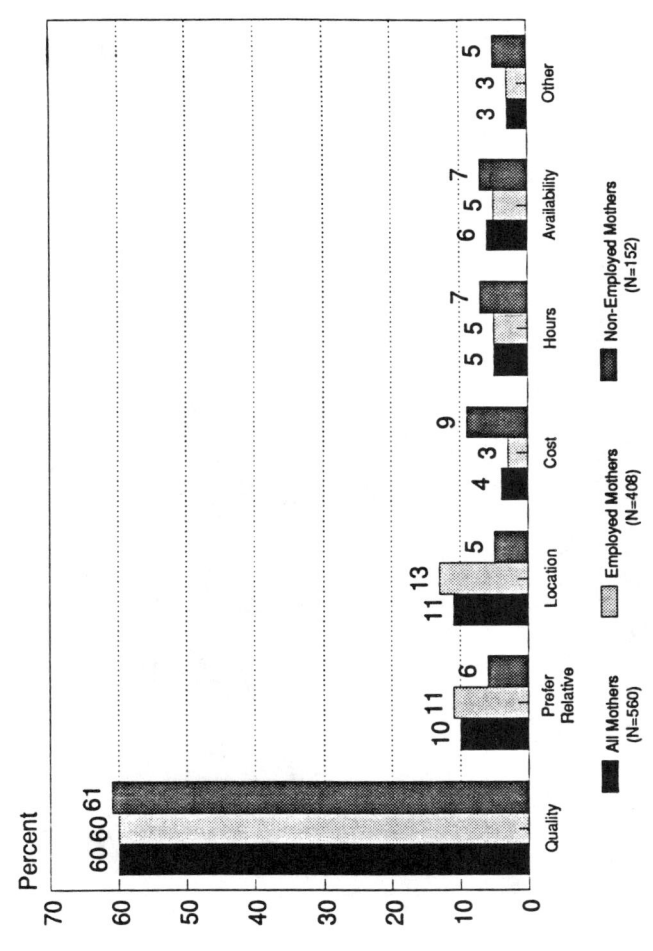

Figure 4.21
Why Prefer an Alternative Type of Care

Source: National Child Care Survey 1990

244 ■ NATIONAL CHILD CARE SURVEY, 1990

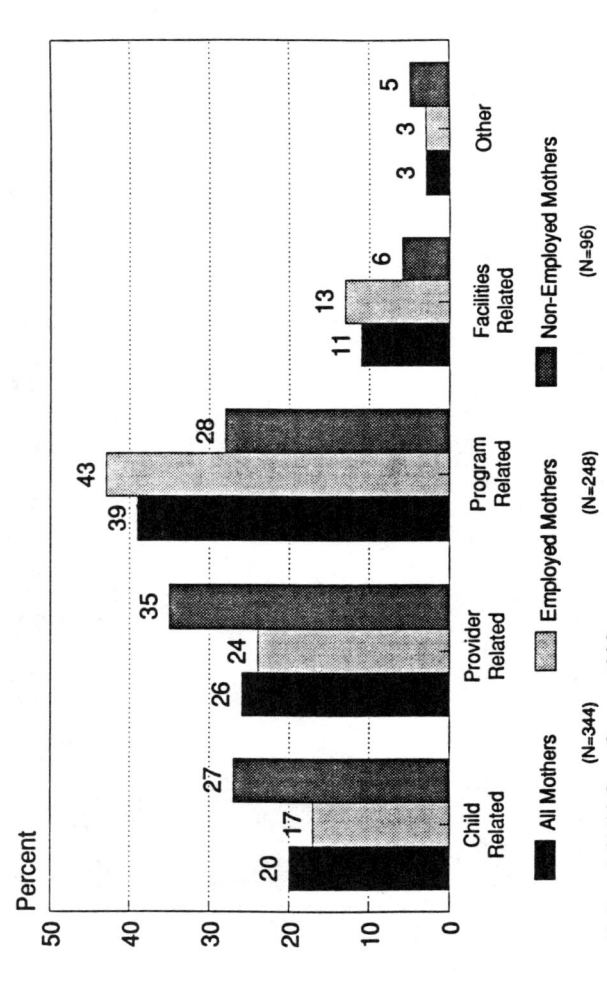

Figure 4.22
Most Important Aspect of Quality
In Preference for Alternative Care Type
By Employment Status of Mother

Source: National Child Care Survey 1990

alternative type of care, the proportion indicating this varied with the age of the child. For children under 1 year old, 42 percent of respondents said quality was the main reason they would prefer a change (table 4.4). In contrast, 69 percent of parents with children between 1 and 4 years old and 55 percent of parents with school-age children (5-12 years) indicated that quality was the reason for preferring some other type of care.

A higher proportion of parents with children under the age of one year than parents of older children indicated a preference for a relative as the reason they would like to change arrangements. This may simply be a proxy for quality. To test this hypothesis, we combined the two categories, "preference for a relative" and "quality." Even then, the results did not change; the proportion indicating that their reason for changing was the quality of the arrangement was still lower for the youngest age group.

Second Reason for Desiring a Change. For those who mentioned a second reason for changing their care arrangement or who cited a second aspect of quality, sample sizes were insufficient for analysis.

SUMMARY AND CONCLUSIONS

Parents participating in the National Child Care Survey, 1990, were asked about both the various types of arrangements and the number of providers they seriously considered in choosing their current care arrangement. Alternative arrangements were considered by 37 percent of families. Families with an employed mother considered child care alternatives more frequently than families with a nonemployed mother (43 percent versus 26 percent, respectively). Those families using relative care considered alternative arrangements *less* often than users of other modes of care. The alternative type of care considered most often by families was care in a center or preschool (50 percent).

Other providers of the same type were considered by 40 percent of parents. Again, families where the mother is employed considered other providers more often than families where the mother is not employed. Almost one-quarter of those families using either centers, in-home providers, or family providers considered both alternative types of care and a variety of providers.

The majority of NCCS parents indicated that they learned about their primary care arrangement from friends, neighbors, or relatives (65 percent); only 9 percent of parents found their current arrangement through a resource and referral service.

The reason most often given by parents for selecting their current arrangement for their youngest child was quality. Families where the mother is employed cited reasons of quality more frequently than families where the mother is not employed (42 percent versus 27 percent, respectively). Likewise, families using more formal care arrangements--centers, family providers, and in-home providers--cited reasons of quality more often than families using relatives to care for the youngest child. The aspect of quality most often mentioned was a provider-related characteristic such as a warm and loving style; this was the most important factor for the majority (70 percent) of parents.

NCCS parents indicated that it took approximately five weeks to settle on a care arrangement for the youngest child. The median time was higher for families where the mother was employed and where the youngest child was of school age.

Overall, the reported level of satisfaction with child care arrangements is quite high; 96 percent of those surveyed indicated that they are either "very satisfied" or "satisfied" with their current care arrangement for their youngest child. At the same time, 26 percent indicated that they would prefer an alternative type or combination of care arrangements for their youngest child. The desire for an alternative care arrangement was higher among families where the mother is employed and where the youngest child has not yet started school.

For those families desiring a change, the type of care they would prefer most often is a center or preschool (49 percent). This finding varies with the age of the child. For children under one year old, the alternative mode of care most often cited was care by a relative. For children between the ages of one and four years, the majority prefer care in a center.

Quality is the reason most often mentioned by parents for desiring a change in care. In contrast to their reason for selecting the current arrangement, the aspect of quality mentioned by the majority of parents wanting a change was program-related. This finding varied with the age of the child; 69 percent of parents with children between the ages of one and four years indicated quality as a reason for changing care, compared to 42 percent of parents with children under one year old.

Note, chapter 4

1. Interviewers were instructed to code the response as "quality" if parents mentioned any of the items cited here earlier under four categories of quality.

Chapter

5

PARENTAL PERCEPTIONS OF CARE

Athough parents may be concerned about the quality of care their children are receiving, they cannot make appropriate decisions if they are uninformed about the availability, cost, and quality of various types of care. Moreover, some types of families may have better access to certain kinds of care than other families. In the first section of this chapter we examine parental perceptions about distance to and cost of the nonparental child care arrangements they are currently using for their youngest child, as well as the availability, distance to, and expected cost of the nonparental arrangements they are not using.[1] Second, we describe parents' perceptions of the group size and child/staff ratio, staff training, transportation aspects, parental participation, and goals of the programs in which their children are enrolled. Third, we discuss parental use of and attitudes about self- and sibling care for their children.

PARENTAL PERCEPTIONS OF CARE USED AND NOT USED

Expected Availability of Care--Nonusers

In terms of perceptions of the availability of types of care not currently used by families, in-home providers are apparently seen as least available, with only 22 percent of those not using an in-home provider saying they knew of one that was available (table 5.1).[2] Center-based programs, on the other hand, were reported to be available by 59 percent of the families not using them. About one-third of those not using relatives and 44 percent of those not using family day care believed these types of care to be available to them.

Figure 5.1 shows perceptions of the availability of alternative types of care according to the type of care parents are currently using. For the sake of comparison, current users were considered to be at the 100 percent level. Among nonusers, center-based programs were perceived to be most available (60-64 percent), regardless of what type of care is currently being used. In-home providers and relatives were perceived by respondents to be the least available types of care, at 17-24 percent and 16-22 percent, respectively.

Income. There were clear differences in perceived availability of relatives and centers by income level. Families with annual incomes above $50,000 were much less likely to report a relative available for care than families with incomes under $50,000 per year (figure 5.2). There is a strong positive relationship between income and perceived availability of center care, with half of families with incomes under $25,000 perceiving a center to be available,

Parental Perceptions of Care ■ 251

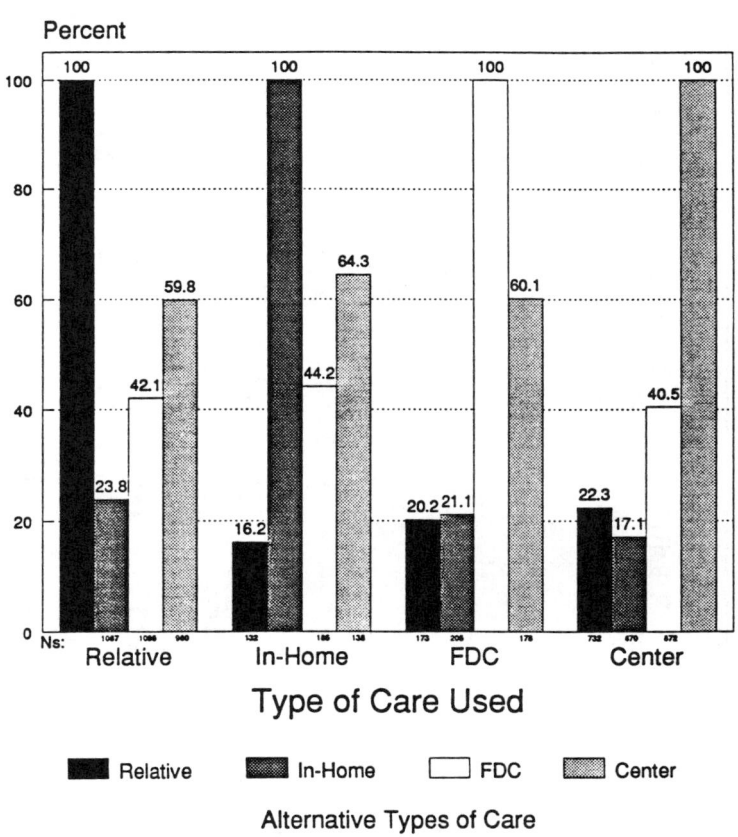

Figure 5.1
AVAILABILITY OF OTHER TYPES OF CARE
BY TYPE OF CARE CURRENTLY USED

Source: National Child Care Survey 1990

252 ■ NATIONAL CHILD CARE SURVEY, 1990

Table 5.1 USER AND NONUSER PERCEPTIONS OF TYPES OF CARE

Characteristics	Relative User[a]	Relative Nonuser	In-Home Provider User	In-Home Provider Nonuser	Family Day Care User	Family Day Care Nonuser	Center/ Preschool User	Center/ Preschool Nonuser
Availability								
Available:								
Yes (%)	--	30.9	--	22.4	--	44.4	--	59.3
No (%)	--	69.1	--	77.6	--	55.6	--	40.7
N	--	3,188	--	4,009	--	3,774	--	3,375
Don't Know	--	11	--	16	--	31	--	34
Refused	--	0	--	1	--	2	--	4
Distance from Home (minutes)								
<10 (%)	60.5	54.5	--	--	73.6	63.9	58.7	58.5
10-19 (%)	19.5	21.9	--	--	17.7	22.6	27.8	29.2
20-29 (%)	10.3	13.0	--	--	6.4	8.3	8.1	8.3
30+ (%)	9.7	10.6	--	--	2.4	5.2	5.4	4.0
N	1,142	983	--	--	573	1,661	918	1,979
Don't know	27	1	--	--	2	14	4	21
Refused	24	0	--	--	4	0	5	1

Price

Based on respondent's current number of hours per week:									
Per hour ($)	1.85	3.83	2.54	4.66	1.63	5.36	1.96	5.41
Per week ($)	28.13	51.66	35.18	66.37	39.58	60.03	42.66	58.78
N	136	1,046	83	3,281	284	2,780	473	2,175
Don't know		646		715		889		1,134
Refused		17		12		14		19
Based on 40-hour week:									
Per hour ($)	1.85	1.56	2.54	2.29	1.63	1.88	1.96	1.66
Per week ($)	28.13	62.27	35.18	91.55	39.58	75.12	42.66	66.29
N	136	1,050	83	3,287	284	2,786	473	2,180
Don't know		646		715		889		1,134
Refused		17		12		14		19

a. User results are based on youngest child under age 13.

Dash (--) means not applicable.

254 ■ NATIONAL CHILD CARE SURVEY, 1990

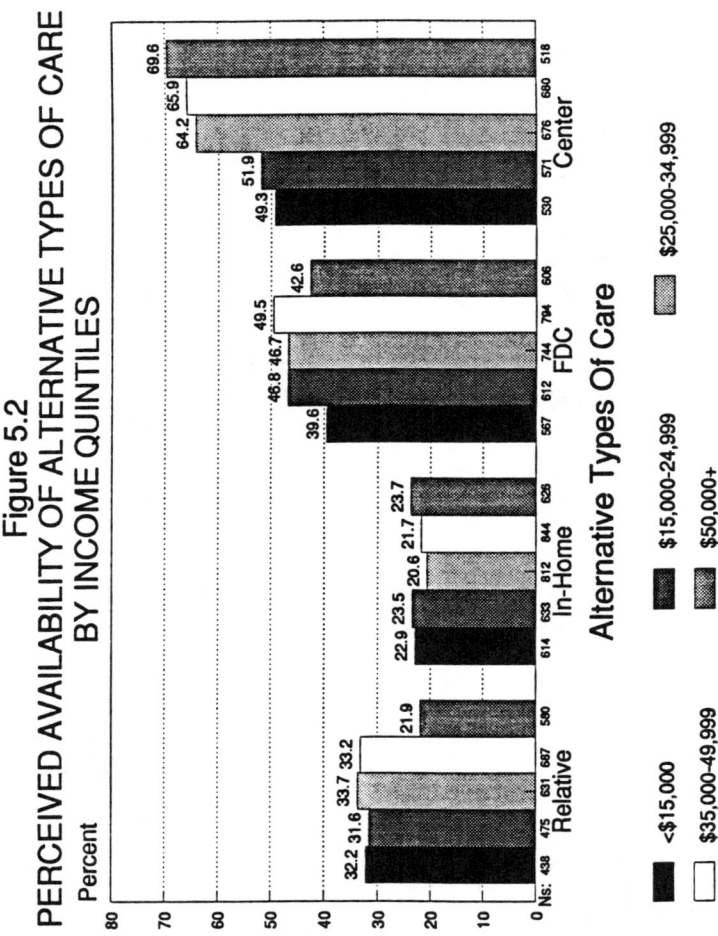

Figure 5.2
PERCEIVED AVAILABILITY OF ALTERNATIVE TYPES OF CARE BY INCOME QUINTILES

compared with 70 percent of families with incomes of $50,000 or more.

Residence. There were no significant differences in perceived availability of alternative types of care by residence.

Distance to Care--Users and Nonusers

Respondents were asked the travel time both to their arrangement and to alternative arrangements. Users and nonusers appear similar in their perceptions of travel times to different types of providers, although parents not using family day care perceive themselves as farther away from that potential provider than families using this care type (figure 5.3). Both users and nonusers agreed that family day-care providers are closest to home, with 74 percent of users and 64 percent of nonusers reporting such providers to be less than 10 minutes away from their homes. Relatives were the next closest type of care for users, with center-based programs immediately behind (60 percent and 59 percent, respectively, are less than 10 minutes away). Nonusers perceived center care to be closer to home than a relative, although there was little difference between the perceived distance from home of the two types of care.

When broken out by the type of care families are currently using, family day-care users reported being closer to their providers than to their alternatives (figure 5.4). Almost three-fourths said their family day-care providers are less than 10 minutes away, whereas a little over half reported a relative or a center or preschool to be this distance from their homes. Families using a nonrelative in the child's home, of course, perceived all alternatives--a relative, family day-care, or center--to be farther away than their current type of care. Users of in-home providers

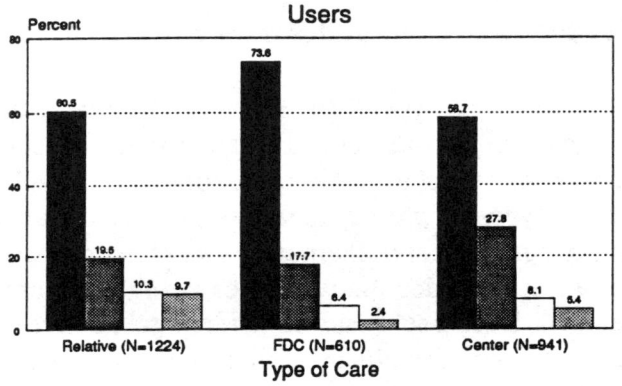
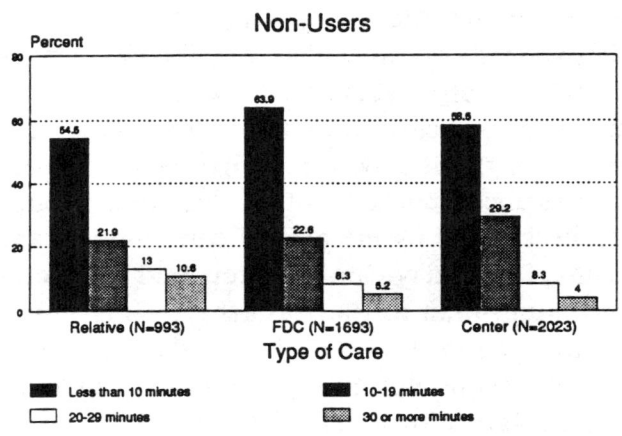

Figure 5.3
PERCEPTIONS OF PROVIDERS' DISTANCES FROM HOME

Source: National Child Care Survey, 1990

Figure 5.4
PERCENT WHO LIVE WITHIN TEN MINUTES OF PROVIDER, BY TYPE OF CARE CURRENTLY USED

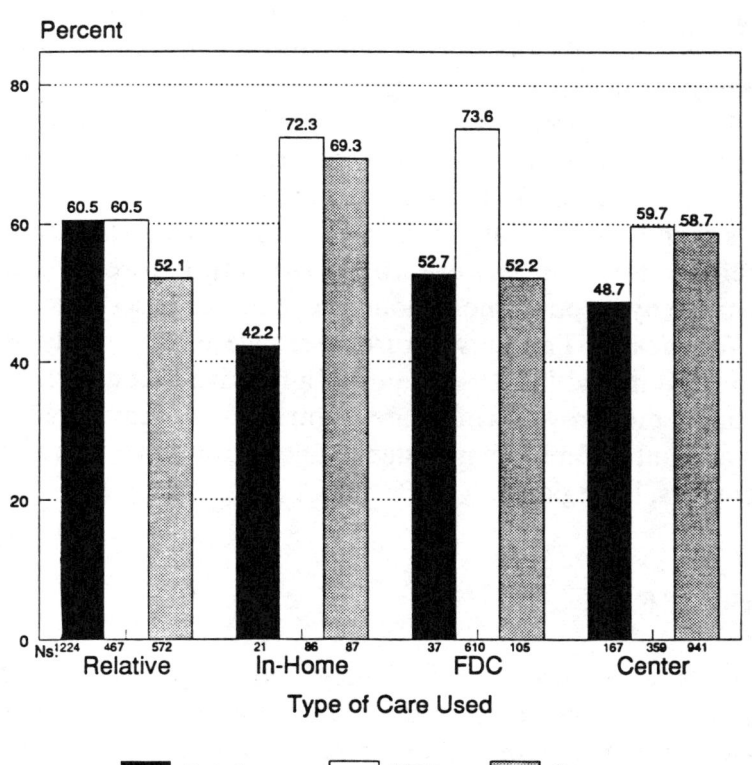

Source: National Child Care Survey 1990

perceived relatives as being the least accessible type of care. Users of relative care indicated being as close to those relatives as to a potential family day-care provider.

Income. There were significant differences in distance to care by income among nonusers of family day-care (figure 5.5). Seventy-two percent of nonusers with incomes greater than $50,000 reported being within 10 minutes of an available family day-care provider, compared to 59 percent of nonusers with incomes below $15,000. There were no significant differences in distance by income among users of family day-care.

Users of center-based care also differed in distance to their providers by income, with 66 percent of those earning more than $50,000, but only 49 percent of users earning less than $15,000, saying they are 10 minutes away from their center. There were no significant differences in distance by income among nonusers of center-based care.

Residence. Families in rural areas were most likely to report living within 10 minutes of a relative that could, or actually did, provide child care (figure 5.6). There were no significant differences in distance to care for either users or nonusers, by region.

Price of Care

Parents were asked how much they would expect to pay for the various types of care they are not now using. Since parents reported expected expenditures in a variety of units, but were not asked to specify number of hours of care, estimated prices of care were calculated in two ways for nonusers. The first method assumes that respondents base their price expectations on a 40-hour-per-week child care schedule (nonusers A). The second method assumes parents

Figure 5.5
PERCENT WHO LIVE WITHIN TEN MINUTES OF PROVIDER, BY INCOME

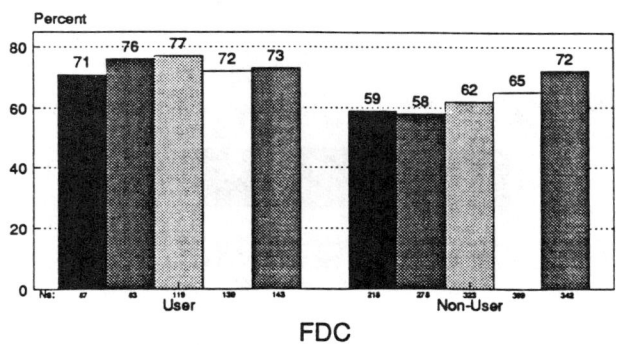

FDC

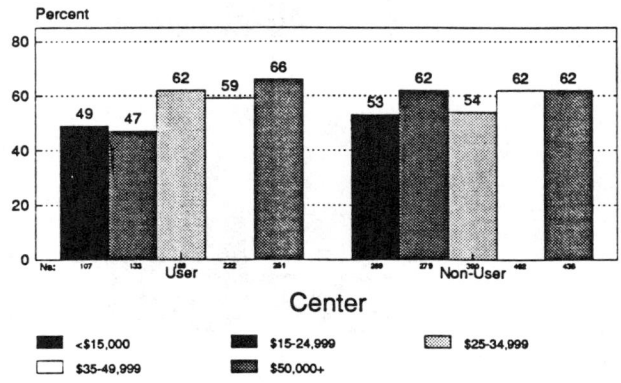

Center

■ <$15,000　　■ $15-24,999　　▨ $25-34,999
☐ $35-49,999　　▩ $50,000+

Source: National Child Care Survey 1990

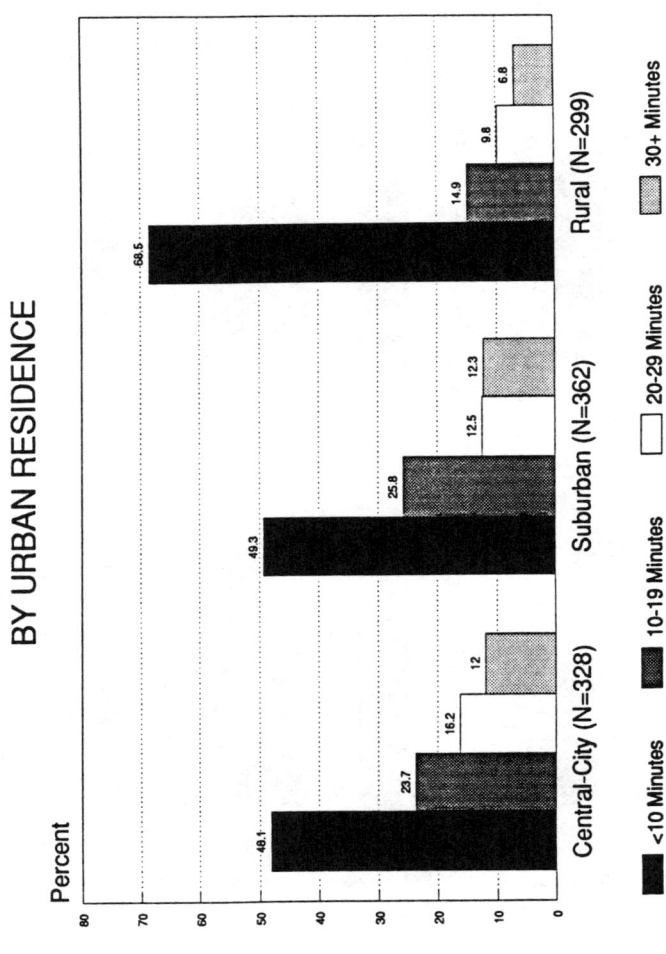

estimate price based on the hours per week their youngest child spends in their current primary arrangement (nonusers *B*) (see figure 5.7). The former probably underestimates hourly expenditures and overestimates weekly expenditures. The latter probably overestimates hourly expenditures and underestimates weekly expenditures.

Many parents said they did not know how much alternative types of care would cost. More than one-third of respondents said they did not know what they would have to pay for a relative or for center-based programs (see table 5.1). Respondents appeared to have an easier time estimating how much in-home providers and family day-care providers would cost, with 18 percent and 24 percent, respectively, saying they did not know.

Figure 5.7 shows estimated hourly and weekly prices of care for users and nonusers. Hourly calculations based on a 40-hour-per-week schedule for nonusers *A* yield prices similar to those that users reported paying. For all types of care except family day-care, nonusers *A* expected to pay a little less per hour (by 9 to 30 cents) than what users pay. Nonusers *A* perceived family day-care to cost, on average, 25 cents more per hour than what users pay. On the other hand, nonusers *B* (calculations based on the number of hours their youngest child spends with their current or primary provider per week) expected to pay far more for all types of care than users reported paying--up to $3.73 more per hour, in the case of family day-care.

Although results show that nonusers *A* are consistently higher than nonusers *B* in their weekly estimates of price across types of care, both types of nonusers estimate alternatives as being considerably more expensive than what users are paying per week. Calculating by 40-hour weeks results in the higher estimates, from $24 more per week than users of centers and preschools pay to $56 more

Figure 5.7
USER AND NON-USER PERCEPTIONS OF PRICES

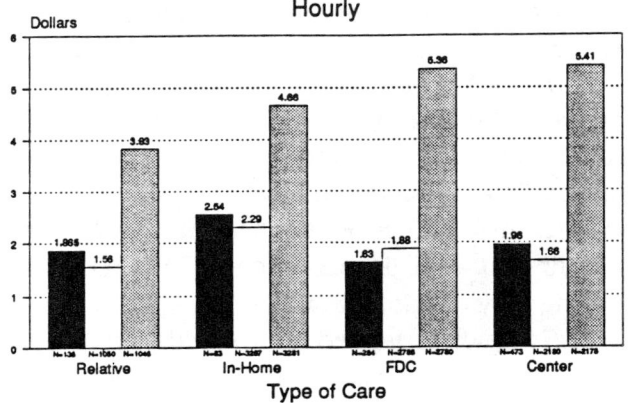

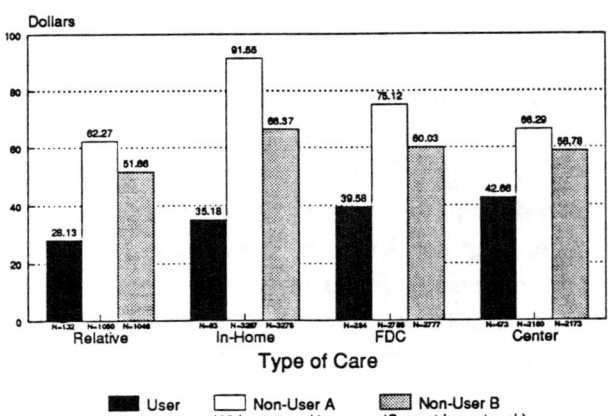

Source: National Child Care Survey, 1990

per week than those currently using in-home providers pay. Nonusers *B* showed price differences by type of care, ranging from centers, at $16 more per week than user expenditures, to in-home providers, who are expected to cost $31 more per week than users are currently paying.

Figures 5.8 and 5.9 show expected hourly and weekly prices for nonusers and the actual expenditure for users broken out by the types of care they are currently using. Calculations based both on 40-hour weeks and current hours per week are presented separately in the figures. When calculated by a 40-hour week, perceptions of hourly prices for alternative types of care show in-home providers as being the most expensive, even for users (figure 5.7). Those using relatives believed that only centers would be less expensive than their current provider (by 25 cents an hour), and users of family day-care believed that only a relative would be cheaper (21 cents). Those using center-based programs believed that, on average, relatives would be 42 cents cheaper an hour than their current arrangement.

Results based upon the actual child care hours currently used are quite different. The expected costs of alternatives increase, generally surpassing what parents are currently paying.

Both methods of calculating cost show that users of child care perceive their alternatives to be more expensive per week than their current arrangement (figure 5.8). Parents perceived their cheapest alternative as costing them up to $47 more per week based upon a 40-hour week, and up to $44 more per week based upon current child care hours. Nonusers tend to believe that in-home providers are the most expensive alternative (in both figures 5.8 and 5.9).

Income. Just as actual expenditures are related to level of income, so are expected expenditures. There is a strong positive relationship between expected expenditures and

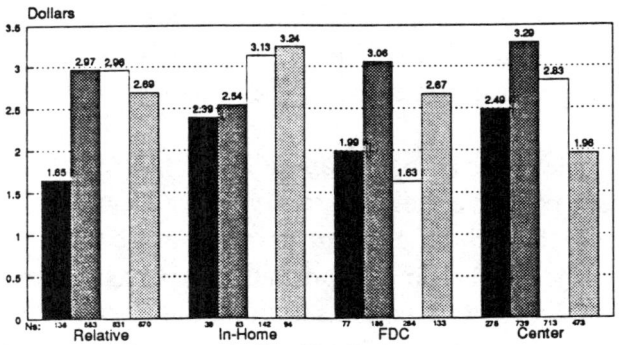

Figure 5.8
PERCEPTIONS OF HOURLY PRICES FOR OTHER TYPES OF CARE
Based on 40 hours per week

Based on current hours per week

Source: National Child Care Survey, 1990

Parental Perceptions of Care 265

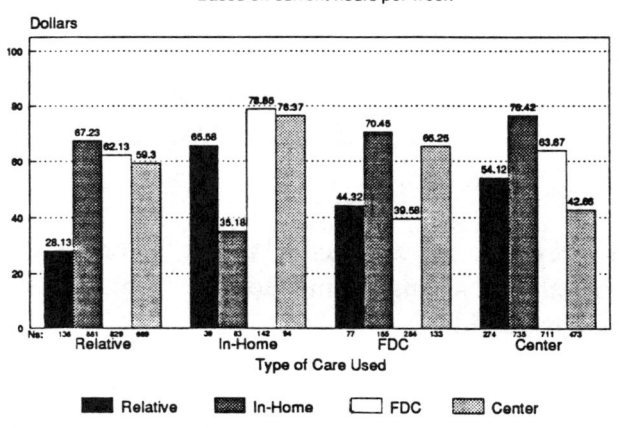

Figure 5.9
PERCEPTIONS OF WEEKLY PRICES FOR OTHER TYPES OF CARE
Based on 40 hours per week

Based on current hours per week

Source: National Child Care Survey, 1990

family income (figure 5.10). As income rises, so do expected hourly and weekly expenditures on care, regardless of type of arrangement. This relationship is most pronounced for in-home providers and least pronounced for center care.

Residence. Families expect to pay more for care if they live in a metropolitan area than in a rural area, and those in central cities expect to pay the most (figure 5.11). In-home provider care shows the largest differences in expected price across urban/nonurban areas of residence. These differences correspond to real differences in fees charged by center- and home-based programs in urban/nonurban areas (see *Profile of Child Care Settings* [henceforth, PCS study] by Kisker, Hofferth, and Phillips, 1991). Families demonstrate strong regional differences in expected expenditures for care. Reflecting actual price differences as found in the PCS study, families in the northeastern and western regions of the United States expect to spend the most for care, for all types of arrangements (figure 5.11).

USER PERCEPTIONS OF CHARACTERISTICS OF CARE

In this survey, parents were asked about the characteristics of the nonparental arrangements they are currently using for their youngest child.

Parental Perceptions of Care ■ 267

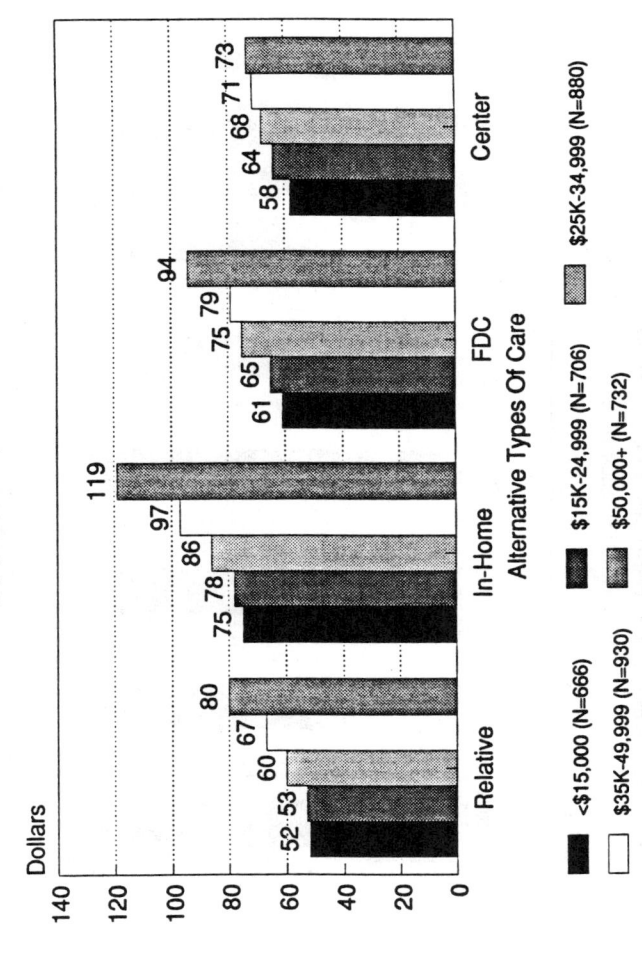

Figure 5.10
EXPECTED WEEKLY EXPENDITURES FOR ALTERNATIVE TYPES OF CARE BY INCOME QUINTILES

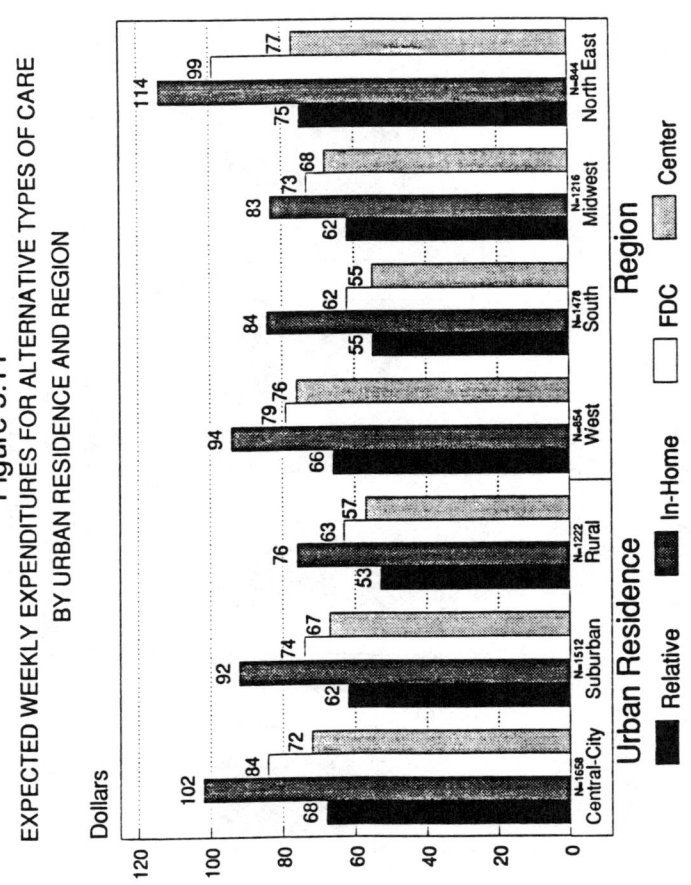

Figure 5.11
EXPECTED WEEKLY EXPENDITURES FOR ALTERNATIVE TYPES OF CARE BY URBAN RESIDENCE AND REGION

Group Size and Child/Staff Ratios

Group sizes are perceived to be smallest for children in the care of a relative or in-home provider--between one and two children, on average (figure 5.12). Group size includes any children of the relative or in-home provider being cared for at the same time. Few parents did not know the number of children cared for together with their own child. Parents reported that children in family day-care are in groups of about four children, on average, whereas children in center-based programs are in groups of about 15 children, on average. The average group size for family day-care reported by providers in the PCS study (Kisker et al. 1991) and taking into account the hours children are in care, is four children, including those of the provider. The average group size for center-based care, again reported in the PCS study, is 16 children. According to these average figures, parents are reasonably good estimators of group size.

For children in the care of relatives and in-home providers, child/staff ratios are the same as group size, since by definition, only one person is caring for the child. However, there may be multiple providers in family day-care homes, and there are almost certainly multiple teachers in centers. Only a few parents (under 2 percent) did not know the number of teachers caring for children in their child's group. Parents reported a child/staff ratio of 3.1 children per staff member in family day-care (figure 5.12). According to the PCS study (Kisker et al. 1991) licensed family providers cared for an average of 3.7 children per provider. Parents reported a ratio of 6.5 children per provider in center-based care. The PCS study reported an average of 8.6 children per staff member. Thus, although parents are quite good at estimating the number of children cared for in a group, they may not be as good at estimating

Figure 5.12
USER PERCEPTIONS OF GROUP SIZES
AND CHILD/STAFF RATIOS

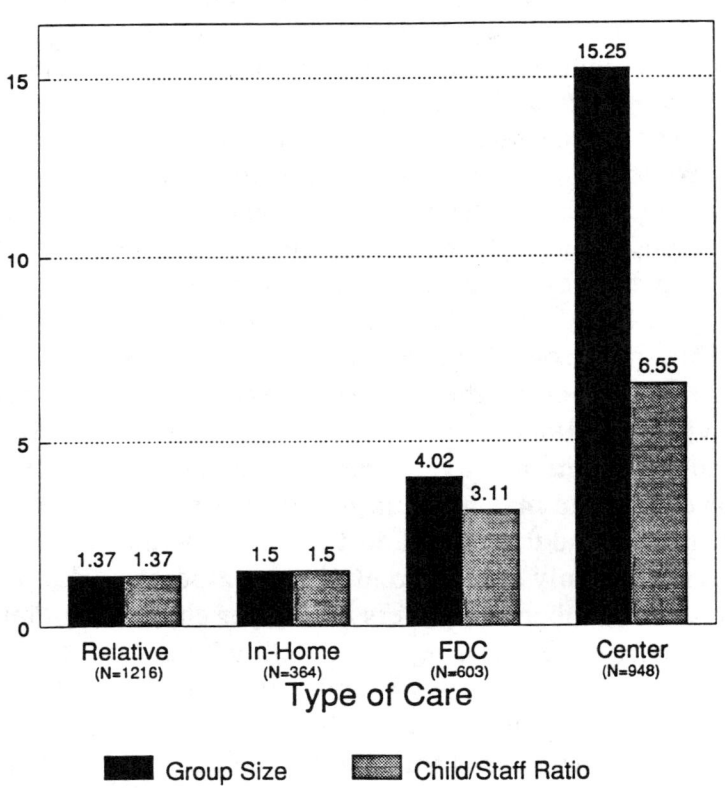

Source: National Child Care Survey 1990

the number of staff members caring for that group, especially when groups are large.

Income. There were significant differences in group sizes and child/staff ratios in family day-care homes for children in families with incomes of less than $15,000 a year versus those with incomes exceeding $50,000 a year (figures 5.13 and 5.14). Both group size and child/staff ratios were significantly higher for families with the highest incomes than for families with the lowest incomes. Earlier evidence suggested that subsidization of low-income families reduces enrollment differences. This evidence suggests that it may also improve the quality of care in some settings by reducing the number of children per staff member.

Provider Education and Training

Parents were also asked whether their providers had any education or training specifically related to young children, such as early childhood education or child psychology. About 12 percent of users of family day-care did not know the answer. Of those who answered, almost 40 percent said that their family day-care provider had some training (figure 5.15). According to the PCS study (Kisker et al. 1991), 64 percent of providers in regulated home-based programs have had some special child care or early education training. The difference is probably due to the inclusion of only regulated programs in the PCS study. Providers in informal, unregulated programs may be less likely to have received some training.

Parents whose children were enrolled in a center, preschool, or before-/after-school program were asked whether the person mainly responsible for caring for the youngest child had received education or training in early childhood

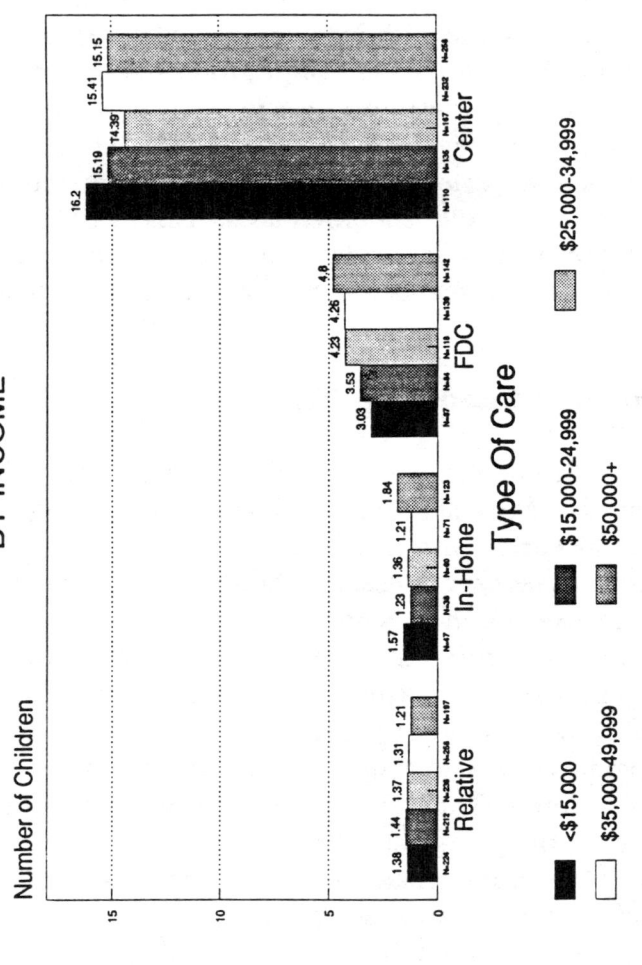

Parental Perceptions of Care ■ 273

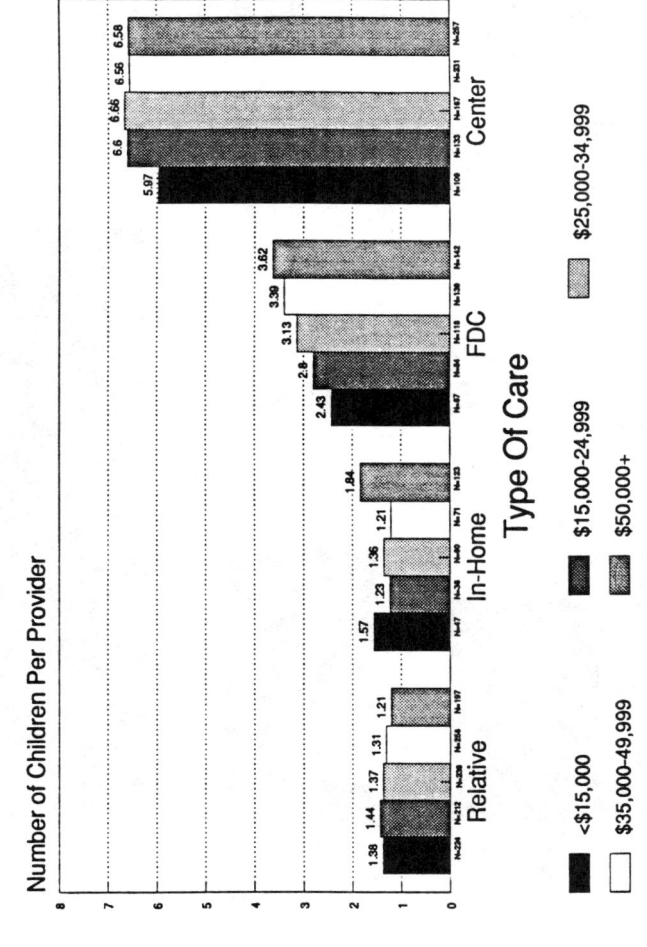

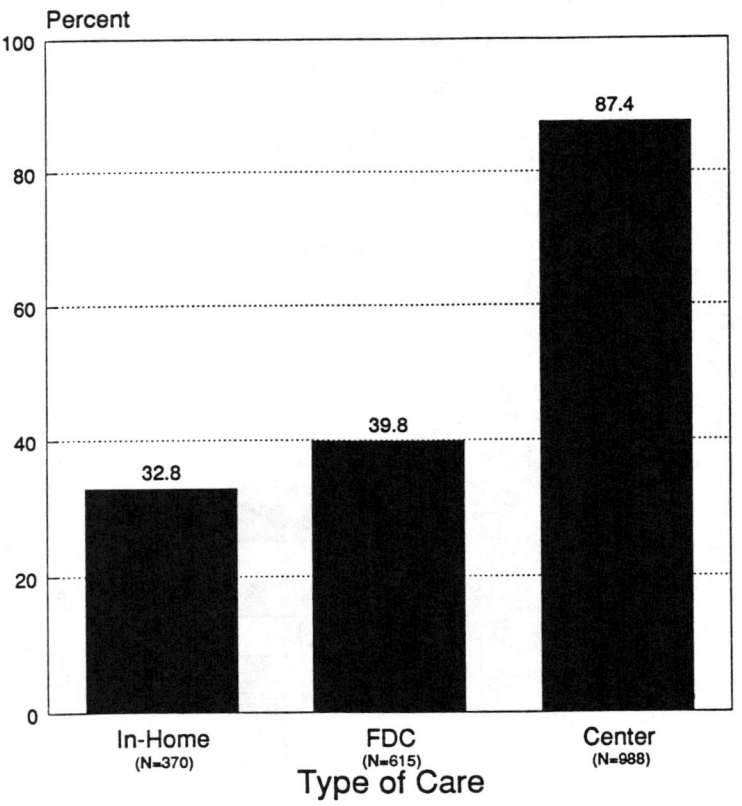

Figure 5.15
USER PERCEPTIONS OF PROVIDERS' EDUCATION AND TRAINING

Source: National Child Care Survey 1990

education or child psychology. Of these parents, about 9 percent did not know the answer and 87 percent said their provider did have some education or training (figure 5.15). This corresponds well with what providers report themselves. In the PCS study, 93 percent of teachers reported having had some special child care or early childhood education or training. There was no significant difference in reported provider training by income level of parent.

Transportation

How do children get to their provider's home? Nine out of 10 youngest children in the family are either driven to the family day-care provider's home or walk there (figure 5.16). In 77 percent of households a parent or other adult drives the child to family day-care. Thirteen percent of the children in family day-care walk to the provider's home. Only 4 percent take public transportation.

For center-based care, 74 percent of youngest children are driven to a center by a parent or other adult; 8 percent use public transportation; 8 percent use center-provided transportation; and 5 percent walk.

Income. Transportation by car to centers and family day-care was positively related to income (figures 5.17 and 5.18). Transportation by car increased from 65 percent to 81 percent as families' incomes rose from less than $15,000 to $49,999. There was a negative relationship between walking to family day-care and income, since this method of transportation fell from 23 percent to 5 percent as income rose from the lowest to the highest groupings.

276 ■ NATIONAL CHILD CARE SURVEY, 1990

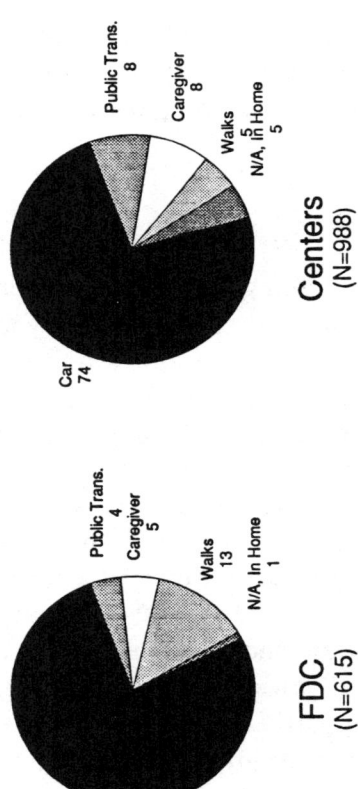

Figure 5.16
TRANSPORTATION TO CARE
FAMILY DAY CARE AND CENTERS

Source: National Child Care Survey, 1990

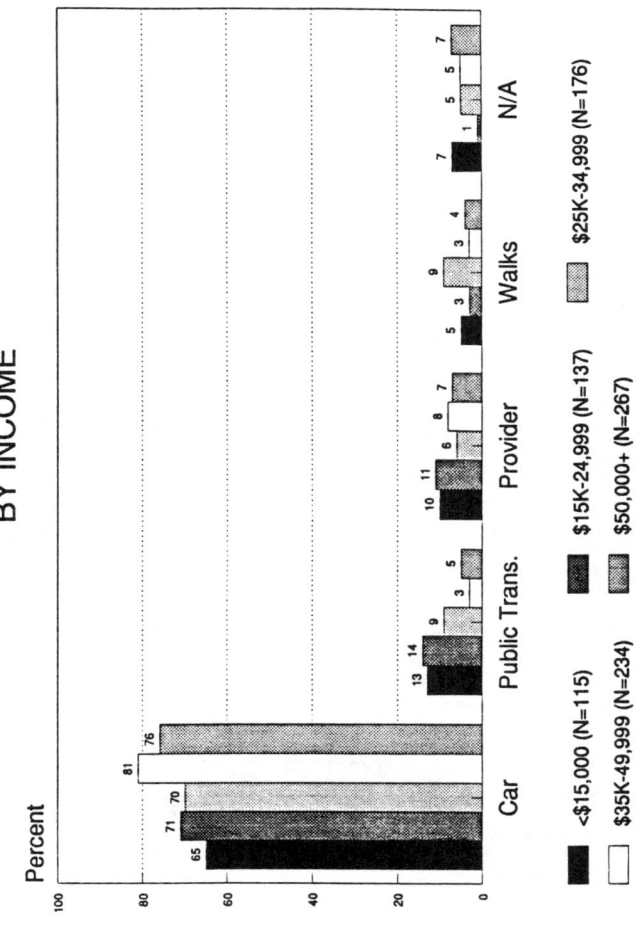

Figure 5.17
TRANSPORTATION TO CENTERS
BY INCOME

**Figure 5.18
TRANSPORTATION TO FAMILY DAY CARE
BY INCOME**

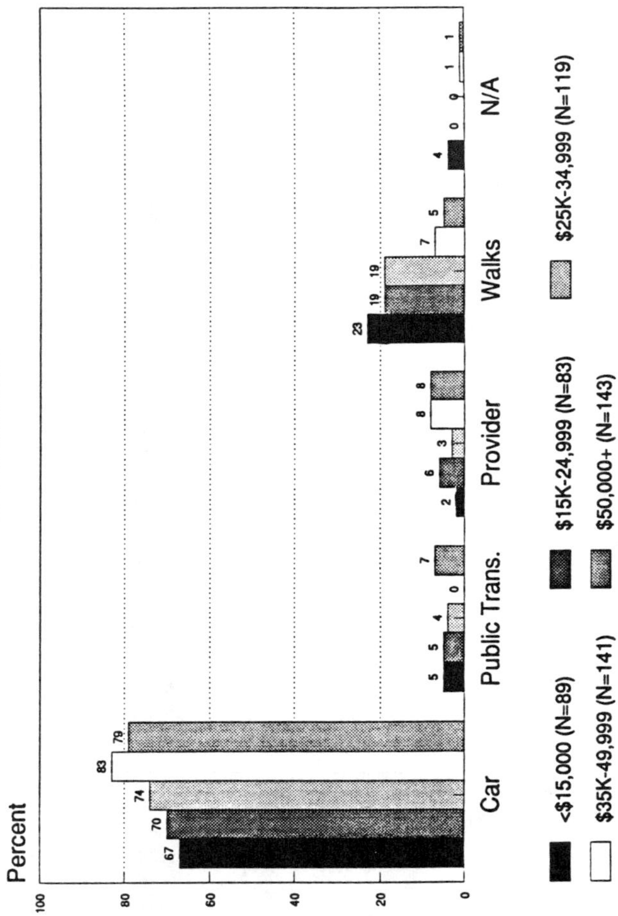

Source: National Child Care Survey 1990

Parental Monitoring

One of the most important ways that parents can monitor the care of their children is to drop by unannounced. Parents were asked whether unexpected visits to providers are "strongly encouraged," "encouraged," "neither encouraged nor discouraged" "discouraged," or "strongly discouraged." The responses for both users of centers and family day-care were similar. Only about 5 percent of parents said that they were "discouraged" or "strongly discouraged" from dropping in unannounced (figure 5.19).

Goal of the Program

Parents who enrolled their child in a center-based program were given a list of goals of early childhood programs and asked to indicate the primary goals of their program. Almost all said that providing a warm and loving environment or promoting general development was a goal (figure 5.20). Three-quarters cited the goal of providing care so that parents can work and a similar proportion cited the goal of preparing children academically. Two-thirds mentioned gaining appreciation for their culture as a goal. Finally, one-quarter cited religious instruction as a goal. These findings are consistent with goals described by providers in the PCS study (Kisker et al. 1991). About 30 percent of providers in that study said that providing some religious instruction was one of their goals.

Income. There is a strong negative relationship between income and the goals of academic preparation and cultural appreciation (figure 5.21). As income declines, more families recorded these as goals of their child care program. There was also a significant income difference for the

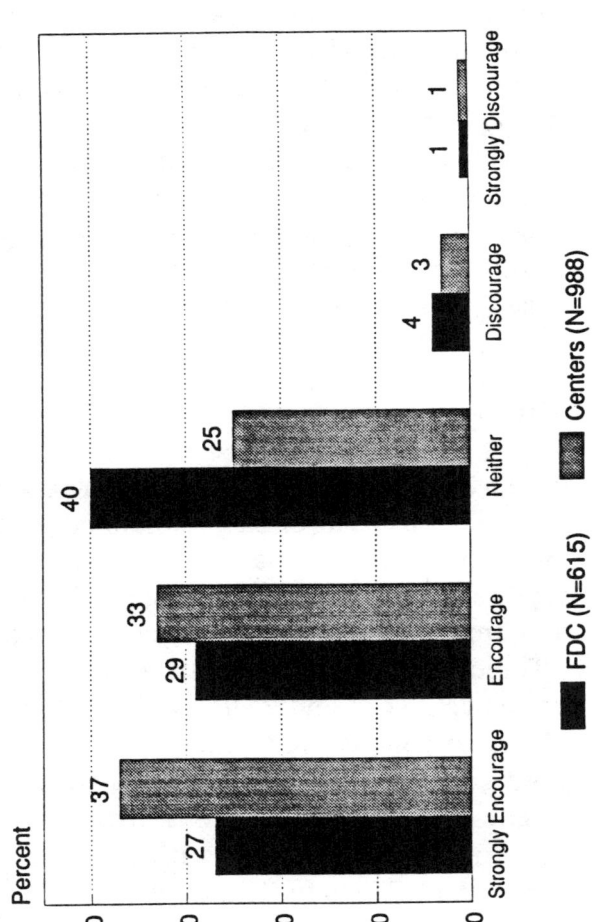

Parental Perceptions of Care

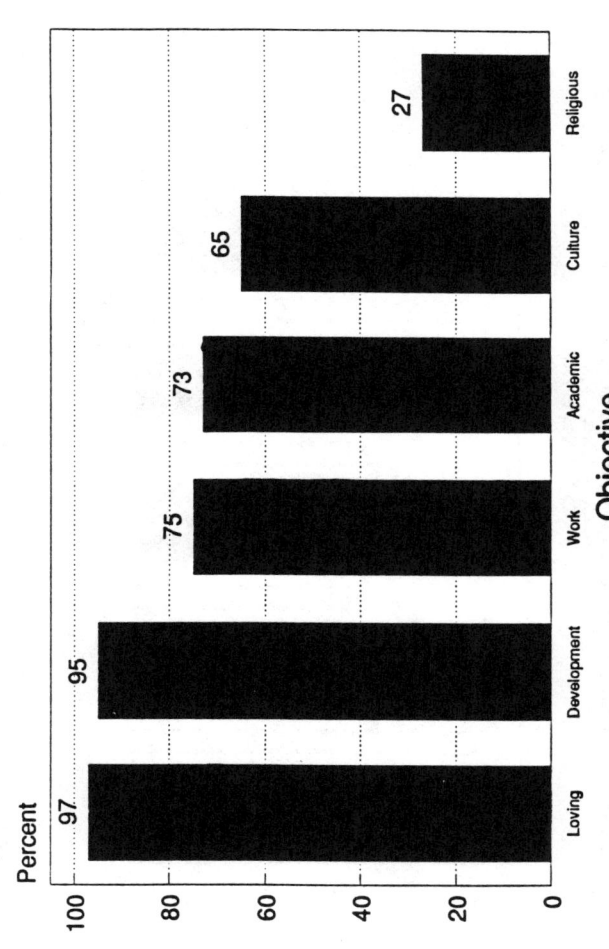

Figure 5.20
OBJECTIVES OF THE PROGRAM CENTERS

Source: National Child Care Survey 1990

282 ■ NATIONAL CHILD CARE SURVEY, 1990

Figure 5.21
PROGRAM GOALS OF CURRENT CHILD CARE ARRANGEMENT BY INCOME

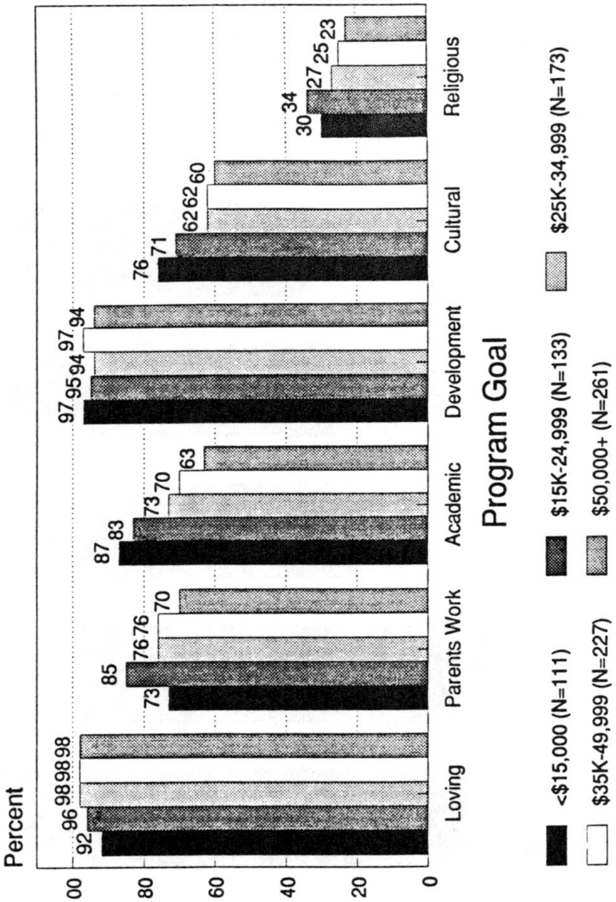

Source: National Child Care Survey 1990

program goal of providing care so parents can work. Eighty-five percent of parents whose incomes fell between $15,000 and $24,999 said this was a goal, compared with 70 percent of parents whose incomes were above $50,000.

SELF-CARE AND SIBLING CARE

Use of Self-Care and Sibling Care

The majority of families using self-care or sibling care for their children do not use either type as a primary arrangement. Six percent of families said they use self-care at some time during the week (figure 5.22), but only 2 percent of families identified it as their child's primary form of care (table 2.2). Another two percent say that they use it as a secondary form--but even when a sum is taken of the number of families who cited self-care as one of their top four forms of care, not all self-care is included. The arrangements discussed earlier in this report (chapter 2) focus on the primary and secondary arrangements for the youngest child. Here, however, to determine the total use of self-care and sibling care, we assigned families first to self-care if they ever use it for their youngest child, then to sibling care if they ever use it. The remaining families (who did not mention self- or sibling care) were assigned to their stated primary arrangement. In this way we obtained the number of families ever using self-care and sibling care for their youngest child. We calculated this first for the youngest child and then for all children. It was possible to separate siblings by age only for youngest children.

284 ■ NATIONAL CHILD CARE SURVEY, 1990

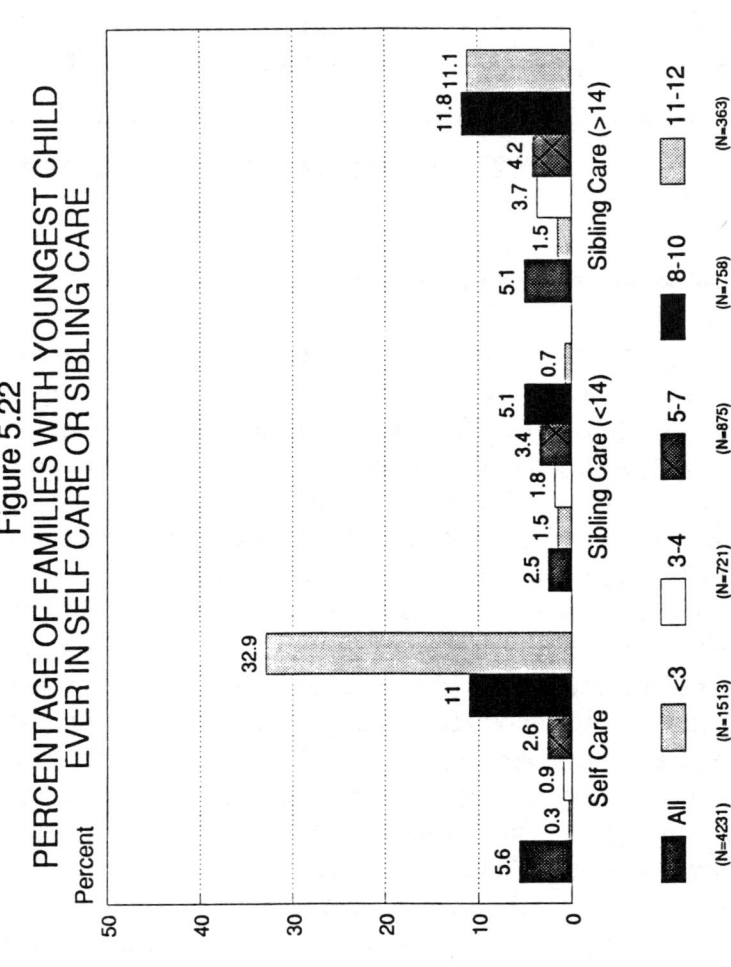

YOUNGEST CHILD

Age of Child. Figure 5.22 shows the distribution of youngest children in self-care by age. Six percent, or 1.5 million, of the youngest children care for themselves at some time during the week. Very few (65,000) youngest children are in self-care before they reach school age. The proportion of children in self-care rises rapidly from 3 percent at ages 5 to 7, to 11 percent at ages 8 to 10, and to 33 percent at ages 11 to 12. By age 12, 4 out of 10 children care for themselves (not shown). Under one percent of youngest children under age 5 and 11 percent of youngest children aged 5-12 are ever in self-care.

Age of Siblings. Another issue of concern is that children are sometimes cared for by siblings who are under age 13 or 14. We found that 3 percent (672,000) of youngest children under age 13 were cared for at some time by a sibling under age 14. The proportion of youngest children in the care of a sibling under age 14 rises from 2 percent under age 5 to 5 percent at ages 8 to 10, after which it gradually declines to zero as the child reaches 12 years old (figure 5.22). Another 5 percent of youngest children under age 13 are cared for by a sibling age 14 or older.

Maternal Employment Status. Figures 5.23 and 5.24 show the proportion of youngest children in self-care and sibling care by the employment schedule of the mother. The proportion of youngest children in self-care is higher among full-time employed mothers than part-time employed mothers or nonemployed mothers. Maternal employment increases self-care most for the 8- to 12-year-old age group. Prior to that age few children care for themselves.

The proportion of children in the care of a sibling who is under 14 years old is higher for part-time mothers than for full-time mothers (4 percent compared with 3 percent,

286 ■ NATIONAL CHILD CARE SURVEY, 1990

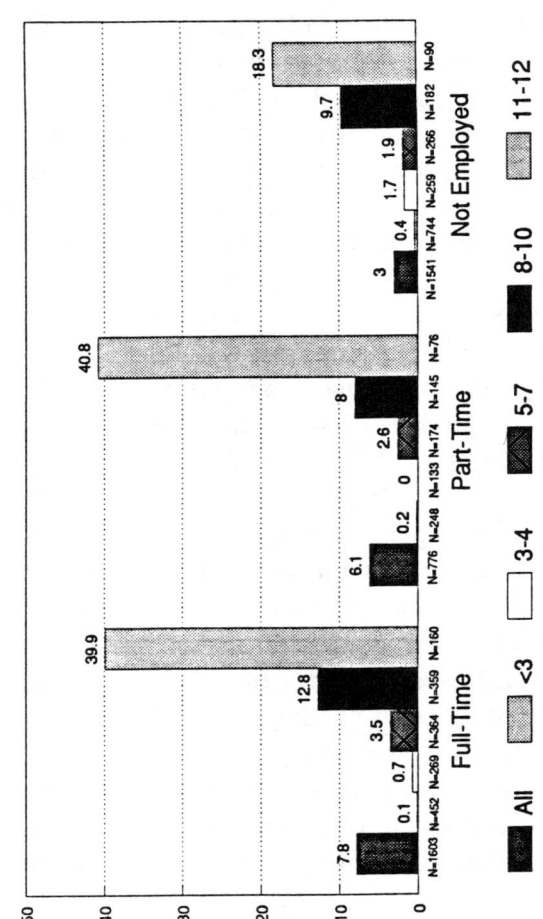

Figure 5.23
PERCENTAGE OF YOUNGEST CHILDREN EVER IN SELF CARE BY EMPLOYMENT STATUS OF MOTHER

Source: National Child Care Survey 1990

Parental Perceptions of Care ■ 287

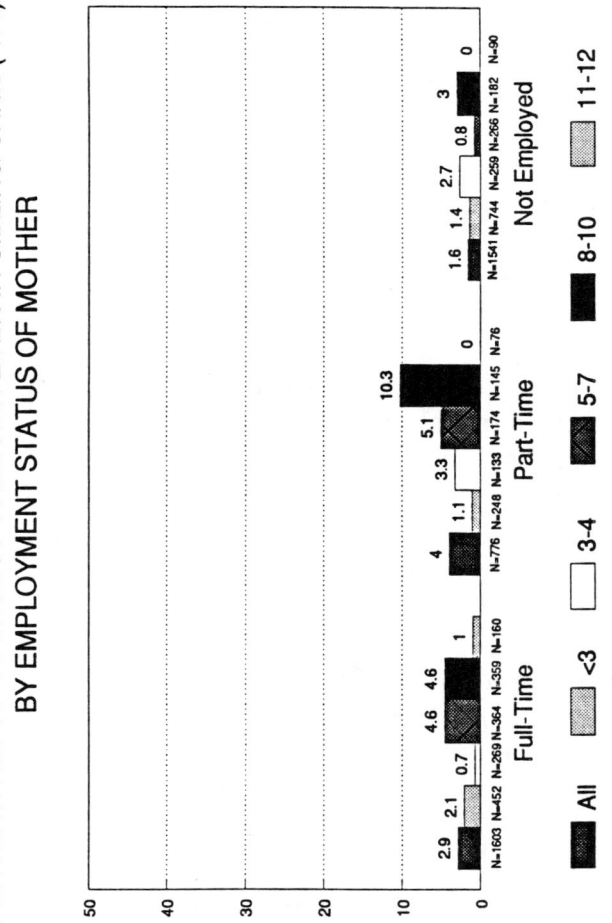

Figure 5.24
PERCENTAGE OF YOUNGEST CHILDREN EVER IN SIBLING CARE (<14) BY EMPLOYMENT STATUS OF MOTHER

Source: National Child Care Survey 1990

respectively) (figure 5.24). However, children of full-time employed mothers are slightly more likely to be in the care of an older sibling than the children of part-time employed mothers (not shown). Under 2 percent of children of nonemployed mothers are in the care of a young sibling some time during the week, and 3 percent are in the care of an older sibling (not shown).

ALL CHILDREN UNDER AGE 13

According to these national data, 3.5 million children under age 13, or 7 percent of all children under age 13, regularly cared for themselves during a typical week in 1990. Of children aged 5-12, 3.4 million (12 percent) are in self-care. These figures are almost double the 1984 figure of 1.8 million children (six percent) aged 5-13 in self-care cited in Cain and Hofferth (1989). It should be noted that both figures include all instances of self-care reported by parents, no matter how brief. Only about 676,000 children, or 1.4 percent of all children under age 13, are in self-care as their primary child care arrangement. Although we have not yet examined the amount of time spent in child care, we expect that it is short. The December 1984 Current Population Survey showed that almost 9 out of 10 children in self-care after school were alone for 2 hours or less, and 2 out of 3 who were in self-care before school were alone for less than one hour (in Cain and Hofferth 1989).

Age of Child. About 71,000 preschool children and 3.4 million school-age children care for themselves at some time during a typical week. Although any number of preschool-age children in self-care is too many, the proportion of preschool-age children in self-care is small. The proportion of children in self-care rises from fewer than 1 percent of preschool-age children to 2 percent of 5- to 7-year-old children, to 11 percent of 8- to 10-year-old children, and to 32 percent of 11- to 12-year-old children (figure 5.25).

Age of Sibling. About 3 million children under age 13, or 6 percent, regularly spend some time in the care of a sibling. Only about 1.4 million, or 3 percent, are in sibling care as their primary arrangement. Unfortunately, for children other than the youngest child, we were unable to determine the age of the sibling.

Maternal Employment Status. As with the youngest child, a higher proportion of the children of employed mothers (9 percent) than nonemployed mothers (4 percent) are ever in self-care, with little difference according to whether the mother is employed full-time or part-time (10 percent versus 8 percent, respectively) (figure 5.26). Fortunately, the major difference in use of self-care is among older school-age children and not among preschoolers. For example, almost 40 percent of 11- to 12-year-old children of mothers employed full-time care for themselves, compared with 22 percent of children of mothers not employed outside the home. Still, it should be noted that despite the presumed availability of the mother, a substantial proportion of school-age children of nonemployed mothers care for themselves on a regular basis before, after school, or at night.

The trends are similar for sibling care (figure 5.27). Eight percent of the children of employed mothers and 4 percent of the children of nonemployed mothers are ever in the care of an older sibling during the week.

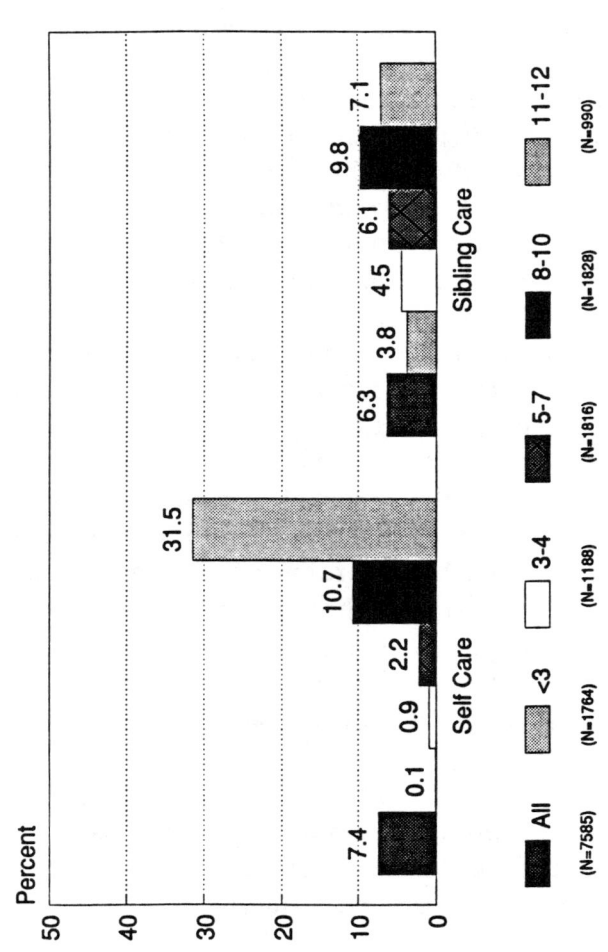

Figure 5.25
PERCENTAGE OF ALL CHILDREN EVER IN SELF CARE OR SIBLING CARE

Parental Perceptions of Care ■ 291

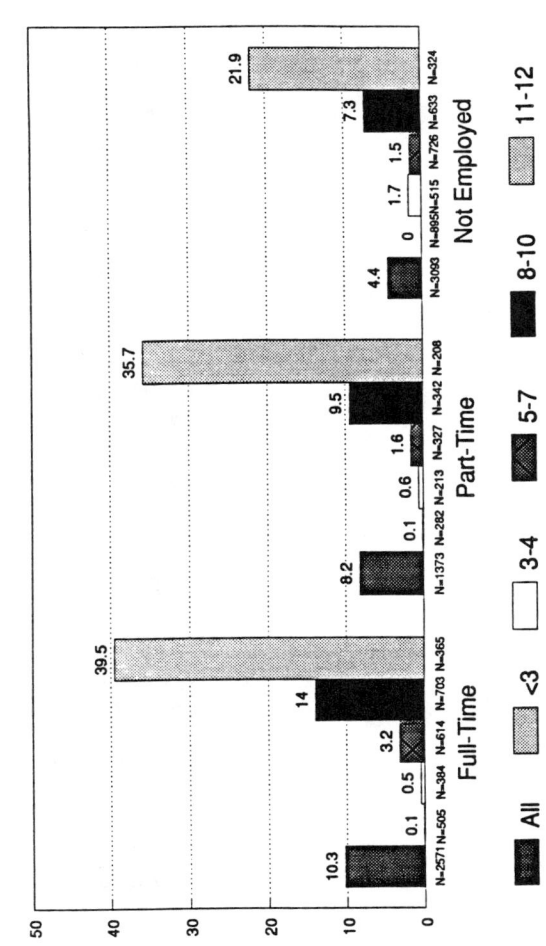

Figure 5.26
PERCENTAGE OF ALL CHILDREN EVER IN SELF CARE BY EMPLOYMENT STATUS OF MOTHER

Source: National Child Care Survey 1990

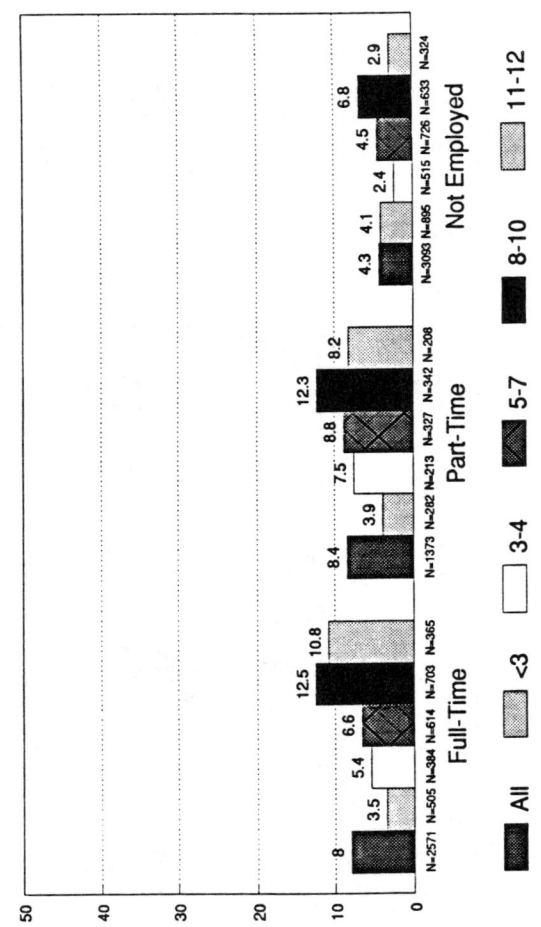

Figure 5.27
PERCENTAGE OF ALL CHILDREN EVER IN SIBLING CARE
BY EMPLOYMENT STATUS OF MOTHER

Source: National Child Care Survey 1990

Age First Left Child to Care for Self

In response to an NCCS survey question, parents reported first allowing their youngest child to care for himself/herself up to one-half hour a day at 9 on average. Table 5.2 shows the distribution of responses to this question among parents who use self-care for their youngest child. About one-third of children first cared for themselves before age 9; 10 percent were under 5 years of age. The bulk of parents started this practice when their children were 9 or 10; another third started after age 10.

The age at which parents reported first leaving their youngest child up to two hours at a time was 9.6 years on average. Examining the distribution in table 5.2, one sees that, compared with the age at which parents said they first left their youngest child up to one-half hour, fewer children were under age nine and more were nine or older when they were first left up to two hours.

The average age at which parents reported leaving a youngest child in self-care for two hours or more was 9.8, almost 10 years of age (figure 5.28). Again, fewer parents allowed very young children to care for themselves, and more waited until their youngest was 11 to 12 years of age.

A substantial number of parents refused to answer these questions. They were more sensitive as the length of time that the children are left to care for themselves increases. Almost one-third of the parents refused to answer the question about the age their youngest child was first left in self-care for two or more hours.

Finally, because not everyone has left a child in self-care, we asked nonusers at what age they would consider leaving their youngest child in self-care (figure 5.28). There was a substantial difference in responses between users and nonusers. The average age nonusers would start

294 ■ NATIONAL CHILD CARE SURVEY, 1990

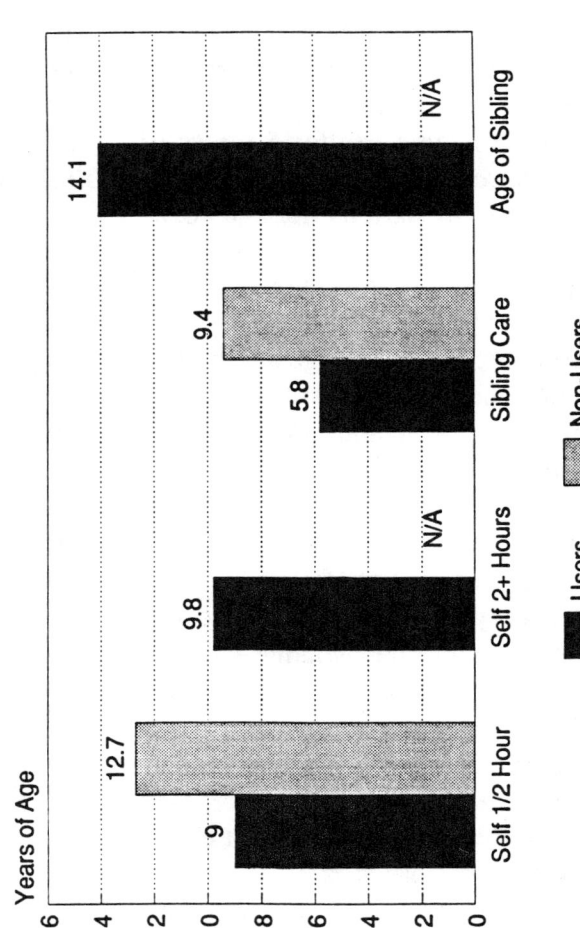

Figure 5.28
AVERAGE AGE FIRST LEFT/WOULD LEAVE YOUNGEST CHILD IN SELF OR SIBLING CARE

Source: National Child Care Survey 1990

Table 5.2 USE AND PERCEPTION OF SELF- AND SIBLING CARE (percentages)

	Self-Care		Sibling Care	
	User	Nonuser	User	Nonuser
			Age at Start of Sibling Care	
Age				
0-5	10.1	0.2	42.9	17.3
6-8	22.5	2.0	34.5	27.2
9-10	39.1	12.7	5.8	9.4
11-12	28.3	33.4	3.6	15.1
13+	--	51.7	--	16.4
Mean age	9.0	12.7	5.8	9.4
Dk., Ref.[a]	(22)	(239)	(23)	(66)
N	(22)	(3,716)	(402)	(1,872)
			Age of Sibling at Start of Care	
Age				
0-5	3.9	--	1.1	--
6-8	18.3	--	0.9	--
9-10	38.0	--	6.9	--
11-12	39.8	--	26.3	--
13+	--	--	64.9	--
Mean age	9.6	--	14.1	--
Dk., Ref.[a]	(31)	--	(21)	--
N	(174)	--	(406)	--

(continued)

Table 5.2 *(Continued)*

	Self-Care		Sibling Care	
	User	Nonuser	User	Nonuser
			Age First Left Child Two-Plus Hours:	
Age				
0-5	4.3	b	b	b
0-6	13.9	b	b	b
9-10	38.8	b	b	b
11-12	43.0	b	b	b
13+	--	b	b	b
Mean age	9.8	b	b	b
Dk., Ref.[a]	(45)	b	b	b
N	(133)	b	b	b
Presence of Neighbor?				
Yes	88.5	b	90.1	b
No	11.5	b	9.9	b
Dk., Ref.[a]	(2)	b	(7)	b
N	(245)	b	(427)	b
Reach You by Phone?				
Yes	98.5		97.4	
No	1.5		2.6	
Dk., Ref.[a]	(2)		(5)	
N	(245)		(429)	

	Self-Care		Sibling Care	
	User	Nonuser	User	Nonuser
Most Important Reason for Leaving Child in Self-/Sibling Care				
Child's maturity	44.4	61.4	3.1	9.5
Sibling maturity	--	--	74.8	70.2
Child's independence	7.0	1.2	1.0	0.7
Safety in home	7.6	7.7	5.5	3.0
Safety in neighborhood	6.0	6.2	0.3	1.7
Reliable neighbor	14.2	16.7	5.7	11.8
No alternative	6.1	0.4	6.9	1.2
Family finances	0.3	0.3	2.3	1.0
Can telephone parent	13.7	5.0	0.5	0.9
Other	0.8	1.1	--	--
Dk., Ref.[a]	(11)	(98)	(23)	(87)
N	(236)	(3,877)	(408)	(1,872)

Source: National Child Care Survey, 1990.

Note: Blank spaces in nonuser column indicate areas not queried in the NCCS.

a. DK., Ref. = Don't know or refused to answer.
b. Not applicable.

is 12.7 years, almost four years older than the age at which children currently in self-care started caring for themselves.

Factors Associated with Leaving Child in Self-Care

We asked both users and nonusers what was or would be the most important factor in allowing the youngest child to care for himself/herself. Although the single largest response for all parents was the child's maturity, the reasons given differed by whether the parent was currently using self-care or not (table 5.2). Two out of five user parents cited the child's maturity. Twenty-eight percent cited a reliable neighbor or the ability to reach the parent by telephone. Almost 14 percent cited safety in the home or neighborhood. Seven percent cited the independence of the child. Six percent said they had no alternative. Only a few cited family finances, but perhaps that was another way of saying they had no alternative. If we sum these two reasons then, almost 6.5 percent of those using self-care used it because they had no alternative.

Among parents not using self-care, three out of five said that the child's maturity was most important. The only other major categories were a reliable neighbor available, safety in home or neighborhood, and ability to reach the parent by telephone.

Finally, we asked users whether, in fact, there was a reliable neighbor available in case of emergency and whether the child could reach the parent by telephone. Nine out of 10 said yes to the first question, and almost all said yes to the latter question.

Age First Left Child in Care of Sibling

Parents reported that the average age at which they started sibling care was 5.8, almost six years of age (table 5.2, figure 5.28). A substantial proportion (almost 43 percent) of families started sibling care when the youngest child was under age five. The sibling who cared for the youngest was 14 years old, on average, at that time. Very few families (9 percent) reported a sibling under age 11 caring for a younger brother or sister. The median age fell between 11 and 12, but enough were older than 12 to raise the mean age of the sibling to 14.

Table 5.3 shows the age distribution of the youngest child by the age of the sibling who first began to care for the child. In two-thirds of the families, the youngest child was at least 5 years of age and the oldest at least 11 when sibling care began.

Finally, nonusers who had at least two children were asked the age at which they would consider first leaving a child in sibling care. The average age reported was 9.4, considerably older than the age (5.8) that users first reported leaving their youngest in sibling care (table 5.2).

Users and nonusers of sibling care were asked what was or would be the most important factor in deciding to allow an older sibling to care for a younger one (table 5.2). Three out of four user parents mentioned the maturity of the sibling. Also mentioned were a reliable neighbor and safety in the home. Nine percent mentioned either no alternative or family finances as the major factor, a figure slightly larger than the proportion of user families (6.5 percent) who said that self-care was their only option. Among nonusers of sibling care, 7 out of 10 mentioned the maturity of the sibling and 1 in 10 mentioned the maturity of the youngest

Table 5.3 AGE OF YOUNGEST CHILD AT START OF SIBLING CARE, BY AGE OF SIBLING AT THE TIME, PERCENTAGES

Age of Youngest Child	Age of Sibling at Start of Care							Sample Size
	<5	5–7	8–10	11–12	13–17	18+	Total	
<3 years	5.1	2.8	8.9	22.8	37.1	23.3	100.0	48
3–4 years	0.0	1.8	2.1	23.8	58.2	14.1	100.0	43
5–7 years	0.0	0.0	13.5	31.1	45.3	10.1	100.0	76
8–10 years	0.0	0.0	2.1	27.5	64.0	6.4	100.0	156
11–12 years	0.0	0.0	0.0	6.7	67.0	26.3	100.0	79
Total	1.0	0.8	7.0	26.3	51.7	13.1	100.0	402

Source: National Child Care Survey, 1990

child. The only other major category mentioned was the availability of a reliable neighbor (12 percent).

Users were asked whether a neighbor was available and if the child could reach the parent by telephone. Nine out of 10 users said that a reliable neighbor was available in an emergency and that the child could reach the parent by phone.

SELF-CARE AND SIBLING CARE: A SUMMARY

Self-care is more widely used in 1990 than has been reported in earlier national surveys. In 1990, 3.5 million children under age 13 (7 percent) were reported to care for themselves on a regular basis during the week, compared with 1.8 million in December 1984 (Cain and Hofferth 1989). Because of the difficulty of and sensitivity involved in assessing the extent to which children are in self-care, we cannot evaluate whether there has been a real increase in self-care over the past five years or whether differences in data collection methods have led to these large discrepancies in self-care estimates. We can make several generalizations, however. First, only a small proportion of these children (676,000) are in self-care as a primary child care arrangement; rather, self-care is a minor arrangement spanning time between other forms of care. Second, the amount of time in self-care is short. Previous research indicates that few children are in self-care for more than two hours at a time.

Almost 8 percent of youngest children are regularly in the care of an older sibling during a typical week, but only about 2-3 percent are in the care of a sibling under age 14. About 6 percent of all children are in sibling care, age of sibling unknown, but only 3 percent are in sibling care as the primary arrangement.

SUMMARY AND CONCLUSIONS

Overall, it is striking that the information provided by parents on the price of care (even for types they do not use) and on the characteristics of their arrangements closely matches national estimates on fees that providers charge, on actual expenditures by users, and on the average characteristics reported by providers. Of course, this does not mean that a single parent's information exactly matches that which her or his provider would give; on average, however, it corresponds. This suggests that many parents are fairly well-informed consumers of child care.

Second, it is important to note that parents' decisions appear consistent from a rational decision-making perspective; that is, parents appear to select care which is closer to home, which costs less, and which is equal in quality to the types they rejected.

Third, parents perceive care by a relative or in-home provider to be least available to them, and care by a center or family day-care provider to be most available, regardless of the type of care they actually choose.

Finally, it is clear that although a great many families use self-care and sibling care for their children, in the large majority of families these constitute only incidental sources of care.

Notes, chapter 5

1. Although we are interested in whether, on average, parents' reports match those of providers, parents' perceptions of a child care provider's characteristics such as price, location, and availability may be more important in parents' decision making than the accuracy of this information.

2. Statistics cited from tables or figures in this chapter are typically rounded off to the nearest whole number.

Chapter

6

PREVIOUS USE OF CHILD CARE ARRANGEMENTS

Child development studies have shown that stability of care is an important factor in healthy child development, both in terms of establishing relationships and in academic success (Howes et al. 1988; Whitebook et al. 1989). There are two different aspects of stability: stability within arrangements and stability across arrangements. This report focuses on the latter. To investigate this issue, the National Child Care Survey, 1990 (NCCS), collected information on the length of care arrangements used during the past year. This information includes arrangements that were ongoing at the time of the survey, as well as those that ended during the 12 months prior to data collection.

Separate information was collected for preschool and school-age children. Parents whose youngest child was either in kindergarten or not yet enrolled in school were asked a series of questions regarding the length of their current care arrangements as well as the number, type, and length of any previous arrangements used during the past 12 months. Respondents were also asked to recall details about the first time their youngest child was left in a regular care arrangement. Finally, parents with a youngest child of school age were asked a series of questions on care arrangements for the summer months.

The first two sections of this chapter describe, respectively, the types of changes in child care over the year prior to the survey and the duration of these arrangements. The third section looks at the first time regular nonparental care was used, and the fourth section examines the summer care arrangements for those children enrolled in school. The last section summarizes the findings.

CHANGES IN CHILD CARE ARRANGEMENTS IN YEAR PREVIOUS FOR PRESCHOOL AGE CHILDREN

Approximately 60 percent of NCCS respondents had a youngest child who was either in kindergarten or who had not yet started school. To better understand any changes in child care arrangements in the 12 months prior to the survey (November 1988-April 1989, depending upon the exact date of the interview), the youngest child in each family was assigned to one of the following five categories:

Same parental arrangement, which includes children who did not have any regular nonparental arrangements over the year previous;

Same nonparental arrangement, which includes children who had been in the same primary arrangement for the year previous;

Started nonparental arrangement, which includes all children who started an arrangement during the year previous;

Ended nonparental arrangement, for children who had been in a regular care arrangement during the year previous but are now cared for only by their parents; and

Switched nonparental arrangement, which includes children who had changed nonparental arrangements during the year previous.

As figure 6.1 shows, 27 percent of children had no regular arrangements during the 12 months previous, and another 29 percent were in the same nonparental care situation. Thirty percent of children began a nonparental care arrangement during the year, whereas only 3 percent of children left regular nonparental care to be cared for solely by their parents. Eleven percent of children switched from one nonparental care arrangement to another.

Maternal Employment Status. The likelihood of changing child care arrangements varies with the employment status of the mother. In families where the mother is employed, a much higher proportion of children either started a nonparental arrangement or were in the same nonparental arrangement for the 12 months previous. Thirty-three percent of children with an employed mother, compared with 25 percent of children of nonemployed mothers, started a nonparental arrangement during the year previous (figure 6.1). Likewise, 38 percent of children with an employed mother but only 18 percent of children with a nonemployed mother, were in the same nonparental arrangement. Not surprisingly, a much larger proportion of chil-

308 ■ NATIONAL CHILD CARE SURVEY, 1990

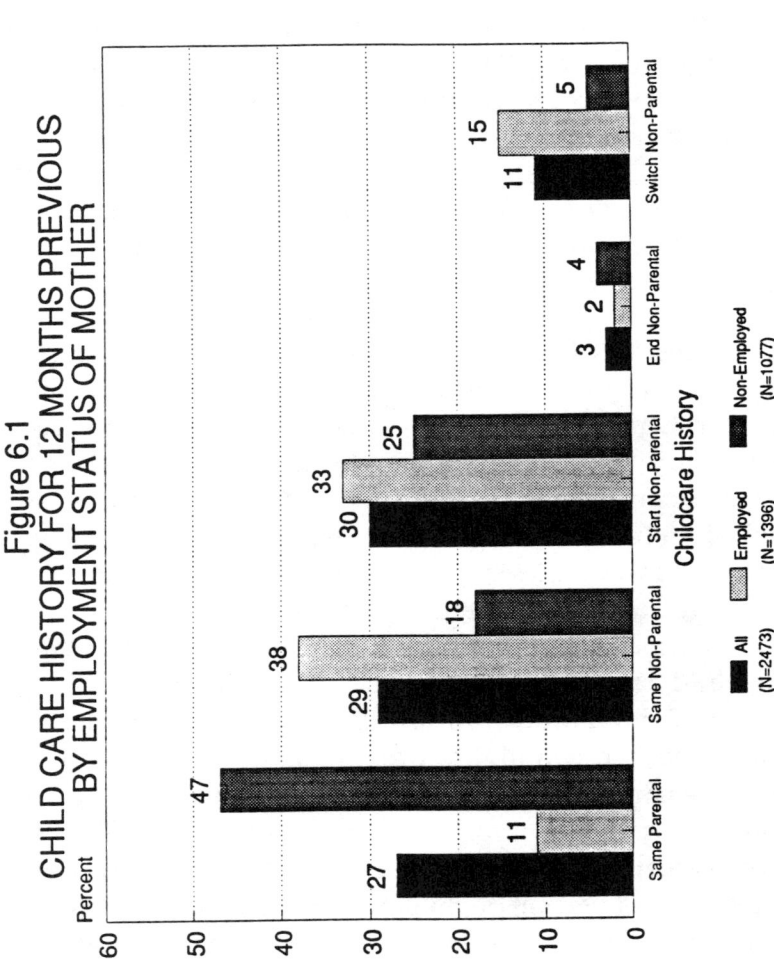

dren whose mothers are not employed outside the home had the same parental arrangement (no regular arrangements)--47 percent--compared to 11 percent of children with employed mothers.

Age of Youngest Child. The likelihood of changing care arrangements also varies with the age of the youngest child. As table 6.1 shows, the proportion of children in the same parental care declines from 45 percent for children under one year of age to 20 percent for 3- to 4-year-old children and to 8 percent for children ages 5 to 6 years. The proportion of children in the same nonparental care situation increases with age from 1 percent of children under 1 year (probably due to the use of a provider that is already providing care for an older sibling) to 38 percent of 1- to 2-year-olds and 41 percent of 3- to 4-year-old children. Thirty percent of 5- to 6-year-olds are with the same nonparental caregiver. In all likelihood this proportion is small because these children recently entered kindergarten. The proportion of children starting care decreases with age from 48 percent of those under one year to 24 percent of 3- to 4-year-old children. For the 5- and 6-year-old children we see an increase in the proportion starting a nonparental care arrangement, also due in large part to enrolling in kindergarten.

Maternal Employment Status and Age of Youngest Child. There are also large differences in patterns of childcare over the past year by age and employment status of the mother (table 6.1). Seventy percent of children under one year of age with an employed mother started nonparental care as compared to 31 percent of children whose mother is not employed outside of the home. Likewise we see a higher proportion of children under one year of age with nonemployed mothers having the same nonparental care--64 percent as compared to 22 percent of children with

Table 6.1 CHILD CARE HISTORY BY AGE OF YOUNGEST CHILD AND FAMILY INCOME (PERCENTAGE)

	Same Parental	Same Non-parental	Start Non-parental	End Non-parental	Switch Non-parental	Total %	Sample Size
All	27	29	30	3	11	100	2,463
<1 year	45	1	48	2	3	100	538
1–2 years	29	38	17	5	11	100	878
3–4 years	20	41	24	3	13	100	674
5–6 years	8	30	42	1	19	100	372
Employed							
<1 year	22	1	70	2	5	100	236
1–2 years	12	48	20	4	16	100	490
3–4 years	9	51	23	2	16	100	427
5–6 years	3	31	43	1	22	100	235
							1,389

Non-emp.							
<1 year	64	1	31	3	2	100	302
1–2 years	51	25	13	7	4	100	388
3–4 years	38	23	27	4	7	100	247
5–6 years	15	26	42	1	15	100	137
							1,075
Family Income							
Under 15,000	29	28	33	4	7	100	468
15,000–24,999	32	27	24	4	12	100	399
25,000–34,999	30	26	31	2	10	100	399
35,000–49,999	24	33	27	5	12	100	495
50,000+	15	34	33	2	15	100	509
							2,463

Source: National Child Care Survey 1990

employed mothers. It is interesting that between the ages of 3 and 4 years an almost identical proportion of children of employed and nonemployed mothers (23 and 27 respectively) started a nonparental care arrangement. For children who switched nonparental care arrangements a larger proportion in all age categories had employed mothers. There were too few children that ended nonparental care arrangements to compare by employment status of the mother and age of youngest child.

Family Income. The probability of changing care arrangements also varies with family income. Families with annual incomes above $50,000 were less likely to have the same parental arrangements over the year previous than were families in the lowest income group (15 percent versus 30 percent, respectively) (table 6.1) The data also show a greater proportion of children from families with higher incomes remaining in the same nonparental care arrangements; 33 percent of families with annual incomes of $35,000 or more stay with the same provider, compared to 27 percent of families with incomes under $35,000. The proportion of children switching nonparental care arrangements also varies directly with income; only 7 percent of children from families with incomes below $15,000 changed nonparental arrangements, compared to 15 percent of children from families with incomes above $50,000.

Type of Care and Race. There are no significant differences in changes in care arrangements by current type of care being used or by race.

EPISODES OF CHILD CARE ARRANGEMENTS FOR PRESCHOOL-AGE CHILDREN

To get the most complete picture of the length of child care arrangements, all episodes of nonmaternal child care used for the youngest child during the 12 months prior to the survey were considered. The National Child Care Survey collected information on up to four ongoing arrangements, as well as up to four other arrangements ending during the year previous. There were so few respondents with more than two previous arrangements that the third and fourth previous arrangements were omitted from this analysis. Hence, the dataset used for this analysis contains up to six possible spells, or episodes, of child care (four current or ongoing arrangements and two previous arrangements) for the youngest child in each family. Table 6.2 details the number of spells in each category.

Table 6.2 DISTRIBUTION OF CHILD CARE SPELLS

Arrangement	Percent	Sample Size
First current	45.2	1,761
Second current	29.3	1,142
Third current	11.8	460
Fourth current	3.3	127
First previous	8.9	345
Second previous	1.5	57
Total	100.0	3,895

Source: National Child Care Survey 1990

The children for whom we have information regarding length of arrangements are those who have not yet started first grade; kindergartners are included in this sample. For those children who started kindergarten within the 12 months prior to the survey date (5- and 6-year-olds), we would expect to see current arrangements lasting less than one year. In fact, we would expect to see arrangements that are between 3 and 8 months in length, as the interviews were conducted between November 1989 and April 1990 and the school year traditionally begins in September.

LENGTH OF CURRENT AND PREVIOUS ARRANGEMENTS

All Families

All Current Arrangements. The majority of arrangements in the NCCS were still ongoing at the time of the interview. Consequently, we could not calculate the true duration for these arrangements beyond their status at the time of the interview. In all likelihood the arrangements were longer than what we observed, but how much longer is unknown. The distribution of all current arrangements is shown in figure 6.2. When all current arrangements are pooled, the median length of an arrangement is 12 months; that is, half lasted less than 12 months and half lasted more than 12 months.

Primary Current Arrangement. The median length of children's primary current arrangement (the one in which they spend the most time) is 10 months, slightly shorter that the median length of all current arrangements (12 months) (figure 6.2).

All Previous Arrangements. The median length of previous arrangements is 8 months, only slightly less than the

Previous Use of Child Care Arrangements   ■ 315

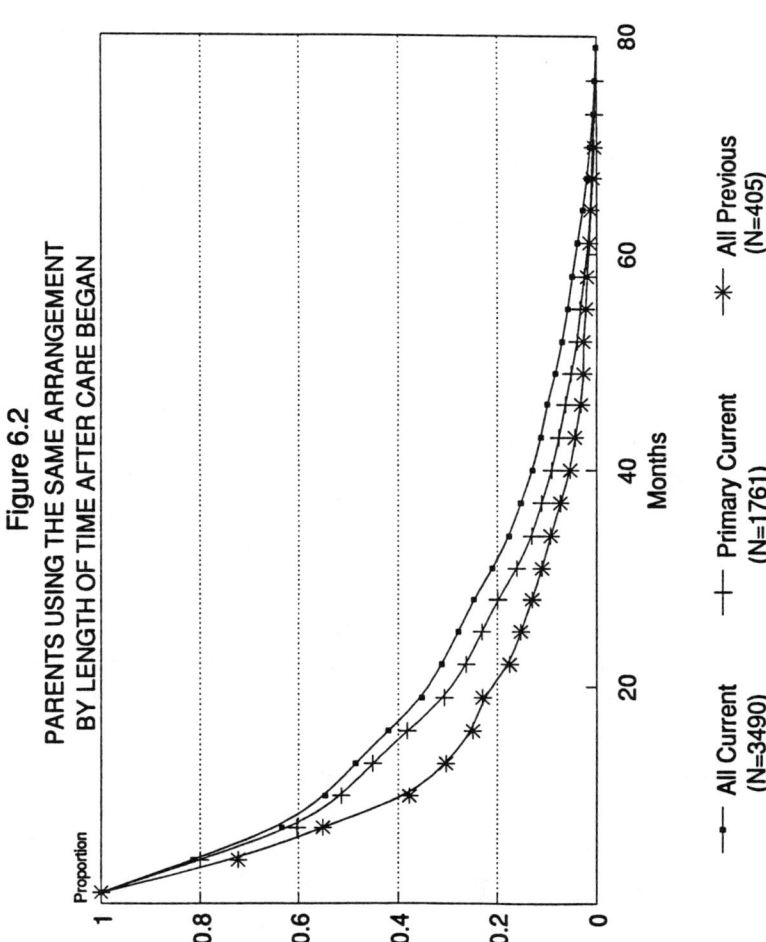

Figure 6.2
PARENTS USING THE SAME ARRANGEMENT
BY LENGTH OF TIME AFTER CARE BEGAN

Source: National Child Care Survey 1990

duration of the current primary arrangement (10 months), but 4 months less than that of all current arrangements (12 months) (figure 6.2). Unlike the information for current arrangements, the median for previous arrangements is known with certainty, because the arrangement had ended by the time of the survey. Given that current arrangements are likely to continue, the difference between current and previous arrangements will be larger than observed. Thus, looking only at completed spells underestimates the length of child care arrangements.

AGE OF CHILD

As one might expect, an important source of variation in length of arrangements is the age of the child. The older the child, the longer the potential length of time the arrangement may have lasted. In this section we discuss the length of arrangements by age of child, and in succeeding sections the age of child is included to control for these differences in potential length of arrangement.

All Current Arrangements. Figure 6.3 shows the median duration of current and previous arrangements by the age of the child. The data show that the median length of the arrangement increases with the age of the child, until the transition into kindergarten. As expected, children 3-4 years old have spent the longest time in their current arrangements; 19 months is the median length of their arrangement, compared with 10 months for 0- to 2-year olds and 8 months for 5 year olds.

Primary Current Arrangement. The length of time children have spent in their primary current arrangement is only slightly shorter than the time they have spent in all arrangements. The median time children ages 0-2 have

Previous Use of Child Care Arrangements 317

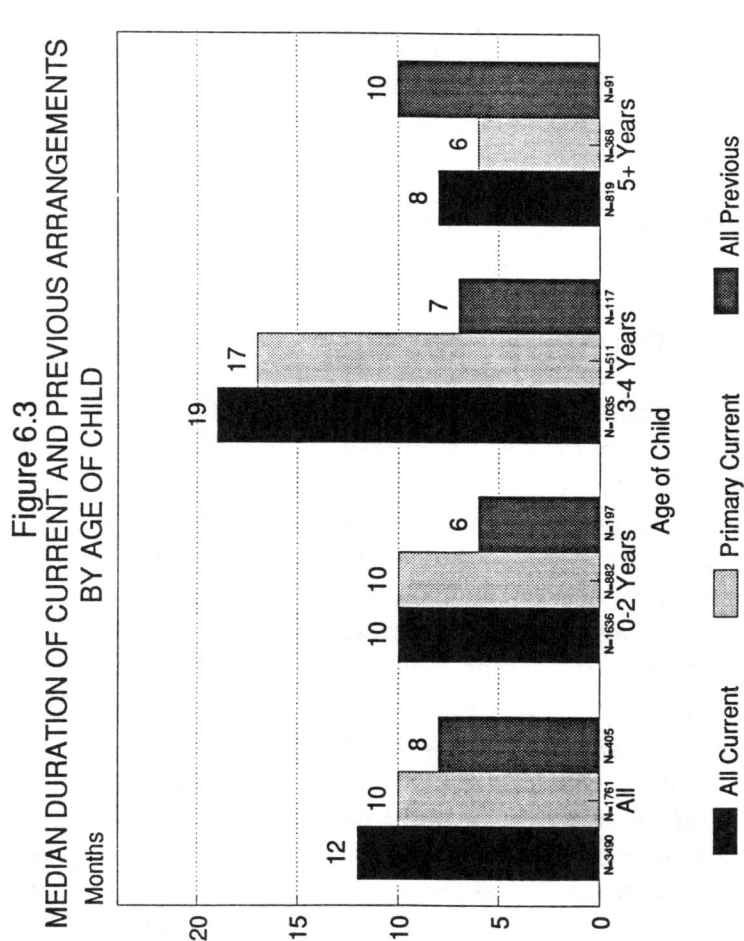

spent is 10 months, while children 3-4 have spent 17 months, and children 5-6 have spent 6 months in their primary arrangement.

All Previous Arrangements. Previous arrangements are, as discussed earlier, shorter than current arrangements, except for children ages 5-6. For this group, previous arrangements lasted longer (10 months) than the previous arrangements of younger children (6 to 7 months).

MATERNAL EMPLOYMENT STATUS AND AGE OF CHILD

Maternal employment status appears to be related to the length of the care arrangement, with arrangements for children of employed mothers lasting longer than those for children of nonemployed mothers (figure 6.4). This makes sense in light of earlier findings indicating that a higher percent of children of employed mothers start nonparental care at earlier ages; if they start care earlier in life the potential duration of the arrangement is longer. For this analysis, we evaluated only current arrangements, since the employment status of the mother may have been different at the time of previous child care arrangements.

All Current Arrangements. The median length of all current child care arrangements is 13 months for children with employed mothers and 9 months for children with nonemployed mothers (figure 6.4). This difference between children with employed and nonemployed mothers holds across the different age groups of children; however, it is largest for 3- to 4-year-old children. The median length of time 3- to 4-year-old children have spent in care at the time of the survey is 21.5 months if they have an employed mother and 14 months if their mother is not employed (figure 6.4).

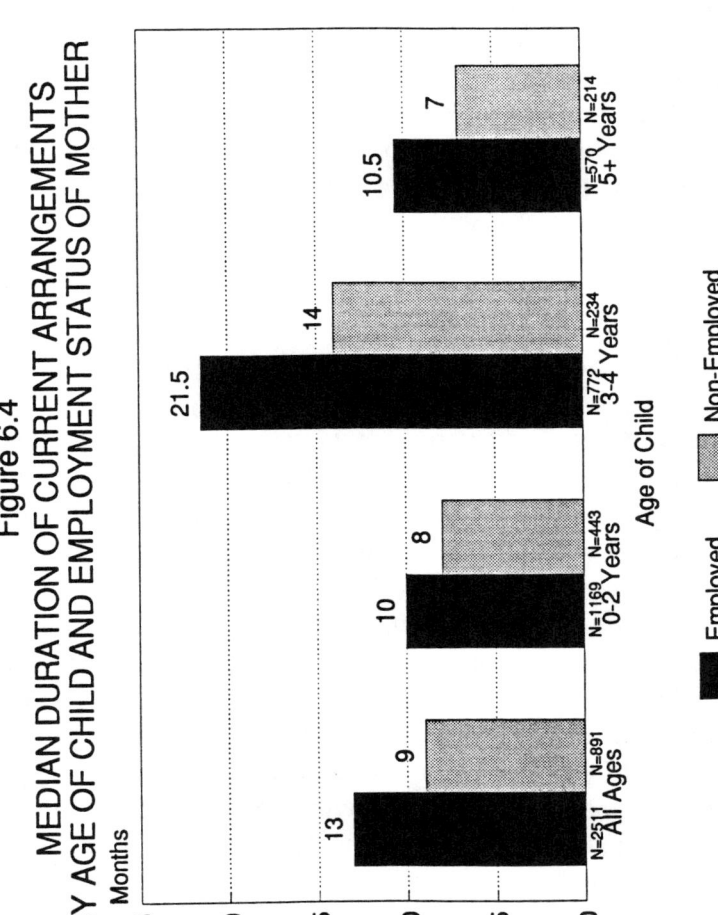

Figure 6.4
MEDIAN DURATION OF CURRENT ARRANGEMENTS BY AGE OF CHILD AND EMPLOYMENT STATUS OF MOTHER

Source: National Child Care Survey 1990

Primary Current Arrangements. The median length of the primary current child care arrangement is 12 months for children with employed and 7 months for children with nonemployed mothers. The same pattern of length of arrangement by maternal employment and age of child holds for primary as for all current arrangements. In particular, the median duration of arrangements for the 3- to 4-year-old children of employed mothers is 19 months whereas it is only 8 months for those of nonemployed mothers (not shown). Length of arrangement differences between the children of employed and nonemployed mothers are very small at ages 0-2 and 5-6.

FAMILY INCOME AND AGE OF THE CHILD

The duration of care arrangements varies with the income of the family (figure 6.5). Here we focus only on current arrangements; differences between the pattern of all current, primary current, and previous arrangements resemble that of the sample as a whole.

All Current Arrangements. The median length of all current arrangements generally increases as income levels rise. Some of this difference is likely to be due to the employment of the mother. For families with incomes below $15,000 per year, the median length of all arrangements is 8 months; for families with incomes of $50,000 or more, the median length is 14 months. As family income rises, so does the duration of arrangements, except for middle income families ($25,000 to $34,999), whose arrangements are almost as short as those of low-income families. We expect low-income families to have shorter arrangements both because fewer mothers in these families are employed and because their financial situation may

Previous Use of Child Care Arrangements 321

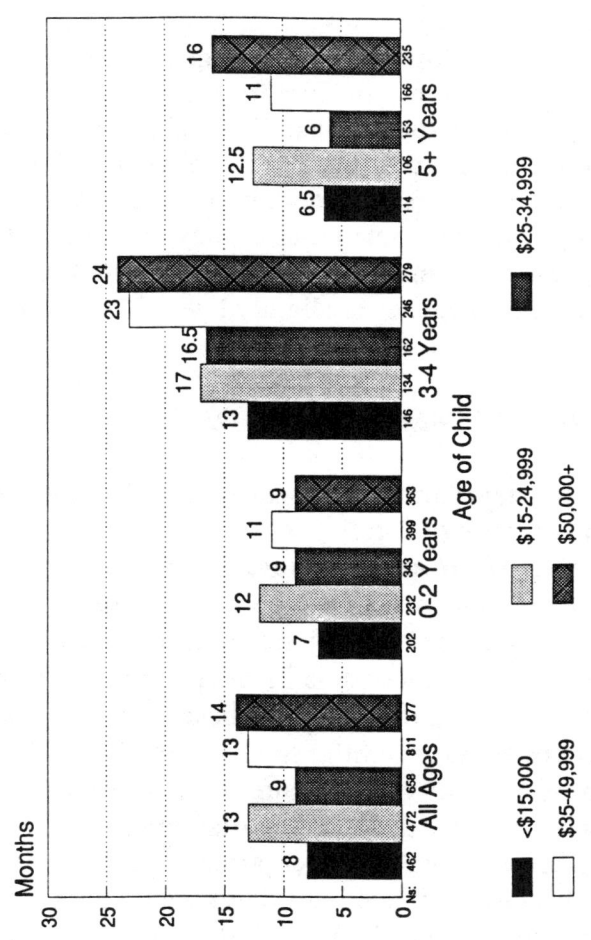

limit their ability to maintain the same arrangement. The shorter arrangements of middle income children is unexpected. Since age of youngest is so important, we next examined income differences within age groups.

There is no trend in length of arrangements by income level among families with a youngest child under age 3 (figure 6.5). Among children ages 3-4, the arrangement lengthens as family income increases, which is consistent with previous expectations. The odd pattern among middle income families described above appears primarily among children ages 5-6. The decline in length of arrangements among middle income families may be due to their moving children into kindergarten at a somewhat later age than either slightly higher or slightly lower income families.

TYPE OF CARE AND AGE OF CHILD

Arrangements are also expected to differ in length according to the type of care.

All Current Arrangements. The duration of current arrangements varies by type of care used. As expected, care by a parent or a relative are the longest lasting forms of care; the median length is 21 months for the former and 15 months for the latter. Center-based, in-home, and family day care all have similar median lengths (8, 10.5, and 10 months, respectively) (figure 6.6). The median length of lessons is 7 months. The median length of time children had been enrolled in kindergarten at the time of the survey was 4 months. Since interviews were conducted between November 1989 and April 1990 of the following year, this appears reasonable.

However, length of each type of arrangement varies by age of child (figure 6.7). In part this is because there is

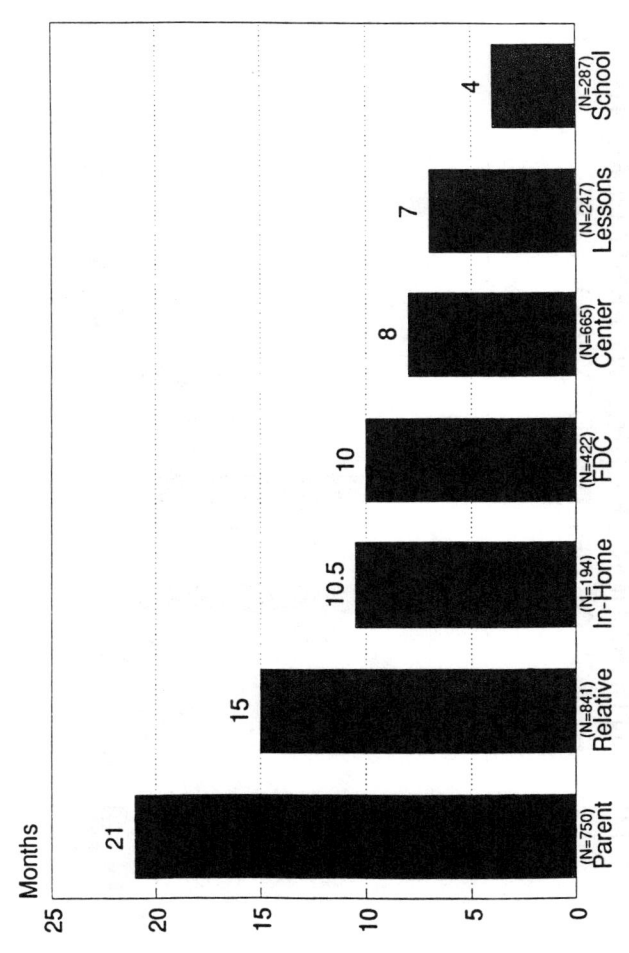

Figure 6.6
MEDIAN DURATION OF CURRENT ARRANGEMENT BY TYPE OF CARE

Source: National Child Care Survey 1990

324 ■ NATIONAL CHILD CARE SURVEY, 1990

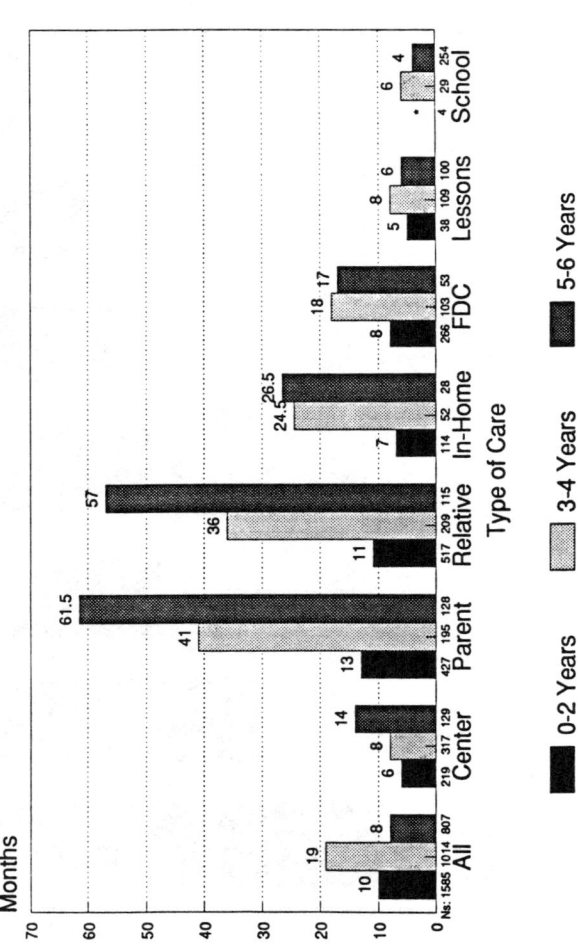

simply more time that could have been spent with a provider, and this is why time spent in the care of a parent or a relative increases dramatically with age. Time spent with an in-home provider also increases sharply with the age of the child, suggesting that it too is a very stable form of care. Time spent in a center-based program or in family day care increases, but not as dramatically as in-home provider care. The median length of time spent in center-based care is less than time spent in family day care, at all ages, particularly for the 3- to 4-year-olds. This simply reflects the fact that many centers do not care for children under the age of two (Kisker et al. 1991). If most children do not start center care until at least two years of age, the amount of time they could spend there is limited. Time spent in lessons is short for all age groups.

All Previous Arrangements. Although previous arrangements tend to be shorter than current arrangements, there is an important exception. For children 5-6 years old the most common type of previous arrangement is center-based care. The length of these previous center-based arrangements is longer than any other previous type of care arrangement (figure 6.8).

Types of Changes

For respondents who indicated changing from one nonparental care arrangement to another nonparental care arrangement, the majority (56 percent) changed to center-based care (figure 6.9). Another 29 percent changed to care by an in-home or family provider, and 15 percent changed to care by a relative.

Of those who changed to a center-based program, 41 percent left a different center, 38 percent had been using an

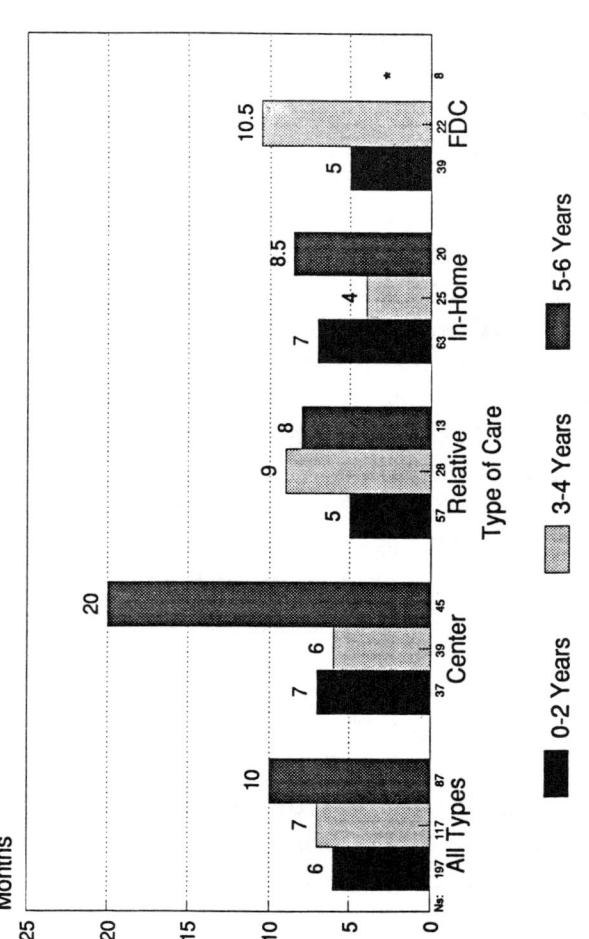

Figure 6.8
MEDIAN DURATION OF PREVIOUS ARRANGEMENTS BY AGE OF CHILD AND TYPE OF CARE

* N <10.
Source: National Child Care Survey 1990

Previous Use of Child Care Arrangements

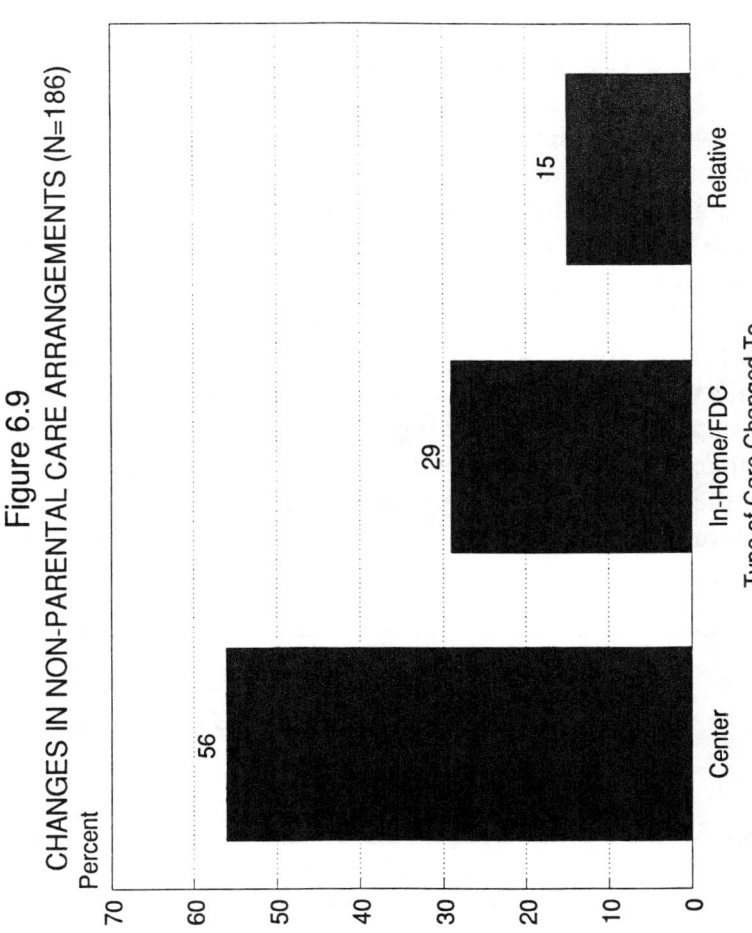

Figure 6.9
CHANGES IN NON-PARENTAL CARE ARRANGEMENTS (N=186)

Source: National Child Care Survey 1990

in-home or family provider, and 23 percent left the care of a relative (not shown). The number of respondents switching between other types of care was too small for further subgroup analysis.

Reason for Ending Previous Arrangements

Data were obtained on why NCCS respondents switched from one nonparental care arrangement to another nonparental care arrangement. Respondents indicated that the main reason the first previous arrangement ended was because it was no longer available or affordable (42 percent) (figure 6.10). The next most common response was that the respondent changed jobs or decided to stay home with the child (21 percent). Seventeen percent indicated that school closing for the summer caused the arrangement to end. A total of 7 percent indicated either that the child was not happy or that he/she was too old for the arrangement. Finally, 13 percent had some other reason for this change.

FIRST USE OF NONPARENTAL CARE FOR PRESCHOOL-AGE CHILDREN

Respondents with a youngest child who had not yet started first grade were asked to recall the age of that child when he or she was first left in regular nonparental care. This question was asked of all respondents with children not yet in first grade, regardless of the type of care currently used.

Previous Use of Child Care Arrangements ■ 329

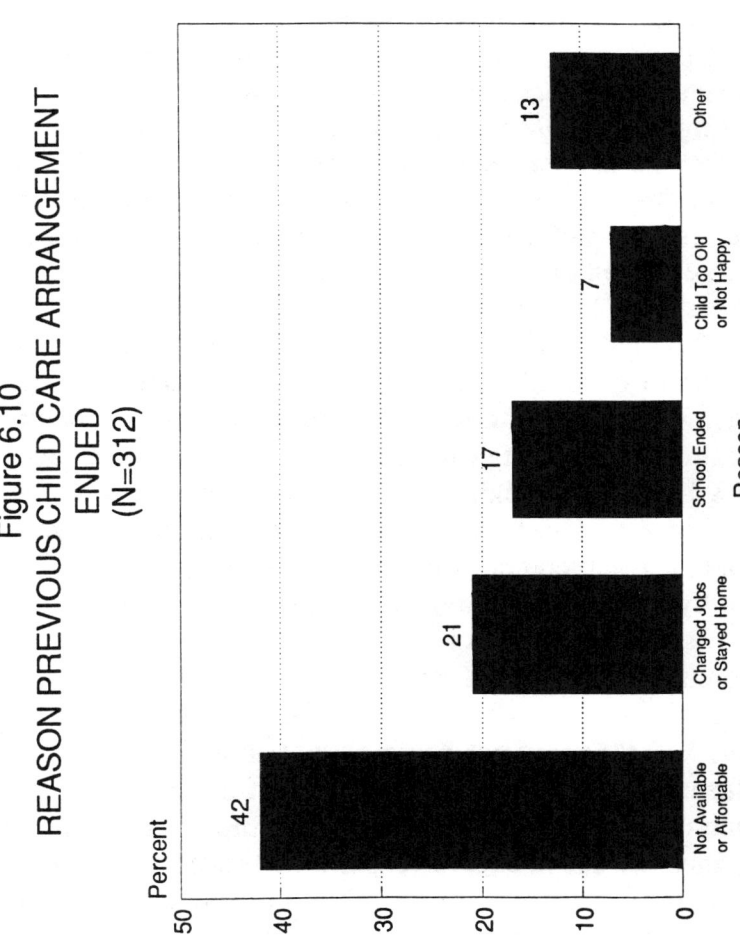

Figure 6.10
REASON PREVIOUS CHILD CARE ARRANGEMENT ENDED
(N=312)

Source: National Child Care Survey 1990

Approximately 60 percent of respondents indicated that their children were regularly left in nonparental care prior to the start of kindergarten (not shown). As seen in figure 6.11, the vast majority of those children (87 percent) were in a child care arrangement by the time they were two years old. Another 11 percent began care between their third and fourth birthdays. Thus, by the age of four, 98 percent of these children had started a nonparental care arrangement.

Maternal Employment Status. As expected, the age when children first used nonparental care varies with the current employment status of the mother. Among those families who had used nonparental care for the youngest child, children of employed mothers started nonparental care earlier in life; 70 percent of children with an employed mother started care during the first year of life, compared to 55 percent of children of nonemployed mothers (figure 6.12). Children of nonemployed mothers had a greater probability of entering care from ages one to two. By age two, 90 percent of children with an employed mother, compared to 80 percent of children with a nonemployed mother, had started nonparental care. Differences in enrollment by maternal employment status had disappeared by age 5, since there was a big increase in the enrollment of children of nonemployed mothers at ages three to four.

Family Income. Children from families with incomes above $50,000 per year begin care at an earlier age than children from families with incomes of $50,000 or less. Figure 6.13 shows that 74 percent of children from families with incomes above $50,000 experienced regular nonparental care during the first year of life, compared to 66 percent of children from middle-income families ($15,000 to $49,999) and 57 percent of children from low-income families.

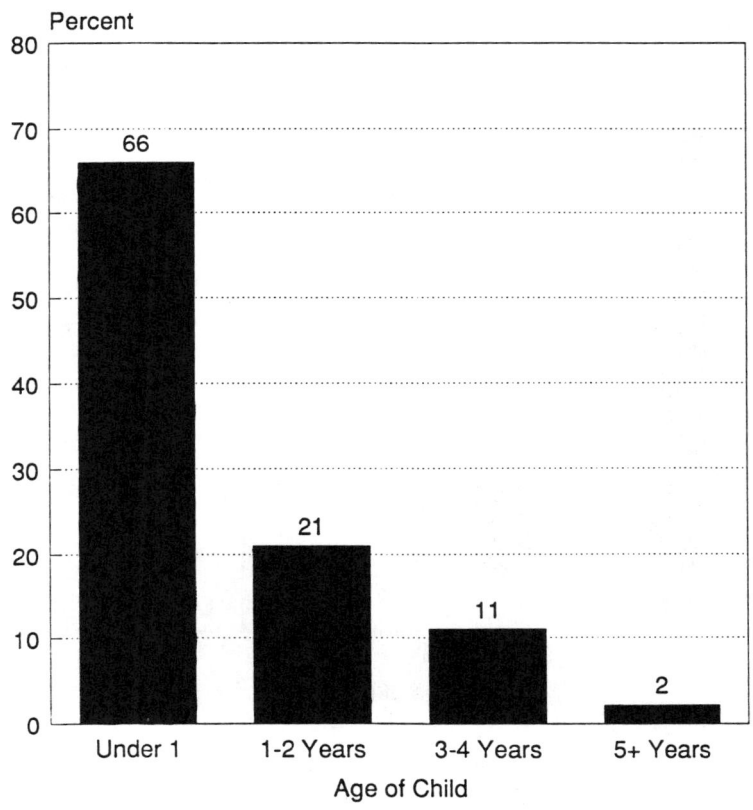

Figure 6.11
AGE OF FIRST NON-PARENTAL CARE
(N=1798)

Source: National Child Care Survey 1990

Figure 6.12
AGE OF FIRST NON-PARENTAL CARE
BY EMPLOYMENT STATUS OF MOTHER

Source: National Child Care Survey 1990

Figure 6.13
AGE OF FIRST NON-PARENTAL CARE BY INCOME

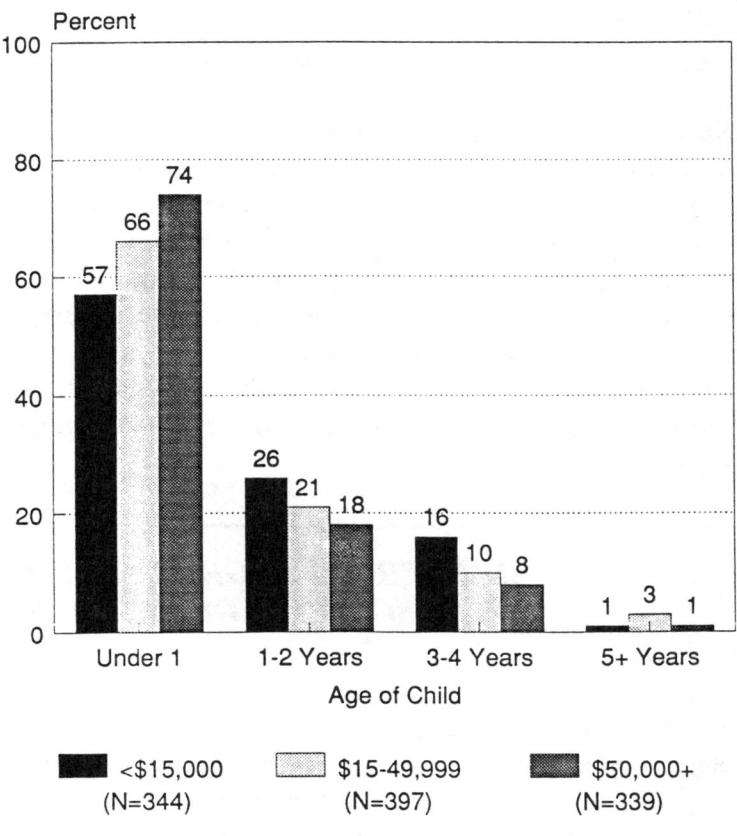

Source: National Child Care Survey 1990

Hours Spent In First Nonparental Care Arrangement

NCCS respondents were also asked to recall the number of hours per week their youngest child spent in his or her first arrangement. Figure 6.14 illustrates that 32 percent of children spent less than 10 hours per week in their first regular arrangement. Another 11 percent of children spent between 10 and 19 hours per week with their first care provider, 18 percent were in care for 20-34 hours per week, and 39 percent spent more than 35 hours per week in nonparental care.

Maternal Employment Status. The number of hours spent in the first regular care arrangement varied with the employment status of the mother. As shown in figure 6.15, the majority of children (60 percent) with nonemployed mothers spent less than 10 hours per week in care, whereas almost half of the children of employed mothers were in care for 35 or more hours per week.

Family Income. The number of hours spent in the first nonparental care arrangement did not vary with family income.

SUMMER ARRANGEMENTS FOR SCHOOL-AGE CHILDREN

If the youngest child was enrolled in school (first grade or higher), respondents were read a list of types of care available during the summer and asked to indicate all that were used for the youngest child. Up to four responses were coded. This section details the number and type of arrangements used for school-age children. However, because the

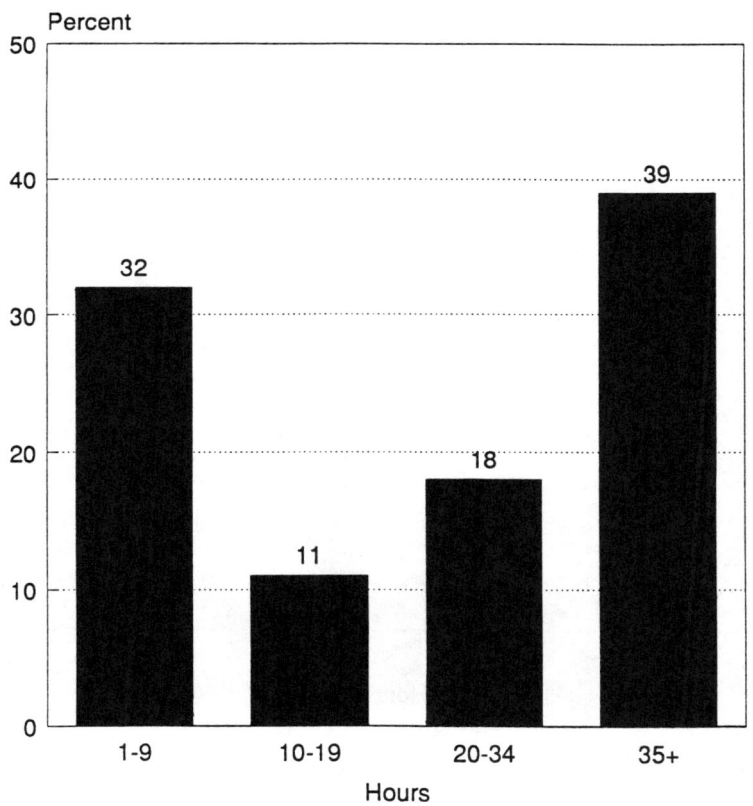

Figure 6.14
HOURS SPENT IN FIRST CARE ARRANGEMENT
(N=1692)

Source: National Child Care Survey 1990

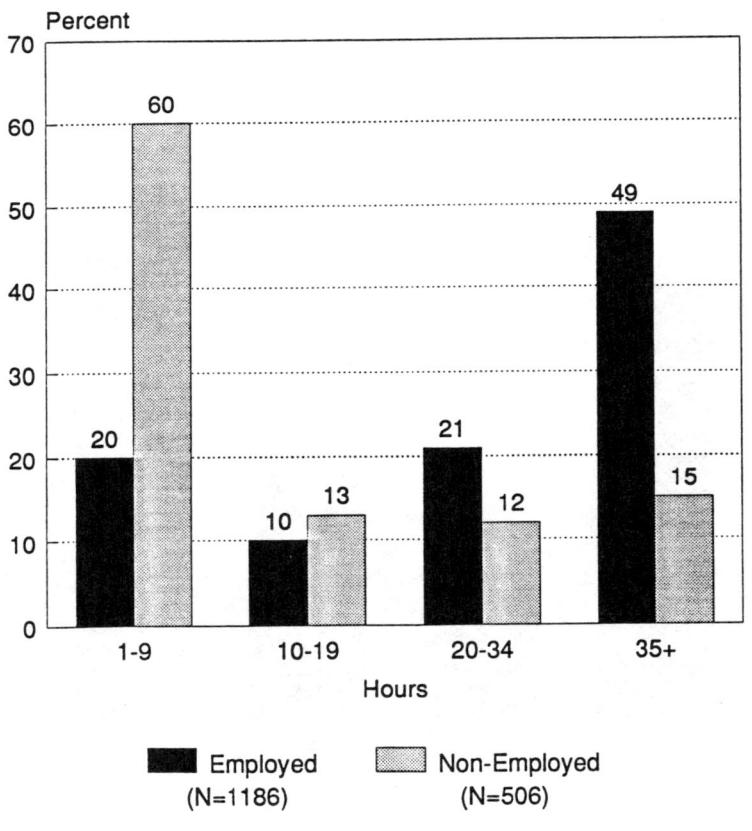

Figure 6.15
HOURS SPENT IN FIRST CARE ARRANGEMENT
BY EMPLOYMENT STATUS OF MOTHER

Source: National Child Care Survey 1990

number of hours per week that each type of care was used is not known, we could not determine which arrangement was used for the greatest amount of time.

Of those interviewed, 28 percent indicated that they had no regular arrangements for their youngest child last summer. Of those who said they used at least one type of care, the most common type was summer camp, at 25 percent. Another 23 percent indicated using a community recreation program. After camps and recreation programs the next most common response was other relatives, at 17 percent. Figure 6.16 illustrates these findings and shows the full range of responses to this question.

Of the 72 percent of respondents who indicated using at least one type of care for the previous summer, only 41 percent indicated using a second type of care. The most common second type of care was by another relative (26 percent), followed by community recreation programs (18 percent), siblings (12 percent), and friends and neighbors (10 percent) (see figure 6.17).

Only 18 percent of respondents indicated a third arrangement. Again, the most common type of third arrangement was by another relative (28 percent). Care by a friend or neighbor was the next most frequently used type of care (18 percent), followed by self-care (10 percent) and sibling care (10 percent) (see figure 6.18 for the full distribution of responses to this question).

Use of a fourth type of care was indicated by only 6.5 percent of respondents. For those indicating a fourth type of care, both self-care and care by a parent at another home were mentioned by 19 percent of respondents. The next most commonly used type was by a friend or neighbor (18 percent), followed by relative care (16 percent) (see figure 6.19 for the full distribution of responses to this question).

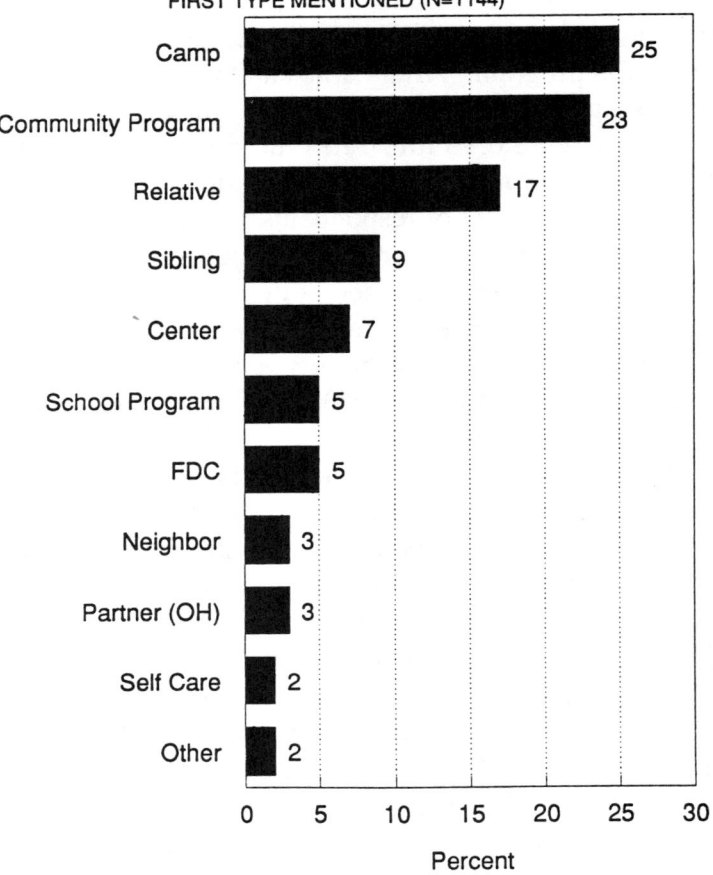

Figure 6.16
SUMMER ARRANGEMENTS FOR SCHOOL AGE CHILDREN:
RESPONDENTS WITH ONE OR MORE TYPE OF ARRANGEMENTS
FIRST TYPE MENTIONED (N=1144)

Source: National Child Care Survey 1990

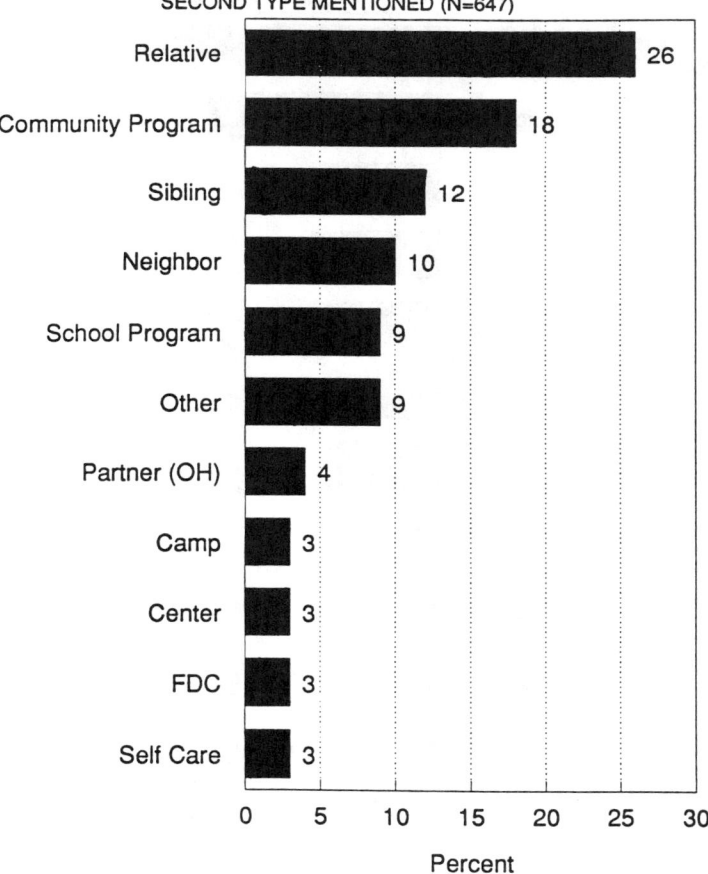

Figure 6.17
SUMMER ARRANGEMENTS FOR SCHOOL AGE CHILDREN:
RESPONDENTS WITH TWO OR MORE TYPE OF ARRANGEMENTS
SECOND TYPE MENTIONED (N=647)

Source: National Child Care Survey 1990

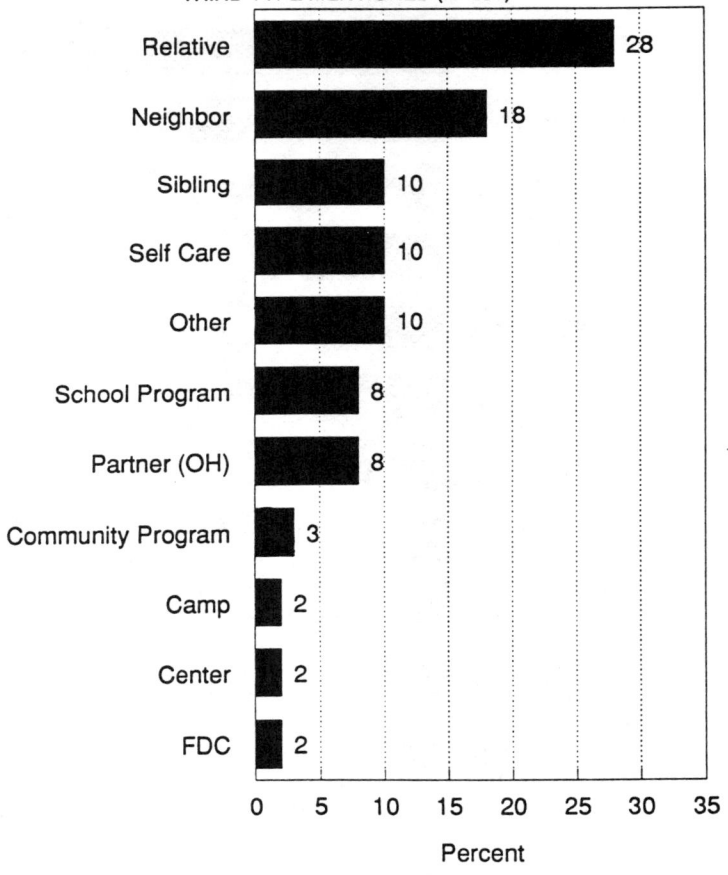

Figure 6.18
SUMMER ARRANGEMENTS FOR SCHOOL AGE CHILDREN: RESPONDENTS WITH THREE OR MORE TYPE OF ARRANGEMENTS THIRD TYPE MENTIONED (N=291)

Source: National Child Care Survey 1990

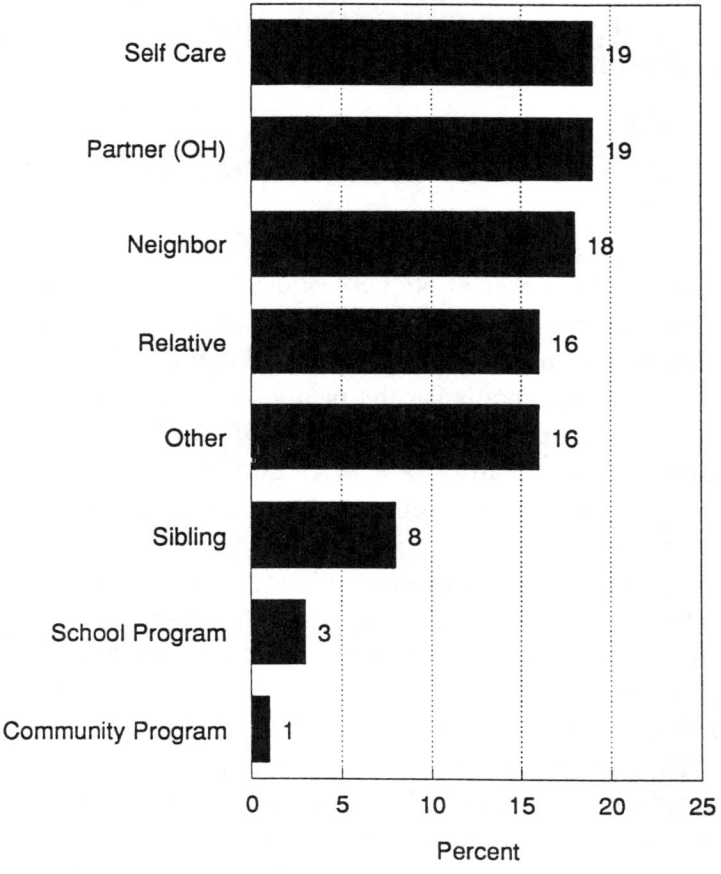

Figure 6.19
SUMMER ARRANGEMENTS FOR SCHOOL AGE CHILDREN:
RESPONDENTS WITH FOUR OR MORE TYPE OF ARRANGEMENTS
FOURTH TYPE MENTIONED (N=105)

Source: National Child Care Survey 1990

Current Type of Care. Current type of care does not appear to be a strong indicator of the type or combination of care types used during the summer. Approximately 20 percent of the sample indicated using the same type of care in the summer as they were currently using, another 25 percent sent their child to camp, and 28 percent indicated there were no regular arrangements. The remaining quarter indicated that their child spent the summer in a wide range of care situations.

SUMMARY AND CONCLUSIONS

Almost 60 percent of NCCS respondents had a youngest child who was either in kindergarten or had not yet started school. Twenty-seven percent of these children had no regular arrangements for the past year; 29 percent were in the same nonparental care situation; another 30 percent began a nonparental care arrangement; 3 percent left regular care; and 11 percent switched nonparental care providers.

The age of the youngest child was an important factor in patterns of care over the past year. Younger children were more likely to start nonparental care than older children, who were more likely to be in the same nonparental care arrangement for the entire 12 months previous.

The mother's employment status in conjunction with the age of the child also influenced the pattern of care for the past year. For example, seventy percent of children under one year of age whose mother was employed started nonparental care as compared to 31 percent of children whose mother was not employed at the time of the survey. By the age of 3 to 4 years an almost identical proportion of children started care regardless of the mother's employment status. Differences across the other categories can also be seen by the employment status of the mother.

The majority of the arrangements in the NCCS were still ongoing at the time of the interview. As such we could only calculate their duration as of the survey date. In all likelihood the arrangements lasted longer than what we observed; therefore, the reported medians for current arrangements underestimate their true duration.

The median length of child care arrangements ranges from 8 to 12 months, depending on whether the arrangement has been completed or is still in use. At the time of the survey, ongoing arrangements had already lasted longer than arrangements which ended in the year previous. There are important differences depending on the age of the child. The median length of current arrangements increases with the age of the child until age 5, at which time it again declines, since children have just begun kindergarten. Children 3-4 have spent 19 months in an arrangement, compared with 10 months for 0- to 2-year-olds and 8 months for 5-year-olds.

Other factors related to length of arrangement are the employment status of the mother, family income, and type of arrangement. Children of employed mothers spend a longer time in their arrangements than children of nonemployed mothers, regardless of age of child, though the differences are largest among 3-4 year olds. The length of the arrangement increases with the income of the family, particularly for 3-4 year old children. Care by family members (parents and relatives) is the longest, lasting 21 and 15 months, respectively. Care by in-home providers, by center-based programs, and by family day care providers lasts somewhat less than a year (10.5, 10 and 8 months, respectively). Lessons are of slightly shorter duration (7 months). As expected, for these preschool-age children, the median length of all arrangements (except lessons) increases with age.

Respondents indicated that previous arrangements ended for a variety of reasons, the most common of which was that the arrangement was no longer available or affordable (42 percent). Another 17 percent indicated that school closing caused the arrangement to end. Taken together, almost 60 percent of arrangements changed for reasons beyond the control of the parents.

When asked about first use of nonparental care, approximately 60 percent of NCCS respondents indicated that they left their youngest child in regular care prior to the start of school. Children of currently employed mothers started to use nonparental care at an earlier age than those of nonemployed mothers, and children of high-income parents began nonparental care earlier than children of low income parents. Children with currently employed mothers spent more hours per week in their first care arrangement than did children whose mothers are not currently employed.

Parents of school-age children were asked about the child care arrangements used during the previous summer. The responses indicated that school-age children spent their time in a variety of care situations. About 20 percent of children used the same type of care as during the school year, another 25 percent went to camp, 28 percent had no regular arrangements, and the remaining children used a variety of care types.

Chapter

7

EMPLOYERS AND CHILD CARE

As the labor force participation of mothers has increased, more and more two-parent families comprise two earners (U.S. Bureau of Labor Statistics 1988). In addition, single mothers are highly likely to be in the labor force. This chapter focuses on issues of interest to dual-earner couples with children, to single employed parents, and to employers: What is the impact of child care problems on employment and how do employers help parents balance the demands of work and family life? In particular, the chapter examines two employment-related issues: (1) the extent to which events such as breakdown of a child care arrangement or a sick child disrupt employment and (2) the extent to which employers provide benefits which may assist employees in managing their family and work responsibilities.

CHILD CARE FAILURES AND TIME LOST FROM WORK

This section examines the incidence of child-care-related disruptions in the work schedules of women employed outside the home. Such disruptions causing employed women to lose time from work are divided into two major categories: (1) a breakdown in the regular child care arrangement because the provider who usually cares for the child is not available, and (2) a breakdown in the regular child care arrangement because the child is ill and is not cared for by the provider.

It should be noted at the outset that most of the data presented in this section are based on sample sizes too small to ascertain statistically significant differences for the purpose of subgroup analysis. Statistically significant differences are noted when they occur. Also, because the data were collected during the more inclement and illness-ridden winter months, breakdowns in regular arrangements may be overestimated.

Failures in Child Care Arrangements Causing Absenteeism from Work

Characteristics of women experiencing work disruptions because of failures in child care arrangements are presented in table 7.1. Of the approximately 2,300 mothers in the National Child Care Survey (NCCS) that are employed outside the home, 15 percent reported losing some time from work during the last month because of a failure in their regular child care arrangement. In comparison, analysis of the 1986-87 Survey of Income and Program Participation (SIPP) child care survey found that child care failures caused 7 percent of employed women to lose some time from work in the month previous (in U.S. Bureau of the Census, 1990). The most likely reason for this discrepancy is that the question regarding lost time differs between the two instruments. The SIPP survey asked respondents only one question regarding lost time from work, whereas the

Table 7.1 EMPLOYED MOTHERS LOSING DAY OF WORK DURING MONTH PREVIOUS BECAUSE OF FAILURES IN CHILD CARE ARRANGEMENTS

Characteristics[a]	Number	Percentage	Characteristics[b]	Number	Percentage
Number of Women	2,299	15.0	*Number of Women*	786	12.0
			Age of Child		
Partner Status			Less than 1 year	78	9.0
Partner present	1,797	15.0	1-2 years	154	13.0
All other	502	14.0	3-4 years	93	13.0
			5-9 years	263	13.0
Number of Children			10-12 years	198	13.0
1	1,201	14.0	*Type of Care Arrangement*		
2	836	16.0	In child's home:		
3+	262	16.0	Relative	107	20.0
			Sitter	87	20.0
Yearly Household Income				20	19.0
			In another home:	219	10.5
Less than $15,000	357	15.0	Relative	104	9.0
$15,000-$24,999	381	13.0	Family day care	115	11.0
$25,000-$34,999	382	14.0	Center/preschool	161	13.0
$35,000-$49,999	489	12.0	Self-care	26	20.0
$50,000+	572	18.0	Parent	180	12.0

Source: National Child Care Survey, 1990

a. Includes all mothers employed outside home. No limit on the number of children or child care arrangements.
b. Limited to women with only one child under age 13 using one type of care.

NCCS survey separated the definition of "lost time from work" into three components: being late for work, leaving early from work, and missing at least an entire day from work. Therefore, in the NCCS, respondents could be included in the "lost time" category: (a) if they had been late, (b) if they left early, or (c) if they missed a day of work during the last month.

When the proportion of women employed outside the home reporting that they missed at least a day of work in the month previous is examined separately, it is comparable to the SIPP survey. Six percent of the NCCS survey respondents reported being absent from work for at least a day during the past month because of a child care failure (table 7.2), compared to 7 percent of the SIPP survey respondents. This suggests that the SIPP records primarily *days* lost rather than *time* lost from work. Because the incidence of *absenteeism* varies so markedly depending on which definition of absenteeism is used, both are included in this analysis.

Family Income. As shown in figure 7.1, women at the highest end of the income distribution scale ($50,000 or more) reported the highest incidence of failures in child care arrangements resulting in time lost from work, but women at the lowest end of the income distribution scale ($15,000 or less) reported the highest incidence of child care failures resulting in missing at least a day of work.

Eighteen percent of those with family incomes of $50,000, compared to 12-15 percent of all other income groups, reported losing time from work during the month previous because of a child care failure (table 7.1, figure 7.1). The percentage differences in work disruptions between women with family incomes of $50,000 or more and those with lower family incomes are statistically

Table 7.2 EMPLOYED MOTHERS LOSING DAY OF WORK DURING MONTH PREVIOUS BECAUSE OF FAILURES IN CHILD CARE ARRANGEMENTS

Characteristics[a]	Number	Percentage	Characteristics[b]	Number	Percentage
Number of Women	2,299	6.0	*Number of Women*	786	6.0
			Age of Child		
Partner Status			Less than 1 year	78	6.0
Partner present	1,797	6.0	1-2 years	154	7.0
All other	502	7.0	3-4 years	93	5.0
			5-9 years	263	6.0
Number of Children			10-12 years	198	4.0
1	1,201	6.0	*Type of Care Arrangement*		
2	836	6.0	In child's home:		
3+	262	9.0	Relative	107	7.0
			Sitter	87	8.0
Yearly Household Income				20	5.0
Less than $15,000	357	10.0	In another home:		
$15,000-$24,999	381	5.0	Relative	219	5.0
$25,000-$34,999	382	7.0	Family day care	104	5.0
$35,000-$49,999	489	4.0	Center/preschool	115	5.0
$50,000+	572	6.0	Self-care	161	5.0
				26	0.0
			Parent	180	7.0

Source: National Child Care Survey, 1990
a. Includes all mothers employed outside home. No limit on the number of children or child care arrangements.
b. Limited to women with only one child under age 13 using one type of care.

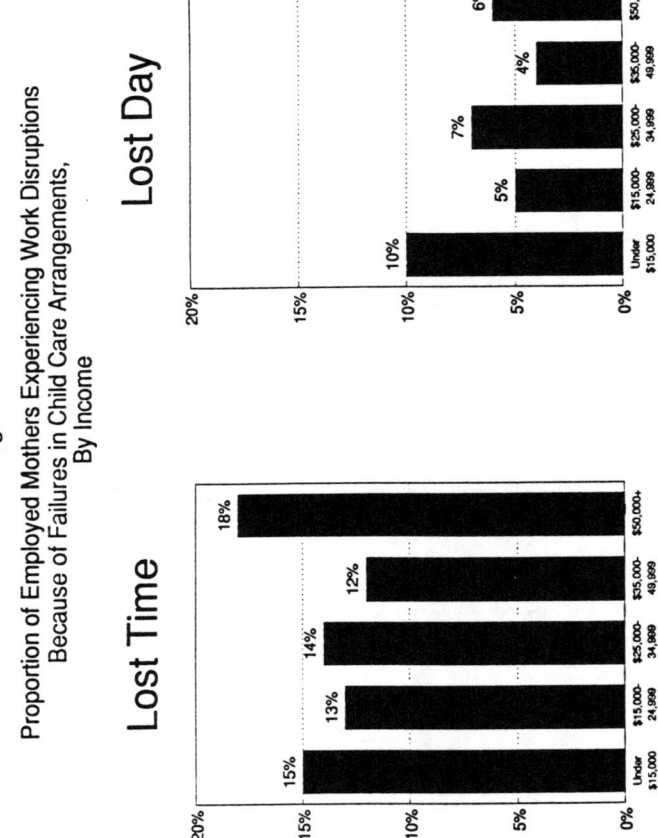

Figure 7.1
Proportion of Employed Mothers Experiencing Work Disruptions Because of Failures in Child Care Arrangements, By Income

Note: Includes all mothers employed outside the home. No limit on the number of children or child care arrangements.
Source: National Child Care Survey 1990

significant, except for those with family incomes of $15,000 or less.

Ten percent of women with family incomes under $15,000 reported missing at least one day of work in the last month owing to a child care failure, compared to 4-7 percent in all other income categories (table 7.2, figure 7.1). (Only the difference between those with incomes less than $15,000 compared to those with incomes between $35,000 and $49,999 is statistically significant).

Number of Children. A slightly higher proportion of mothers with more than one child experienced a failure in a child care arrangement resulting in lost time from work (16 percent) than those with only one child (14 percent) (table 7.1). Similarly, a higher proportion of mothers with more than two children missed at least one day of work (9 percent) than those with one or two children (6 percent) (table 7.2).

Partner Status. Partner status appears to be unrelated to whether employed mothers are more or less likely to lose time from work owing to a child care failure. Among those with partners, 15 percent reported losing time from work, compared to 14 percent without partners (table 7.1), and 7 percent of single mothers missed at least one day of work compared to 6 percent of employed mothers with partners (table 7.2).

Age of Child. To increase the accuracy of the conclusions about the relationship between child care failures and the age of the child, analysis was limited to employed women with only one child and one child care arrangement. Overall, the incidence of absenteeism from work due to breakdowns in children's care arrangements varied only a small amount by the age of the children in care. Women with infants experienced the lowest incidence of lost time from work (9 percent) compared to 13 percent for each of the other age groups (table 7.1). In addition, women with school-age children 10-12 years of age were least likely to miss an entire day of work (4 percent) owing to a child care failure (table 7.2), but these differences are not statistically significant.

Type of Primary Care Arrangement. The relationship between the incidence of child care failures and the primary type of care arrangement is of particular interest in the event that certain types of care appear more stable than others. Here, again, the analysis is limited to employed women with only one child and one arrangement.

In general, lower incidences of lost time from work were associated with placing children in an arrangement physically outside the child's home (10.5 percent) rather than within it (20 percent) (table 7.1, figure 7.2). This difference is statistically significant. The highest proportion of women experiencing child care failures had a relative (20 percent) or nonrelative (19 percent) care for the child in the child's home. A similarly high proportion of women experienced a breakdown in the arrangement when they depended on the child to care for himself/herself (20 percent). A much lower proportion of women experienced care-related work disruptions if their children were cared for in a center (13 percent), by a family day-care provider (11 percent), or a relative in another home (9 percent).

For those who reported missing at least one day of work in the month previous, this general in-home/out-of-home care distinction remains, although the difference is not so striking. Among mothers with one child and one care arrangement, the highest proportion missing work as a result of a child care failure was among employed mothers who relied on a relative in the child's home (8 percent) or a parent (7 percent). For all other types of care arrangements, only 5 percent reported missing a day of work (table 7.2).

Employers and Child Care

Figure 7.2
Proportion of Employed Mothers Experiencing Work Disruptions Because of Failures in Child Care Arrangements, By Type of Care

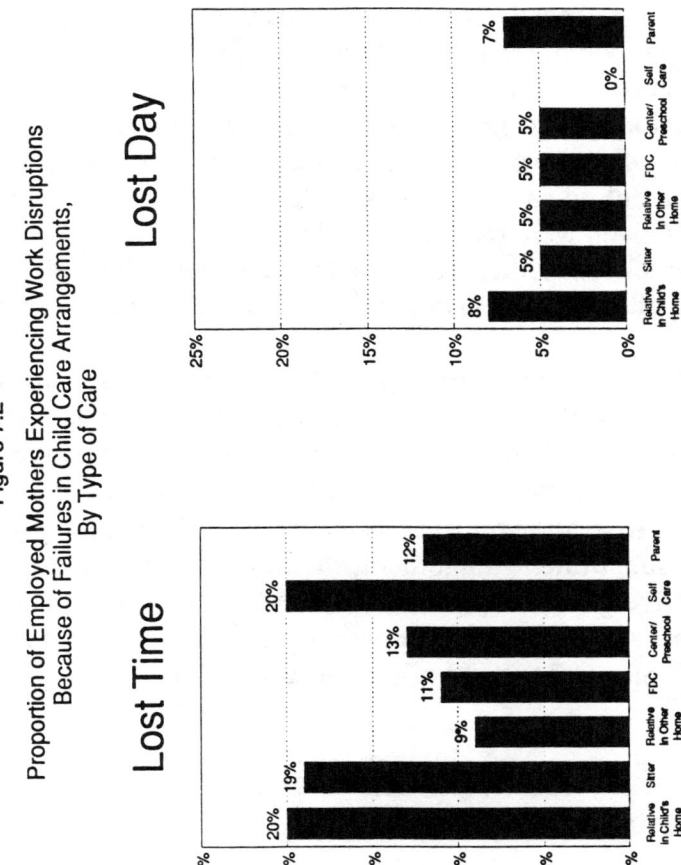

Note: Includes all mothers employed outside the home. No limit on the number of children or child care arrangements.
Source: National Child Care Survey 1990

Number of Times Mothers Missed Work. Employed mothers reported missing at least one day of work because of a failure in the care arrangement an average of 1.58 times during the month previous (not shown). This average does not represent the actual number of days missed from work, but, rather, the number of times this happened in the reference month. That is, one time (or episode) might actually represent several days missed from work.

Reason for Failure in Care Arrangement. Employed women who missed at least one day of work were asked why their child care arrangement failed. The two primary reasons given were that the provider was ill (23 percent) or that the school/facility was closed (21 percent). Another 10 percent cited the illness of a provider's family member (not shown).

Alternative Care Arrangement Used. Employed women were also asked if an alternative care arrangement was used the last time their regular arrangement failed, so that they did not miss work. Almost half (46 percent) reported that an alternative arrangement was never used. For those who used a substitute arrangement, the most common type of alternative care was provided by relatives (28 percent) or neighbors (8 percent). The woman's husband or partner stayed home in 7 percent of the cases (not shown).

Absenteeism from Work Caused by Child's Illness

Of the nearly 2,300 mothers employed outside the home, 35 percent reported that in the month previous their child (or one of their children) was sick on a day they were supposed to be at work (not shown). About half (51 percent) of those with a sick child actually missed work to care for that child (table 7.3). On average, these mothers missed 2.2 days during the month previous to care for a sick child (not shown).

Family Income. Women with family incomes less than $35,000 appear less likely to miss a day of work owing to a child's illness than those with higher family incomes. Forty-four percent of those with incomes less than $15,000 did not go to work when their child was sick, compared to 53 percent of those with incomes greater than $50,000.

Partner Status. More mothers stayed at home with a sick child if they had a spouse or partner (52 percent) than if they did not (45 percent) (table 7.3).

Age of Youngest Child. Mothers with very young children appear to be more likely to stay at home with a sick child than those with children three years of age and older. However, the sample sizes are too small to determine whether the differences are statistically significant. For those with only one child and one care arrangement, almost three-quarters of mothers with children less than one year old missed work because their child was sick, and 59 percent of women with toddlers also stayed home for the same reason. In comparison, the proportion of mothers with children in the older age groups who missed work ranged from 49 percent (5-9 years old) to 34 percent (10-13 years old) (table 7.3).

Type of Regular Care Arrangement. Among women with only one child and one arrangement, a greater percentage of those who regularly placed their child in care outside the child's home, particularly those with a family day-care provider (61 percent) or a center (55 percent) took time off from work to care for their sick child than those who used relatives (46 percent of those using relatives in another home; 34 percent of those using relatives in the child's home) (table 7.3).

Table 7.3 EMPLOYED MOTHERS WITH SICK CHILD WHO LOST TIME FROM WORK DURING MONTH PREVIOUS BECAUSE OF CHILD'S SICKNESS

Characteristics[a]	Number	Percentage	Characteristics[b]	Number	Percentage
Number of Women	794	51.0	*Number of Women*	218	49.0
Partner Status			*Age of Child*		
Partner present	167	45.0	Less than 1 year	18	73.0
All other	628	52.0	1-2 years	51	59.0
			3-4 years	24	37.0
Number of Children			5-9 years	79	49.0
1	350	52.0	10-12 years	46	34.0
2	339	52.0	*Type of Care Arrangement*		
3+	106	44.0	In child's home:	137	34.0
			Relative	31	34.0
Yearly Household Income			Sitter	6	35.0
Less than $15,000	113	44.0	In another home:	56	55.0
$15,000-$24,999	128	47.0	Relative	22	46.0
$25,000-$34,999	134	52.0	Family day care	34	61.0
$35,000-$49,999	168	55.0	Center/preschool	51	55.0
$50,000+	224	53.0	Self-care	8	51.0
			Parent	148	45.0

Source: National Child Care Survey, 1990
a. Includes all mothers employed outside home. No limit on the number of children or child care arrangements.
b. Limited to women with only one child under age 13 using one type of care.

Alternative Care Arrangement Used. Of the 794 women in the survey who reported their child was sick on a day they were supposed to be at work, over half (51 percent) stayed home from work to care for their sick child. Of those that went to work, over a third (36 percent) left their child with relatives, whereas almost a quarter (23 percent) used their regular arrangement. Another 21 percent reported that their partner stayed home to provide care (not shown).

RECEIPT OF EMPLOYER BENEFITS BY PARENTS

Besides the federal and state governments, private employers also provide benefits that may directly or indirectly assist employees in managing their family and work responsibilities. Table 7.4 presents an overview of current child care, parental leave, and other employer policies affecting work and family life. These data are from three large national surveys of employers conducted from 1987 through 1989 by the U.S. Bureau of Labor Statistics, in the U.S. Department of Labor (U.S. Bureau of Labor Statistics 1989, 1990; Hayghe 1988), and from the National Child Care Survey, 1990. Types of benefits are divided into three groups: child care policies, parental leave policies, and other policies. Child care policies include employer-sponsored centers or reimbursements for care at a local center, flexible spending accounts, information and referral services, and child care counseling. Parental leave policies include paid and unpaid maternity and paternity leave. Other policies include flextime, voluntary part-time work, job sharing, work at home, and flexible leave.

Table 7.4 PROPORTION OF ESTABLISHMENTS OFFERING CHILD CARE, AND PARENTS REPORTING RECEIVING LEAVE AND OTHER WORK/FAMILY BENEFITS, 1987-90

	1987[a]	1988[b]	1989[c]	1990[d]
Child Care Policies (%)				
Employer-Sponsored Center for Reimbursement	5.2	4	5	10
Flexible Spending Account Available	--	--	23	8
Information and Referral	5.1	--	--	9
Counseling	5.1	--	--	--
Other	1.0	--	--	--
Other Policies (%)				
Flextime	43.2	--	11	21
Voluntary Part-time	34.8	--	--	36
Job Sharing	15.5	--	--	--
Work at Home	8.3	--	--	10
Flexible Leave	42.9	--	--	29
Other	2.1	--	--	1
Parental Leave Policies				
Unpaid Maternity Leave	18%	--	37%	--
	19 wks		20 wks	
Paid Maternity Leave	16%	2%	33%	1%
	17 wks		18 wks	
Unpaid Paternity Leave	--	--	--	--
Paid Paternity Leave	--	--	--	--

Note: Dashes (--) denote data not available.
a. Establishments with 10 employees or more (Hayghe 1988).
b. Establishments with 100 employees or more (BLS 1989).
c. Establishments with 100 employees or more (U.S. Bureau of Labor Statistics [BLS] 1990).
d. Parents of children under age 13 (National Child Care Survey, 1990).

Table 7.4 shows that in the late 1980s about 5 percent of employers sponsored child care centers on site or reimbursed employees for care. Five percent of employers provided information and referral and 5 percent provided counseling services.[1] Few employers provided paid maternity/paternity leave, but as many as one out of three provided unpaid maternity leave. Finally, 4 out of 10 employers provided flextime or flexible leave, one in three offered voluntary part-time work, and a few provided opportunities for job sharing or work at home (16 percent and 8 percent, respectively).

On-site Child Care. In 1990, 10 percent of NCCS parents said that child care was available through their or their spouse's employer at the location where they work (table 7.5, figure 7.3). Seven percent reported that child care was available at the mother's place of work, 2 percent at the father's workplace, and 1 percent at both workplaces. Since the majority of respondents are mothers, we suspect that mothers are less likely to know about the availability of a benefit through the father's workplace; this factor may therefore contribute to the consistently lower reporting of benefits available through the father's workplace. The proportion who did not know about the availability of a benefit through the partner's employer was always much higher than for the respondent's employer. The proportion of parents who reported not knowing was low: under 1 percent of respondents did not know whether child care was provided by their own employer, and about 2 percent did not know whether it was provided by the partner's employer (not shown). Surprisingly, there were no differences in availability of child care at the workplace by income (figure 7.4).

The proportion of NCCS parents (10 percent) who reported workplace care is substantially higher than the proportion of establishments (with 100 or more employees)

Table 7.5 PROPORTION OF PARENTS REPORTING BENEFITS AVAILABLE THROUGH THEIR OWN OR SPOUSE'S EMPLOYER, BY HOUSEHOLD INCOME

Benefit	Total	Under $15,000	$15,000–$24,999	$25,000–$34,999	$35,000–$49,999	$50,000+
Child Care at Workplace						
Mother only	6.5	6.0	6.8	7.6	6.2	6.6
Father only	2.3	3.4	2.5	1.9	2.1	2.2
Both	0.8	0.5	0.3	0.9	0.8	1.2
Neither	90.4	90.1	90.4	89.6	90.9	90.1
Total	100.0	100.0	100.0	100.0	100.0	100.0
Sample size	3,591	488	584	621	787	864
Use Workplace:						
Yes	31.2	40.8	31.8	37.2	29.9	25.7
No	68.8	59.2	68.2	62.8	70.1	74.3
Total	100.0	100.0	100.0	100.0	100.0	100.0
Sample size	331	46	55	62	71	81

Flexible Spending Account (FSA)						
Mother	4.9	2.4	3.4	4.9	5.6	6.9
Father	2.4	0.3	0.1	1.5	4.0	4.4
Both	1.0	0.4	0.4	0.1	1.0	2.5
Neither	91.7	96.9	96.1	3.5	89.5	86.2
Total	100.0	100.0	100.0	100.0	100.0	100.0
Sample size	3,528	484	576	611	776	846
Use FSA:						
Yes	22.0	8.9	10.9	19.4	16.1	31.4
No	78.0	91.1	89.1	80.6	83.9	68.6
Total	100.0	100.0	100.0	100.0	100.0	100.0
Sample size	278	13	22	37	79	111
Cafeteria Plan						
Mother only	2.7	2.8	2.5	2.5	2.4	3.3
Father only	1.8	0.6	0.7	1.0	1.8	3.9
Both	1.0	0.7	0.1	1.0	0.8	2.2
Neither	94.4	95.9	96.7	95.5	95.0	90.7
Total	100.0	100.0	100.0	100.0	100.0	100.0
Sample size	3,515	485	573	613	767	845
Trade Benefits:						
Yes	6.3	8.9	8.7	3.2	8.2	6.1
No	93.7	91.1	91.3	96.8	91.8	93.9
Total	100.0	100.0	100.0	100.0	100.0	100.0
Sample size	184	18	19	26	39	72

(continued)

Table 7.5 (Continued)

Benefit	Total	Under $15,000	$15,000–$24,999	$25,000–$34,999	$35,000–$49,999	$50,000+
Offer Money						
Mother	0.9	1.5	0.7	1.4	0.6	0.7
Father	0.6	0.5	0.4	1.0	0.3	0.8
Both	0.1	0.0	0.0	0.0	0.1	0.1
Neither	98.4	98.0	98.9	97.6	98.9	98.4
Total	100.0	100.0	100.0	100.0	100.0	100.0
Sample size	3,558	490	582	616	776	860
Vouchers						
Mother	0.4	0.0	0.2	0.1	0.9	0.4
Father	0.2	0.2	0.3	0.3	0.1	0.2
Both	0.2	0.4	0.0	0.5	0.3	0.1
Neither	99.2	99.4	99.5	99.1	98.7	99.3
Total	100.0	100.0	100.0	100.0	100.0	100.0
Sample size	3,552	490	581	617	775	857

Information and Referral						
Mother only	4.9	3.3	4.8	4.3	5.4	5.9
Father only	3.0	2.3	3.0	2.5	2.5	3.9
Both	1.0	0.4	0.4	0.5	1.2	2.0
Neither	91.1	94.0	91.8	92.6	90.8	88.2
Total	100.0	100.0	100.0	100.0	100.0	100.0
Sample size	3,496	483	568	611	762	842
Flextime						
Mother only	10.9	9.2	12.0	10.1	11.8	11.5
Father only	6.5	2.7	6.1	5.3	7.4	8.7
Both	3.0	1.1	1.8	1.8	3.7	6.0
Neither	79.6	87.0	80.2	82.8	77.1	73.8
Total	100.0	100.0	100.0	100.0	100.0	100.0
Sample size	3,531	486	578	617	769	852
Unpaid Leave						
Mother only	15.4	15.8	13.1	15.0	17.7	16.4
Father only	7.4	2.0	7.3	7.1	8.5	10.2
Both	4.8	1.7	3.3	3.6	6.7	7.4
Neither	72.4	80.5	76.3	74.3	67.1	66.0
Total	100.0	100.0	100.0	100.0	100.0	100.0
Sample size	3,482	476	567	605	759	851

(continued)

Table 7.5 (Continued)

Benefit	Total	Under $15,000	$15,000–$24,999	$25,000–$34,999	$35,000–$49,999	$50,000+
Part-time Work						
Mother only	23.5	29.8	23.3	23.0	25.7	20.2
Father only	7.0	5.3	7.1	5.6	7.4	8.3
Both	4.8	2.3	4.4	4.0	6.1	7.1
Neither	64.6	62.6	65.2	67.5	60.8	64.3
Total	100.0	100.0	100.0	100.0	100.0	100.0
Sample size	3,514	480	570	615	770	852
Work at Home						
Mother only	5.2	2.4	4.2	3.9	7.2	7.0
Father only	3.4	1.1	1.7	1.7	4.3	6.8
Both	1.0	0.6	0.5	0.5	0.8	2.2
Neither	90.4	95.9	93.5	93.9	87.8	84.0
Total	100.0	100.0	100.0	100.0	100.0	100.0
Sample size	3,560	489	580	616	782	860

Other Benefit					
Mother only	0.6	1.0	0.8	0.5	0.3	0.6
Father only	0.4	0.2	0.2	0.6	0.4	0.8
Both	0.1	0.0	0.1	0.0	0.1	0.0
Neither	98.9	98.8	98.8	98.9	99.2	98.7
Total	100.0	100.0	100.0	100.0	100.0	100.0
Sample size	3,545	489	579	615	775	856
Any Benefit						
Yes	51.6	48.0	49.6	48.7	55.7	57.2
No	48.4	52.0	50.4	51.3	44.3	42.8
Total	100.0	100.0	100.0	100.0	100.0	100.0
Sample size	3,589	490	584	622	788	867

Source: National Child Care Survey, 1990

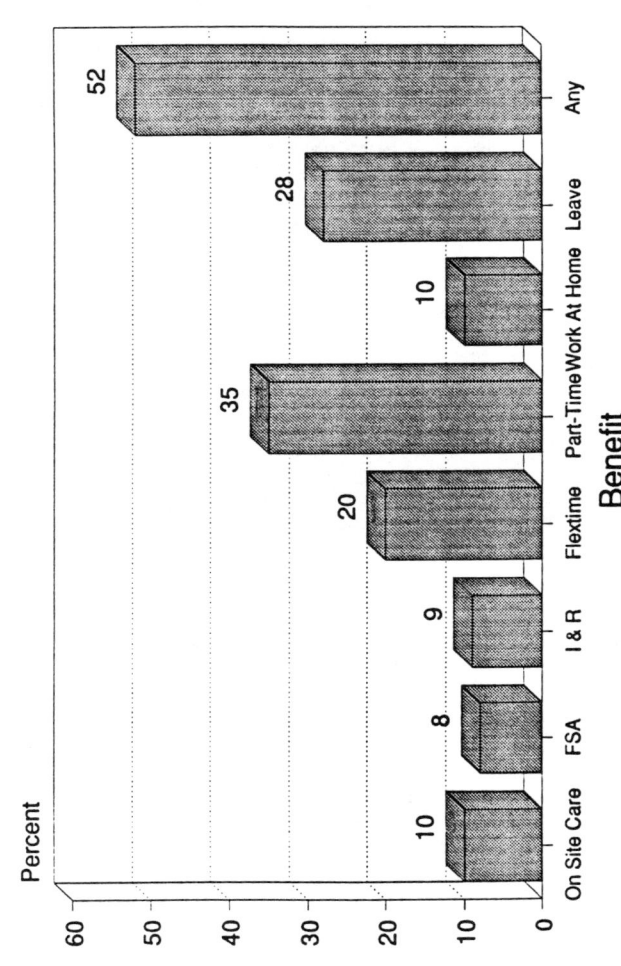

Figure 7.3
PERCENTAGE OF FAMILIES WITH
WORK/FAMILY BENEFITS

Source: National Child Care Survey 1990

Employers and Child Care

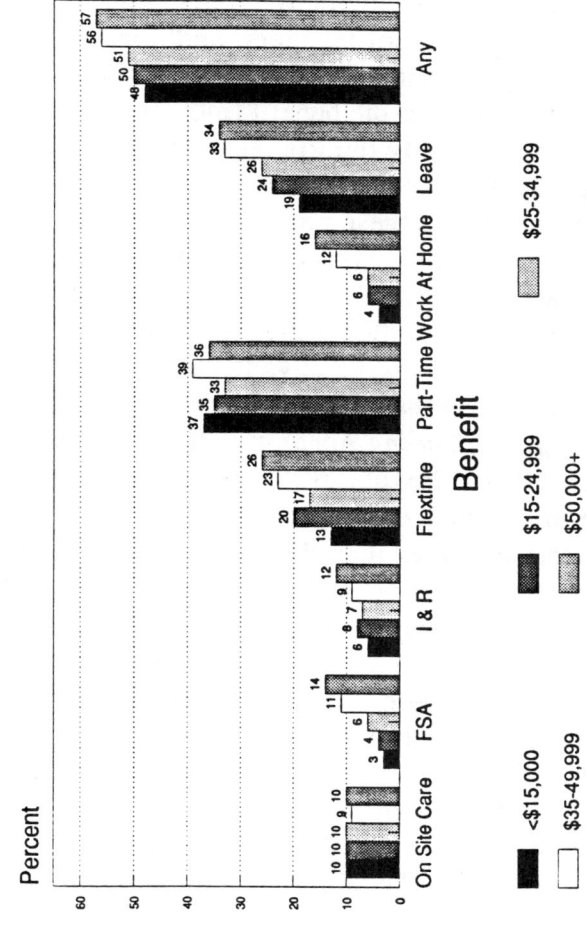

Figure 7.4
PERCENTAGE OF FAMILIES WITH WORK/FAMILY BENEFITS BY HOUSEHOLD INCOME

Source: National Child Care Survey 1990

offering such programs in 1989 or earlier (5 percent), suggesting a concentration of parents, particularly mothers, in establishments with such programs (table 7.4). Other analyses (not presented here) have indicated that 11 percent of employed mothers are employed in occupations that typically provide on-site child care, such as child care providers, preschool teachers, and nurses (unpublished analyses by the authors). In addition, since there are two potential sources of the benefit (mother or father), the likelihood that a family reports receiving a benefit should be higher than the likelihood of a single firm providing it.

Do parents use these programs? A high proportion--31 percent--of parents who had child care available at the workplace used it (table 7.5). Use of this care varies by income level, with a higher proportion of low income families (41 percent) taking advantage of this child care than high income families (30 percent).

Flexible Spending Accounts. Eight percent of parents reported that a flexible spending account (FSA) was available through their employer (table 7.5). This percentage is considerably lower than the proportion of employers who reported offering it in the late 1980s (23 percent, table 7.4). This difference may be due partly to a higher concentration of parents in small firms or to the fact that parents are simply not familiar with this program. This benefit is certainly less visible and more different to comprehend than others. Compared with other benefits, a higher proportion of parents did not know whether this benefit was offered: 2 percent of respondents did not know whether their own employer provided the benefit, and 4 percent did not know whether the benefit was provided by the spouse's employer (not shown).

The availability of the flexible spending account varies with income. Only 3 percent of low-income families said that it is available, compared with 14 percent of families in the top income quartile (figure 7.4). Of those who said it was available, 22 percent of families used the benefit (table 7.5). The higher the income level, the more likely is the family to use such an account. Nine percent of low-income families and 31 percent of families with incomes of $50,000 and over used the account. Since 1989, families can use either the Child and Dependent Care Federal Income Tax Credit or the flexible spending account, but not both. The former is of more benefit to the lowest-income taxpayers, and the latter is of more benefit to high-income taxpayers. Thus, these findings are reasonable.

Cafeteria-Style Benefit Plan. Six percent of parents said that their company provided benefits in a cafeteria-style plan (table 7.5). Again this response varied slightly by income, with 9 percent of high-income parents and 5 percent of low-income parents so characterizing their benefits. Of those who said that their benefits are flexible, only 6 percent said that they traded other types of benefits for child care (table 7.5).

Money or Vouchers. Less than one percent of parents said that the employers offered money or vouchers for child care (table 7.5).

Information and Referral. Eight percent of parents said that their employer offered information and referral (I & R) services for finding child care (table 7.5).

Flextime. Twenty percent of parents claimed that one parent or both worked for an employer who permitted flextime. A higher proportion of high-income (26 percent) than low-income families (13 percent) had this option available to them (figure 7.4, table 7.5).

Unpaid Leave. Twenty-eight percent of parents said that unpaid leave was available to them through their workplace (table 7.5).

Part-time Work. Thirty-five percent of parents said that part-time work was available from either their own or their partner's employer (table 7.5). There were no differences by income level.

Work at Home. Ten percent of families reported that they could work at home (table 7.5). This percentage varied dramatically by income level, with 4 percent of low-income families reporting that one of their employers permitted them to work at home, compared with 16 percent of upper-income families.

Other Child Care Benefits. One percent of families reported other types of benefits through one partner's employer (table 7.5).

No Benefits. Half of parents reported having at least one of the above-mentioned child care or related benefits available from either of their employers. There was no significant difference by income level (table 7.5).

LEAVE POLICIES

Although parental leave has, in practice, been treated as a separate issue, it is an important part of overall child care policy for three basic reasons. The first of these is that growth in the employment of mothers, which is heavily concentrated among mothers with infants (Hofferth and Phillips 1987), means that more children need care but fewer mothers are available to provide that care.

Second, the more intensive needs of infants require more staff, and, therefore, care for them is much more expensive than care for older children. Child/staff ratios for infants are the lowest of all age groups, with three states requiring one staff member for every three infants (Morgan 1987). With staff costs comprising the bulk of the expense of care, this means infant care is very resource intensive. The number of providers offering high-quality, personally attentive care for infants is widely agreed to be small.

Third, there has been concern about the well-being of children who spend many hours a week in nonrelative, out-of-home care, particularly if it is not of high quality (Hayes et al. 1990).

This section describes parents' reports of the leave time they took and employer benefits to pay for this leave.

Use of Leave Time

Half of all mothers who had ever worked since their first child was born took some leave after the birth of their youngest child (table 7.6, figure 7.5). Although a smaller proportion of families with incomes under $15,000 took leave than those with incomes of $50,000 or higher, the difference is not significant because of small sample sizes.

Of those mothers who took maternity leave, one-third took up to 12 weeks of leave (table 7.7). Twenty-nine percent took 13 to 26 weeks, 13 percent took 27 to 52 weeks, and 25 percent took more than 52 weeks. There are some differences by income. Sixty-five percent of upper-income families took leave of 6 to 26 weeks, compared with about 50 percent of low-income families. Low- and moderate-income families either took very short or very long leaves; the former may be because they couldn't afford more, and the latter may be a cause of their low incomes.

Table 7.6 PROPORTION OF MOTHERS TAKING LEAVE AFTER YOUNGEST CHILD WAS BORN, BY HOUSEHOLD INCOME

	Total	Under $15,000	$15,000–$24,999	$25,000–$34,999	$35,000–$49,999	$50,000+
Yes	50.0	47.9	46.1	51.8	49.1	54.8
No	48.1	52.1	53.1	46.6	49.2	40.6
Currently on leave	1.8	0.0	0.7	1.6	1.7	4.6
Total	100.0	100.0	100.0	100.0	100.0	100.0
Sample size	598	82	105	112	144	119

Source: National Child Care Survey, 1990

Employers and Child Care ■ 373

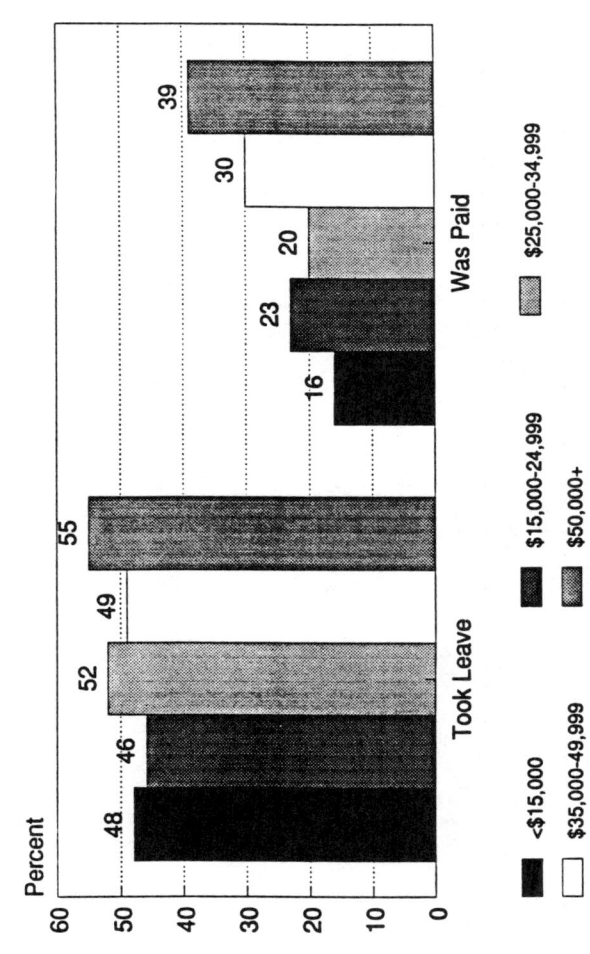

Figure 7.5
LEAVE AFTER BIRTH OF YOUNGEST CHILD MOTHER

Source: National Child Care Survey 1990

Table 7.7 NUMBER OF WEEKS OF LEAVE TAKEN AMONG MOTHERS TAKING LEAVE BY HOUSEHOLD INCOME

Weeks	Total	Under $15,000	$15,000–$24,999	$25,000–$34,999	$35,000–$49,999	$50,000+
Up to 5	10.2	11.8	16.7	14.3	5.4	2.9
6–12	22.8	14.7	20.8	16.1	28.8	30.9
13–26	29.2	35.3	18.8	25.0	28.8	33.8
27–52	12.6	11.8	16.7	12.5	13.7	10.3
53+	25.2	23.5	31.2	32.1	24.6	22.1
Total	100.0	100.0	100.0	100.0	100.0	100.0
Sample size	294	34	48	56	73	68

Source: National Child Care Survey, 1990

Of parents who took leave, 28 percent reported that their leave was paid (table 7.8). This proportion was lower for low-income families than upper-income families (16 compared to 39 percent, respectively). Of those who had paid leave, 23 percent took annual leave, 48 percent took sick/disability leave, 18 percent had some type of parental leave and 10 percent named another type of leave (table 7.9). The sample sizes were too small to examine income differences.

Of mothers who took leave, 45 percent said that they kept their health insurance while they were on leave, 16 percent said that they lost their insurance, and 39 percent had no health insurance to lose (table 7.10). These proportions differ by income. A higher proportion of upper-income mothers kept their insurance (59 percent), compared with low-income families (19-30 percent). A higher proportion of low-income mothers (71 percent) than high income mothers (27 percent) did not have insurance to begin with.

Those few mothers on maternity leave were asked whether their same or a similar job was guaranteed for them when they returned. All but one said that the same job was guaranteed for them upon their return.

SUMMARY AND CONCLUSIONS

Our survey results indicate that child care failures caused 15 percent of mothers employed outside the home to lose some time from work and 7 percent to miss at least one day of work during the month previous. Employed mothers missed at least one day of work for this reason an average of 1.6 times.

Table 7.8 PAID AND UNPAID LEAVE AMONG MOTHERS TAKING LEAVE

Was Leave Paid?	Total	Under $15,000	$15,000–$24,999	$25,000–$34,999	$35,000–$49,999	$50,000+
Yes	27.9	16.3	22.8	20.4	30.3	39.5
No	72.1	83.7	77.2	79.6	69.7	60.5
Total	100.0	100.0	100.0	100.0	100.0	100.0
Sample size	297	35	48	56	73	70

Source: National Child Care Survey, 1990

Table 7.9 PAID LEAVE TAKEN BY MOTHERS, BY TYPE OF LEAVE

	Total
Vacation Leave	23.1
Sick/Disability Leave	48.2
Parental Leave	17.8
Some Other	10.1
Total	100.0
Sample Size	111

Source: National Child Care Survey, 1990.

Child care failures resulting in work disruptions are experienced among mothers of all income levels, but low-income mothers appear to be especially vulnerable, particularly in terms of missing a day of work altogether. Women with family incomes of $50,000 or higher were most likely to miss some time from work because of a failure in their child care arrangement (18 percent). However, women with low family incomes (less than $15,000) were more likely to miss an entire day of work than any other income group (10 percent). Many low-income jobs may not provide much flexibility in terms of work schedules, thus producing a higher incidence of absenteeism among low-income workers with a child care failure. Failures of child care arrangements were more common among those in the child's home than outside the child's home. Formal outside-the-home market arrangements may be more reliable than informal arrangements.

Table 7.10 HEALTH INSURANCE KEPT OR LOST THROUGH EMPLOYER BY MOTHERS TAKING LEAVE

Kept Health Insurance?	Total	Under $15,000	$15,000–$24,999	$25,000–$34,999	$35,000–$49,999	$50,000+
Yes, kept it	45.2	19.1	30.4	42.5	53.5	58.9
No, lost it	15.9	9.7	18.9	21.8	16.5	14.5
Didn't have insurance	38.9	71.2	50.7	35.7	30.0	26.6
Total	100.0	100.0	100.0	100.0	100.0	100.0
Sample size	275	29	45	53	67	65

Source: National Child Care Survey, 1990

Although only a little more than one-third of employed mothers reported that they had a sick child during the month previous, over one-half of those respondents missed at least one day of work to stay home and care for their child. On average, these mothers missed 2.2 days of work in the last month for this reason. Thus, child care failures owing to the unavailability of the regular provider or a child's illness caused one-quarter of women employed outside the home to miss at least a day of work in the past month.

How does the picture from parents match that from employers? According to this national data, 50 percent of all families have available some employee benefit or policy to help balance their work and family life, and 50 percent do not have such a benefit or policy. The largest proportion, 20-36 percent, say that part-time work, unpaid leave, or flextime are available to them. Around 10 percent say that their employer sponsors an on-site center that has a reimbursement account or provides resource and referral services. This figure is twice as high as what employers report, but this is not unexpected. Parents may select employers that provide the benefits they need, and, in addition, two-parent families (77 percent of the sample) have twice the probability of obtaining a benefit through an employer if both spouses are employed than does a single employee.

Generally, these findings confirm that many employee benefits are less available to low-income families than to high-income families. Not only do low-income families earn less, but when family emergencies, such as a family illness or the breakdown of a child care arrangement, arise, low-income mothers may have little choice but to lose a day of work and pay.

Finally, about half of all mothers took some leave after the birth of their youngest child. Only about 3 out of 10 were paid during this absence from work. Of those who were paid, the majority were paid through a combination of vacation and sick/disability pay. Few mothers had paid parental leave available to them.

Note, chapter 7

1. Statistics cited from tables in this chapter are typically rounded off to the nearest whole number.

Chapter

8

OPINIONS ON FEDERAL CHILD CARE POLICY: FAMILIES WITH CHILDREN UNDER AGE 13

At the time the National Child Care Survey (NCCS) was designed and fielded (1989-90), policymakers were debating a number of major child care issues. Almost 7 billion dollars was spent by the federal government to assist families with their child care needs. The bulk of expenditures, 4 billion dollars, benefited middle- and upper-income families in the form of revenue lost through the Child and Dependent Care Federal Income Tax Credit, allowing families to reduce the amount of tax paid in proportion to their actual child care expenditures. Although low-income families were potentially eligible, if their tax liability was small, they received little benefit from the nonrefundable credit. Thus, there was considerable discussion about the extent to which additional federal assistance should be targeted to low-income households. In addition, there was concern that two-parent families with only one wage earner were being unfairly penalized because they had chosen to forgo the additional earnings of a second earner to raise their children themselves. A mechanism like the earned income tax credit that only required one parent to be employed (in two-parent families), and that did not place any restrictions on how the funds were spent, was favored. Thus, on the one hand, a vocal group was pushing for expansion of child care benefits to all families with an employed mother, while on the other hand another vocal minority was objecting to benefits going *only* to families with an employed mother. Meanwhile, a budget deficit severely limited the amount of outlays possible.

A second issue in the debate was whether child care assistance should be targeted, again to save money, to families with the youngest children. Several bills in the U.S. Congress, for example, proposed to alter the earned income tax credit by providing supplemental funds for low-income families with children under age three.

Although the National Child Care Survey, 1990, primarily obtained information from parents to permit evaluation of parental use of and demand for child care, a small set of opinion items was added with funding from the Office of the Assistant Secretary for Planning and Evaluation, Department of Health and Human Services. In 1990 there were about 27.6 million households with a youngest child under age 13, constituting about 30 percent of all U.S. households. A sample of these households was asked their opinion about a number of aspects of federal child care policies for American families. This chapter reviews the responses to those items.

SHOULD SUPPORT BE TARGETED TO LOW-INCOME FAMILIES?

The NCCS first asked parents whether they believe that federal child care policies should support families of all income levels, low-income families only, or not support child care at all. Slightly more than half (54 percent) of American parents with children under age 13 responded that federal policies should support families of all income levels (table 8.1). One out of three, 36 percent, said that these policies should support low-income families only, and 7 percent said that the federal government should not support child care at all. Four percent said that they did not know or refused to answer. These results suggest widespread support for federal assistance to parents for child care and greater support for universal assistance than for targeting.

It can be hypothesized that parents responded to these questions primarily from a sense either of self-interest or altruism. After examining parents' responses by their economic and demographic characteristics, we found somewhat more support for the "self-interest" rather than the "altruism" hypothesis; parents were more likely to indicate that federal support should be provided to groups similar to themselves.

Income. For example, a higher proportion of low-income families than upper-income families said that they supported targeting assistance to low-income families (44 percent versus 32 percent) (figure 8.1). Although slightly more upper- than lower-income families supported child care for all income levels, this difference was not statistically significant. Upper-income parents (incomes of $50,000

Table 8.1 SHOULD FEDERAL CHILD CARE SUPPORT BE TARGETED TO FAMILIES OF ALL INCOME LEVELS, LOW INCOME LEVELS ONLY, OR NONE AT ALL?

	All Income (%)	Low Income (%)	None (%)	Refused or Don't Know (%)	Total (%)	N
All	53.5	35.5	6.9	4.1	100	4,392
Family Type						
Mother only	49.4	44.4	2.8	3.4	100	837
Mother and father	55.3	32.6	8.0	4.1	100	3,383
Household						
Employed mother	56.5	33.3	6.6	3.6	100	2,595
Nonemployed mother	50.3	37.6	7.5	4.7	100	1,619

Income						
<$15,000	48.2	44.5	3.7	3.7	100	874
$15,000–$24,999	52.0	38.7	5.9	3.4	100	706
$25,000–$34,999	55.9	30.7	9.0	4.4	100	687
$35,000–$49,999	57.6	32.1	7.6	2.8	100	852
$50,000+	56.5	32.1	8.6	2.9	100	918
Age of Youngest						
Less than 1 year	63.5	29.0	4.0	3.4	100	605
1–2 years	55.4	34.5	6.3	3.8	100	965
3–4 years	55.8	33.5	7.3	3.4	100	739
5–9 years	51.5	37.3	6.8	4.4	100	1,462
10–12 years	43.0	40.8	10.8	5.3	100	604

Source: National Child Care Survey, 1990

Figure 8.1
SHOULD SUPPORT BE TARGETED TO FAMILIES OF ALL INCOME LEVELS, LOW INCOME LEVELS, OR NONE AT ALL?

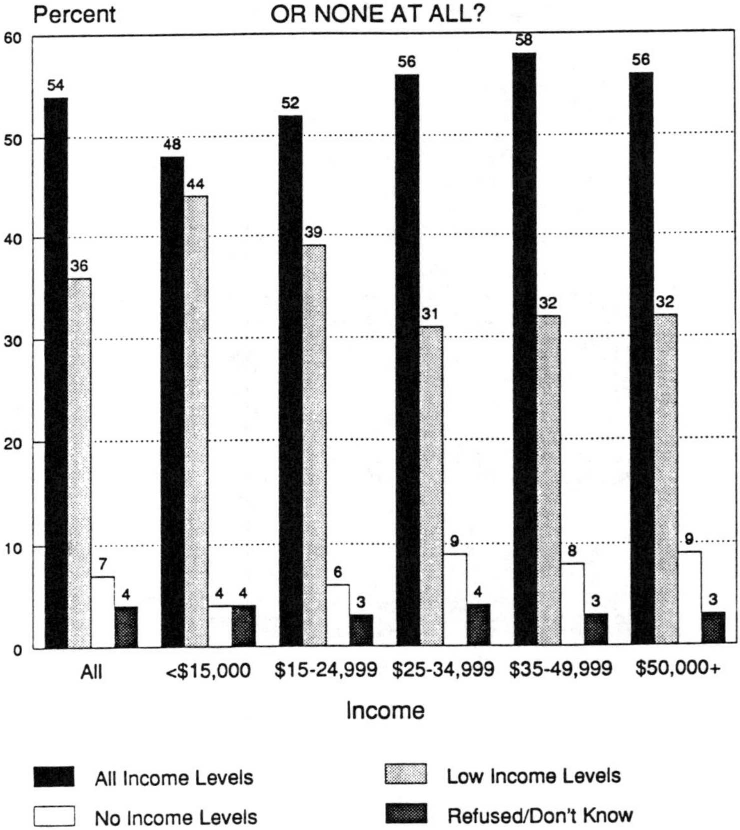

Percent

Income	All Income Levels	Low Income Levels	No Income Levels	Refused/Don't Know
All	54	36	7	4
<$15,000	48	44	4	4
$15-24,999	52	39	6	3
$25-34,999	56	31	9	4
$35-49,999	58	32	8	3
$50,000+	56	32	9	3

Source: National Child Care Survey 1990

or more) were significantly more likely than low-income parents ($15,000) to say that the federal government should not support child care at all (9 percent versus 4 percent). This may reflect their lower need for assistance or simply a difference in belief about the role of the federal government in child care. There were no significant differences by income in the percentage who did not know or refused to answer.

Age of Youngest Child. The only other characteristic significantly associated with targeting is the age of the youngest child (figure 8.2). The older the child, the larger the proportion of parents who thought that assistance should be targeted to low-income families only--41 percent versus 29 percent. In addition, more of these families with older children also stated that the federal government should not support child care at all (11 percent versus 4 percent). This may be a rational response to needing less assistance with child care as children grow older and care for themselves. Parents may forget how much help they received when their children were younger, or they may say they did it themselves and that others can do the same.

Family Type. Single-parent families were slightly less likely than two-parent families to say that federal policy should support all families (49 percent versus 55 percent), and were more likely than two-parent families to say that support should be targeted to low-income families (44 percent versus 33 percent) (figure 8.3).

Maternal Employment Status. Differences by the employment status of the mother were not significant.

Figure 8.2
SHOULD SUPPORT BE TARGETED TO FAMILIES OF ALL INCOME LEVELS, LOW INCOME LEVELS, OR NONE AT ALL?

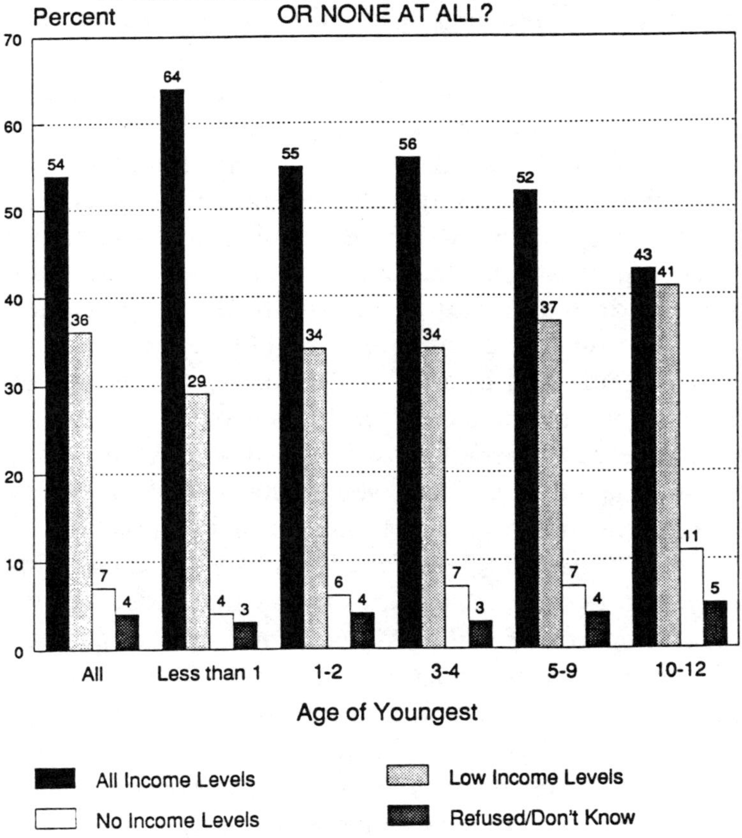

Source: National Child Care Survey 1990

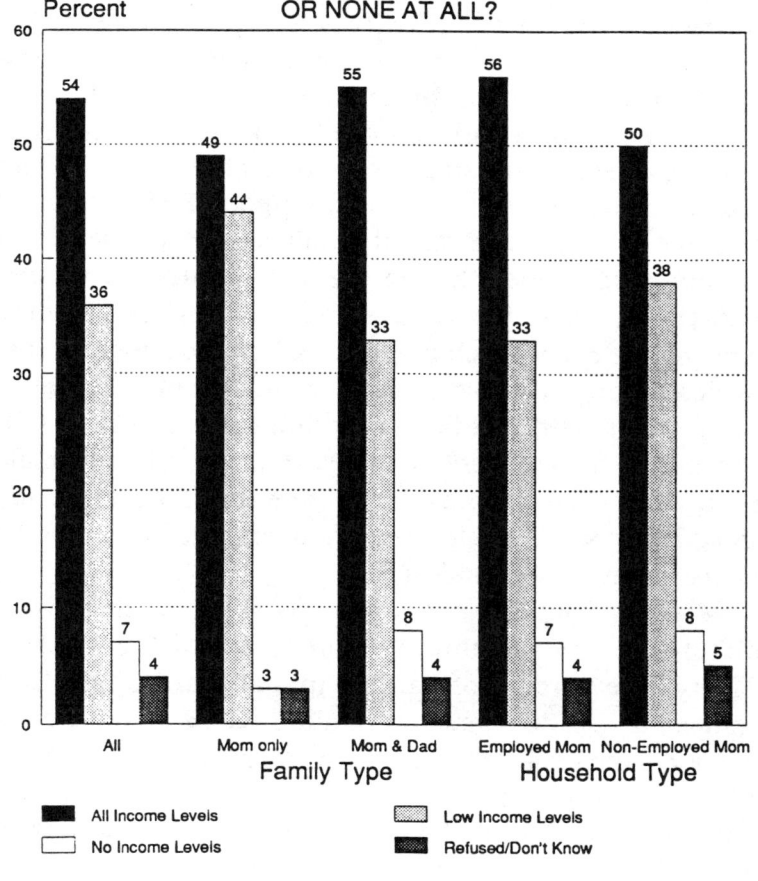

Figure 8.3
SHOULD SUPPORT BE TARGETED TO FAMILIES OF ALL INCOME LEVELS, LOW INCOME LEVELS, OR NONE AT ALL?

Source: National Child Care Survey 1990

DOES THE MOTHER HAVE TO BE EMPLOYED?

The survey next asked parents whether federal child care policies should support all two-parent families or only those two-parent families in which both parents are employed. If the respondent had supported targeting assistance to low-income families in question one, then the words *low-income* were inserted into the question. The parallel question for single-parent families was whether federal child care support should support all single-parent families or only single-parent families in which the parent is employed. Since the mother is generally the second earner, this question focuses on whether respondents believe that maternal employment should be a prerequisite for federal child care assistance. Two-thirds of respondents (64 percent) said that federal policies should support all two-parent families, not just those with two earners (table 8.2). A similar proportion believe that federal policy should support all single-parent families whether or not the mother is employed (table 8.3).

Maternal Employment Status. As expected, there were differences by the employment status of the mother. Thirty-five percent of parents in dual-earner families, compared with 26 percent of families with a nonemployed mother, stated that only families with an employed mother should be assisted (figure 8.4). The response was similar regardless of whether the hypothetical family was a two-parent or one-parent family.

Income. Generally, the lower the income level, the less respondents favored targeting and the more they favored universal assistance, regardless of the mother's employ-

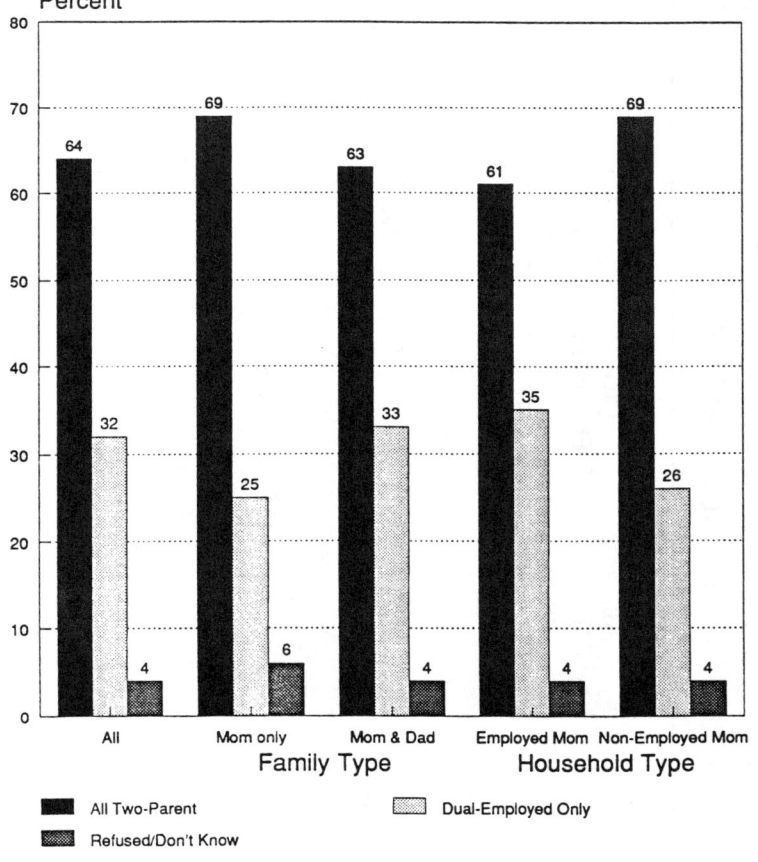

Figure 8.4
SHOULD SUPPORT BE TARGETED TO ALL TWO-PARENT FAMILIES, OR ONLY THOSE IN WHICH BOTH PARENTS ARE EMPLOYED?

Source: National Child Care Survey 1990

Table 8.2 RESPONSE TO SURVEY QUESTION: MUST BOTH PARENTS BE EMPLOYED TO RECEIVE FEDERAL CHILD CARE SUPPORT?

	All Two-Parent (%)	Dual Employed (%)	Refused or Don't Know (%)	Total (%)	N
All	64.2	31.7	4.1	100	3,908
Family Type					
Mother only	68.6	25.0	6.4	100	785
Mother and father	63.1	33.4	3.6	100	2,973
Household					
Employed mother	61.3	34.8	3.9	100	2,330
Nonemployed mother	69.2	26.3	4.5	100	1,422

Income				
<$15,000	68.4	26.1	5.4	100	810
$15,000–$24,999	66.5	29.2	4.3	100	640
$25,000–$34,999	62.6	33.5	3.9	100	595
$35,000–$49,999	61.7	34.8	3.4	100	764
$50,000+	59.8	37.3	2.8	100	813
Age of Youngest				
Less than 1 year	70.8	25.6	3.6	100	559
1–2 years	66.9	30.4	2.8	100	868
3–4 years	65.9	29.8	4.3	100	660
5–9 years	61.1	34.0	4.9	100	1,299
10–12 years	58.6	36.3	5.1	100	506

Source: National Child Care Survey, 1990

Table 8.3 RESPONSE TO SURVEY QUESTION: MUST THE SINGLE PARENT BE EMPLOYED TO RECEIVE FEDERAL CHILD CARE SUPPORT?

	All Single Parents (%)	Employed Single Parents (%)	Refused or Don't Know (%)	Total (%)	N
All	64.3	32.9	2.9	100	3,908
Family Type					
Mother only	71.9	26.5	1.6	100	785
Mother and father	62.2	34.6	3.1	100	2,973
Household					
Employed mother	62.0	35.2	2.9	100	2,330
Nonemployed mother	68.0	29.2	2.8	100	1,422

Income				
<$15,000	70.1	27.3	2.5	810
$15,000–$24,999	64.1	33.1	2.8	640
$25,000–$34,999	64.0	33.1	3.0	595
$35,000–$49,999	61.1	36.2	2.7	764
$50,000+	60.3	37.5	2.2	813
Age of Youngest				
Less than 1 year	71.5	27.1	1.3	559
1–2 years	65.4	32.8	1.8	868
3–4 years	64.7	32.6	2.8	660
5–9 years	62.8	33.5	3.7	1,299
10–12 years	58.4	37.3	4.3	506

Source: National Child Care Survey, 1990

ment status. For example, 26 percent of families making under $15,000 per year, compared with 37 percent of families with incomes of $50,000 per year, favored targeting assistance to families with an employed mother only (figure 8.5). Consistent with these differences by income, single-mother families were also less likely to favor targeting than two-parent families. These responses differ from responses to question one, in which lower-income families were more likely than higher-income families to favor targeting assistance to low-income families. Perhaps having already targeted their own income group, low-income families then feel comfortable with more universal assistance.

Age of Youngest Child. Families with older children regularly favored targeting assistance to families with an employed mother. This response is consistent with responses to question one, and may be explained by the higher labor force participation of mothers of older children (figure 8.6).

Difference between Targeters and Nontargeters. There were consistent differences between respondents in their answers to these questions. Those who said that federal assistance should be targeted to low-income families in the first question (targeters) were more likely to want to target assistance in their responses to later questions than those who favored universal benefits (nontargeters). Although the levels of responses differed by the response to the first question, the pattern of responses was the same by demographic characteristics. The proportion of targeters who believed that only dual-earner, two-parent families should receive federal assistance was consistently higher (by about 12 percentage points) than the proportion of nontargeters (not shown). In addition, the responses were similar,

Opinions on Federal Child Care Policy

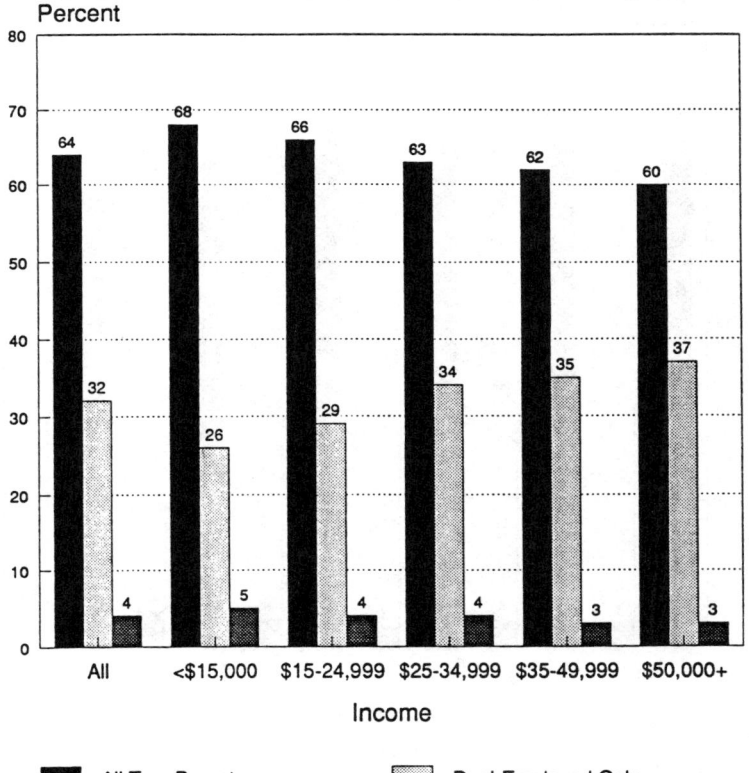

Figure 8.5
SHOULD SUPPORT BE TARGETED TO ALL TWO-PARENT FAMILIES, OR ONLY THOSE IN WHICH BOTH PARENTS ARE EMPLOYED?

Source: National Child Care Survey 1990

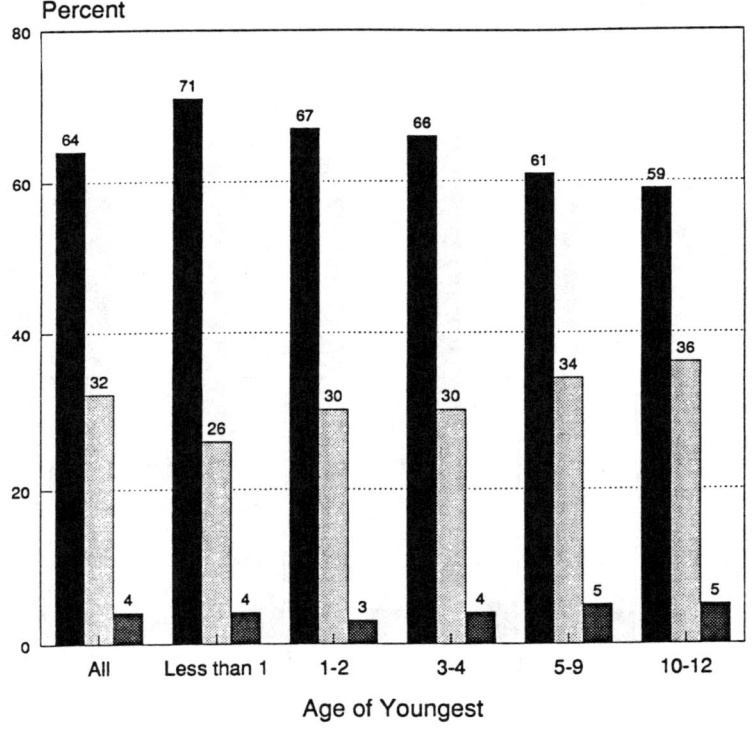

Figure 8.6
SHOULD SUPPORT BE TARGETED TO ALL TWO-PARENT FAMILIES, OR ONLY THOSE IN WHICH BOTH PARENTS ARE EMPLOYED?

Source: National Child Care Survey 1990

regardless of whether the hypothetical mother was in a two-parent or single-parent family.

One important difference between targeters and nontargeters should be pointed out. Families with high income levels ($50,000 or more) who favored universal benefits believed that all single parents should receive federal child care assistance, regardless of the employment status of the mother (not shown). There were few opinion differences by income level among those in favor of universal benefits. In contrast, among those who believed in targeting assistance to low-income families, families with high incomes were the most likely to want to target child care assistance to employed single mothers only, much more so than those with low incomes.

SHOULD SCHOOL-AGE CHILDREN BE INCLUDED?

The third survey question was whether federal child care policy should support all families with children under age 13, or only families with preschool-age children. The answer to this question was clear. An overwhelming majority of parents (86 percent) said that federal assistance should support families until their children reached age 13 (table 8.4). Families with younger children were more likely to favor targeting support to families with children under age 5 than families with only older children (figure 8.7), but the difference was not very large. There were few other differences in responses to this question, regardless of the respondent's previous preference for targeting, income, or demographic characteristics. It appears that policies to

Table 8.4 RESPONSE TO SURVEY QUESTION: SHOULD SUPPORT BE TARGETED TO ALL FAMILIES WITH CHILDREN UNDER AGE 13, OR ONLY TO THOSE WITH CHILDREN UNDER AGE 5?

	All Children <13 (%)	Only Children <5 (%)	Refused or Don't Know (%)	Total (%)	N
All	85.5	12.8	1.7	100	3,908
Family Type					
Mother only	84.5	13.7	1.8	100	785
Mother and father	85.9	12.4	1.7	100	2,973
Household					
Employed mother	86.4	11.9	1.6	100	2,330
Nonemployed mother	84.3	14.0	1.7	100	1,422

Opinions on Federal Child Care Policy

Income				
<$15,000	86.4	11.2	2.4	100	810
$15,000–$24,999	85.4	13.8	0.8	100	640
$25,000–$34,999	84.9	13.5	1.6	100	595
$35,000–$49,999	84.3	14.0	1.7	100	764
$50,000+	88.1	10.8	1.2	100	813
Age of Youngest				
Less than 1 year	84.8	14.0	1.1	100	559
1–2 years	82.7	16.6	0.6	100	868
3–4 years	87.4	11.0	1.5	100	660
5–9 years	85.8	11.7	2.5	100	1,299
10–12 years	88.0	9.5	2.4	100	506

Source: National Child Care Survey, 1990

Figure 8.7
SHOULD SUPPORT BE TARGETED TO ALL FAMILIES WITH CHILDREN UNDER 13, OR ONLY TO THOSE WITH CHILDREN UNDER 5?

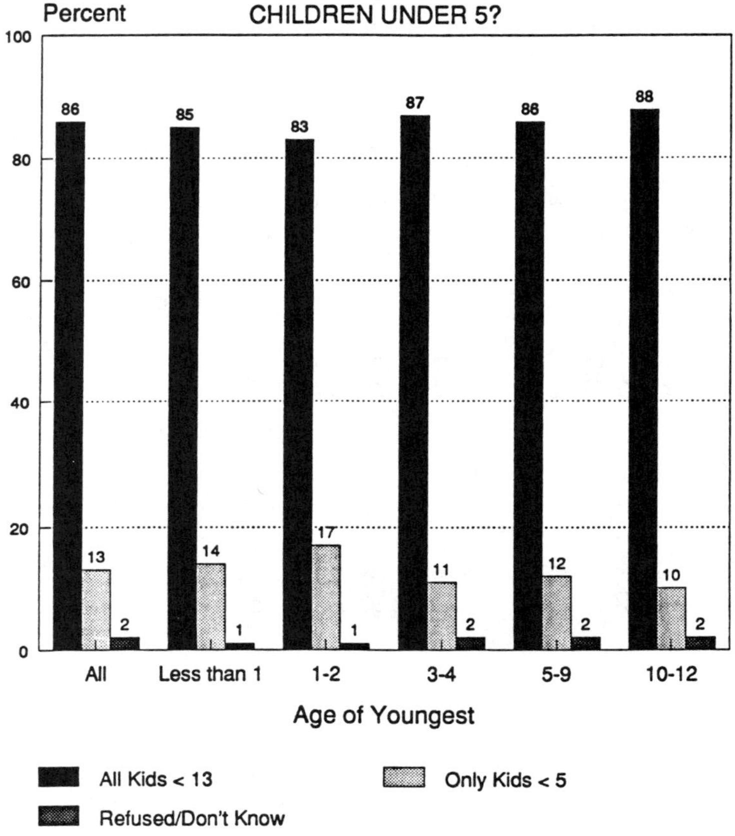

Source: National Child Care Survey 1990

support child care for school-age children would be welcomed by eager parents.

SHOULD EMPLOYERS PROVIDE CHILD CARE BENEFITS?

The last question asked parents whether they believed that employer-provided child care benefits should be available to all families with one employed parent, only to those in which both parents are (or the single parent is) employed, or whether employers should not provide child care benefits to any of their employees.

Overall, 53 percent of respondents said that employers should provide child care benefits to all families with one employed parent, 29 percent said that both parents (or one, if a single-parent family) need be employed, and only 11 percent said that employers should not provide child care benefits at all (table 8.5, figure 8.8). Again, this suggests that there is broad support for employer-provided child care benefits. The proportion who said that employers have no business providing benefits to anyone, although larger than for the first questions, was still small.

Income. Differences by income were small. Upper-income respondents were slightly more likely to say that employers should not provide child care benefits than were lower-income respondents.

Age of Youngest Child. The only demographic factor affecting whether a respondent favors or opposes employer-sponsored child care benefits was age of youngest child (figure 8.8). Families with older children were twice as likely as families with children under age one to say that

Table 8.5 RESPONSE TO SURVEY QUESTION: SHOULD EMPLOYERS PROVIDE CHILD CARE BENEFITS?

	To All Families (%)	Dual Employed (%)	None (%)	Refused or Don't Know (%)	Total (%)	N
All	52.8	29.0	11.1	7.2	100	4,392
Family Type						
Mother only	58.3	26.2	9.1	6.5	100	837
Mother and father	51.6	30.1	11.3	7.0	100	3,383
Household						
Employed mother	51.8	30.5	11.6	6.1	100	2,595
Nonemployed mother	54.6	27.6	9.7	8.0	100	1,619

Income						
<$15,000	58.3	24.6	9.0	8.1	100	874
$15,000–$24,999	53.3	28.1	11.6	7.0	100	706
$25,000–$34,999	51.0	33.3	10.1	5.6	100	687
$35,000–$49,999	50.5	33.0	10.6	5.9	100	852
$50,000+	53.0	30.5	11.9	4.6	100	918
Age of Youngest						
Less than 1 year	58.3	30.1	7.7	3.9	100	605
1–2 years	57.5	30.0	6.4	6.1	100	965
3–4 years	55.1	27.3	11.3	6.3	100	739
5–9 years	48.1	29.5	13.1	9.2	100	1,462
10–12 years	47.5	27.4	16.5	8.5	100	604

Source: National Child Care Survey, 1990

Figure 8.8
SHOULD EMPLOYERS PROVIDE CHILD CARE BENEFITS TO ALL FAMILIES, ONLY THOSE IN WHICH ALL PARENTS ARE EMPLOYED, OR NONE AT ALL?

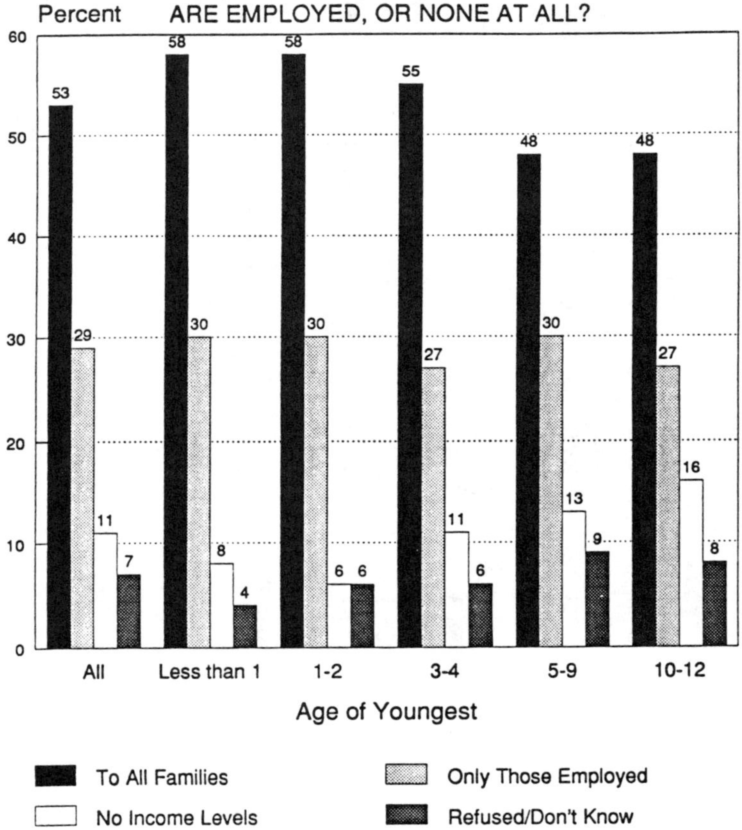

Source: National Child Care Survey 1990

employers should not be providing such benefits. Again, this provides support for the self-interest hypothesis; the former are less likely to need the benefits.

SUMMARY AND CONCLUSIONS

To obtain some indication of public opinion regarding federal and private employer child care policies, respondents to the NCCS were asked their views on various policies. Responses to these questions indicated that among families with a youngest child under age 13, there is broad-based support for both federal and employer-based child care policies. Nine out of ten support such policies. The greatest opposition was to private employer policies; however, only about 1 in 10 respondents, on average, expressed such opposition. In support of our hypothesis that self-interest rather than altruism motivates public opinion regarding child care policy, high-income families and families with only older children were the most opposed to any participation of the federal government or private employers in providing child care benefits. For example, 16 percent of respondents whose youngest child was age 10-12 said that employers should not provide child care benefits to any families, compared to 8 percent of families with the youngest under age one.

Among those who supported federal child care efforts, the majority favored universal benefits over targeting to low-income parents. Targeting was favored more by parents of older children and by those with incomes below $15,000 per year.

In general, among families who supported federal assistance in child care, a higher proportion also favored making benefits available regardless of the employment status of the mother, rather than targeting benefits only to families in which the mother is employed. Not surprisingly, families with employed mothers were more in favor of targeting than families with nonemployed mothers, but the difference was not large.

Finally, the overwhelming majority (85 percent) of parents with children under age 13 favored providing assistance to all families with children under age 13, not just to families with children under age 5. There were no significant differences by family characteristics. (There was a slight tendency for families of older children to favor all families more than families with only younger children, but the difference was not significant.) Thus, while most beliefs reflected self-interest, some altruism may be evident in the overwhelming support in this sample with children under age 13 for providing assistance to families with older as well as younger children.

Chapter

9

SUMMARY AND CONCLUSIONS

The National Child Care Survey, 1990, interviewed by telephone a nationally representative sample of 4,392 U.S. families with children under age 13 to learn about (1) who cares for children, (2) how much parents spend on child care, (3) how parents choose arrangements and programs to care for their children, (4) what they perceive their child care options to be, (5) previous use of child care arrangements, (6) how American families balance work and family responsibilities, and (7) American parents' perceptions of public- and private-sector child care policies. This survey represents approximately 27 million households with children under age 13, or 3 out of 10 U.S. households.

One of the major features distinguishing this study from others is the inclusion of parental care as child care. A second feature is the inclusion of all families, not just families with an employed mother. Therefore, these findings truly represent how U.S. families care for children in the early 1990s.

CHILD CARE ARRANGEMENTS

Parents are the principal source of child care in American families. In 45 percent of families, the primary child care arrangement is at least one parent. Nonparental arrangements play an important part in children's lives. Twenty-six percent of children under age 13 are cared for in a formal center-based program or activities such as lessons during nonschool time; 14 percent are cared for by a relative; 7 percent by a family day-care provider; 3 percent by an unrelated provider in the child's home; fewer than 2 percent care for themselves; and 3 percent are in other arrangements.

The type of care used differs depending on whether the mother is employed or not and the age of the youngest child. Employed mothers and mothers of preschoolers are more likely to use nonparental care than are nonemployed mothers and mothers of school-age children. Of course, even when the mother is employed, parents remain the primary caregivers for children. Still, employed mothers of preschool age children rely equally on center-based programs and on parental care as their primary arrangements while working (28 percent of their youngest children are in center-based care and 28 percent are in parental care), whereas the majority of nonemployed mothers rely most often on parental care (67 percent).

Even though most nonemployed mothers care for their children themselves, almost one out of three nonemployed mothers relies on center-based programs for 3- to 4-year-old children (compared with 43 percent of employed mothers). When all uses of either school or preschool are considered, the proportion of all children in programs rises to 41 percent by age 3 and 61 percent by age 4.

For employed mothers, use of center-based programs for preschool-age children has increased consistently over the past 25 years, from 6 percent in 1965 to 28 percent in 1990. Accompanying this increase has been a decline in care by in-home providers and relatives. Use of family day-care has remained constant. Parental care as a primary arrangement for employed mothers appears to have grown somewhat over the past 15 years, reflecting increased time spent by both fathers and mothers in caring for their preschool-age children.

Although school-age children are much less likely than preschool-age children to be enrolled in center-based before- or after-school programs, the use of center-based programs appears to have risen over the past five years, perhaps reflecting an increase in the availability of center-based before- and after-school programs. In 1990, 16 percent of school-age children were enrolled in a center (excluding lessons), compared with 7 percent in 1984-85.

In addition, a number of parents rely on activities such as lessons and sports, not only as educational and cultural supplements but also as child care arrangements for children after school. Twenty-one percent of school-age children are enrolled in these activities.

Of potential policy importance is the lack of a difference between lowest and highest income families in center-based program enrollments. Although there are some income differences in enrollments in preschool and before-/after-school programs in centers, these differences are relatively small. In fact, for children of nonemployed mothers, enrollments by families at the lowest income levels are significantly higher than enrollments by middle-income families. This may suggest that although subsidization has not completely eliminated differences by income, governmental assistance has reduced a part of the differential.

However, sharp income differences remain in use of activities such as lessons and sports. For example, among school-age children of employed mothers, 21 percent of children whose annual family incomes are $50,000 or more take lessons. In contrast, only 5 percent of children whose annual family incomes are under $15,000 take lessons. Among children of nonemployed mothers, the difference is just as great. Twenty-nine percent of children of mothers whose annual family income is $50,000 or above take lessons, compared with 12 percent of children in households with annual incomes under $15,000. These differences reflect the educational levels of low-income mothers as well. What is not known is the effect on children of taking lessons. Lessons offer a structured after-school activity, as well as opportunities for cultural education, socialization, and practice of physical and intellectual skills. Lessons may be an important aspect of the lives of school-age children, one in which, apparently, there are sharp differences by socioeconomic levels.

Preschool-age children and children of employed mothers spend more time in nonmaternal care than school-age children or children of nonemployed mothers. The youngest preschool-age child of an employed mother spends an average of 35 hours per week in primary care, including all types of care, regardless of whether the parents pay for that care. Children in a center-based program or a family day-care home are in care for an average of 37 hours per week, compared with about 30 hours per week spent by children in the care of a relative, in-home provider, or parent. Contrary to our expectations, younger preschool children spend more time in their primary arrangement than older preschool children. Young preschool children with nonemployed mothers spend about 20 hours per week in care on average, ranging from 15 hours per week in center-based care, family day-care, relative care, or in-home provider care to 29 hours per week in care by the other parent.

School-age children with an employed mother spend an average of 13 hours per week in care, and five-year-olds spend more time in care than older children. If they have a nonemployed mother, they spend only about 6 hours per week in a regular arrangement.

PARENTAL EXPENDITURES

Most parents care for their children themselves, and thus pay nothing for child care. Employed mothers are more likely than nonemployed mothers to pay for child care, especially if the youngest child is under five years old. Fifty-six percent of employed mothers make monetary payments for their primary care arrangement for their youngest preschool-age child, as do 69 percent of full-time employed mothers and 33 percent of part-time employed mothers. Only 14 percent of nonemployed mothers pay for the primary child care arrangement for their youngest preschool-age child. Thirty-six percent of employed mothers and 21 percent of nonemployed mothers of school-age children pay for their primary care arrangement.

Among those who pay, employed mothers generally pay less per hour than nonemployed mothers. For example, families with an employed mother spend $1.56 per hour for the primary arrangement of their youngest preschool-age child, compared to $2.38 per hour for nonemployed mothers. However, children of employed mothers typically spend more time in paid care (37 hours) than do children of mothers who are not employed (13 hours). Therefore, employed mothers pay more on a weekly basis.

Among the different types of care, in-home providers, which cost $2.30 per hour on average, are the most expensive arrangement for employed mothers with a preschool-age child. Relatives provide the least expensive care for employed mothers with a preschool-age child, at $1.11 per hour. Center-based programs and family day-care providers fall in-between, at $1.67 per hour and $1.35 per hour, respectively.

Care for school-age children is more expensive--$2.78 per hour for children of employed mothers and $4.38 per hour for children of nonemployed mothers. School-age children of employed mothers are in a paid arrangement more hours per week (13 hours) than school-age children of nonemployed mothers (4 hours).

When all children in the family are considered, employed mothers with a preschool-age child pay more per week ($63) than mothers who are not employed ($35). Overall, employed mothers with a preschool-age child spend about 11 percent of their weekly family income on child care. Nonemployed mothers with a preschool-age child spend about 6 percent of their family income on child care. Families with a school-age child spend about 4-5 percent of their family income on child care, regardless of whether or not the mother is employed.

Although they are less likely to pay for care, if they pay, single mothers and poor families spend a substantially greater share of their income on child care than two-parent or non-poor families, regardless of employment status or the youngest child's age. For example, single mothers with a preschooler spend 20 percent of their income and families with annual incomes under $15,000 spend 22-25 percent of their income on child care. In contrast, families with a preschool-age child and with annual incomes of $50,000 or more pay only about 6 percent of their income for child care.

Few families (5 percent) claim they receive direct financial assistance with their child care expenses. In contrast, 35 percent of employed parents with a preschool-age child and 27 percent of employed parents with a school-age child claim the federal Child and Dependent Care Credit.

Hourly expenditures on center-based and family daycare remained stable from 1985 to 1990, whereas hourly expenditures for in-home providers increased sharply from 1975 to 1990, so that in-home care has become the most expensive form of child care on an hourly basis.

CHOICE AND SATISFACTION

Parents were asked about both the types of arrangements and the number of providers they seriously considered in choosing their current care arrangement. Other types of arrangements were considered by 37 percent of families. Families with an employed mother considered other types of providers more frequently than families with a nonemployed mother (43 percent versus 26 percent, respectively). Families using relative care considered other arrangements *less* often than users of other modes of care. The alternate type of care most often considered by families was care in a center or preschool (50 percent).

Other providers of the same type were considered by 40 percent of parents. Again, families where the mother is employed consider other providers more often than families where the mother is not employed. Almost one-quarter of those families using either centers, in-home providers, or family day-care providers considered both alternative types of care and a variety of providers of the same type.

Parents reported that it took approximately five weeks to settle on a care arrangement for their youngest child. The median time was higher for families in which the mother was employed and the youngest child was of school age.

The majority of NCCS parents (65 percent) indicated that they learned about their primary care arrangement from friends, neighbors, or relatives; only 9 percent of parents found their current care arrangement through a resource and referral service.

Quality was the characteristic cited most often by parents in selecting their current arrangement for their youngest child. Families where the mother is employed cited quality more frequently than families where the mother is not employed (42 percent versus 27 percent, respectively). Likewise, families using more formal care arrangements--centers, family day-care providers, and in-home providers--mentioned quality more often than families using relatives to care for their youngest child. The aspect of quality most often cited was a provider-related characteristic such as a warm and loving manner; this was the most important factor for the majority of parents (70 percent).

Overall, the reported level of satisfaction with child care arrangements is quite high; 96 percent of those surveyed indicated that they are either "very satisfied" or "satisfied" with their current care arrangement for the youngest child. Nevertheless, 26 percent would prefer an alternative type or combination of care arrangements for their youngest child. The desire for an alternative care arrangement was higher among families where the mother is employed and where the youngest child has not yet started school.

For those families desiring a change, the preferred mode of care is a center or preschool (49 percent). This finding varied with the age of the child. For children under one year of age, the alternative mode of care most often cited was care by a relative. For children between the ages of one and four years, the majority preferred care in a center.

Quality was the reason most often mentioned by parents for desiring a change in care. Families with an employed mother cited program-related factors, such as cognitive and social development and school preparation, as their main reasons for desiring a change. Families with a nonemployed mother cited provider-related reasons such as a warm, loving manner. A substantial proportion of families with a nonemployed mother cited child-related factors, such as child/staff ratio and group size, and program-related factors.

PERCEPTIONS OF ALTERNATIVES

Overall, the information parents provide on the price of care (even for types they do not use) and on the characteristics of their arrangements matches overall estimates on the fees that providers charge, on actual expenditures of users, and on the average characteristics that providers report. Of course, this does not mean that an individual parent's information corresponds exactly with that given by his or her provider, but it matches on average. This suggests that, for the most part, parents are informed consumers when it comes to choosing child care arrangements.

Parents' decisions in terms of location and cost also appear consistent from a rational decision-making perspective. That is, parents pick an arrangement on the basis of its characteristics. As a result, for reasonably comparable care, parents perceive the arrangement they have chosen to be closer to home and to cost less than the arrangements they do not choose.

Parents perceive care by a relative or in-home provider to be least available to them, and care by a center or family day-care provider to be most available, regardless of the type of care they actually choose.

Finally, although numerous families use self-care and sibling care for their children, in the majority of families these constitute only incidental sources of care; fewer than 2 percent report using self- or sibling-care as a primary arrangement.

Regarding self-care, 3.5 million U.S. children under age 13 (7 percent) are in self-care on a regular basis. This is almost twice the number identified in the December 1984 Current Population Survey (CPS) (Cain and Hofferth 1989), suggesting an increase in self-care or at least an increase in parents who report it. Only about 600,000 children are in self-care as a primary arrangement, however. Other data show self-care as likely to be of short duration, under two hours per day.

The average age at which parents first allowed their youngest child to care for himself/herself up to one-half hour per day was age 9. The longer the period, the older the child. For parents who had not yet used self-care, the average age they said they might start it was 12.7 years of age, almost four years later than the age at which children now in self-care started caring for themselves. The single most important factor they would consider was the child's maturity, but a reliable neighbor and the ability to reach a parent by telephone were factors next in importance. Parents began relying on sibling care when their youngest child was 5.8 years of age, on average. The sibling was 14 years old, on average. Nonusers reported that they would wait until their youngest was 9 years old before allowing an older sibling to be in charge.

PREVIOUS CHILD CARE ARRANGEMENTS

Almost 60 percent of NCCS respondents had a youngest child who was either in kindergarten or had not yet started school. Twenty-seven percent of these children had no regular arrangements for the past year; 29 percent were in the same nonparental care situation; another 30 percent began a nonparental care arrangement; 3 percent left regular care; and 11 percent switched nonparental care providers.

The age of the youngest child was an important factor in patterns of care over the past year. Younger children were more likely to start nonparental care than older children, who were more likely to be in the same nonparental care arrangement for the entire period.

The mother's employment status in conjunction with the age of the child also influenced the pattern of care for the past year. For example, 70 percent of children under one year of age whose mothers were employed started nonparental care, as compared to 31 percent of children whose mothers were not employed at the time of the survey. By the age of 3 to 4 years mother's employment status made virtually no difference to the proportion of children who started nonparental care. Differences across other categories can also be seen by the employment status of the mother. The median length of child care arrangements ranges from 8 to 12 months, depending on whether the arrangement has been completed or is still in use. At the time of the survey, ongoing arrangements had already lasted longer than arrangements which ended in the previous year. There were important differences depending on the age of the child. The median length of current arrangements increased with the age of the child until age five, at which time it again declined, since children had just begun kindergarten. Children 3-4 had spent 19 months in an arrangement, compared with 10 months for 0- to 2-year-olds and 8 months for 5-year-olds.

Other factors related to length of arrangement are the employment status of the mother, family income, and type of arrangement. Children of employed mothers spend a longer time in their arrangements than children of nonemployed mothers, regardless of age of child, although the differences are largest among 3- to 4-year-olds. The length of the arrangement increases with the income of the family, particularly for 3- to 4-year-old children, with care by family members (parents and relatives) being the longest, lasting 21 and 15 months, respectively. Care by in-home providers, by center-based programs, and by family day care providers lasts somewhat less than a year (10.5, 10, and 8 months, respectively). Lessons are of slightly shorter duration (7 months). As expected, for these preschool-age children, the median length of all arrangements (except lessons) increases with age.

Respondents indicated that previous arrangements ended for a variety of reasons, the most common of which was the arrangement was no longer available or affordable (42 percent). Another 17 percent indicated that school closing caused the arrangement to end. Taken together, almost 60 percent of arrangements changed for reasons beyond the control of the parents.

When asked about first use of nonparental care, approximately 60 percent of NCCS respondents indicated that they left their youngest child in regular care prior to the start of school. Children of currently employed mothers started to use nonparental care at an earlier age, as did children of higher-income parents. Children with currently employed mothers spent more hours per week in their first care arrangement than did children whose mothers are not currently employed.

Parents of school-age children were asked about child care arrangements used during the previous summer. The responses indicated that school-age children spent their time in a variety of care situations. Twenty-eight percent indicated they had no regular arrangements for their school-age children. Of those that said they used at least one type of care, about 20 percent used the same type of care as during the school year, another 25 percent went to camp, 23 percent indicated using a community recreation program, 17 percent relied on relatives, and the remaining children used a variety of care types.

EMPLOYERS AND CHILD CARE

Child care failures caused 15 percent of employed mothers to lose some time from work and 7 percent to miss at least one day of work during the last month. Employed mothers missed at least one day of work for this reason an average of 1.6 times per month. Child care failures resulting in work disruptions are experienced among mothers of all income levels, but low-income mothers appear to be especially affected, particularly in terms of missing a full day of work. Women with family incomes of $50,000 or higher were most likely to miss some time from work because of a failure in their child care arrangement (18 percent). However, women with low family incomes (less than $15,000) were more likely to miss an entire day of work than any other income group (10 percent). Many low-income jobs may not provide much flexibility in terms of work schedules, thus producing a higher incidence of absenteeism among low-income workers with child care problems. Failures of child care arrangements were more common among families in which the child was cared for at home than outside the child's home. Formal, outside-the-home market arrangements may be more reliable than informal arrangements.

Although only a little over one-third of employed mothers reported that they had a sick child during the past month, over half of those respondents missed at least one day of work to stay home and care for their child. On average, these mothers missed 2.2 days of work for this reason.

Thus, child care failures due to the unavailability of the regular provider or a child's illness led one-quarter of women employed outside the home to miss at least a day of work in the past month.

What types of child care benefits are available to assist families in balancing work and family demands? According to NCCS data, half of all U.S. families have some employer benefit or policy which helps them manage child care and other family responsibilities. The largest proportion of families, 20-36 percent, say that part-time work, unpaid leave, or flextime are available to them. Ten percent say that their employer sponsors an on-site center, a figure twice as high as that reported by employers. Parents may select employers that provide the benefits they need, and, in addition, two-parent dual-earner families have a higher probability of obtaining a benefit through an employer than does a single employed parent.

Generally, these findings confirm that many employee benefits are less available to low-income families than to high-income families. Not only do low-income families earn less, but when family emergencies, such as a family illness or the breakdown of a child care arrangement, arise, low-income mothers may have little choice but to lose a day of work and pay.

Finally, about half of all mothers took some leave after the birth of their youngest child. Only about 3 out of 10 were paid during this absence from work. Of those who were paid, the majority were paid through a combination of vacation and sick/disability pay. Few mothers have paid parental leave available to them.

OPINIONS ON CHILD CARE POLICY

To obtain some indication of public opinion regarding federal and private employer child care policies, respondents to the NCCS were asked their views on various policies. Responses to these questions indicate broad-based support for both federal and employer-based child care policies among families with a youngest child under age 13. Five out of ten parents supported an active public role in assisting all families with child care and four of ten would assist low income families. The largest opposition was to private employer policies; however, only about 1 in 10 families, on average, were opposed to such policies. In general, high-income families and families with only older children were those most opposed to any participation by the federal government or private employers in providing child care benefits. For example, 16 percent of respondents whose youngest child was aged 10-12 felt that employers should not provide child care benefits to any families, compared with 8 percent of families with their youngest child under age 1.

Among those who supported federal child care efforts, the majority favor universal benefits over policies which benefit only low-income families. Targeting was favored more by parents of older children, who have fewer child care expenses, and by those with incomes below $15,000 per year, who must spend a relatively high proportion of their family income for child care.

In general, among families who supported government assistance in child care, a higher proportion also favored making benefits available regardless of the employment status of the mother, rather than targeting families in which the mother is employed. Not unexpectedly, families with employed mothers were more in favor of targeting than families with a nonemployed mother, but the difference was not large.

Finally, the overwhelming majority (85 percent) of parents of children under age 13 favored providing assistance to all families with children under age 13, not just to families with children under age 5.

The responses suggest overwhelming support for public policies to assist families in meeting their child care needs. While most beliefs reflected self-interest, some altruism may be evident in the overwhelming support in this sample with children under age 13 for providing assistance to families with older as well as younger children.

CONCLUSIONS

Almost all children in the United States live with and are primarily cared for by their parents. However, American families care for their children in different ways. Some use exclusive parental care supplemented with enrichment activities, and some use a combination of parents and relatives supplemented with center-based programs. Others use full-day care in a family day care home or center-based program. When both school and preschool programs are considered, enrollments in programs rise rapidly between ages three and five. In part, the care choices parents make for their children depend on the way mothers spend their own time--in employment, in other activities, or in homemaking--and on the ages of children.

School serves as the most important form of nonparental care for school-age children. Kindergartners (5-year-olds) are in a transition year. Since kindergarten is generally a part-day program, parents of 5-year-olds generally need to supplement this program with other types of care. Nine out of 10 five-year-olds are enrolled either in school or a preschool.

The increased use of center-based programs that occurred from the 1970s to the mid-1980s has not slowed. This report documents a continued movement toward use of center-based programs for children of all ages and types of families, which is consistent with the increase in the supply of and stability in price of such care. Center-based care is generally viewed by most parents as available. This report also documents the declining role played by nonrelative, in-home providers in American families and the increasing cost to those who use them. Family day-care remains an important part of the child care market, but primarily for preschool-age children of employed mothers. Family day-care is an option for most families, in that they perceive it as the most available of care. However, parents also have some misconceptions about it. Even though it is one of the least expensive forms of care, nonusers mistakenly think that it is more expensive than center-based care. In real dollars, parents today spend no more for family day-care than they did 15 years ago.

Although relatives are perceived as the least expensive form of care, they are also least likely to be available, and are less used as time goes by. Therefore, parents will have to use more formal modes of care.

In making their decisions, therefore, families make complicated trade-offs between location, cost, convenience, quality, and preference for someone they know and are comfortable with. This study finds that parents are overwhelmingly concerned about the quality (broadly conceived) of the care their children receive. Beyond quality, they are concerned about location and cost as well. Fortunately, parents appear fairly knowledgeable about some of the important characteristics of the programs they are using for their children, particularly the size of the group and the education and training of the provider.

About half of families with children under age 13 have access to some benefit or policy through their employer to assist them in balancing work and family responsibilities. Most families need this assistance, since in a given month one out of four families experiences a breakdown of child care or a child's illness, causing a parent to lose at least a day of work. Although many of the potential income-related differences in access to child care have been reduced or eliminated through federal assistance, low-income families still bear a considerable burden in their attempts to raise children and support themselves. Public opinion among parents strongly supports public policies to assist these families.

APPENDIX A

DESIGN EFFECTS TABLES FOR SURVEY PERCENTAGES

The tables in this appendix provide generalized 95 percent confidence limits for survey percentages. A separate table is provided for each of five sample groups: (1) the entire sample of 4,392 households; (2) 1,272 youngest children under age five, employed mother households; (3) 1,122 youngest children under age five, nonemployed mother households; (4) 1,302 youngest children aged 5-12, employed mother households; and (5) 550 youngest children aged 5-12, nonemployed mother households. The 95 percent confidence limits apply to all sample households in a group, as well as subclasses of the group.

To construct these tables, we computed standard errors for each group using nine survey variables. The selected variables included child care arrangement and demographic and socioeconomic status variables. We then derived an average design effect for each group. The design effect equals the ratio of the cluster sampling variance to the sample variance yielded by a simple random sample. The average design effect for a group was then used to derive an average design effect for each subclass. In so doing, we assumed that the subclasses tended to be spread across the

100 Mathematica Policy Research (MPR) primary sampling units. If a subclass is actually only located in a small number of primary sampling units, then the actual standard errors are larger than those given in the table.

Appendix A

Table A.1 ENTIRE SAMPLE: CONFIDENCE LIMITS

Sample Size	Average Design Effect	95% Confidence Limits (%)					
		5% or 95%	10% or 90%	20% or 80%	30% or 70%	40% or 60%	50%
4,392	1.68	9.8	1.2	1.5	1.8	1.9	1.9
4,000	1.61	0.9	1.2	1.6	1.8	1.9	2.0
3,000	1.46	0.9	1.3	1.7	2.0	2.1	2.2
2,000	1.30	1.1	1.5	2.0	2.3	2.4	2.5
1,000	1.14	1.4	2.0	2.6	3.0	3.2	3.3
500	1.06	2.0	2.7	3.6	4.1	4.4	4.5
400	1.04	2.2	3.0	4.0	4.6	4.9	5.0
300	1.03	2.5	3.4	4.6	5.3	5.6	5.7
200	1.01	3.0	4.2	5.6	6.4	6.8	7.0
100	1.00	4.3	5.9	7.8	9.0	9.6	9.8
50	1.00	6.0	8.3	11.1	12.7	13.6	13.9

Note: For a given sample size, the chances are 95 in 100 that the actual population percentage lies in the range formed by the sample percentage minus the number given in the table and the sample percentage plus the number given in the table.

Table A.2 YOUNGEST CHILD UNDER AGE FIVE, WORKING MOTHER: CONFIDENCE LIMITS

	Average Design Effect	95% Confidence Limits (%)					
Sample Size		5% or 95%	10% or 90%	20% or 80%	30% or 70%	40% or 60%	50%
1,272	1.50	1.5	2.0	2.7	3.1	3.3	3.4
1,000	1.38	1.6	2.2	2.9	3.3	3.6	3.6
500	1.16	2.1	2.8	3.8	4.3	4.6	4.7
400	1.12	2.3	3.1	4.2	4.8	5.1	5.2
300	1.08	2.6	3.5	4.7	5.4	5.8	5.9
200	1.03	3.1	4.2	5.6	6.5	6.9	7.0
100	1.00	4.3	5.9	7.8	9.0	9.6	9.8
50	1.00	6.0	8.3	11.1	12.7	13.6	13.9

Note: For a given sample size, the chances are 95 in 100 that the actual population percentage lies in the range formed by the sample percentage minus the number given in the table and the sample percentage plus the number given in the table.

Table A.3 YOUNGEST CHILD UNDER 5, NONWORKING MOTHER: CONFIDENCE LIMITS

Sample Size	Average Design Effect	95% Confidence Limits (%)					
		5% or 95%	10% or 90%	20% or 80%	30% or 70%	40% or 60%	50%
1,122	1.48	1.6	2.1	2.8	3.3	3.5	3.6
1,000	1.42	1.6	2.2	3.0	3.4	3.6	3.7
500	1.18	2.1	2.9	3.8	4.4	4.7	4.8
400	1.13	2.3	3.1	4.2	4.8	5.1	5.2
300	1.09	2.6	3.5	4.7	5.4	5.8	5.9
200	1.04	3.1	4.2	5.6	6.5	6.9	7.1
100	1.00	4.3	5.9	7.8	9.0	9.6	9.8
50	1.00	6.0	8.3	11.1	12.7	13.6	13.9

Note: For a given sample size, the chances are 95 in 100 that the actual population percentage lies in the range formed by the sample percentage minus the number given in the table and the sample percentage plus the number given in the table.

Table A.4 YOUNGEST CHILD 5 TO 12, WORKING MOTHER: CONFIDENCE LIMITS

Sample Size	Average Design Effect	95% Confidence Limits (%)					
		5% or 95%	10% or 90%	20% or 80%	30% or 70%	40% or 60%	50%
1,302	1.16	1.3	1.8	2.3	2.7	2.9	2.9
1,000	1.12	1.4	2.0	2.6	3.0	3.2	3.3
400	1.04	2.2	3.0	4.0	4.6	4.9	5.0
300	1.02	2.5	3.4	4.6	5.2	5.6	5.7
200	1.01	3.0	4.2	5.6	6.4	6.8	7.0
100	1.00	4.3	5.9	7.8	9.0	9.6	9.8
50	1.00	6.0	8.3	11.1	12.7	13.6	13.9

Note: For a given sample size, the chances are 95 in 100 that the actual population percentage lies in the range formed by the sample percentage minus the number given in the table and the sample percentage plus the number given in the table.

Appendix A ■ 435

Table A.5 YOUNGEST CHILD 5 TO 12, NONWORKING MOTHER: CONFIDENCE LIMITS

Sample Size	Average Design Effect	95% Confidence Limits (%)					
		5% or 95%	10% or 90%	20% or 80%	30% or 70%	40% or 60%	50%
550	1.28	2.1	2.8	3.8	4.3	4.6	4.7
500	1.25	2.1	2.9	3.9	4.5	4.8	4.9
400	1.18	2.3	3.2	4.3	4.9	5.2	5.3
300	1.12	2.6	3.6	4.8	5.5	5.9	6.0
200	1.05	3.1	4.3	5.7	6.5	7.0	7.1
100	1.00	4.3	5.9	7.8	9.0	9.6	9.8
50	1.00	6.0	8.3	11.1	12.7	13.6	13.9

Note: For a given sample size, the chances are 95 in 100 that the actual population percentage lies in the range formed by the sample percentage minus the number given in the table and the sample percentage plus the number given in the table.

APPENDIX B

SAMPLE BIAS FROM THE EXCLUSION OF NONTELEPHONE HOUSEHOLDS

As in all telephone surveys, a major concern with the use of random digit dial (RDD) is the unknown bias that may result from the exclusion of nontelephone households from the survey population. The main source of data for the analysis of bias due to nontelephone coverage is the 1988 National Health Interview Survey (NHIS). The NHIS is a continuous, household survey of the civilian noninstitutionalized population living in the United States. Telephone ownership is asked routinely and is ascertained for 99 percent of the completed NHIS interviews. The survey sample is designed from data from the U.S. Bureau of the Census, which characteristically underrepresent households without telephones. To correct for this problem, NHIS estimates are adjusted each quarter to Census Bureau estimates of the population.

In 1986, approximately 7.2 percent of households in the United States did not have a telephone (Groves and Lyberg 1988). This percentage varies by region, with the South having the highest rate of noncoverage (10.4 percent) and the Northeast having the lowest rate (4.5 percent). The 1986 NHIS revealed that telephone coverage increases with increasing family income and education. Coverage for persons in families with annual incomes of $20,000 or more is 96 percent (Groves and Lyberg 1988). Of those without telephones, the majority have low incomes, are black, and are under the age of 35.

In 1988, the NHIS included a child care supplement that collected information on child care usage for children under 6 years of age. To evaluate the extent of the bias from nontelephone households in the National Child Care Survey, 1990 (NCCS) sample, the 1988 NHIS data were used to compare child care information for households with and without telephones. A subsample of youngest children from the NHIS was selected to make the data comparable to that of the NCCS, 1990.

Child care usage patterns for telephone and nontelephone households are quite different, with nontelephone households using care arrangements, particularly formal arrangements (centers and family day-care providers), at a much lower rate. Table B.1 illustrates this point; almost twice as many (61 percent) of nontelephone households indicate no regular child care arrangements for the youngest child, compared to 38 percent of the homes with phones.

The 1988 NHIS data confirmed Groves' earlier finding that the most important factor determining telephone status was income; 69.6 percent of the nontelephone households (with the youngest child under age 6) have incomes below $15,000. Further analysis reveals that the pattern of child care use for nontelephone families is similar to that for the low-income population with telephones (see table B.2).

Table B.1 CHILD CARE ARRANGEMENTS BY TELEPHONE STATUS

Type of Care Used by Youngest Child	Nontelephone Households	Telephone Households	All Households
Center	8.8	17.4	16.5
In-home care	2.1	4.6	4.3
Family day care	7.8	14.7	14.0
Father	6.1	7.9	7.7
Mother while working	1.1	3.2	3.0
Other relative	11.9	12.7	12.6
No regular arrangement	61.0	37.9	40.2
Other	1.2	1.8	1.7
Sample size	413	3,802	4,215

Source: National Health Interview Survey, National Center for Health Statistics, 1988.

A t-test for the statistical difference between the two groups (assuming random sampling) indicates that the pattern of lower usage of center care by nontelephone households continues even when income differences are removed. Nontelephone households also more often rely on care by the mother (no regular arrangement).

Table B.2 CHILD CARE ARRANGEMENTS FOR FAMILIES WITH INCOMES BELOW $15,000

Type of Care Used by Youngest Child	Nontelephone Households (%)	Telephone Households (%)
Center[a]	7.9	12.4
In-home care	1.8	2.4
Family day care	6.6	9.6
Father	4.7	5.9
Mother while working[b]	0.1	2.3
Other relative	11.9	12.9
No regular arrangement[c]	65.8	52.7
Other	0.6	1.9
Sample size	307	697

Source: National Health Interview Survey, National Center for Health Statistics, 1988.

a. Significant at .05 level.
b. Subgroup n is under 12.
c. Significant at .001 level.

APPENDIX C

BACKGROUND ON NATIONAL CHILD CARE SURVEY

This study had two main goals. First, we sought a comprehensive picture of how children in the United States are being cared for. To satisfy this goal, for each household in the survey we obtained a schedule of care for all children under age 13. (This age cutoff was chosen because it corresponds to the ages that families can claim the child care tax credit on their income tax.) As part of the schedule, we asked when the child was in each child care arrangement during the past week.

The second goal was to obtain a variety of detailed information regarding child care arrangements, such as how the care was found, how satisfied parents are with their child care arrangements, and the cost of care. To minimize the time burden for respondents, these questions were asked only for the youngest child in the household.

In addition to asking parents about child care, we also wanted to gather child care information from people and institutions providing care. We designed a second survey to collect data from day care centers and a third survey to collect information from family day-care providers. The following sections define the categories of child care arrangements, present the guidelines used by the interviewers, and provide a glossary of terms used in the study.

CATEGORIES OF CHILD CARE

When we speak of child care, we mean any time someone other than the primary caregiver is watching a child on a regular basis. The primary caregiver is assumed to be the mother or stepmother, if living in the household. If no mother is present, the father is the primary caregiver. If he is not living in the household, then whoever takes care of or has primary responsibility for the child is the primary caregiver.

Families use child care for a variety of reasons, including those of employment, school, or engaging in other activities. Likewise, families use different types of care; some use care for just a few hours a week, whereas others require 40 or more hours per week. Some have one arrangement and some use several arrangements. In general, care for preschoolers falls into the following categories:

Center-Based Programs. Established settings where children are cared for in a group away from their homes for all or part of the day. There are many different kinds of center-based care, including nursery schools, preschools, and parent cooperatives. Some of these centers are set up primarily to provide work-related care, and others are designed to prepare children for their school years. Centers provide care for groups of children ranging in age from infancy through school age.

Head Start. A comprehensive program offering help with educational needs, health, nutrition and social services for low-income children between the ages of three and five. Head Start is typically a half-day, part-week program that relies heavily on parental involvement.

Family Day-Care (FDC) Home. (Also called Family Child Care.) A private home where an adult cares for children from infancy through school age on a regular basis. The care is provided at the home of the caregiver (*not* in the child's home). The family day-care provider is often a mother who has children of her own for whom she is also caring. Family day care can be licensed or unlicensed. The number of children in a family day-care home varies with the situation. If two or more women join together to operate an FDC home, it may be referred to as a group home or minicenter. The family day-care provider can be a relative, friend, or neighbor of the children, or someone that the family did not previously know.

In-home Care. Generally a nonrelative who takes care of *one family's children* in the children's own home. Sometimes a provider brings her own child/children along to a home. Another common situation is for two families to share an in-home provider.

Care by Spouse/Partner. Care by the father, husband, or partner on a regular basis when the mother is not at home.

Relative Care. Care by a grandmother, aunt, cousin, or other relative, on a regular basis in the child's home or in the relative's home.

In addition to the types of care just listed, school-age children may be cared for in a variety of other ways. Some of the more common arrangements are:

Before- and/or After-School Programs. Special programs providing care to school-aged children before or after school. Many schools have a special program to complement half-day kindergartens that also fall into this category. These programs are most often run by the school itself, by parent groups, or by a local day-care center. *Some children may go to a family day-care home for before- or after-school supervision; we consider this type of care family day care, not before- or after-school care.*

Sibling Care. An older sibling is responsible for a younger family member. Sibling care includes care by stepsisters and stepbrothers.

Self-care. The child is responsible for his or her own care. Children who are responsible for themselves after school are often referred to a "latch-key kids," since they let themselves into their own homes.

Lessons, Clubs, Sports. School-age children may participate in a variety of activities after school, varying by day of the week and season of the year.

Any activities such as soccer, music lessons, scouts, and so forth, should be included in this category.

INTERVIEWER GUIDELINES FOR THIS STUDY

What Is Considered Child Care?

For the purposes of this study, we are interested in any type of child care used on a regular basis. By this we mean child care at least once a week for the past two weeks. It does not matter what the parent is doing during this time; all that matters is regularity. Some examples of regular care include:

- A grandparent or other person who watches a child one or more times a week (this could be a tricky one, but use the rule of thumb that if care occurs on the *same day every week*, then it counts);

- A nursery school;

- A teenage babysitter who works on a regular schedule.

- A neighbor with whom a parent might swap care on a regular basis;

- For children from divorced families, this could be care by the noncustodial parent living in a different residence.

Categorizing Child Care Arrangements

We refer to each type of care used by a child as an "arrangement." If a child goes to nursery school two days a week and watches him or her one other day, that child has two different arrangements--nursery school and grandparent. For the purposes of the survey, we also have a "no regular arrangements" category. This should be the type of care category recorded when respondents say that the children are home with them all the time.

Who Should Answer the Survey?

Our first choice for the respondent is the mother of the children, whom we assume to be the primary caregiver. If the mother lives in the household but is not available, we will offer to call back. If we reach a responsible adult who wishes to answer the survey, we will let him or her do so. To maintain consistency, when someone other than the mother or father is the respondent but the mother lives in the household, we will still ask the mother's employment and employment history. If the mother does not live in the household, then the primary caregiver becomes the focus of these questions.

Defining Changes in Arrangements

Usually it will be clear when an arrangement has changed: for example, the child will be a new person attending a different center/school. However, at times, this may not be clear: for example, a child attends kindergarten at a daycare center. The rule here is that if the place changes, it is considered a new arrangement. Applying that rule, children who attend kindergartens at a day-care center they had been attending as a preschooler have not change their arrangement.

GLOSSARY

AFDC: Aid to Families with Dependent Children. A federal welfare program administered by the Department of Health and Human Services that provides funds for low-income, especially female-headed, families with children. Such families may receive subsidized child care.

Child and Dependent Care Credit: Under current federal income tax law, when both parents work or a single parent works, families can deduct a portion of their child care costs from their income taxes. The amount of the credit will vary depending on income and cost.

Cooperative: Usually a day-care center, preschool, or nursery school where parental participation is required along with or in lieu of payment.

Flexible Spending Account: A child care benefit offered by some employees, by which the amount of money spent on child care is taken out of the employee's gross income. Under such a plan, employees pay no federal or Social Security taxes on money they spend for child care up to $5,000 per year.

Flextime: A plan by which employees may adjust their working hours. For example, if one misses work on Monday because of a sick child, one might be able to work on Saturday to make it up.

Full-time: Thirty-five or more hours' work per week.

Infant: A child from birth up to eleven months in age.

Information and Referral: Also known as resource and referral. A network of information regarding child care. Information includes listing of programs, agencies, and individuals that provide care and counseling on how to locate and evaluate care. Information and referral services can be run by governments or by private firms or businesses.

Parents' Day Out. Another form of nursery/preschool program. These programs are usually less formal and are available for only a few hours each week.

Part-time. Less than 35 hours' work per week.

Preschooler. A child from 36 months to 71 months in age, or until he or she starts kindergarten.

Toddler: A child from 12 months to 35 months in age.

Vouchers: Method of child care payment that can be provided by an employer or a social service agency. The recipient gives the voucher to the child care provider in lieu of cash payment.

APPENDIX D

CARE BY MOTHER AND FATHER

In 93 percent of the households sampled in the NCCS, 1990, the mother was the respondent, in 4 percent her spouse was the respondent, and in the remaining 3 percent either the father or another household member was the respondent. The relationship of each household member to the child was also obtained. Therefore, it was possible to properly link the information to the mother, father, or another household member. The only difficulty the respondents had was in determining when their partner should be considered a child care arrangement. This was particularly the case when the mother was not employed, since in such instances there was no reference activity to link with father care. Interviewers used two criteria to determine whether a person should be considered a regular caregiver. First, care had to occur on a regularly scheduled basis, by which was meant at least once a week for the past two weeks. Second, the respondent could not also be in the household at the time. Therefore, these data do not provide any information about the division of labor between husband and wife in the household when both are present.

Analysis of the responses was problematic when defining parental care in the 4 percent of households where the father answered the questions. To simplify the analysis, the questions were parallel for wives and husbands. Just as the wife might report that her husband cared for the children while she was employed, so the father would be required to report that his wife was the caregiver when he was employed outside the home. This was not an easy concept to communicate to respondents, since they did not usually consider the other parent as a caregiver. In the analysis, because a mother who cared for the children herself reported "no regular arrangements" and in order to consistently code parental care, we recoded "no regular arrangement" as mother or father care, depending on who the respondent was. This was the approach used in compiling the descriptive data on child care arrangements discussed in detail in chapter 2, as well as that utilized in succeeding chapters.

REFERENCES

REFERENCES

Cain, Virginia S. and Sandra L. Hofferth. 1989. "Parental Choice of Self-care for School-Age Children." *Journal of Marriage and the Family* 51 (Feb.):65-77.

Groves, Robert M., and Lars E. Lyberg. 1988. "An Overview of Nonresponse Issues in Telephone Surveys." In *Telephone Survey Methodology*, edited by R. Groves et al., pp. 191-211. New York: John Wiley & Sons.

Hayes, Cheryl D., John L. Palmer, and Martha J. Zaslow, eds. 1990. *Who Cares for America's Children?: Child Care Policy for the 1990s*. Washington, DC: National Academy Press.

Hayghe, Howard. 1988. "Employers and Child Care: What Roles Do They Play?" *Monthly Labor Review* 111 (September):38-44.

Hofferth, Sandra. 1988. "Child Care in the United States." In *American Families in Tomorrow's Economy, Proceedings of Hearing before the Select Committee on Children, Youth, and Families, July 1, 1987* (pp. 166-87). Washington, DC: U.S. Government Printing Office.

Hofferth, Sandra L., and Deborah A. Phillips. 1987. "Child Care in the United States, 1970 to 1995." *Journal of Marriage and the Family* 49(Aug.):559-71.

Howes, C., C. Rodning, D.C. Galluzzo, and L. Myers. 1988. "Attachment and Child Care: Relationships with Mother and Caregiver." *Early Childhood Research Quarterly* 3:403-416.

Johansen, Anne, Arleen Leibowitz, and Linda Waite. 1990. "Tax Credits, Preferences, and Child Care Choice." Paper presented at the annual meeting of Association for Public Policy and Management, San Francisco, October.

Kisker, Ellen Eliason, Sandra L. Hofferth, and Deborah A. Phillips. 1991. *A Profile of Child Care Settings: Early Education and Care in 1990*, volume 1. Princeton: Mathematica Policy Research.

Louis Harris and Associates. 1987. *Report on Survey Method: The 1987 CDC Survey of Day-Care Exposure and Morbidity in the U.S.* New York: Louis Harris and Associates.

Low, Seth, and P. Spindler. 1968. *Child Care Arrangements of Working Mothers in the United States.* Washington, DC: U.S. Department of Health, Education and Welfare, Children's Bureau; and U.S. Department of Labor, Women's Bureau.

Morgan, Gwen. 1987. *The National State of Child Care Regulation 1986.* Watertown, MA: Work/Family Directions.

Robins, Philip K. 1990. "Child Care Policy and Research: An Economist's Perspective." Paper presented at the Carolina Public Policy Conference on the Economics of Child Care, University of North Carolina, Chapel Hill, May.

Sonenstein, Freya L. 1991. "The Child Care Preferences of Parents with Young Children: How Little is Known." In *Parental Leave and Child Care: Setting a Research and Policy Agenda*, edited by J. Hyde and M. Essex, pp. 337-353. Philadelphia, PA: Temple University Press.

References

Thornberry, Owen T., Jr., and James T. Massey. 1988. "Trends in United States Telephone Coverage Across Time and Subgroups." In *Telephone Survey Methodology*, edited by R. Groves et al., pp. 25-50. New York: John Wiley & Sons.

UNCO, Inc. 1975. *National Childcare Consumer Study: 1975*, vols 1-4. Washington, DC: UNCO.

U.S. Bureau of the Census. 1982. *Trends in Child Care Arrangements of Working Mothers*. Current Population Reports, series P-23, no. 117. Washington, DC: U.S. Government Printing Office.

U.S. Bureau of the Census. 1983. *Child Care Arrangements of Working Mothers: June 1982*. Current Population Reports, series P-23, no. 129. Washington, DC: U.S. Government Printing Office.

U.S. Bureau of the Census. 1987. *Who's Minding the Kids? Child Care Arrangements: Winter 1984-85*. Current Population Reports, series P-70, no. 9. Washington, DC: U.S. Government Printing Office.

U.S. Bureau of the Census. 1988. *School Enrollment--Social and Economic Characteristics of Students: October 1985 and 1984*. Current Population Reports, series P-20, no. 426. Washington, DC: U.S. Government Printing Office.

U.S. Bureau of the Census. 1990. *Who's Minding the Kids? Child Care Arrangements 1986-87*. Current Population Reports, series P-70, no. 20. Washington, DC: U.S. Government Printing Office.

U.S. Bureau of Labor Statistics. 1988. "Labor Force Participation Unchanged among Mothers with Young Children." *News*. Bulletin No. 88-431. Washington, DC: U.S. Department of Labor.

U.S. Bureau of Labor Statistics. 1989. *Employee Benefits in Medium and Large Firms, 1988.* Bulletin 2336. Washington, DC: U.S. Department of Labor.

U.S. Bureau of Labor Statistics. 1990. "Employee Benefits Focus on Family Concerns in 1989." *News.* Bulletin, March 30.

Waksberg, J. 1978. "Sampling Methods for Random Digit Dialing." *Journal of the American Statistical Association* 73(362).

Whitebook, Marcy, Carollee Howes, and Deborah Phillips. 1989. *Who Cares? Child Care Teachers and the Quality of Care in America.* Final Report: The National Child Care Staffing Study. Oakland, CA: Child Care Employee Project.

LIST OF TABLES AND FIGURES

LIST OF TABLES

1.1	Sampling Frame and Response Rates: National Child Care Survey, 1990	14
2.1	U.S. Households with Children under Age 13	28
2.2	Primary Child Care Arrangements for All Children under Age 13	29
2.3	Primary Child Care Arrangements for All Children under Age 13, by Age	31
2.4	Primary Child Care Arrangements for All Children under Age Five	33
2.5	Primary Child Care Arrangements for All Children under Age Five, by Mother's Employment Schedule	34
2.6	Primary Child Care Arrangements for All Children under Age 13, by Age, Employed Mother	36
2.7	Primary Child Care Arrangements for All Children under Age 13, by Age, Nonemployed Mother	38
2.8	Primary Child Care Arrangements for All Children Aged 5-12	39

2.9	Primary Child Care Arrangements for All Children Aged 5-12, by Mother's Employment Schedule	40
2.10	Primary Child Care Arrangement for Youngest Child, by Family Type, All Families	43
2.11	Primary Child Care Arrangement for Youngest Child, by Age	44
2.12	Primary Child Care Arrangement for Youngest Child under Age Five	46
2.13	Primary Child Care Arrangement for Youngest Child under Age Five, by Mother's Employment Schedule	49
2.14	Primary Child Care Arrangement for Youngest Child, by Age, Employed Mother	50
2.15	Primary Child Care Arrangement for Youngest Child under Age Five, by Family and Area Characteristics, Employed Mother	54
2.16	Primary Child Care Arrangement for Youngest Child, by Age, Nonemployed Mother	59
2.17	Primary Child Care Arrangement for Youngest Child under Age Five, by Family and Area Characteristics with Nonemployed Mother	60
2.18	Primary Child Care Arrangement for Youngest Child, Aged 5-12	66
2.19	Primary Child Care Arrangement for Youngest Child, Aged 5-12, by Mother's Employment Schedule	70

List of Tables and Figures ■ 457

2.20	Primary Child Care Arrangement for Youngest Child Aged 5-12, by Family and Area Characteristics with Employed Mother	72
2.21	Primary Child Care Arrangement for Youngest Child Aged 5-12, by Family and Area Characteristics with Nonemployed Mother	78
2.22	Proportion of All Households with Only One Arrangement, by Type of Arrangement	82
2.23	Secondary Child Care Arrangement for Youngest Child, by Age, All Families	83
2.24	Proportion of Households with Only One Arrangement, by Type of Arrangement, Youngest under Age Five	85
2.25	Secondary Child Care Arrangement for Youngest Child under Age Five	86
2.26	Proportion of Households with Only One Arrangement, by Type of Arrangement, Youngest Child Aged 5-12	91
2.27	Secondary Child Care Arrangement for Youngest Child Aged 5-12	92
2.28	Number of Arrangements for Youngest Child, All Households	98
2.29	Primary Child Care Arrangement for Youngest Preschool Child, Employed Mother, 1965-90	99
2.30	Primary Nonschool Child Care Arrangement for Youngest School-Age Child, Employed Mother, 1985-90	103

2.31	Hours per Week, Primary Child Care Arrangement for Youngest Child, Employed Mother	106
2.32	Weekly Child Care Hours, by Age of Youngest and Mother's Employment Status	108
2.33	Hours per Week, Primary Child Care Arrangement for Youngest Child, Nonemployed Mother	110
3.1	Percentile Distribution of Mean Hourly Expenditure for Primary Care Arrangement for Youngest Child under Age Five, Employed Mothers Paying for Care Only	135
3.2	Percentile Distribution of Mean Hourly Expenditure for Primary Care Arrangement for Youngest Child Aged 5-12, Employed Mothers Paying for Care Only	149
3.3	Percentile Distribution of Mean Hourly Expenditure for Secondary Care Arrangement for Youngest Child, by Age of Child and Maternal Employment Status, Mother Paying for Care Only	158
3.4	Mean Weekly Child Care Expenditure for All Children and Percentage of Total Weekly Income for Youngest Child under Age Five, by Race, Poverty, and Family Income, Employed Mothers Paying for Care Only	164
4.1	Types of Care Seriously Considered, by Maternal Employment Status	204
4.2	Most Important Reason for Choice of Current Care Arrangement, by Type of Care	217

List of Tables and Figures

4.3	Comparison of Satisfaction/Preference Data, 1975 and 1990	233
4.4	Most Important Reason for Preferring Different Arrangement, by Age of Youngest Child	242
5.1	User and Nonuser Perceptions of Types of Care	252
5.2	Use and Perception of Self- and Sibling Care	295
5.3	Age of Youngest Child at Start of Sibling Care, by Age of Sibling at the Time	300
6.1	Child Care History by Age of Youngest Child and Family Income	310
6.2	Distribution of Child Care Spells	313
7.1	Employed Mothers Losing Some Time during Month Previous because of Failures in Child Care Arrangements	347
7.2	Employed Mothers Losing Day of Work during Month Previous because of Failures in Child Care Arrangements	349
7.3	Employed Mothers with Sick Child who Lost Time from Work during Month Previous because of Child's Sickness	356
7.4	Proportion of Establishments Offering Child Care, and Parents Reporting Receiving Leave and Other Work/Family Benefits, 1987-90	358
7.5	Proportion of Parents Reporting Benefits Available through their Own or Spouse's Employer, by Household Income	360

7.6	Proportion of Mothers Taking Leave after Youngest Child was Born, by Household Income	372
7.7	Number of Weeks of Leave Taken among Mothers Taking Leave, by Household Income	374
7.8	Paid and Unpaid Leave among Mothers Taking Leave	376
7.9	Paid Leave Taken by Mothers, by Type of Leave	377
7.10	Health Insurance Kept or Lost through Employer by Mothers Taking Leave	378
8.1	Should Federal Child Care Support Be Targeted to Families of All Income Levels, Low Income Levels Only, or None at All?	384
8.2	Response to Survey Question: Must Both Parents Be Employed to Receive Federal Child Care Support?	392
8.3	Response to Survey Question: Must the Single Parent Be Employed to Receive Federal Child Care Support?	394
8.4	Response to Survey Question: Should Support Be Targeted to All Families with Children under Age 13, or Only to Those with Children under Age 5?	400
8.5	Response to Survey Question: Should Employers Provide Child Care Benefits?	404

LIST OF FIGURES

2.1	Proportion of Children Enrolled in Regular School or Center-Based Program, by Age	25
2.2	Primary Care, Youngest Preschool Child Employed and Nonemployed Mothers	48
2.3	Primary Care for Youngest Child under 13	51
2.4a	Primary Care for Youngest Preschool Child by Education, Employed Mothers	56
2.4b	Primary Care for Youngest Preschool Child by Income, Employed Mothers	57
2.5a	Primary Care for Youngest Preschool Child by Education, Nonemployed Mothers	62
2.5b	Primary Care for Youngest Preschool Child by Income, Nonemployed Mothers	64
2.6	Primary Care for Youngest School Age Child: Employed and Nonemployed Mothers	68
2.7a	Primary Care for Youngest School Age Child by Education, Employed Mothers	71
2.7b	Primary Care for Youngest School Age Child by Income, Employed Mothers	74
2.8a	Primary Care for Youngest School Age Child by Education, Nonemployed Mothers	77

2.8b	Primary Care for Youngest School Age Child by Income, Nonemployed Mothers	80
2.9	Secondary Care, Youngest Preschool Child: Employed and Nonemployed Mothers	87
2.10	Secondary by Primary Arrangement: Youngest Child under Five with Employed Mother	88
2.11	Secondary by Primary Arrangement: Youngest Child under Five with Employed Mother	90
2.12	Secondary Care, Youngest School Age Child: Employed and Nonemployed Mothers	93
2.13	Secondary by Primary Arrangement: Youngest Child 5-12 with Employed Mother	95
2.14	Secondary by Primary Arrangement: Youngest Child 5-12 with Nonemployed Mother	96
2.15	Primary Care, Youngest Preschool Child, Employed Mothers, 1965-90	100
2.16	Primary Care for Youngest School Age Child, Employed Mothers, 1985-90	104
3.1	Distribution of Payment for Primary Arrangement by Maternal Employment Status, Youngest Child under Five	121
3.2	Percentage Paying for Primary Arrangement by Type of Arrangement and Maternal Employment Status, Youngest Child under Five	123
3.3	Percentage Paying for Primary Arrangement by Time Spent in Care, Youngest Child under Five	125

List of Tables and Figures

3.4	Distribution of Payment for Primary Arrangement by Maternal Employment Status, Youngest Child Age 5-12	127
3.5	Percentage Paying for Primary Arrangement by Type of Arrangement and Maternal Employment Status, Youngest Child Age 5-12	128
3.6	Percentage Paying for Primary Arrangement by Time Spent in Care, Youngest Child Age 5-12	129
3.7	Distribution of Payment for Secondary Arrangement by Maternal Employment Status, Youngest Child under Five	131
3.8	Distribution of Payment for Secondary Arrangement by Maternal Employment Status, Youngest Child Age 5-12	132
3.9	Mean Hourly Expenditure for Youngest Child under Five by Maternal Employment Status, those Paying for Care Only	134
3.10	Mean Hourly Expenditure for Youngest Child under Five by Type of Primary Arrangement, Employed Mothers Paying for Care Only	139
3.11	Average Hourly Expenditure for Youngest Child under Five, Employed Mothers Paying for Care Only	141
3.12	Mean Hourly Expenditure for Youngest Child under Five by Type of Primary Arrangement, Nonemployed Mothers Paying for Care Only	144

3.13 Mean Hourly Expenditure for Youngest Child Age 5-12 by Maternal Employment Status, those Paying for Care Only 146

3.14 Mean Hourly Expenditure for Youngest Child Age 5-12 by Type of Primary Arrangement, Employed Mothers Paying for Care Only 148

3.15 Average Hourly Expenditure for Youngest Child Age 5-12, Employed Mothers Paying for Care Only 153

3.16 Mean Weekly Expenditure for all Children in the Family by Maternal Employment Status, Mothers with Youngest Child under Five Paying for Care Only 162

3.17 Mean Weekly Expenditure for all Children in the Family by Primary Arrangement of Youngest Child, Mothers with Youngest Child under Five Paying for Care Only 163

3.18 Mean Weekly Expenditure for all Children in the Family, Employed Mothers with Youngest Child under Five Paying for Care Only 167

3.19 Mean Weekly Expenditure for all Children in the Family by Maternal Employment Status, Mothers with Youngest Child Age 5-12 Paying for Care Only 169

3.20 Mean Weekly Expenditure for all Children in the Family by Primary Arrangement of Youngest Child, Employed Mothers with Youngest Child Age 5-12 Paying for Care Only 171

List of Tables and Figures

3.21	Mean Weekly Expenditure for all Children in the Family, Employed Mothers with Youngest Child Age 5-12 Paying for Care Only	172
3.22	Mean Percentage of Family Income Spent on Child Care by Maternal Employment Status, Mothers with Youngest Child under Five Paying for Care Only	175
3.23	Mean Percentage of Family Income Spent on Child Care by Race/Ethnicity and Family Income, Employed Mothers with Youngest Child under Five Paying for Care Only	177
3.24	Mean Percentage of Family Income Spent on Child Care, Employed Mothers with Youngest Child under Five Paying for Care Only	178
3.25	Mean Percentage of Family Income Spent on Child Care by Maternal Employment Status, Mothers with Youngest Child 5-12 Paying for Care Only	180
3.26	Mean Percentage of Family Income Spent on Child Care, Employed Mothers with Youngest Child Age Age 5-12 Paying for Care Only	182
3.27	Percentage Receiving Direct Financial Assistance for the Care of the Youngest Child, by Family Income	185
3.28	Percentage of Employed Mothers using 1988 Child Care Income Tax Credit	187
3.29	Mean Weekly Payment for Youngest Child under Five, Employed Mothers Paying for Child Care, 1975-90	189

3.30	Mean Hourly Payment for Youngest Child under Five, Employed Mothers Paying for Child Care, 1975-90	191
3.31	Mean Hours in Care for Youngest Child under Five, Employed Mothers Paying for Child Care, 1975-90	192
3.32	Mean Weekly Payment for Youngest Child 5-12, Employed Mothers Paying for Child Care, 1975-90	194
3.33	Mean Hourly Payment for Youngest Child 5-12, Employed Mothers Paying for Child Care, 1975-90	195
3.34	Mean Hours in Care for Youngest Child 5-12, Employed Mothers Paying for Child Care, 1975-90	197
4.1	Seriously Considered Alternative Types of Arrangements by Current Type of Care, Employed Mothers	205
4.2	Seriously Considered Alternative Types of Arrangements, by Family Income and Maternal Employment Status	206
4.3	Seriously Considered Alternative Types of Arrangements, by Age of Youngest and Maternal Employment Status	208
4.4	Alternative Types of Providers Considered	209
4.5	Seriously Considered Other Providers, by Current Type of Care and Employment Status of the Mother	210
4.6	Number of Other Providers Considered	212
4.7	How First Learned of Current Child Care Arrangement for Youngest Child	214

List of Tables and Figures

4.8	Most Important Factor in Choice of Current Arrangement, by Employment Status of Mother	216
4.9	Most Important Factor in Choice of Current Arrangement, by Income	219
4.10	Most Important Aspect of Quality in Choice of Current Care Arrangement, by Employment Status of Mother	221
4.11	Provider Related Characteristics of Quality (Choice of Child Care Arrangement)	222
4.12	Second Most Important Aspect of Quality in Choice of Current Care Arrangement, by Employment Status of Mother	224
4.13	Second Important Factor in Choice of Current Arrangement, by Employment Status of Mother	225
4.14	Second Reason for Choosing Primary Arrangement, by First Reason	227
4.15	Weeks to Commitment, by Age (Youngest Child)	230
4.16	Families Preferring Alternative Type or Combination of Care, by Age of Youngest Child and Employment Status of Mother	235
4.17	Families Preferring to Change Arrangement, by Current Type of Care	236
4.18	Preferred Alternative Type of Care	237
4.19	Preferred Alternative Type of Care, by Age of Youngest Child	239

4.20	Families Preferring Center-Based Care, by Income	240
4.21	Why Prefer an Alternative Type of Care	243
4.22	Most Important Aspect of Quality in Preference for Alternative Care Type, by Employment Status of Mother	244
5.1	Availability of Other Types of Care, by Type of Care Currently Used	251
5.2	Perceived Availability of Alternative Types of Care, by Income Quintiles	254
5.3	Perceptions of Providers' Distances from Home	256
5.4	Percent Who Live within Ten Minutes of Provider, by Type of Care Currently Used	257
5.5	Percent Who Live within Ten Minutes of Provider, by Income	259
5.6	Perceived Distance from Nearest Available Relative, by Urban Residence	260
5.7	User and Non-User Perceptions of Prices	262
5.8	Perceptions of Hourly Prices for Other Types of Care: Based on 40 Hours per Week	264
5.9	Perceptions of Weekly Prices for Other Types of Care: Based on 40 Hours per Week	265
5.10	Expected Weekly Expenditures for Alternative Types of Care, by Income Quintiles	267

List of Tables and Figures ■ 469

5.11	Expected Weekly Expenditures for Alternative Types of Care, by Urban Residence and Region	268
5.12	User Perceptions of Group Sizes and Child/Staff Ratios	270
5.13	Total Children Supervised by Provider, by Income	272
5.14	Child/Staff Ratios, by Income	273
5.15	User Perceptions of Providers' Education and Training	274
5.16	Transportation to Care, Family Day Care, and Centers	276
5.17	Transportation to Centers, by Income	277
5.18	Transportation to Family Day Care, by Income	278
5.19	Dropping in Unannounced, Family Day Care and Centers	280
5.20	Objectives of the Program, Centers	281
5.21	Program Goals of Current Child Care Arrangement, by Income	282
5.22	Percentage of Families with Youngest Child ever in Self Care or Sibling Care	284
5.23	Percentage of Youngest Children ever in Self Care, by Employment Status of Mother	286
5.24	Percentage of Youngest Children ever in Sibling Care (under 14), by Employment Status of Mother	287

5.25	Percentage of all Children ever in Self Care or Sibling Care	290
5.26	Percentage of all Children ever in Self Care, by Employment Status of Mother	291
5.27	Percentage of all Children ever in Sibling Care, by Employment Status of Mother	292
5.28	Average Age First Left/Would Leave Youngest Child in Self or Sibling Care	294
6.1	Child Care History for 12 Months Previous by Employment Status of Mother	308
6.2	Parents Using the Same Arrangement by Length of Time after Care Began	315
6.3	Median Duration of Current and Previous Arrangements by Age of Child	317
6.4	Median Duration of Current Arrangements by Age of Child and Employment Status of Mother	319
6.5	Median Duration of Current Arrangements by Age of Child and Household Income	321
6.6	Median Duration of Current Arrangement by Type of Care	323
6.7	Median Duration of Current Arrangement by Age of Child and Type of Care	324
6.8	Median Duration of Previous Arrangements by Age of Child and Type of Care	326
6.9	Changes in Nonparental Care Arrangements	327

List of Tables and Figures

6.10	Reason Previous Child Care Arrangement Ended	329
6.11	Age of First Nonparental Care	331
6.12	Age of First Nonparental Care by Employment Status of Mother	332
6.13	Age of First Nonparental Care by Income	333
6.14	Hours Spent in First Care Arrangement	335
6.15	Hours Spent in First Care Arrangement by Employment Status of Mother	336
6.16	Summer Arrangements for School Age Children: Respondents with One or More Types of Arrangement	338
6.17	Summer Arrangements for School Age Children: Respondents with Two or More Types of Arrangement	339
6.18	Summer Arrangements for School Age Children: Respondents with Three or More Types of Arrangement	340
6.19	Summer Arrangements for School Age Children: Respondents with Four or More Types of Arrangement	341
7.1	Proportion of Employed Mothers Experiencing Work Disruptions Because of Failures in Child Care Arrangements, by Income	350
7.2	Proportion of Employed Mothers Experiencing Work Disruptions Because of Failures in Child Care Arrangements, by Type of Care	353

7.3	Percentage of Families with Work/Family Benefits	366
7.4	Percentage of Families with Work/Family Benefits, by Household Income	367
7.5	Leave after Birth of Youngest Child, Mother	373
8.1	Should Support be Targeted to Families of all Income Levels, Low Income Levels, or None at all? By Income	386
8.2	Should Support be Targeted to Families of all Income Levels, Low Income Levels, or None at all? By Age of Youngest	388
8.3	Should Support be Targeted to Families of all Income Levels, Low Income Levels, or None at all? By Family and Household Type	389
8.4	Should Support be Targeted to all Two-Parent Families, or only those in which both Parents are Employed? By Family and Household Type	391
8.5	Should Support be Targeted to all Two-Parent Families, or only those in which both Parents are Employed? By Income	397
8.6	Should Support be Targeted to all Two-Parent Families, or only those in which both Parents are Employed? By Age of Youngest	398
8.7	Should Support be Targeted to all Families with Children under 13, or only to those with Children under Five? By Age of Youngest	402

8.8 Should Employers Provide Child Care Benefits to all Families, only those in which all Parents are Employed, or None at all? 406

HQ 778.7 .U6 N38 1991

NATIONAL CHILD CARE SURVEY, 1990

DATE DUE

JAN 13 '97			
MAY 20 '97			
JAN 05 '98			
NOV 23 1998			
MAR 05 2002			

Demco, Inc. 38-293